HERO:
DAVID BOWIE

HERO: DAVID BOWIE

Lesley-Ann Jones

HODDER

First published in Great Britain in 2016 by Hodder & Stoughton
An Hachette UK company

First published in paperback in 2017

1

A CIP catalogue record for this title is available from the British Library

ISBN 978 1 444 75883 2
eBook ISBN 978 1 444 75884 9

Typeset in Plantin Light by Hewer Text UK Ltd, Edinburgh

Printed and bound by CPI Group (UK) Ltd, Croydon, CR0 4YY

Hodder & Stoughton policy is to use papers that are natural, renewable
and recyclable products and made from wood grown in sustainable
forests. The logging and manufacturing processes are expected to
conform to the environmental regulations of the country of origin.

Hodder & Stoughton Ltd
Carmelite House
50 Victoria Embankment
London EC4Y 0DZ

www.hodder.co.uk

IN MEMORIAM

DAVID ROBERT JONES
8 January 1947 – 10 January 2016

Contents

Bowie Is Dead

He died in his own bed in New York City, two days after his sixty-ninth birthday and the release of his twenty-seventh studio album, *Blackstar*: his personal requiem and his 'parting gift' to the world. The announcement, made on his official social media accounts, was unemotional and succinct:

> 10 January 2016: David Bowie died peacefully today, surrounded by his family after a courageous eighteen-month battle with cancer. While many of you will share in this loss, we ask that you respect the family's privacy during their time of grief.

'Very sorry and sad to say that it's true,' wrote his son, the BAFTA award-winning film maker Duncan Jones, on Twitter. 'I'll be offline for a while. Love to all.'

Disbelief and denial consume. We are arrogant in our ignorance. We didn't know that he was terminally ill. They're saying it was liver cancer, but isn't that usually secondary? Wouldn't his primary have been lung? We speculate, pointlessly. Not even Brian Eno knew before it happened, and he worked with Bowie for decades. 'It was a complete surprise,' Eno admits. Artist George Underwood had no idea either, and he'd been David's closest friend since they were eight years old.

'It's very difficult when your best friend dies,' George laments from his sofa on the day, tears running behind his specs. 'I feel completely in shock.' He will be more composed, and more forthcoming, when I spend the day with him.

In other news come warnings of a brutal snow bomb poised to unleash chaos on this scepter'd isle, this earth of majesty, this seat of Mars ... this England[1] – bringing the worst weather for more than half a decade. We had five years left to cry in. We never knew.

Leonardo DiCaprio is royally eclipsed, despite his triple Golden Globes triumph for *The Revenant* the night before, pointing to first-ever Oscars success ahead. The historic global summit of all thirty-eight national Primates of the Anglican church, in Canterbury, to discuss their division over the acceptance of gay clergy, is ignored. Yet these three headlines seem pertinent to the revelation that the immortal Starman, the godfather of freaks, the saviour of outsiders, alternative thinkers and sexual vacillators, the dispossessed, the young, the past-it and the never-will-be dudes, has flared, flickered and gone out for good. Hot tramp, we loved him so.

The grief is tsunamic. Twitter and Facebook are in meltdown, as are millions of fans. In Manhattan, they clamour at the doors of 285 Lafayette Street, the apartment block topped with the penthouse where David dwelled in luxury with Iman, his former supermodel wife of twenty-four years, and their fifteen-year-old daughter Lexi.

In Berlin, the devoted gather on the street outside David's former home, Hauptstrasse 155 in the Schöneberg district, to contribute their candles and flowers. Others head for the Hansa Tonstudio on Köthener Strasse near Potsdamer Platz, where he recorded during the Seventies.

In the Netherlands, queues converge at the entrance to the Groninger art museum, where the 'David Bowie Is' touring exhibition is on show.[2] The museum responds by offering a book of condolence for fans to sign, and by throwing open its doors on a Monday, when it is normally closed.

In Los Angeles, the bereft create a shrine around Ziggy's star on the Hollywood Walk of Fame. David's plaque, which sits opposite 7021 Hollywood Boulevard between Paula Abdul and Faye Dunaway to the east, and Pierce Brosnan and Fred Allen to the west, is obliterated by lit offerings and cellophaned florals, toy aliens, cigarette lighters and tiny bottles of Jameson's Irish whiskey. A questionable gift, this last, given that David had been teetotal and a member of AA (the alcoholics' support network, not the Automobile Association) for many years. Fans shuffle about garlanding glitter into the air like fairy dust, and playing Bowie tracks on iPhones. Why did they come?

'He's helped make me a lot more confident and OK with embracing my weird,' offered one.

'He allowed me to accept myself and who I really wanted to be,' wept another. They speak for many.

In Newcastle, New South Wales, the faithful convene to post messages on a mural of Bowie in the guise of the Goblin King from the 1986 movie *Labyrinth*. David made promo videos in the Australian state, including the memorable piece for 1983's 'Let's Dance'. It was shot in far northern Carinda, a tiny town with a population of fewer than two hundred. Its only hotel was used as the location, and is now a destination of pilgrimage for Bowie fans. During the shoot, remembers director David Mallet, the locals were less than happy about it.

'David hadn't been in the public eye for two or three years when we made this video,' he says. 'He'd been writing and being a bit of a recluse. So it wasn't a comeback, but the first thing that people had seen for quite a while. It was a total change musically, for Bowie, and a total change for all of us making videos. It was one of the earliest that was made on 35mm film.'

It had been Bowie's idea to shoot the video in Australia.

'The record was clear and crisp and right in front of you. And I thought, this needs clear and crisp film, not old video tape. So off we go to Australia, where the light is fantastic, and we come back with "China Girl" and "Let's Dance".

'The scene in the bar in "Let's Dance" was genuine local people in their bar at ten in the morning. They hated David Bowie, and they hated us horrible Nancy boys making a film, so much. Although in the film, they look as though they are bopping away and enjoying it. In fact, they were completely taking the piss. It was all David's idea, and it was basically to do with some Aborigines going on a sojourn, a walkabout. And ending in Sydney, a big conurbation, that was the premise of it all.'

David's affinity with Australia was established. He bought a lavish apartment in the Kincoppal waterfront complex at Sydney's Elizabeth Bay, which he kept for ten years, only selling it after he had met and married the former supermodel Iman.

In London, we take him at his word, and we dance: in the street, into the night, and all the way home come dawn. A couple of thousand flock to Brixton's Ritzy cinema for a gathering arranged via Facebook, with instruments, speakers, food, booze, 'and most importantly, love', for an impromptu knees-up in the rain. It's an ocean of emotion. Daring revellers boogie atop red telephone kiosks, while rousing choruses are raised by the tearful throng.

A soaring 'There's a Starman, waiting in the sky!' is captured by both television cameras and radio mics, and repeated endlessly over the internet and on the airwaves. Opposite the underground station, near the corner of Tunstall Road, a huge, colourful mural of not-quite Bowie's face by Australian street artist James Cochran becomes the focal point, where fans display the requisite night-lights and blooms.

Down in Beckenham, Kent, where David created Camelot within the moth-eaten Gothic splendour of Haddon Hall, where he launched the Free Festival and founded the Arts Lab back in the Sixties, the tributes are more modest but no less heartfelt. More tapers, more tulips, deposited on the pavement in front of chain restaurant Zizzi. Once a High Street pub, it bears his tribute plaque, erected by Copers Cope Area Residents Association and the Noble House Pub Company:

DAVID BOWIE

ROCK MUSICIAN
LIVED IN BECKENHAM
& LAUNCHED HIS CAREER
IN THE THREE TUNS
1969–1973

This is where the wistfully remembered Arts Labs were held. 'Zizzi Stardust', quips one worshipper as he stoops to examine the tiny red telephone boxes, faded album covers and hand-penned notes that the fans have left there. An elderly lady in bottle-green knitwear and trainers recounts the story of a 'local lass', Mary Finnigan, 'who lived with David here in Beckenham all those years ago, and who loved him, and who kept it a secret for a long, long time, but who has now written her own little book about it all.' Inside among the ghosts, diners eat at tables etched with Bowie song titles and sassy artworks, on the very spot where their idol played an elementary 'Space Oddity' when he was an Absolute Beginner.

Over at 'Bec Rec', the park on Croydon Road, the gates have been left unlocked for the night, allowing fans to enter and pay their respects at the bandstand where he performed in 1969. The gig was later immortalised in his song 'Memories of a Free Festival'. The next day, Bromley Council announces its plans to 'redouble' its efforts to make the renovated Victorian bandstand a 'fitting and enduring tribute' to the late icon's memory. This bandstand being the only one of its kind in the country, it is worth saving in any case, regardless of any latter-day rock heritage. A 'Bowie's Beckenham Oddity' event is announced, for 13 August. We scribble it into our diaries, of course. But will we be there?

The BT Tower displays a glowing electronic tribute, as it tends to on momentous occasions. Notice boards on the London underground are scrawled with expressions of hero-worship penned by commuters. Pubs all over the country, and bars and hotels around the world, play his music round the clock. And there is a wonderful, unprecedented send-off from the media. Television schedules are panic-overhauled, in order to present wall-to-wall pundits pontificating on the so-called icon and his legacy. Radio schedules are hastily reconfigured, entire shows given over to no-chat back-to-back tracks. The print press cranks into ebullient overdrive, publishing Souvenir Editions!, Exclusive Pull-Outs! and Candid Photo Supplements!, of the kind usually reserved for deceased senior Royals. *The Times* produces a fabulous wrap-around cover, the *Guardian* a twelve-page supplement, and the *Independent* eclipses the lot of them with a brilliant editorial tribute. Cynic-hack-me recognises these as primarily commercial opportunities: less a case of giving loyal readers a keepsake to treasure, more a cold-blooded cashing-in of a chance to flog more newspapers. But once a hack, always a hack. I join in, responding to a commission from the *Daily Mail* to contribute a spread on the David Bowie I knew.

The overwhelming outpouring of grief over Bowie is described in some quarters as 'out of all proportion to the loss'. It is 'unprecedented'. Is it? Are we being drama queens? Our hero's death may well prove, in time, to be reminiscent of JFK's in 1963, in that we'll all remember exactly where we were when we heard of it. Will we? I don't remember Kennedy's death, but I was only a child. I do remember John Lennon's assassination in New York, the closest comparable event that I can think of. To this day, I never leave the city without making a detour to the Strawberry Fields memorial in Central Park.

I remember Diana, Princess of Wales – in whose presence David performed at Wembley Stadium on 13 July 1985, for Live Aid. The tragic Paris car accident that claimed her life, her boyfriend Dodi Fayed's and their driver Henri Paul's on 31 August 1997, was when the UK lost the plot on a titanic scale. I took my newborn son

Henry to Kensington Gardens, and photographed him in his baby carrier among the bouquets. What a crass thing to do, I cringe now at the thought. We watched Diana's mourn-porn Westminster Abbey funeral on television along with nineteen million others, succumbing to grief as her brother, Earl Spencer, delivered his provocative eulogy condemning the Royals. We wept at the sight of Elton John bashing out on the piano his hastily reworded 'Candle in the Wind', which became a best-selling farewell to the princess, as 'Goodbye, England's Rose'.

I found it difficult to comprehend at the time, and I still do, the mass hysteria that ensnared us. The collective taking-leave of senses and the intensity of our mourning rendered us temporarily insane. But was that genuine mourning, or was it sentimentality? Seduced by the media into sorrow that we had no right to feel – Diana was not in our lives, she was not our sister, daughter or mother, she was a photograph, a news bulletin, no more accessible than a character on *EastEnders* or *Coronation Street* – we questioned our 'heartbreak' only when it dawned on us that our anguish had faded as fast as it had flared. We rarely speak of her today – other than, perhaps, in the context of Kate'n'Wills. We've 'moved on'.

The legacy of the self-styled People's Princess is primarily imagery. Beyond the endless 'iconic' photos, the outfits, the shoes, the hair-dos and the Harbour Club membership, what did she achieve? No offence intended. But the heir and the spare aside, her odd meander among the landmines and getting hands-on with AIDS victims was the size of it. She left no music, no film, no art for us to cherish, to remember her by. To continue to enjoy. Bowie, like his friend Lennon, left so much. Does our grief for him seem more justified? At risk of wrath, I must say that it does to me. Bowie's death is our own death, in some respects. It marks the loss of our youth, of all our yesterdays, of our wildest dreams.

There is no funeral for David. Not even a private ceremony. No fuss. He would never have wanted that. His body is cremated on 12

January in New Jersey. It is revealed that he wanted his ashes scattered in Bali, 'in accordance with the Buddhist rituals', and also in the Catskill Mountains north of New York City – where he loved the air, the light and the countryside, where he recorded *Heathen*, and where he owned, in Ulster County, what turned out to be his favourite of the many homes he had owned during his lifetime. His will, a twenty-page document filed under his legal name, David Robert Jones, declares his estate to be worth approximately $US100 million. He left their SoHo home to his wife, along with half the remainder of his wealth. His forty-four-year-old son Duncan would receive twenty-five per cent. His daughter Alexandria, fifteen, is left twenty-five per cent, along with her father's Catskills retreat. $US1 million goes to Marion Skene, Duncan's childhood nanny, whom he long regarded as his 'second mother'. $US2 million is the sum left to David's long-serving Girl Friday Coco Schwab, together with shares that he owned in Opossum Inc. Incredulity breaks out among fans all over the internet when it is discovered that the company has zero public disclosure, cannot be found trading in any market, and presents no public accounts. Some do the inevitable mad thing and start conspiracy theories, suggesting that it's all a sign, and that their hero must still be alive. Get a grip.

On 15 February, the 58th annual Grammy Awards are held at the Staples Center, Los Angeles. Numerous dearly departed are honoured, Bowie above all. Lady Gaga's ten-hit mash-up tribute to him takes the unofficial biscuit as Best Circus Cabaret. What a laugh. What was producer Nile Rodgers thinking? Maybe he wasn't.

'Jaw-droppingly bad,' is respected American music commentator Bob Lefsetz's verdict. 'Why didn't they just hire the original, Liza Minnelli, to do this faux-tribute to a bleeding-edge artist? Medleys never work. If she'd just sung "Space Oddity" *sans* make-up and production, it would have been better. Who's responsible for this? Couldn't Nile Rodgers have said no? . . . Gaga is treated like a superstar, as opposed to someone with one hit album. Hell, this was a job for Annie Lennox, someone from the old days who's still got it.'

' "Over-excited or irrational, typically as a result of infatuation or excessive enthusiasm; mentally confused",' tweets David's son, Duncan Jones. 'Damn it! What IS that word!?'

The Chic star naturally defends the performance he orchestrated.

'I did four projects with David including his biggest by far!' says Rodgers. 'I think I had an amazing relationship with him. Don't take it so seriously! . . . it's from the heart. It gives me a musical opportunity to say hello and goodbye to an artist who changed my life.'

Days later, Gaga's still sore . . . though not at the reviews, which Stefani couldn't care less about. She's still smarting from the tattoo she'd had done on her side at an ink parlour in West Hollywood two days before the show, her latest of many, featuring David's 'Aladdin Sane' lightning-bolt face: '. . . the image that changed my life.'

Infinitely more authentic is a three-night performance from 18 February by the Losers' Lounge in lower Manhattan: a traditional revue which honours pop stars and cult artists, led by former Psychedelic Furs keyboardist Joe McGinty at Joe's Pub on Lafayette Street.

London has a go, and does it better. During the BRIT Awards at the O2 Arena in Greenwich nine days later, the tribute introduced by, you guessed, Annie Lennox, is dignified and complete.

'The legacy of his extraordinary sound and vision will be loved and revered for as long as the earth still spins,' she declares.

Accepting the Icon award on David's behalf, actor Gary Oldman divulges that Bowie considered the hideousness of terminal cancer to have its compensations.

'I've got my cheekbones back,' was the way he told it, his close friend reveals.

The understated performance of 'Life on Mars?' by nineteen-year-old New Zealander Lorde is poignant. The 2014 BRIT

International Female Solo Artist winner, signed by Universal at the age of twelve, was the youngest solo artist to achieve a Number One single on the US Billboard Hot 100 in twenty-seven years. Her music was heard on *The Hunger Games: Mockingjay – Part One* soundtrack. She is, said Bowie himself, 'the future of music'. Her band on the night are the *crème* of David's own loyal backing musicians: pianist Mike Garson, who first played with Bowie in 1972, guitarists Earl Slick (1974) and Gerry Leonard (2001), drummer Sterling Campbell (1994), bassist Gail Ann Dorsey (1995) and keyboard player Catherine Russell (2002).

'David, you were mortal,' concludes Oldman, fiercely holding back tears, 'but your potential was superhuman, and your remarkable music is living on. We love you and we thank you.'

Duncan Jones approves.

On 31 March, a many-months-in-the-planning Bowie tribute gig is reconfigured as a sell-out memorial concert and staged over two nights at New York's Carnegie Hall and at Radio City Music Hall, featuring Tony Visconti's band Holy Holy, Cyndi Lauper, Debbie Harry and Blondie, the Roots, the Mountain Goats, the Pixies, Michael Stipe, Mumford & Sons, the New York City Children's Chorus, and many more.

On 14 April, Prince covers "Heroes" during his concert at the Fox Theater, Atlanta, in tribute to his friend. One week later, he too is dead.

John Giddings, organiser of the annual Isle of Wight Festival, announces his intention to honour David during the 9–12 June 2016 event at Seaclose Park, at which the Who, Queen with Adam Lambert, Stereophonics, Richard Ashcroft, Iggy Pop et al perform.

'We're printing twenty thousand Ziggy Stardust masks, and giving all the money to the Stand Up To Cancer charity,' John reveals. 'I was David's agent for thirty years. I love him.'

Glastonbury boss Michael Eavis adds that tributes will be paid at this year's festival, 22–6 June, at Worthy Farm, Pilton, Somerset, in the presence of Adele, Muse, Madness, Coldplay and seemingly endless others, and at which David's friend Philip Glass will perform his acclaimed 'Heroes' Symphony.

'We'll do the whole Bowie set from 2000 on one of the film screens when the stages are shut down,' Eavis confirms. 'It was an amazing gig, and I'm so glad he did that when he did – it was the last chance. David is one of my favourite artists of all time.'

There is far more about him than anyone can read, watch, absorb, ponder, listen to. We're all too soon Bowie'd out. How to make sense of it all? Someone might know. I stop by the Facebook page of David's most important record producer ever, Tony Visconti. Among much else to consider and digest, I come across this:

'He was an extraordinary man, full of love and life. He will always be with us. For now, it is appropriate to cry.'

To cry, and to remember.

Local Hero

This is about a hero. A remarkable man with a most unremarkable surname. We encountered him in the least likely location imaginable: our own backyard. The media were not yet obsessed with celebrities, and his level of fame was low-key. When his star exploded on the global stage, it felt as though we who saw him first were sharing him with the world.

Hy Money introduced me to David. I knew her as 'Lisa's Mum'. Lisa and I were best friends at Oak Lodge County Primary School, West Wickham in Kent. Her mother Hyacinth, a self-taught musician, artist and photographer, was shipped alone to England from India at the age of eighteen, with a pittance in her pocket and a phone number. She married the first man who asked her out, and had four children. The only Asian in our staid white town – which considered itself contemporary but which was stuck in the Fifties, a bastion of bunting, Boy Scouts and Mothers' Union cake sales – she was racially abused. When we went pirouetting through the streets dressed in the contents of Hy's dressing-up box, other mothers shooed their children indoors.

The first time I ever played an instrument – it was only a tambourine – was in her home, at one of her soirées. Shortly after her last-born started school, Hy began taking pictures for a local newspaper, the *Beckenham Record*. She would one day make a name for herself as the UK's first female sports photographer, at Crystal

Palace F.C. – having fought off lensmen who complained to their union and tried to get her banned, insisting that not only was a football pitch touchline no place for a woman, but that she was 'stealing their wages'.

Hy's fame was a few years off when, one Sunday afternoon in 1969, she took Lisa and me to a performance by Lithuanian sitar player Vytas Serelis, at the Three Tuns Folk Club in a pub on Beckenham High Street. She was there to photograph him. This ancient Indian instrument had been introduced to the world by Ravi Shankar, she explained. When it was used by both the Beatles and the Rolling Stones on recordings, its lush, drone-y sound infiltrated the mainstream. None of which meant much to two little mates from school. Marc Bolan and David Bowie were there too, that day, but they could have been anybody.

David co-founded the Beckenham Arts Lab at the Three Tuns soon afterwards. Lisa and I progressed to different grammar schools. David and fellow local musician Peter Frampton were suddenly in the news, and we were all thrilled about that. My new classmates and I set out to discover where David lived, which was in Haddon Hall, an imposing Gothic mansion on Southend Road, Beckenham. We took to door-stepping him and his new wife Angie there after school. Angie bestowed many signed photographs, for which we were always exceedingly grateful, but the best thing she ever did for us was to be out one day when we called.

That was the day when David answered the door in a lemon-silk, embroidered kimono, clutching a bottle of black varnish with which he was painting his nails. He was using a cocktail stick for want of a brush. That was strange enough, but then so was the colour. Black nail polish wasn't common back then. We were into shades of mauve and lilac at the time, but of course we couldn't wear it to school. He invited us in for tea, and was mortified to find that they were out of milk. We sat cross-legged on the floor and talked about ghosts, 'Space Oddity', his hopeless acting career and UFOs.

The first records I bought were not Bowie's. I didn't wake up to the pop charts until 1970. The first-ever single I got with my pocket money, from Woolworth's on West Wickham High Street, was 'Down the Dustpipe' by Status Quo – which BBC Radio 1's star turn, Tony Blackburn, couldn't stand. Several months later, with my birthday-card dosh, I invested in 'I Hear You Knocking' by Dave Edmunds, which John Lennon said he loved, so we knew it was good. I also bought 'When I'm Dead and Gone' by McGuinness Flint, and T. Rex's debut, 'Ride a White Swan'. Singles cost about seven shillings, pre-decimal: 35p. LPs were just under £2.00. Great Britain went metric a year later.

My first LPs were *Bridge Over Troubled Water* (Simon & Garfunkel), *Fog On the Tyne* (Lindisfarne,) and Wings' *Wild Life*. I saved up to buy records from the music department in Medhurst's, a large store on the Market Square at the top end of Bromley High Street, which is now a branch of Primark. David used to buy his records there, too. You could try them before you bought, in special listening booths. *Top of the Pops* on Thursday nights, BBC1, was unmissable: it's all we talked about in the playground the next day.

We all saw David Bowie perform 'Starman' on *Top of the Pops* on 6 July 1972, of course – but we were less than blown away by it. Although that specific appearance is widely proclaimed to have been the definitive performance, a turning point in popular music, the moment the 'whole world' changed . . . it didn't seem such a big deal to us. It's because that *Top of the Pops* performance of 'Starman', the one with Bowie and his guitarist Mick Ronson coming on to each other only five years after homosexuality between consenting males over the age of twenty-one had been decriminalised, the one about which entire tomes have been written, was not 'The First Time'.

I'm not the only one who remembers watching it: Bowie and the Spiders from Mars performed 'Starman' on Granada TV's *Lift Off with Ayshea* on 15 June 1972. Tragically, ITV deleted the master tape, but surviving photos suggest blatant flirtation between Bowie and Ronson on the day.

Many have expressed doubt, down the years, that this performance ever happened, because there remains no physical proof of it. But those of us who saw it beg to differ. A glimpse of the images is all that is needed to determine the differences between this and the later *Top of the Pops* rendition. In *Lift Off*, Bowie is strumming a brown (not his blue) acoustic guitar. Drummer Mick 'Woody' Woodmansey is wearing a different outfit, and has not yet lightened his hair. And there are giant, hexagram 'Star of David' stars in the 'sky' behind the band. In Tibetan lore – David had at one time been obsessed with the Buddhist religion and culture – this is the star of the 'origin of phenomenon'.

Marc Riley, former guitarist and keyboard player with Mancunian post-punk rockers The Fall, who went on to become a plugger, alternative rock critic and BBC radio presenter, remembers the show clearly. It obviously had more impact on him than on me: '. . . on came this . . . *thing*, with his weird mates,' he remembers. 'I was absolutely gobsmacked. My gran was shouting insults at the TV (which she usually saved for Labour's Party Political Broadcasts), and I just sat there agog. I was experiencing a life-changing moment. I know it sounds ridiculous, but it really did knock me for six.'

The *Top of the Pops* performance came three weeks later. 'For the second time in my life,' recalls Riley, 'I was transfixed by a bloke in a quilted jumpsuit and red leather boxing boots! There's no doubt that Bowie's appearance on *Top of the Pops* was a pivotal moment in British musical history. Like the Sex Pistols at the Lesser Free Trade Hall in Manchester in 1976, his performance lit the touch paper for thousands of kids who up till then had struggled to find a catalyst for their lives.'

But there was no extreme playground reaction at the Ravensbourne School, Bromley the next day. Not after either performance. I have no recollection of anyone in our gang mentioning 'Starman' in the context of 'turning point', or a life-ch-ch-changing experience, or of it being 'when the Seventies truly began'.

Besides, Marc Bolan had been camping it up on telly for well over a year by then. It was Bolan performing 'Hot Love' on *Top of the Pops* who originally took our breath away. Marc was so beautiful, you could barely bring yourself to look at him. The glitter under his eyes was a simple touch of style, a gimmick, but it seemed so profound and meaningful at the time. When he tucked his curly electric guitar lead down the back of his trousers for one of the *Top of the Pops* performances of 'Get It On' (July 1971), we fantasised that the power source must be his bum.

I reckon that 'Starman' performance on *Top of the Pops* is extolled to such a degree simply because the footage still survives. Ever since the show in question was initially re-screened (during the early Eighties?), music experts and culturalists from here to Boswell, Indiana (the 'hub of the universe') have been queuing up to wax lyrical about how it changed their lives, whether or not they saw it themselves at the time. I decided it might be interesting to ask Nicky Graham, former Spiders from Mars keyboard player turned music business mogul, who actually played in that legendary *Top of the Pops* performance. I wondered whether he remembered any immediate reaction to Bowie and the Spiders' appearance, rather than the hysteria that came years later. His answer, here in this book, is a surprising one.

So 1971 and 1972 belonged to Bolan. 'Hot Love', 'Get it On', 'Jeepster', 'Telegram Sam', 'Metal Guru', 'Children of the Revolution': we couldn't get enough of him, just as he couldn't get enough of himself. 1973 was the game-changer, when music started consuming my life. Out went *Bunty*, *Jackie* and *Girls' World*. In came the *Melody Maker* and the *New Musical Express*. Up in the loft went the Thunderbirds, the Sindys and the outfits my mother had sewn for them. In the bin went the moth-eaten gonks and unkempt trolls. In came vinyl. I swapped my Lady Penelope pink Rolls-Royce for a record player, and my National Health 'Joe 90' specs for coloured contact lenses.

It was all happening. Edward Heath was in Number Ten, and

Richard Nixon and the Watergate scandal dominated America. We joined the EEC, which later metamorphosed into the European Union. My sportswriter father went to Jamaica to report on George Foreman almost slaughtering Joe Frazier to take the heavyweight world boxing title at the Sunshine Showdown. The new London Bridge opened, cue huge excitement, as did the ill-fated World Trade Center twin towers in New York – at the time the tallest buildings in the world. A year later, as part of a schools exchange programme with Stella Maris High School on Long Island, I stood with my friends on top of the South Tower in the breathtaking Top of the World observatory, never imagining what would happen there twenty-seven years later.

Significant singles that year were Tony Orlando & Dawn's 'Tie a Yellow Ribbon Round the Old Oak Tree', Sweet's 'Ballroom Blitz', Elton John's 'Crocodile Rock' and Roberta Flack's 'Killing Me Softly'. Elvis Presley's TV special *Aloha From Hawaii via Satellite* (which my Auntie Ann loved) was the first worldwide telecast by an entertainer. It was viewed, perhaps perversely, by more people than had watched the 1969 moon landings. Bowie's chum Lou Reed was bitten on the butt by a fan during a gig in Buffalo, New York.

These were the factoids I relished, recording them for posterity in exercise books – for an entire year in purple and orange mirror-writing, with self-penned Spirograph patterns down the sides. Virgin Records launched, with Mike Oldfield's *Tubular Bells*. Queen released their debut, eponymous album, its stand-out single 'Seven Seas of Rhye'. The Who brought out *Quadrophenia*, and Roxy Music were everywhere and nowhere baby, with *For Your Pleasure*, and that exotic Amanda Lear creature on the front. Woman? Man? Bird? Plane? Who knew? David did, he was sleeping with it, despite being married to Angie. It was not for us to judge.

Bowie collapsed with exhaustion at a concert in Madison Square Garden ('Gimme your hands!'), and in May played the first-ever rock gig at the Earls Court Exhibition Centre. I didn't get a ticket, but I *was* at Hammersmith Odeon on 3 July, for the retirement of the Spiders. I've read all manner of outrageousness about that one in recent times. If fans really were cranking the shank and fellating total strangers in scenes of gay, bi and hetero abandon all over the auditorium, it wasn't coming to an aisle near me. Perhaps, like so much else in those days, it went over my head.

I have a list in the back of my purple diary from that year, of the albums I got in 1973. As well as the Beatles' *Red Album* and *Blue Album* (I came to the Fab Four party late), I bought *Aladdin Sane*, *The Rise and Fall of Ziggy Stardust and the Spiders from Mars* and *Hunky Dory*. All Bowie's, and in that order. I also bought *Red Rose Speedway* and *Band on the Run* by Wings, my other great love at the time. For Bolan, it was as good as all over by March 1973, when he released his single '20th Century Boy'. I chucked him for Bowie, and never looked back. Not until I wrote his biography in 2012.

David was our epiphany. People like him didn't exist in the semi-detached, net-curtained, knitted-doll-toilet-roll-cover world. Had it turned out that he really was from a parallel universe, I doubt that I would have been in the least surprised. He was twenty-three, still a boy, and yet married. Mortal, flawed, a scrawny chancer, and yet apparently enchanted. He was friendly enough. A little indifferent. He preened and he postured. His attitude was very 'look at me'. He sat around nattering and giggling, rolling and popping his lips as if having just applied lipstick. He picked at his cuticles, flicked his hair, batted his eyelashes, hugged his knees. Perhaps he was even posing as one of us, mirroring the behaviour of gawky tweenage girls. Trying us on for size, seeing what quirks he might pilfer.

He seemed slightly 'off': a 'bird of paradise with a broken wing,' I wrote later. 'Perfectly beautiful, except for the awful teeth.' I was on the fence, that's for sure: did I think deep-down that I ought to disapprove? That must have crossed my mind, because I also described him as 'a ruthless fantasist', a 'calculating cynic', 'lascivi-ous', and 'the worst kind of obsessive: one with a negligible attention span.' I speculated that there 'may well be a conscience in there somewhere'; but that, despite the image, he seemed 'compassionate, nostalgic and home-loving'. A bundle of contradictions, then. Maybe that was just me.

Androgynous get-up and posing aside, the lasting, paradoxical impression was of how normal he was. That complicated, contradictory, cheeky, charming, disarming Bowie-by-Bromley – 'Dave', as he signed himself, often in red pen – I was to find, over the years to come, never really changed.

He quizzed me about my hair, mere tufts at the time, which was taking ages to grow back after surgery. I was mortified by the question, but he'd put me on the spot. I'd suffered a post-op condition called Telogen effluvium, which basically meant that my hair had fallen out from shock. I'd spent much of the previous year in hospital, then convalescing at home. My appendix had ruptured, a few days before the Easter holidays. They operated on Good Friday. Peritonitis kicked in: in those days a killer. Our vicar at St Francis of Assisi arrived at the Intensive Care Unit at Farnborough Hospital. I was not expected to make it through the night. But I survived, a freak: scarred, skeletal and three-quarters bald.

The cool girls at my new school kept their distance. I made three friends, and I know them still. David was sympathetic. He too, he said, had undergone painful surgery at Farnborough Hospital, just across the road from where my parents still live. That was after a smack in the mush from George Underwood, the school chum who remained his friend to the end. It was the punch that apparently resulted in the most distinguished look in rock. There is more to the episode, well of course, than meets the eye.

'My cousin saw you in Margate,' I blurted. 'She's still got the ticket.' Cringe. A 'carried a watermelon' moment.

'Margate!' he grinned. 'I'm very fond of down there. Oh, I do like to be beside the seaside! It's that great look-out-there-nowhere-longingness.'

What on earth did *that* mean? I didn't dare ask. I scribbled the phrase in my rough book as soon as I got back on the bus, but I never did find out.

'Maybe I'll move there one day,' he mused. 'It'd be a great place to bring up kids. I do feel an affinity. I have a real fondness for the old seaside schtick, all that music-hall, end-of-pier stuff. It's very real. My nan was a nurse at the Seabathing (Hospital) on the front, before the First World War. She used to sing me little ditties. One of them was about Margate. 'A *breeze*! A *breeze*! Who sails today the ocean's swelling waters',[1] he mock-warbled, crooking his elbows and rocking his arms in time, like something out of Gilbert & Sullivan's *H.M.S. Pinafore*. 'I wish I could remember how it went. My grandparents got married there, and lived there for a while.'

'Mine still do,' I told him. It was true. My own grandmother, Nancy Jones, worked with her brother and sister-in-law, Gladys and Glyn Powell, at their guest house on Westbrook Bay. My grandfather Emlyn ran the putting green opposite the beach, just down from Margate station.

'I've potted a few balls there in my time,' David nodded. 'I'm such a kid, I never can resist a round of pitch and putt!'

Margate had been a quiet fishing village until sea bathing became a popular pastime in the early eighteenth century. The landscape painter J.M.W. Turner was a regular visitor from the 1820s and more than a hundred of Turner's works were inspired by the sea and the storms at Margate.[2] By the 1900s, the town was on the map. By the early Sixties, it had acquired the saucy-postcard kitsch that epitomises the English seaside resort; the end-of-pier, fish-and-chip-ness that David so loved.

In 1965, he was the lead singer with a Margate Mod band, the Lower Third. Back then, the town was a primary destination for Mods, who would pour in *en masse* on scooters, especially on Bank Holiday Mondays. Brawls with Rockers on motorbikes would ensue, as they also did in Brighton and other seaside towns, which scandalised the country for a time. The Lower Third had a regular slot at a local hotel. They played nine or ten gigs throughout the summer season at Cliftonville Hall, as well as a string of other engagements around the country. Had I been a few years older, no doubt I would have seen them play. I'd spent every half-term and holiday with my grandparents in Margate since I was small. The memory shimmers with endless summers of rubber buckets, choc-ices and donkey rides on sand; of the Margate Caves and the Tivoli Park circus, the Shell Grotto, the Winter Gardens, the pier – lost to a storm in 1978 – and the penny arcade.

Run for the shadows. I fantasised for days after that visit to Haddon Hall. I dared to imagine growing up to be like him. Fat chance. I was plain and four-eyed, barely artistic, and never in a million musical. We didn't have the money for lessons. I longed for so much that was never going to happen. Being a girl, I was most unlikely to engage in the family trade. Football had once conferred a glimmer of limelight on our Joneses. My putting-green grand-father Emlyn had once played for Everton, his brother Great Uncle Bryn for Arsenal. Uncle Cliff, a star at Spurs, had been the best left-winger on earth, in his day. They call Gareth Bale 'the new Cliff Jones' today. Darling of 'the Double' team of 1960–61, he was capped fifty-nine times for Wales. Bryn and Cliff secured the fami-ly's place in the history books, for having twice produced the world's most expensive player. My father Ken, a marginal pro, retired early after injury, reinvented himself as a sports reporter, became a columnist, and spent ten years on the road with Muhammad Ali. Fleet Street seemed not too far-fetched an ambi-tion, then. Perhaps, I dared hope, it was in the genes.

After music writer Michael Watts's landmark Bowie interview in the *Melody Maker* on 22 January 1972, in which our hero threw caution from the window to 'confess', 'I'm gay, and always have been, even when I was David Jones,' he became fair game. It was exactly what he'd wished for and provoked. It was now fashionable in the media to exaggerate him beyond reasonable doubt. To portray him as a sex-crazed kook and a drug-addled alien. To put unuttered (and sometimes unutterable) words into his mouth. Anything went, and everything worked. He became a superstar, and fell head over heels in love with himself, along with half the population of planet Earth.

During his extreme cocaine addiction in the late Seventies, he lost sight of himself for a while. He somehow wrenched himself from the vacant glitz of Los Angeles and relocated to the epicentre of austerity, Berlin – which he had to do, in order to survive. While a Modern Languages student on a year out, I ran into him one December in Chartier on the Faubourg Montmartre, Paris, which in those days was a budget eaterie a Jagger's throw from my digs. Today, it is a 'legendary brasserie', still cheerful, though nowhere near as cheap; still feeding students and artists as well as locals and tourists. David was flat-capped, unadorned, unaccompanied, barely recognisable. He looked snivelly, on the edge of a cold. He was scoffing *cassoulet* and swilling *vin blanc de table*. I sat and had a glass with him.

'The barnet made a comeback, then,' he grinned. Nice pun.[3] Incredible memory, too, I thought to myself. And still making a joke of everything. But wasn't he afraid of getting mobbed, in a place like this?

'Nah,' he said with a shrug. 'They don't know it's me.'

'I knew it was you.'

'You knew me before.'

'Before what?'

'You know. Before the madness. They'd never expect to see me in here, so they're not looking for me, if you know what I mean. I keep my head down.'

'And your hat on.'

'And me 'air on. Very me, don't you think?'

'No.'

He doodled houses, trees, starbursts and wings with a black Bic on the paper tablecloth. I wish I'd kept it. I have the menu, at least. I noticed that he was a southpaw, cack-handed like me. It was another thing we had in common (and probably a 'sign': which everything is to a teenager, when every emotion is through the roof). He chain-smoked Gitanes, removing one from the packet with his teeth, lighting it with a match, sucking down a few drags, tapping the ash into a tin ashtray before grinding the half-smoked fag there, and lighting another. He held them the way lefties hold pencils, or like a bookie, with his fingertips – the burning end facing into his palm. Why?

'This was how you knew which were the Nazi spies in the old war films. And you knew which ones were the Yanks, because they did it the other way!'

'Why do you do it?'

'What?'

'Smoke so much.'

'Habit I s'pose. It's my mum and dad's fault. I used to nick theirs, and it went from there. It was the thing to do, it made you look grown-up, we thought, all us kids . . . and it was not an expensive habit, in the days when you could still buy single ciggies or a couple at a time, down the newsagents. Hard to believe now, that, isn't it. Stupid thing is, I used to have a right go at my mother for smoking. I don't know why I do it at all, really. You think it's going to relax you, but it doesn't.'

'Do you smoke like this all day?'

'I don't usually start until I've had me breakfast.'

Smoking seemed to come more naturally to him than breathing. I couldn't help wondering how his voice might sound without it, let alone what his breath must taste like. He'd been at some awards thing, he said, and was on his way back to Geneva to spend Christmas with the family at home in Blonay, a village above the lake near Montreux. He'd nipped to Paris to find a few presents in the Galeries Lafayette on the Boulevard Haussmann, a less than ten-minute walk from where we sat.

'It used to have a staircase in the middle like a cruise liner's,' he said, 'but they ripped it out a couple of years ago. God knows why, it was the best in Europe, must've been. Wonder what they did with it. Wouldn't have minded that in my gaff. As if it would fit! Still, it's worth going there just to look up at the dome, even if you don't want to buy anything. Better than St Paul's.'

He began talking animatedly about Jan Cox, an obscure American mystic whom he'd recently discovered – and about a Dutch painter of the same name, who at the time was living in Belgium.[4]

'Weird, that,' he said. 'I discovered them both at the same time. I went looking for the one but I found the other, which led me back to the one I was trying to find in the first place. There is no such thing as coincidence. A lot of people are afraid of mystics, wouldn't you say? In some ways, they have more to fear from painters. If only they knew.'

We wished each other a Merry Christmas . . . 'and a Happy Blue Year.'

'Ta-ta,' he said, touching his cap, aping the barrow-boy. I left him standing there on the pavement in the cold as I turned to go. Like the sky, I was lachrymose.

In September 1977, he released his signature, perhaps his most famous song: ' "Heroes" '. He got himself back. He divorced Angie, took custody of their child, and stayed on in Switzerland, selling their 'cuckoo-clock house' in 1982 and moving to the Château du Signal near Lausanne. In July 1981, when I accompanied the late DJ Roger Scott to Montreux to interview members of Queen at Mountain Studios, a drunken session at the sadly defunct White Horse pub resulted in the jam that led to the recording of 'Under Pressure'. It appeared on Queen's album *Hot Space*, and was their second Number One, and David's third.

When Bowie stepped back into the spotlight in 1983, he looked superhuman: a bronzed and glowing, golden-haired Apollo, with not a trace of Ziggy, zombie or Duke. I got to see him on the Serious Moonlight tour. In 1984, Bowie's *Melody Maker* confidant Michael Watts hired Capital Radio's Nicky Horne, Gary Crowley and me to co-present *Ear-Say*, the rock magazine series he was editing for Channel 4 television. Michael and I became friends. He was with me when my father fell under a train at London Bridge in December 1992, and lost his writing arm.

The next time I saw David was in 1987, on the Glass Spider tour. It opened in the Netherlands that May, when I was six months' pregnant with my first child. The late Sir David English, then editor of the *Daily Mail*, tried to disqualify me from the job, arguing that Associated Newspapers' insurance wouldn't cover me to fly. What's more, he'd be surprised if the airline would agree to carry me. There's always a way round it. I'd take the train to Harwich, an overnight ship to the Hook of Holland, and a further train to Rotterdam. Post-gig, the hacks, snappers and hangers-on would be wending our way to the Amsterdam Hilton. Christ, you know it ain't easy.

This rebel rebel rocked up at David's dressing-room door backstage at the Feyenoord football stadium, 'De Kuip', wearing one blue and one brown contact lens. When he answered the door, he met my mismatched gaze, his eyes fell to my bump, and he said, 'You again. Very funny, shall we just do this?' Post gig, which was a strange one, I found myself wandering the concrete corridors of the stadium alone. Reluctant to join the pumped-up throng outside, I lacked a lift back to the hotel. It was David who saw me to safety, calling for a police escort for 'the lady with the baby'. He was involved with one of his dancers, Melissa Hurley, and had already spoken of marriage. Perhaps he was broody.

Their relationship didn't work out. Neither did Tin Machine. He'd only wanted to re-create the magic of being in a rock'n'roll band, he said, but the moment had passed. The fans were not into it.

I saw him a few times more in New York, sometimes at Indochine, an elite French–Vietnamese restaurant on Lafayette Street close to the Astor Place Theatre. It was a favourite haunt. He ate like a bird. Drank rarely. Preferred water, and strong coffee. He was always squeaky-showered and shaven. He now chain-smoked Marlboro, still stubbing out after a couple of drags.

At the turn of the Nineties, I stayed in his house on the Caribbean island of Mustique. What had made him build his own place there? 'A whim', he called it. 'I love a good cliché. The house is the most delightful cliché. And the light there is terrifying.'

I flew with my daughter Mia (as yet unborn when I interviewed him in Rotterdam) to Barbados, where a Merlyn Commander conveyed us to the ultimate destination. Mustique had been put on the map by Her Majesty's late sister Princess Margaret and her set. His home, Britannia Bay House, was paradise: five-star everything. All ours, gratis, for a month.

David married the former supermodel Iman in 1992, and went to ground after that – or rather skyward, into a ninth-floor apartment in the Essex House Hotel on Central Park South. In 2000, their longed-for daughter was born. Becoming a father for the second time at fifty-three – Zowie/Joey/Duncan had arrived when David was only twenty-four – he felt blessed by the opportunity to redeem himself as a parent. Two years later they moved house, to a vast, glamorous apartment at 285 Lafayette Street, SoHo, with a rooftop garden and an A-list of residents, a brief stroll up the road from Indochine. In summer 2004, he took a wake-up call: the first of a series of heart attacks.

Despite increasing ill-health, it was the final third of Bowie's personal life that turned out to be the most positive and fulfilling. He had made a fortune and he lived richly, because he could. He had found true love, which he'd longed for, having been casual about relationships in his youth. The Joneses, as they were always known, purchased an estate a hundred miles upstate in the Catskills, near Woodstock. David had recorded his album *Heathen* in the neighbourhood in 2001, and felt at home there. Musicians who worked with him in the twilight years report that he retained his sense of humour, remained self-deprecating, tongue-in-cheek and quintessentially 'London–English', and was never up himself – or only now and then, and mostly in jest. Behind the Bowie, he was still David Jones (and never did change his name by deed poll). Whoever David Jones was. Did *he* even know? Had his whole life been a search for an illusion? As he was fond of saying, even the act was an act. He was only ever 'just an entertainer'.

He died on Sunday, 10 January. The news seeped out at around 3 a.m. in New York's Eastern time zone: 7 a.m. GMT. At 07.02, I got an email from an American friend who keeps hedge-fund hours:

'David Bowie passed away,' she wrote. 'How sad ... It's quite shocking. I didn't know he was ill.'

Nor did anyone but the closest. All sworn. Just as he wanted. Just as he'd lived. By his own rules.

To attempt to tell his epic tale with every date, fact, location, figure and complete supporting cast would take longer to write than Bowie lived. This is not that. Neither is it a go-to manual for note-by-note dissection of his vast catalogue of songs, nor for pathological interpretation of every lyric. Nor is this the place for a roll-call of every musician he ever recorded and performed with. This hangs humbly on my memories and personal experiences of the man and his music, and on those of a handful who were once close to him. The revelations made by individuals who have said little or nothing about Bowie before, are frank, funny and heart-rending.

Millions adored him. Most never got near him. To have experienced the Bowie phenomenon up close and personal still feels surreal. I'll always wonder about those hours spent in London, Paris, Montreux, Birmingham, Rotterdam and New York with this lost, tormented, serene and instinctive soul. He stabbed in the dark like the rest of us. But he found ways that were unprecedented of distilling the essence of life and the conundrums of the universe. His ability to express them rocked, and changed us all.

INNER-CITY INFANT

I

1947–1953

He was a baby boomer: one of millions of babies born during the post-Second World War surge that occurred across the globe between 1946 and 1964, particularly in the West, which peaked in the UK in March 1947. King George VI, the father of Queen Elizabeth II, was on the throne. Clement Attlee was in Number Ten: the first Labour Prime Minister to serve a five-year term.

Atrocious timing, stork. It was a cold coming he had of it. Britain was in the grip of its harshest winter for years. Major power cuts were about to be imposed in England and Wales, due to fuel shortages caused by the weather. The BBC Television service, which had begun regular broadcasts just over a decade earlier, was suspended until well into March.

David Robert Jones was born at home in post-Blitz Brixton, south of London's Thames, on a bitter Wednesday morning, 8 January 1947. It was also Elvis Presley's twelfth birthday. Although clearly a vintage year for rock'n'roll – Steve Marriott, Elton John, Gerry Rafferty, Brian May, David Essex and Marc Bolan all landed that year, too – it was anything but glam.

Brixton had once been a grand, progressive neighbourhood, after the opening of the Vauxhall Bridge in 1816 connected it to central London and lured the middle classes across the river. The turn of the century brought widespread social upheaval, when the middle classes abandoned their mansions and a vast working-class population moved in. By 1925, the area was a bustling shopping and cultural centre. But then came the Luftwaffe.

Though the booms had long faded, in 1947 children still played on bomb sites that wouldn't be cleared for years. Slums were being demolished, council housing was going up, and shell-damaged houses were flogged off for a song. In the late Forties and early Fifties, many West Indian immigrants settled in the area, and have been there ever since.

The damp rose relentlessly in the Joneses' new home. Paint peeled, the woodwork was worm-riddled, and lino curled underfoot. Some of the windows were still criss-crossed with tape, a wartime hangover, applied to prevent glass bursting during air raids. There was no central heating: warmth came from a coal fire burning in a single grate. Like most families of their kind, they heated only one room.

David's mother had him at home because she had no choice. There was not yet a National Health Service. That thing most taken for granted, our modern welfare state, was still more than a year away. Some mothers were lucky enough to give birth in hospital. The majority still faced the agony at home, attended by one of a brisk army of district nurses and midwives, who breezed about on bikes; or with their mum, or a kindly sleeves-up neighbour. Birth was women's work, managed with hot water and a bar of carbolic soap. No pain relief. Picture the tin bath hanging on the wall out the back. They all had one. Fathers were banished for a smoke in the yard. Their sole responsibility throughout labour was to keep the home fire flaming, so that the placenta could be burned after birth. No frills.

A robust utility pram, perhaps second-hand, most likely borrowed, sat waiting for baby David in the gloomy hallway. He would remember that pram with a shudder in years to come. There was no washing machine or tumble drier to deal with the endless soiled towelling nappies and baby clothes, which were mostly home-made out of cast-off men's vests and bedsheets. Laundry was washed and mangled by hand, and hung to dry in the yard or on a brass airer round the fire. Nobody had a car. Housewives and mothers walked everywhere, using prams as pushchairs and shopping trollies. There was no supermarket to nip to, long queues at the butchers' and the bakers' endured, and there were still ration books for most things: for bread until the following year, sugar until 1953, and for meat and all other comestibles until 1954. David's mother was still lining up to buy apportioned food until he was seven.

The year of 1947 was one of sweeping change: social and environmental, cultural and political. After the First World War, Britain had lost her influence in industry and the armed forces. The aftermath of the Second saw the rapid decline of the Empire. The greatest global power for more than a century, it would soon be reduced to a Commonwealth. India, the jewel in the crown, was lost in 1947. Earl Mountbatten of Burma was her last Viceroy. Pakistan also gained independence. On the domestic front, the school-leaving age was raised to fifteen, and in September, the University of Cambridge voted to allow women to become full students for the first time. But freedom was not a given: only on 15 June that year would restrictions on foreign travel imposed during the war be lifted. In August, the first Edinburgh Festival of the Arts and the Edinburgh International Film Festival were launched. Princess Elizabeth, our future Monarch, announced her engagement to Lt Philip Mountbatten (the Duke of Edinburgh-to-be), and married him in Westminster Abbey on 20 November. The ceremony was watched by four hundred thousand viewers, and is our oldest-surviving telerecording.

Into all this David came, a nation on the brink of change and unprecedented development. He was his mother Peggy's third child, his father John's second. His parents were not married.

It's a tangled tale. David's father, real name Haywood Stenton Jones, was a shoe manufacturer's son from Doncaster, a south Yorkshire market town about a hundred and seventy miles north of

London. He was born in 1912, making him thirty-five at the time of David's birth. After receiving a good inheritance in his early twenties, John hiked south to seek work in the entertainment business. His head was soon turned by Hilda Sullivan, the young singer he married in December 1933. He threw himself into making her a star. Two thirds of his investment later, his 'turn' was still unknown. Undeterred, he opened his own nightclub in Soho with the grand he had left, promoting his wife as the resident songbird. The venture failed miserably.

In September 1934, John became a full-time employee of Dr Barnardo's, a London-based charity for orphaned and vulnerable children, and was made responsible for PR. His marriage to Hilda limped along, the on-off union challenged by both lack of funds and infidelity. John's 'Midland bonk', an unknown Birmingham woman, bore him a child, Annette Jones, whom his wife Hilda bizarrely agreed to adopt. When the couple went their separate ways soon afterwards, Hilda hung onto the baby. John shot off to war in 1939, and in 1945 wound up in Tunbridge Wells, Kent – where he met David's mother.

Margaret Burns, known as Peggy, was born in Folkestone on the Kent coast, seventy miles south-east of London, in 1913. Hailing from east of the River Medway, she was a Maid of Kent (as opposed to a Kentish Maid, who hails from the west). When she and John met in Tunbridge Wells, she was a waitress, an usherette, or both at the local cinema. A year younger than John, she had already had two children out of wedlock. Her first was a boy, Terence, by a Frenchman called Jack Rosemberg, who abandoned Peggy before the birth. Terry went by his mother's surname. Her second child, a daughter named Myra Ann born nearly six years later, was put up for adoption and never seen again.

Peggy moved with her new beau to north London – to live, unbelievably, with John's wife Hilda. In 1947, they all bought the house at Stansfield Road together. It cost £500, and was a suggested legacy for Annette. Haywood remained married to Hilda. The arrangement got complicated when David was born. After that, Hilda threw in the towel and put in for a divorce which was finalised that August. John and Peggy were married weeks later, at Brixton Register Office, on 12 September 1947. Peggy's mother acted as witness. David was nearly nine months old.

Much has been made, down the years, of the fact that David's birth was not registered, despite the legal requirement to do so, until he was thirteen years old. It was assumed that registration must have been overlooked, and that his parents only applied to do it more than a dozen years down the line when they found that they needed to in order to get him a passport, 'for a family trip to France'. This is incorrect. For a start, his parents would never have been able to enrol him at any school without a birth certificate. In fact, David did have one from birth like virtually everybody else in the UK, despite his illegitimacy – still a matter of shame in those days. His parents could of course have been prosecuted for not registering him, failure to do so being a criminal offence.

My curiosity was sparked when I examined an official copy of David's certificate. The date, place of birth, gender and birth names are shown very clearly in the first three columns – as are the names of his parents. His mother is named 'Margaret Mary JONES, formerly BURNS', even though she and John were not married at the time of David's birth. Two columns along, clear amendments to the original certificate details have been made. A new address is given under 'M.M. Jones, Mother': '4 Plaistow Grove, Bromley, Kent' (their eventual address), and is verified 'by declaration dated 4 April 1960'. To the right, the next column entry reads 'Fifth April 1960 on the authority of the Registrar General'. Why would Margaret Mary have become 'formerly' Burns, why would an address have been added, and for what reason would such amendments have been made?

Two lawyers I consulted had no clue. The third introduced me to a contact at the relevant Government department, who trawled the records (off the record). The explanation, via a circuitous route, turned out to be simple.

'You *can* re-register a birth,' said my informer.

'This is common when the original entry had an error. What you've got here is that in 1960, for whatever reason, someone applied to re-register this birth, and to have the original certificate altered. It is strange to add a new address on. Usually, when changes are made to a certificate and a new one issued, the Registrar would handwrite explanatory notes underneath or on the side of the original. I will check the original entry for you.'

He did so. Days later, all became clear.

'The law allows for re-registration of a birth in order to make a baby a child of the marriage,' he explained. 'So when parents marry after the birth of their baby, re-registration of the birth of legitimated persons is allowed. But during the years immediately after World War Two, parents were not allowed to re-register a child if there was a third party involved: say for example one of the partners had been married to another person. A block on this kind of activity was applied. This was the Government keeping tabs on people in the early post-war years. The block was later removed. After the Births and Deaths Registration Act of 1953, things became more straightforward. As the procedure stands, parents are obliged to register within forty-two days of a birth, to provide both a legal record and also protection of the child concerned.'

What about the declaration having been made on 4 April 1960, but authority having been given on 5 April 1960?

'Very simple,' he said. 'The mother went into her local Register Office – Bromley – to make the declaration. Details were then conveyed to HQ to be verified by the Registrar General, who alone could give authority to the application.'

Peggy entered into her only marriage with a ten-year-old and a past. Quite how questionable a past would not become apparent until much later. Certainly her own growing-up was blighted by the effects of 'the family affliction', a condition which research indicates was almost certainly schizophrenia, and which affected several of her family members. In years to come, it would preoccupy the adult David, when his obsession with 'madness' became a major theme in his work. The clues are all there in 'All the Madmen', 'Jump They Say', 'I'm Deranged', 'Ashes to Ashes', and many other of his songs.

Peggy's mother Margaret Heaton was a Manchester lass who had moved to Margate to work as a nursing auxiliary in the Royal Seabathing Hospital. Her soldier-boy pen-pal Jimmy Burns followed her to the south coast, and they were married at All Saints Church, Westbrook, in 1912. But the Great War loomed. What once had seemed like an idyll beside the seaside now posed a threat, given the proximity of the Channel. The couple moved deeper into Kent, to Southborough, Tunbridge Wells, and had six children: Peggy (David's mother), Nora (Victoria Honoria), James, Una, Vivienne and Eileen Patricia, known as Pat.

David's grandmother Margaret is remembered as having exhibited behaviour understood today to be schizophrenia. The illness tends to run in families, is said to be caused by a combination of genetic and environmental factors, and can be triggered by extreme stress or emotion. Victims suffer from hallucinations, delusions, behavioural changes, and confused and even suicidal thoughts. Margaret apparently found it difficult to express affection and emotion, disliked physical contact, and was angry and sometimes violent, especially as she aged.

Her family believed that at least three of her children inherited the tendencies. Nora, Una – the unmarried mother of David's cousin Kristina (the two would later become close), and Vivienne all experienced attacks and had visions. The most extremely affected, Nora was lobotomised, and packed off to an institution in Yorkshire. David later referred to them as his 'mad aunts', and to the affliction as 'this nuttiness'. He seemed resigned to the fact that his family on his mother's side was tainted by mental illness. He would at times become deeply concerned by it. 'Sometimes when

I'm drunk or stoned, I can almost feel it in me,' he told his first wife
Angie on the day they met.

The eldest, Peggy – David's mother – appeared to have been
spared. But the effect of so much misery and anxiety impacted
upon her ability to raise her children affectionately. She is described
as having been 'hands-off', and a 'cold' mother. This was evident in
her behaviour towards her elder son Terry.

Born in 1937, the result of a brief liaison, baby Terry was looked
after by Peggy's mother. He was a happy little boy, by all accounts.
His youngest aunt, Pat, doted on him. When Peggy 'went off to that
London' with John, Terry remained with his grandparents in
Southborough. After David was born, Peggy wanted Terry to come
and live with the family. John resisted, but Peggy got her way.

Terry was ten years old, shy, awkward, and wary of his step-
father. He was registered at school as Terry Jones (but would later
reclaim the surname Burns). As he grew up, he is said to have felt
increasingly frustrated and rejected, especially by John. David
would later describe his father as having had 'a lot of love in him,
but he didn't know how to show it.' His mother seems to have failed
to stick up for Terry, who withdrew into his shell. It was not a happy
home. Though the half-brothers (David would later refer erroneously to Terry as his 'step-brother') were a decade apart in age, they
shared a bedroom. David worshipped Terry, but couldn't help him.
Terry brooded, internalising his pain and frustration, and started
having blackouts at school. Though he had shown academic promise in earlier years, his focus and confidence deserted him. He left
at fourteen, with nothing to his name. His eventual descent into
mental illness would be absolute.

Could David have been afflicted?

'It's a very complicated question,' says eminent consultant
psychiatrist Dr Cosmo Hallström.

'If you have a first-degree relative with schizophrenia, your
chances are one in eight – thirteen per cent, roughly – of getting the
illness yourself. The most important risk factor is genetic. His aunts

and his grandmother probably had it. They were second-degree relatives, so the risk goes down. But if your brother has it, your risk is fifteen to twenty per cent of getting it. The figures are approximate. If your brother has it *and* your mother has it, you are definitely in line for it. David Bowie had reasonable cause to be concerned.'

How many different genes can cause schizophrenia?

'At the moment, a hundred and eight have been identified. You need fifty or so to be at risk.'

And the difference between madness and creativity?

'The sixty-four thousand dollar question. Schizophrenia in its early stages is all very interesting. New ways of seeing things, emotional dysregulation, boundaries being broken down and so on. As it takes hold, you stop doing things, you stop being creative, you sit around staring at walls. There is poverty of thought, action and word. It is rare to be creative in the late stages of the illness. You find you can't work, earn money or retain relationships. It's a sad situation.

'But medicine is all about sadness,' Dr Hallström adds. 'David Bowie would certainly have feared schizophrenia. Many people do fear getting it. Most people ignore it and carry on. If you spend your time worrying that you might get it, you're abnormal. The saddest thing in this family's case is that there was no medical option back then. You might have gone for psychotherapy, or you might have been given asylum in an institution. There was nothing in between.

'There is a great tendency to look back and say, this and that happened, and therefore that's why. If you start looking for links, you will find them. Many thousands, millions of children have experienced abandonment, or were raised in cold-hearted homes. They don't all turn out to be phenomenal creative artists who leave astonishing musical legacies and are universally loved. There is a theory that it is impossible to be a great artist unless you have experienced a dysfunctional upbringing. I don't agree with that, because

I'm a scientist. I don't deal in theory. But the kind of parenting that David Bowie received will certainly have affected his development.'

David's first day at Stockwell Infants School is recorded as 12 November 1951, curiously. He would not turn five until January 1952. There appears to be no reason for the anomaly; the British state school year begins with fresh intake during the Michaelmas term in September. The most likely explanation is disagreement over whether he should commence his education in the autumn of 1951, when he was a little too young, or wait until the following year.

David never revealed adverse memories of his brief tenure at Stockwell Infants. The reason for his departure after just one year was his mother's unhappiness. An under-funded 'sink school' in an area of deprivation was less than she wanted for her third-born, the child upon whom she had pinned her hopes to the exclusion of almost all else. Peggy nursed dreams of returning to her beloved Garden of England, her birth county of Kent, where they could re-invent themselves as a respectable middle-class family, and where David would be free to flourish at a nice little village school. Although her husband never expressed longings to move back to his native Yorkshire, it was said that he much preferred the buzz of Brixton and its proximity to the bright lights. The lure of London's West End never faded for John, who still harked back to the good old days when he strove to launch 'his Hilda' as a singer. A compromise was called for, and would come.

Brixton today is hip and happening, a hectic hoopla, an arty and outré melting-pot. It differs substantially from the Brixton in which David was born. In early interviews, he liked to give the impression that he'd lived rough and tough in some edgy English Harlem, and that he'd acquired 'black' rhythms and sensibilities by direct exposure to them as a child. His recollections were fanciful, designed to convey an impression of street-cred and cool.

'It left great, strong images in my mind,' he told *Time Out*'s Timothy White in an interview in 1983. 'All the ska and blue beat clubs were in Brixton, so one gravitated back there. Also, it was one of the few places that played James Brown records.'

Alas, he would not have been immersed in Brixton's music scene while he lived there. When the family sold up and moved out, he was only six years old.

SUBURBAN
SCHOOLBOY

1953–1961

The compromise was Bromley, an old market town registered in an official charter during the first millennium as 'Bromleag': 'a wood-land clearing where broom grows'. It came to prominence as a main coaching inn on the beaten track to Hastings, and landed a literary claim to fame in Jane Austen's *Pride and Prejudice*. The renowned Ravensbourne Morris Men dancers were founded in Bromley the year that David was born. Some of those original members, now in their eighties, are still dancing, outside the Greyhound pub on Keston Common every Boxing Day. It has long been a local tradition to trek there and watch them, which David and his family did.

By 1953, Bromley was something of a no-man's land, falling short of Kent proper but being not quite part of the metropolis. This future major London borough on the hem of the capital's petticoats lay less than ten miles south-east of Brixton, but could not have been more different environmentally, economically or socially. It was leafy, conservative, family-oriented, safe – much as it is today, despite the town planning, expansion and relentless 'improvement' that eviscerates the heart and soul of a place. Comedian Frankie Boyle would later denounce it as 'a lobotomy made out of bricks'. Today, you'll find a large shopping mall, and many pubs, restaurants and bars, a high proportion of which present live music. Alas, the Royal Bell Hotel is now closed. The old

Market Square tavern in which I pulled pints, the summer before college, was quite the hub in David's day. He and George Underwood used to hang in the downstairs bar, known as the 'Cellar Bar'.

'You couldn't have missed me!' laughs George today. 'I used to get in there wearing all kinds in the Sixties. One day I sprayed my hair silver and wore a cavalry outfit with chainmail epaulettes. It was a pyjama top as a shirt, trousers with straps that went under the boot, that whole 'Sergeant Pepper' influence.[1] We'd go up to Notting Hill and buy all this uniform-style gear to pose around in. It was all about being noticed and talked about.'

When the Bell was a Berni Inn – part of a popular nationwide steakhouse chain – you could eat well for a quid 'on the first floor at the back': prawn cocktail, steak and chips and Black Forest gateau, followed by cream-topped Irish coffee in a wine glass, served with After Eights. This, for years, was the classic Bromley night out.

Towards its demise, the pub was also a trendy 'Sky Bar', and breathed its last as 'Bromleys' night club. Precise punctuation was not the only element it lacked. The building is Heritage Grade II listed, immune from demolition, and may eventually be redeveloped as a mini-arts centre. Many agree that it should be named in honour of Bowie. There are several theatres, including the Churchill, next to the Library Gardens that David loved; two main railway stations, four football clubs, and more cultural connections than you might expect.

Father of science fiction H.G. Wells was born in Bromley, and children's authors Enid Blyton and Richmal Crompton lived there, as did David Nobbs, the creator of *The Fall & Rise of Reginald Perrin* for television. An unlikely tenant was Aleister Crowley, notorious drug-addled, bisexual occultist, known in his day as 'the wickedest man in the world', and of whom Bowie would briefly become a follower. Down House in Bromley's Downe village was once the home of Charles Darwin, and is now a museum dedicated to his work. Sir George Martin, the fabled 'fifth Beatle' and producer of the Fab Four's endless hits, attended Bromley Grammar School.

Not everyone loved Bromley. The author Hanif Kureishi grew up there during the Sixties, and poked fun at his home town (and infuriated his family) in his novel *The Buddha of Suburbia*. It was adapted as a four-part TV serial for BBC2, for which David composed the theme, going on to write an entire album by the same name which featured the television soundtrack, and which was produced and mixed at Mountain Studios, Montreux. It was released in 1993, and again in 2007.

The Seventies saw the rise of the sub-cultural 'Bromley Contingent' – frustrated children of suburbia on a mission to rise from suffocating sameness and make their unforgettable mark. Remind you of anyone? This celebrated clique of divas, hipsters and punk groupies, including Siouxsie Sioux, later of Banshees fame, Poly Styrene and Gen X-er Billy Idol, were the original devotees of the Sex Pistols and their musical and sartorial masterminds, Malcolm McLaren and Vivienne Westwood.

In 1965, Bromley would be absorbed as part of Greater London. In the early Fifties, when the Joneses arrived, it was still small-townsville, with a wartime mentality and a May Queen. It also brimmed with lower middle-class baby boomers.

The most shocking aspect of the family exodus to suburbia was that Peggy's son Terry was not invited. A mere fifteen years old at the time, he had already left school and had a humdrum job. His relationship with his step-father John was so poor that Peggy felt it best to leave him behind. Perhaps his troublesome personality and increasingly odd behaviour were to blame. Terry was lodged with the next-door neighbours in Stansfield Road. He would never overcome the ultimate rejection, despite the fact that his parents later relented, and took him in.

Moving from house to house and from school to school, the family made room for David's half-sister Annette at one point, while she was training as a nurse. By June 1955, when David was eight, they were installed at 4 Plaistow Grove: a modest, terraced, bathroom-less house which today would change hands for more than £350,000. It was much smaller accommodation, but a smarter location. The Joneses had at last gone up in the world. Nearby Sundridge Park railway station, which was built for the private use of the aristocratic Scott family, had been redeveloped and opened to the public. The self-indulgent Prince of Wales – King Edward VII for just nine years at the turn of the twentieth century, thanks to the interminable reign of his mother, Queen Victoria (does history repeat?) – often visited the area for game-shooting week-ends. The neighbourhood also boasted an exclusive golf club.

Peggy Jones purchased gloves and hats, and smiled, and aspired, and how. She and John were inclined to take tea at the Bromley Court Hotel, a short-lived privilege. Not long after their arrival in the borough, the hotel was given over to weekend jazz stomps, when it began welcoming the best of the touring rhythm and blues acts.

The railway stations were important. They secured Bromley's status as a dormitory town. The daily London commute was a doddle. A train from Bromley South would deposit you virtually in Trafalgar Square within the half-hour, or at Victoria in twenty minutes. Not impossibly far-flung, John Jones was as happy as he could be with the compromise; as was Peggy, having got her way, fulfilling her dream of returning to her native Kent.

Terry moved back in with his family, but his tenure was short. He departed in November 1955 to commence National Service with the RAF.[2] David enrolled at Burnt Ash Junior School,[3] where he struck up one of his two most important lifelong friendships. The first was Geoff MacCormack, who lived round the corner from David, would join the St Mary's church choir with him, and eventually provide backing vocals on tour with David and on various of his recordings. The other, also a St Mary's chorister, was George Underwood.

David met George, not at Burnt Ash Juniors, but in the Wolf Cubs.

'We were eight, nine-ish, and in the Eighteenth Bromley at St Mary's church hall,' recalls George. 'We met and that was it: we were best friends from then on. We were always together. Our first-ever conversation was about music – skiffle – which was all the rage at the time. It was a revival, really, as it had been a big thing in America much earlier. It was basically a blend of blues, jazz and folk, and you played it on home-made instruments. It was the forerunner of punk. Punk was all about anybody being able to do it, and so was this. All you needed was your mum's washboard – a flat, ridged, wooden thing you scrubbed clothes on – and a tea-chest bass. We heard Lonnie Donegan's skiffle group and Lead Belly's "Rock Island Line" on Radio Luxembourg, and we went, "We can do that!"

'Rock Island Line' was the first recording to achieve gold status in the UK, selling more than a million copies worldwide. It started a craze that became a nationwide obsession. At one point, there were reckoned to be between thirty and fifty thousand skiffle groups around the country. Chas McDevitt's Skiffle Group, Johnny Duncan and the Bluegrass Boys, and the Vipers were among the more prolific. When the *Six-Five Special* produced by Jack Good launched on BBC TV in 1957 – the first British youth music programme with a skiffle recording as its title track and featuring skiffle acts as well as pop artists such as Terry Dene, Petula Clark, Marty Wilde and Tommy Steele – seventeen-year-old John Lennon had already started to perform with his Liverpool skiffle group the Quarrymen.[4]

'The next thing we knew, the cubs were having a camp down at Bognor Regis. Spud-bashing and all that nonsense. David and I weren't really interested. But by the time the next camp came up, on the Isle of Wight the following summer in 1958, we were on a mission.

'David brought an old tea-chest bass that his dad had helped him make, using a broom handle, and a ukulele for me. We did our first-ever performance around the camp fire, playing "Davy Crockett" and the like, and they lapped it up. There was a coffee bar near our camp that had a jukebox, and we used to get in there whenever we could escape from the Ging-Gang-Goolie brigade.'

The writing was on the wall from then on.

As well as their shared love of music, did David and George have similar personalities?

'No one was quite like David!' George laughs. 'Even when he was young. He was enthusiastic beyond the norm. When he was keen on a subject – American football, baseball, Jack Kerouac – after his brother Terry gave him his copy of *On the Road*. Whatever it happened to be, David would enthuse to the point that he'd be telling you what to do, and almost forcing you to get involved in it with him. He got very obsessed about things for very short periods of time. Then it would wear off almost as fast as it had come on, and he'd be on to something else. He was a faddist. We became friends because we had the same sense of humour. We had a similar surreal take on things, and took hardly anything seriously. We were a couple of kooks, I suppose.

'We called each other by our middle names, Robert and Michael. We also used backslang sometimes, which my dad taught me. He was a wholesale greengrocer, and that was how the market traders talked to each other. Reverse talk. It was called "K Cab G-Nals" [kay-cab-gee-nals] which was really backslang. You take a word and split it in half, swap it around, then take the last letter and emphasise it. So glasses are S-slags. Paper is R-pap, and so on. No one ever had a clue what we were on about. That was how David and I talked to each other.'

As if joined at the hip, the pair spent every free moment together.

'I did go round to his, but he was round at mine, most of the time. His mother was not as nice as mine. She was quite difficult. There was no love in that house. That's why he came round mine all the time. To get away from her. She was a really miserable person, Mrs Jones. I used to think maybe she had a chip on her shoulder about something.'

Having sat their Eleven-Plus exams in January 1958, both boys were destined for the new Bromley Technical School on Oakley

Road near Keston Mark, which opened that September. More often than not, they'd get the bus there together.

'It was great, finally being at the same school, because all we wanted to do was spend all our time together anyway,' recalls George. 'We were fortunate enough to be the first intake of pupils at this lovely brand-new school. In particular, I remember the famous staircase where we used to play guitars and harmonise, because it had this great acoustic. We'd congregate there and play Everly Brothers and Buddy Holly. David was as happy as a sandboy. Then one day he came into school, and seemed very down.'

More than used, by now, to his best friend's eccentricities and mood swings, George didn't take much notice.

'I thought it would blow over, whatever "it" was. But he was very distressed, much more so than usual whenever he got upset over anything. After a while, I really felt I had to say something. So I asked him what was up. He said, "I've got a problem, George, and I just don't know who to talk to." He was tearful, and seemed scared. So I said, "I'm your friend, David. You can talk to me." That was when he said, "I think my mother might have been a prostitute."

'I didn't know what to say! I gave him a look, and just shrugged. I mean, he was always being dramatic, and he did exaggerate sometimes and cry wolf a bit. You had to know when he was being serious and when to take him with a pinch of salt, which I usually did. I said, "Come on, David, don't be daft, she can't have been," or something like that. But he was insistent. He said, "No, no, I'm telling you. You've got to believe me, George, because it's really true. I just didn't know who to tell, but I had to tell somebody." He was very upset indeed, he believed it was true, and he persuaded me in the end.

'Apparently he'd found these letters hidden in their house, spelling it all out. How his mother, when she was a young woman, had been a hooker.'

Why is George revealing this now?

'I don't see how it can hurt, to be honest. And maybe I feel a bit guilty about it. I probably didn't react enough. That was my fault, I should have taken more notice of him. He needed a shoulder to cry on, and I didn't really give him that. I thought he was just trying to get attention.'

Did George know what a prostitute was?

'Of course I did. We were twelve, thirteen years old, we weren't babies. He never showed me the letters: I never asked to see them. None of my business, really, but he was obviously very upset. I don't think I was gentle enough with him, when I think back now. I dismissed it. He needed me to be supportive, and I let him down. I didn't really want to hear about it, to tell you the truth. The next time I saw his mum, I couldn't look her in the eye. But that was nothing new. I don't think she liked me very much. She didn't like anyone. I don't believe she even liked herself. When I thought about it years later, once I knew a bit more about relationships and so on, it made all sorts of sense about how he was with his mother, and her dreadful coldness towards him and everyone else.'

Dana Gillespie, the world-renowned blues singer and actress who met David a few years later, would recount a similar story. As one of his earliest girlfriends, she accepted an invitation to visit his parents in Plaistow Grove.

'I had to go on British Rail on my own all the way to Bromley. This was in the days before *Coronation Street*,[5] when we didn't know what all that was like,' baron's daughter Dana tells me. 'Nowadays, thanks to programmes like that, you get a glimpse of how the other half live. They lived in a row of tiny houses, all joined together. His mum and dad sat there in chairs with antimacassars[6] over the back. They made us tuna-fish sandwiches, which we ate in silence. I tried to make conversation with them, but they were very hard to talk to. It was an unbelievably cold house. No love in it. At least, it didn't feel as though there was. When his parents went out of the room, David whispered to me, "Whatever it takes, I'm going to get out of here. If it's the last thing I do, I've got to get away."

'The only subject either of us ever cared about at school was art,' George Underwood reveals. 'The music we did in our own time, but otherwise we were painting and drawing relentlessly. I think we both knew from really early on that we'd end up doing one or the other for a living.'

Though David's relationship with his mother appeared to be deteriorating by the day, there was brief respite in the return of his beloved older brother. But Terry, now twenty-one, was already showing signs of mental illness. In spite of this, he managed to land himself a clerical job in London.

George has particularly fond memories of David's father.

'He was a lovely man, if quite quiet. He always looked out for us. He still worked for Dr Barnardo's. David came into school one day and said, "Do you want to come and meet the Cisco Kid on Saturday at Dr Barnardo's?" Of course I did!'

The Cisco Kid, a long-running American Western TV series, was the first-ever to be filmed in colour. It featured the eponymous lead character played by actor Duncan Renaldo, and his 'short, fat side-kick', Pancho.

'Renaldo was a very charming man,' recalls George. 'We were especially impressed because he was from America, that always unattainable place that we used to obsess over. Anything from America was super-doopah. While we were there, the Kid took us aside, and said, "I want to tell you a secret. You know Pancho . . . ," that was the little guy, ". . . well, he was the original Cisco Kid. Not many people know that." We thought it was so funny, we laughed all the way back!'

By far the boys' finest stroke of luck at Bromley Technical School was having Owen Frampton[7] as their form tutor and art master.

'He was an inspired art teacher and a lovely man,' remembers George, with genuine affection. 'For him, it was never just about getting the best out of us in terms of painting and drawing. He made it a mission to prepare us for the workplace. He opened our eyes to the real world as well as to the abstract world. As we got older, he'd start talking to us about placements and studios. He'd research opportunities, and put us in touch with people. A high percentage of us went on to art school – I did, David didn't, although he always said he did – which is incredibly impressive. That was all down to Owen, and I owed him a lot. We all did.'

Now thirteen years old, the boys began to take a fervent interest in their appearance. It was all about the point of the shoe, the cut of the slack, the tint of lock.

'We had to keep a lid on it during school hours,' chuckles George. 'But off duty we were becoming a right couple of geezers. Not that I could entice David out to parties very often. Only rarely. More often than not, he'd be tucked away in his room, with his nose stuck in some book.'

That year, 1961, turned out to be significant for three reasons. Firstly, in July, just after the end of term, David was taken to the Queen's Theatre in London's West End to see what he later considered to be a 'groundbreaking' show. *Stop the World, I Want to Get Off* starred Anthony Newley, the stage and screen actor and songwriter who co-wrote 'Feeling Good', a massive hit for Nina Simone, and the James Bond *Goldfinger* theme with John Barry. David would look back on the performance as 'a personal turning point' and 'inspirational'. Mike Vernon, the producer of Bowie's first album, would describe David as 'a young Anthony Newley'.

Secondly, his best friend George was offered the role of frontman in local line-up the Konrads, when their original singer dropped out. For David, this could only be a kick in the face. Thirdly, perhaps most crucially, David discovered the saxophone. He would later claim to have been variously inspired by Little Richard's backing band, a string of obscure American musicians, and the Beat poets and authors such as Kerouac. Whoever or whatever first sparked his interest, his father was listening. There was a cool white acrylic Grafton sax with gleaming gold keys under the tree when David awoke on Christmas Day.

YOUNG DUDE

3
1962–1965

What made David select the saxophone over the guitar, say, or the piano?

'It's the easiest instrument to play,' explains revered session musician John Altman. He should know, having played it with everyone from Little Richard, Jimi Hendrix, Bob Marley and Eric Clapton to Tina Turner, Rod Stewart and Fleetwood Mac. He also worked twice with Bowie.[1]

'It's one of the few instruments on which you can become reasonably competent pretty damn quickly. Despite the different pitches and timbres, all saxophones finger the same. Unlike the trumpet, which has only three valves, the trombone, for which you have to move your arm, or the violin, which involves a lot of guesswork and interpretation, a sax is uncomplicated. You put your mouthpiece in your mouth and blow, move your fingers and different notes come out. I remember when I was thirteen, getting my first sax on a Friday night, and playing a gig on the Saturday. I could already play the recorder, a similar thing. After that, it was just a question of refining it.'

For something you simply blow into, it's the most varied of all the woodwinds, Altman adds.

'Think of the greats. Stan Getz sounds different from Ben Webster, who is not the same as John Coltrane, who is unlike Coleman Hawkins, who cannot be compared to Michael Brecker.

From soprano to alto to tenor to baritone saxes, you run the whole gamut of pitch from very high to very low. Each one has its own maestros. Each player makes his or her own sound. This is because it's not about the instrument, it's about your *embouchure*: the way you form your mouth into making the notes.

'We all have a different speaking voice, and we all have a unique *embouchure*. On a guitar, we'd play the same chord and we'd sound identical. The saxophone was the perfect instrument for David, because it played to his strengths. He knew it was the stand-out instrument in any line-up. It allowed him to be an individual.'

There are other advantages.

'It's almost always an instant attraction with the sax,' he says. 'It's shiny and sexy. Sax players get the girls; the whole thing of playing an instrument with your mouth is obvious. Plus, we don't get "brass lips": all trumpeters insert the mouthpiece in a certain way that leaves an indentation in the lip, which can be a real turn-off. Sax players don't suffer from that.

'The great Ronnie Ross was his sax tutor, unfathomably. Ronnie was the top baritone saxophonist in the country, with an international reputation. David had lessons with him when he was thirteen years old. I could never work out how he managed it.'

Not content with the Christmas-present Grafton sax, David was soon badgering his father for an upgrade. A shopping trip together to Tottenham Court Road resulted in the hire-purchase of a brand new Conn. David was still thinking about applying himself to lessons when 'the incident' occurred, said to have caused David's permanently enlarged pupil and giving the impression of different-coloured eyes.

'Overblown? It has been for me,' sighs George Underwood. 'Whenever people talk to me about my art, they always have to mention "the eye thing". It's probably helped my career. I can't really say it's got in my way, I just don't want it on my gravestone. I'm sure Carol Goldsmith doesn't want to dwell on it either.'

It was at George's fifteenth birthday party in February 1962 that the seeds were sown. Both David and George fancied schoolgirl Carol. George secured a date with her, and confided in David that he'd be taking her to the youth club the following Friday. Envy and mischief consumed David, who phoned his friend on the day with the message that Carol had cancelled. When George arrived at the club, her best friend informed him crossly that Carol had hung around for an hour, but had left because she thought he'd stood her up.

'You don't do that to your best friend,' winces George. 'Come the Monday, he was boasting on the bus that *he* was going out with Carol. My anger had got the better of me by the time we got to school, and I punched him. They took him to Farnborough Hospital for treatment. A few days went by, and he had it bandaged. And then he was rushed to Moorfields Eye Hospital. His dad called, and my dad answered the phone. I was in trouble.'

David would milk the matter for years to come, adding 'complicated surgery' and 'lengthy recuperation spells' to the wretched tale. His eye condition is described as having been anything from a 'paralysed pupil' to anisocoria (not *aniscora*, as sometimes quoted). But several eye specialists I spoke to are not so sure.

'Anisocoria is an extremely common eye condition affecting a good fifth of the population,' said one leading ophthalmic surgeon who agreed to comment anonymously. 'It simply describes a visible difference between the sizes of an individual's two pupils. Mechanical anisocoria can be caused by surgery, trauma or infection. Then there's Horner's Syndrome, in which one constricted pupil sometimes suggests the illusion of enlargement of the other. And Adie tonic pupil, in which there is delayed dilation. All of these have been referenced in the case of David Bowie. I happen to believe that it wasn't actually any of them.

'It's impossible to say for certain without having examined him, of course. But the explanations given seem most unlikely to me. In the case of trauma – the punch, say – the damage is not to the eye or its "supporting muscles", but to the parasympathetic nerves that control the pupil at the back. He was born just after the war, when syphilis was still rife, and when penicillin was not routinely available. It seems highly likely that he was a victim of congenital syphilis. Complications including neurosyphilis and meningovascular syphilis can lead to sight impairment, and also affect mental health. The chances are that he was treated in infancy, but that certain damage was sustained, which could have led eventually to this anomaly – punch or no punch. Many pregnant women in those days had no idea that they were infected with syphilis, nor that it was possible to pass on the infection to their unborn child. Where syphilis is latent, which it can be for long periods, there are no symptoms.'

An 'accident' waiting to happen?

'If his mother was a prostitute, syphilis would have been an occupational hazard,' comments consultant psychiatrist Cosmo Hallström.

'But this isn't just about his eye, is it. If your mother is of that persuasion, it's really going to affect your growth and development. Most people whose mothers were prostitutes tend to have problems. It's not generally considered to be a desirable life trait in order to enhance the welfare of your children – and yet not quite bad enough to have your kids taken away from you. We know that children model themselves on their parents. Thus, the old adage "choose your parents wisely". *Why* was this woman a prostitute? Poverty cannot have been the only reason. It rarely is. The majority would not do certain things for certain money, however dire their circumstances. Would knowledge of his mother's past have had an effect on David's evolving sexuality? Probably.'

'I felt often – ever since I was a teenager – so adrift, and so not part of everyone else,' David would reveal, years later. 'With so many dark secrets about my family in the cupboard. It made me feel very much on the outside of everything.'

And in 1997, in *Interview* magazine, he referred to 'an awful lot of emotional and spiritual mutilation' going on in his family during his evidently austere upbringing. Of the alien characters in his songs, he would observe:

'They were metaphysically in place to suggest that I felt alienated; that I felt distanced from somebody, and that I was really in search of some kind of connection.'

Like Vincent van Gogh, he recognised that he was damaged, and turned to face the strange. He was bold enough to express his fears and negative feelings in his work. He also felt the need to expose Earth as a doomed domain consumed by its own decadence, which was the reason why it was reaching for the stars.

'The content of most of what I write – there's been a continuity of alienation and isolation throughout everything I've written,' he said.

It went some way towards explaining the creation of characters behind which to hide, in order to remain attached to his sanity: 'Off stage, I'm a robot. On stage, I achieve emotion. It's probably why I prefer dressing up as Ziggy to being David.'

And as far forward as 2002, the theme and even the language had not been mellowed by time: 'My entire career, I've only really worked with the same subject matter,' he would admit. 'The trousers may change, but the actual words and subjects I've always chosen to write are things to do with isolation, abandonment, fear and anxiety.'

It was his half-brother Terry who 'really started everything for me,' David didn't mind admitting. 'He was into all these different Beat writers and listening to jazz, musicians like John Coltrane and Eric Dolphy.'

As a jazz fan, Terry suggested that David should take sax lessons with Ronnie Ross. David would later claim to have looked him up in the phone book himself. Whichever it was, the lessons lasted only about eight weeks, before David felt he knew enough, and stopped going. Just as he was starting rehearsals with George and the other Konrads to play covers at the June 1962 school fete, the Beatles were completing their first recordings with producer George Martin at EMI's studios on Abbey Road.

The Konrads were so well received on fete-day that they were galvanised into gigging around local venues, including Chislehurst Caves, where we'd attend Friday night discos in the Seventies; the Beckenham Ballroom at Beckenham Junction station, where the Stones' Bill Wyman used to dance when he was still Bill Perks from Penge;[2] Shirley parish hall; Cudham village hall, where we camped as Guides; Justin Hall at St David's College in West Wickham, where I did ballet for years; and upstairs at the Royal Bell on Bromley Market Square. But by the end of the year, band politics defeated George, who quit to join the Spitfires. That Christmas saw the first of David's self-reinventions. He would hitherto be known as 'Dave Jay'.

He left school in July 1963 at the age of sixteen, with a single O level, in Art. Despite many allusions in interviews to 'art college', he never attended one. He took a short-lived job, instead, as a trainee visualiser at the Nevundy–Hurst studio on London's Old Bond Street, which his art teacher Owen Frampton had helped to secure.

But as he would tell society portrait photographer Fergus Greer during a *Sunday Times* Review section photo session in the Nineties, 'I realised very early on that I was never going to make much money from art. So I went into music. We all knew that was where the serious dough was.'

The Konrads kept rolling. An introduction to Stones' manager Eric Easton led to a recording session at Decca's north London studios. The song, co-written by David, was 'I Never Dreamed'. Nothing came of it. David was losing enthusiasm for the band, and went back to the drawing board with George. Together with a percussionist, they stepped out as Dave's Red & Blues, and as the Hooker Brothers. They entertained a few private parties, and played the Bromel Club at the Bromley Court Hotel,[3] where David's mother had once so loved to take tea.

Shortly after the friends formed the King Bees together in 1964

– David was now Davie Jones – came his first encounter with Marc Bolan. Mike Pruskin, an eighteen-year-old wannabe publicist who was assisting Marc with both management and rent, introduced his friend to Leslie Conn. The Dick James Organisation talent scout turned Bolan down flat, but had his beady eye on David, who had been brought to his attention by washing-machine magnate John Bloom.[4] Conn promptly booked the boys for a wedding anniversary bash, but had to halt their set after only fifteen minutes because their heavy R&B sound proved too much for the clan. The King Bees did get a management contract out of Conn, however, as well as a single. 'Liza Jane' was their debut release. It flopped. David quit shortly afterwards to join the Manish Boys, a folk-soul-blues outfit from Maidstone, Kent. But their single 'I Pity the Fool' fell off the side, too.

David joined the Lower Third, the aforementioned Margate Mod band, whom he met in the La Gioconda café, a popular hangout for musicians on Denmark Street, London's 'Tin Pan Alley'. They were a sight for sore eyes gadding about in their American wartime ambulance, which they slept in, toured in, and much besides. Their single 'You've Got a Habit of Leaving' (credited to Davy Jones – yet another name change) failed to chart, and Leslie Conn killed their contract. David announced that he'd be quitting pop to 'study mime at Sadler's Wells', but did in fact keep on for a time with the Lower Third.

He also changed his name yet again, and one last time, to David Bowie: his inspiration the fabled Bowie knife. This fixed-blade weapon was designed in the late-eighteenth–early-nineteenth century for James 'Jim' Bowie, the American pioneer and folk hero who played a prominent role in the Texas Revolution, and who died at the Battle of the Alamo against overwhelming Mexican forces in 1836.

Arguments have raged for decades over how to say David's adopted moniker. The name of the knife is usually pronounced 'Boe-ie' or 'Boo-ie', a nod to its Scottish/Irish Celtic origins; but

David would insist he didn't mind how people said it. It is sometimes rendered as 'Bow-ie', rhyming with 'Wow-ee', and even as 'Boy', as in the south Cornish town Fowey – which is pronounced 'Foy' . . . still with me?

The freak twist of fate is that Jim Bowie himself was in fact half-Jones! He was born in Logan County, Kentucky, in 1796, to father Rezin Pleasant 'Reason' Bowie, of Scottish descent, and mother Elve ap-Catesby Jones, 1766–1837. Elve was the daughter of Welsh immigrant John Jones, born in South Wales in the mid-1700s.[5] Records vary as to how many children Elve and Rezin Bowie had together, the highest number recorded being eleven. Discrepancies are likely due to the very high rate of infant mortality in those days, and thanks to inadequate record-keeping. If eleven children were indeed born to the couple, Jim Bowie was their ninth. Their first-born was called . . . David Bowie.

Pioneer Jim Bowie, whose surname our hero would purloin, had an elder brother with the same full name as that which twentieth-century David Jones assumed. So the Jones boy became a Bowie, while the Bowie veins ran with Jones blood. The coincidence would surely have delighted David. I fell about when I discovered it.

David's out-of-depth new manager Ralph Horton was soon ushering him into another group, the Buzz, and attempted to enlist the help of Simon Napier-Bell, at that time the high-profile manager of the Yardbirds.

'Ralph Horton had been a plumber and I was a famous pop manager,' remembers Simon today. 'I read years later that he'd also worked as a tour manager. No one took him seriously. He wanted a partner who knew what he was doing. I was invited round to a grubby, shabby basement flat in Belgravia. In the corner of the room there was a not particularly attractive young man who I'd never seen before. Ralph introduced him as David, and said he was going to be a superstar. Then Horton made me an offer. "If you agree to co-manage David, you can also have sex with him," he said.

'I thought, what an outrageous thing to say. How very un-British. Not only that, but David didn't pipe up and object, so presumably he was in on it, and had agreed to the deal. It was enough to make me run, which I did. As far as I was concerned, I was never offered a fifty-per-cent share of Bowie's management (nor a taste of his sexual favours), but simply asked to take on a total unknown, whose current manager seemed to be little more than a pimp. Later, of course, Bowie moved his management to Ken Pitt. I often wondered whether Horton had made the same offer to him, and whether that was the basis for the change of management.

'When I thought about it much later, however, I decided I'd turned down two things that might actually have been worthwhile. So when I met Ralph Horton again, thirty-five years later, while he was running a restaurant in Thailand [where Simon lives], he tried to make me feel regretful about my decision by telling me how perfect the Bowie bits had been. Not only had I turned down a young man with an exceptionally large penis – although I must say that I prefer a penis with a bit of character, a bend here or there, or a lump on one side – but I had also turned down someone who turned out to be a rather good artist, about three managers later.'

In September 1965, Horton would make a co-management approach to another successful manager (and agent), Kenneth Pitt.

After another flop single, 'Do Anything You Say', it was on into the Riot Squad. David and Marc Bolan took to meeting regularly for coffee at La Gioconda on Tin Pan Alley – where, some time later, a terrifying encounter with George Underwood took place.

'What happened was, the King Bees had split up, and David had gone behind my back and found himself another band,' says George. 'This was the kind of thing he did. Leslie Conn, the manager, felt a bit sorry for me. One day, he said to me, "Mickie Most[6] is looking for a solo artist – why don't we go and see him, do a little audition for him?" So we did. I felt awkward: I had a new haircut and a new guitar. But Mickie liked me, and wanted to record me. Peter Grant [the future Led Zeppelin manager] and Leslie Conn were also there, as they were going to co-manage me.

'Mickie said, "What do you think of the name Calvin?" Quick as a flash, Leslie whispered in my ear, "It's the name of his little boy!" "Yeah, lovely," I responded. "We want to give you a James Dean image," Mickie went on, "so what about James Calvin?" and I said, "What about Calvin James?" I left there with a new name, a new image and a five-year recording contract with the legendary Mickie Most, which was the best you could get.'

Shortly after an appearance on TV's *Thank Your Lucky Stars*, George ran into David on Denmark Street.

'He was seething with jealousy, almost spitting blood. And he said he was going to kill me – because it had all fallen in my lap, while he was still struggling. It was like David had paid his dues, and I hadn't.'

As always, they got over it.

On 8 February 1965, Davie Jones and the Manish Boys played London's Marquee Club.[7] There to witness the performance was precocious beauty Dana Gillespie.[8]

'I'd started going down there with a friend when I was thirteen, fourteen,' Dana remembers. 'I'd been a pupil at Francis Holland [a private girls' school], but I wanted to be on the stage. I got a place at Arts Educational [the world-famous performing arts college of which Lord Lloyd-Webber is patron, and where my son is currently a student], had a job in a record store in South Kensington after school, and I was very forward for my age. Big-titted, tight tops, lots of peroxide-blonde hair. You couldn't miss me. I was mad about the Yardbirds – Eric Clapton and I had the same birthday, though he's four years older. I didn't know who the King Bees were supporting that night, but they were quite impressive. David came on stage in knee-length suede tasselled boots and a big, loose shirt with a waistcoat. His lemon-yellow hair fell to the shoulders, and he looked rather dreamy to me.

'After their set, I was standing at the back brushing my hair, when David came up behind me, took the brush from my hand, and started doing it for me. "Can I come home with you tonight?" he said. Of course he could. He'd missed his last train back to Bromley, where he still lived with his parents. I'm a South Ken/ Knightsbridge girl, I had no idea where Bromley even was. We walked all the way from Soho to my parents' house in Thurloe Place. I smuggled him up to my bedroom, where I kept my drum kit and my Spanish nylon-stringed guitar.'

Dana was by no means your average fifteen-year-old. Her aristocratic parents had graduated to new partners, and the couples occupied a floor each in their palatial house. She describes her parents as having been 'cool' and 'very wise': 'They never said "no" to me, probably knowing that I'd have gone off and done it anyway.'

She and David had to snuggle up in her narrow single bed.

'In the morning, I woke up, saw him there beside me, and thought, oh, holy shit. a), I've got to get to school, and b), I've got to get him out of the house. But I needn't have worried: my father told me afterwards that they thought he was a girl!'

David became a regular visitor to the Gillespie home thereafter, and often stayed over.

'Sometimes he'd pick me up from school. When he was with the Lower Third, the band went on gigs in an old ambulance. David said it had sometimes been used for sex at Piccadilly Circus. You need to live, in order to be able to produce the songs! Music was king in my life. David was the first guy I'd met who felt the same way as I did about it. He was a little older, and already "in the scene", which was very exciting for me. We'd go off to the *Ready Steady Go!* television studio, just to hang out in the green room, and we'd frequent the Gioconda café, where everyone used to pick up managers and session musicians. Drummer Frank King was my drum teacher.

'David taught me my first chords on the guitar. He also taught me how to listen to bass lines, and suggested songs for me, of which I recorded a few. He encouraged my songwriting hugely. We'd go down to Carnaby Street, where he'd be having a military jacket or an outfit made up. I'd always be dressed in jeans and a top: I wasn't a Sandie Shaw or a Dusty Springfield or a Lulu, in cute little dresses. We'd go to the Marquee, the Whiskey-A-Go-Go and the Roundhouse. I was in those places every night. How did I handle it? It was the pill-popping era, but I wasn't popping any. Nor was I a drinker, and never have been. That has really saved my life.

'I knew from the outset that David was obsessed when it came to his career. He would do literally anything to get what he wanted. I'd have to say he was ruthless in that respect. He was very attractive to women *and* men, and he knew it. He didn't openly go near the bi thing until the MainMan days to come. He looked in the mirror a lot – much more than I did. He really cared about his appearance, and how he came across.

'I don't remember any of it as ugly, sleazy or decadent. It was what it was. It didn't bother me that he was sleeping with other people. So what? I never saw a relationship as being the ultimate goal. For me, it was purely about *music*. For him, it was all about music and his *career*.'

4

1965–1967

Ralph Horton introduced David to Tony Hatch[1] at Pye Records, and Hatch recognised almost immediately that David was on an 'intergalactic trajectory'.

'He wasn't the kind of artist who would audition well in the studio,' the celebrated songwriter and producer remembers, 'so Ralph took me to see him and the Lower Third at the Marquee. I thought, yes, we've got something here. Most definitely. For a start, he stood out. There weren't a great many London bands around at the time. Everyone thought the "real" artists were coming out of Liverpool, Manchester and Sheffield. I liked the London-ness about him. He was writing about what was around him, his own life and times and experiences.'

First impression?

'I couldn't say he was arrogant, nor a humble mouse. But he was confident. I had a gut feeling about him. I totally believed in him, and wanted him to succeed. Writing your own songs was key. The problem I had with the Searchers, for example, was that they didn't write. I was excited about David because I knew I wouldn't have to go looking for songs for him – just as it all fell in George Martin's lap when the Beatles arrived with this great fountain of material.'

Rarely had Hatch witnessed such enthusiasm. David was just seventeen, you know what I mean.

'In the studio, he *really* enjoyed himself,' Tony told me. 'We got on well together. It was a great disappointment to me that it didn't work out. Looking back, I can see that he wasn't quite ready. For the process, I mean. Going into the studio, submitting to it completely, you need that little bit extra for that. I was hoping that, being at the coalface, he would be able to mine the best bits. It didn't quite come. Not that this was his fault. Pye were in a hurry for the hits. In the Sixties, there were still only four major record labels – EMI, Pye/Warner Bros/Reprise, Decca and Philips – and they were all competing among themselves. I needed time to "grow" David, in order to get the best out of him. Pye didn't have the patience or the resources to allow me to nurture him. Studios, pressing, distribution, PR, it all adds up. We were spending a fortune and getting not much back.

'So we were forced to cull a few promising artists. David was one of them. I probably could have fought his corner, but as an in-house producer, I had a very full plate. It was wonderful when the independents started to come along, because it granted producers much more creative freedom.'

Hatch craved success for David perhaps more than David longed for it himself.

'He was an off-beat character, but he had it,' sighs Hatch. 'He most definitely had it. I knew I could have worked with him long-term, and that we would have worked well together, because I would have allowed him creative freedom. I would never have persuaded him to do something against his will. When "Space Oddity" became a hit a few years later, I thought, *fantastic*. It's a brilliant song. Its changing moods really resonated with me. I'd done that in "Downtown", which is also very theatrical. It has a huge tune, it is epic songwriting. I'm still a little disappointed that he hadn't come up with a "Space Oddity" in the Pye studios. But of course, had they given us time, it would have come. With someone like Bowie, you really are making it up as you go along. There is no better way to work.'

The final hours of 1965 and the first of 1966 were spent in the birthplace of French rock: at the Golf Drouot, a tiny club in the ninth arrondissement of Paris. In the Fifties, it had been an elegant tearoom, Le Cup of Tea. Peggy Jones would have been in her element. The name was a nod to its past, when the restaurant that once stood on the site, Le Café d'Angleterre, had its own miniature indoor golf course, a twee distraction while one awaited one's *foie gras hors-d'oeuvre*. Transformed by entrepreneur Henri Leproux into a rock venue in 1961, it became a teenage mecca, with a jukebox and live acts; the Parisian equivalent of London's Marquee or the 2i's coffee bar. It fell foul of licensing laws in the late Seventies, and closed for good in 1981. A commemorative plaque was unveiled at the site in 2014. In its heyday, it was frequented by 'French Elvis' Johnny Hallyday and his cohorts. Gene Vincent, Free and the Who all played there – as, significantly, did Vince Taylor.[2]

'I met him a few times in the mid-Sixties, I went to parties with him,' David would later recall. 'He was out of his gourd. Totally flipped. The guy was not playing with a full deck at all. He used to carry maps of Europe around with him, and I remember him opening a map outside Charing Cross tube station, putting it on the pavement and kneeling down with a magnifying glass. He pointed out all the sites where UFOs were going to land. He was the inspiration for Ziggy. Vince was a rock'n'roll star from the Sixties who was slowly going crazy. Finally, he fired his band and went on-stage one night in a white sheet. He told the audience to rejoice, that he was Jesus. They put him away.'

David Bowie and the Lower Third's performance that New Year's Eve was a smash. They took advantage of the opportunity to experiment, and were gratified to find an audience hooked. The reception galvanised them for other performances over the next few days. David described the club as 'totally inspirational'. He would enthuse just as effusively about his first visit to Paris. In reality, the band's off-duty experience was confined to a stomp in the cold and drizzle along the seedy Boulevard de Clichy, then as now a maelstrom of garbage, neon, pimps, peep shows and kebab outlets.

The quartier was presided over by the decaying Elysée Montmartre, the city's original can-can theatre: not, as usually claimed, the Moulin Rouge. Thirty-three years later, David would perform at the Elysée Montmartre during the tiny Hours tour, on 14 October 1999. The concert was filmed and recorded, with three songs later appearing on the CD single of 'Survive'.

Beyond the Pigalle, cobbled streets, tight alleys and many steps ascended to the Butte and Sacré Coeur. David was enchanted. He conjured himself into a Forties film noir, an Henri Cartier-Bresson photograph. Those first impressions would never leave him, he later said. He would come to rhapsodise over visits to composer Erik Satie's house, to Symbolist painter Gustave Moreau's apartment, and to the Père Lachaise cemetery on Boulevard de Menilmontant in the twentieth. He 'felt at home', he declared, among the tombs of Oscar Wilde and Maria Callas, of Chopin, Molière, Proust, Piaf and Jim Morrison.[3]

His fondness for the French capital surfaced in style twenty-six years later, when he returned in October 1991 with his girlfriend, retired supermodel Iman, during the Tin Machine 'It's My Life' tour. As they sailed down the Seine on a cool, quiet night, David sang to his lover during dinner, adapting the lyrics to the song 'April in Paris' from the 1930s Broadway hit musical *Walk a Little Faster*. When their boat passed under the medieval Pont Neuf, he proposed.[4]

'Luckily, it worked,' he confided in my former Editor at the News of the World, Piers Morgan. 'Everything was perfect. We were eating dinner by candlelight as the boat drifted down the river, and I just stood up and started singing "October in Paris".' As one does.

It was the first of a brace of French proposals. The second took place at the Paris l'Olympia on 29 October, where he plighted his troth live on stage. Once again, he could not have chosen a more romantic or resonant setting. That old music hall in the ninth, on the Boulevard des Capucines, was where chanteuse Edith Piaf had affirmed her great fame. It had welcomed one of David's many idols, Marlene Dietrich. Jacques Brel gave his most memorable concerts there, in 1961 and 1964. Miles Davis, James Brown, Jimi Hendrix, Liza Minnelli, the Beach Boys and the Jackson Five had all appeared there – as had the Beatles, who in 1964 alone performed dozens of shows. There were very good ghosts.

Can I get a witness. David asked for Iman's hand a second time, before a throng of enraptured fans, thrilled to be in on the act. Reader, the multi-millionaire mannequin said yes to the multi-millionaire rock superstar. Then he took up his sax and played.

By 1965, twenty-eight-year-old Terry Burns was fading fast. The cool, handsome but troubled older brother who had derived such pleasure from introducing his eager teenage sibling to West End jazz joints, hip hang-outs and the Beat poetry and literature he himself loved, was now teetering on the brink of mental breakdown. The next two years would bring his deep and rapid decline. He was seeing visions, hearing voices, and suffering acute schizophrenic attacks. He began in-patient treatment at Farnborough Hospital, returning home to Plaistow Grove at weekends. David has been accused down the years of having grown distant from his brother during that period, whether out of shame, fear, confusion or all three. In fact, he was as caring as any eighteen-year-old boy could be, in the circumstances. When Terry became an inmate of Cane Hill asylum, his younger brother was one of his most regular and devoted visitors.

'Cane Hill was part of the so-called "lunatic fringe": a ring of psychiatric hospitals once found around our major cities,' explains consultant psychiatrist Cosmo Hallström. 'On the periphery, out of sight, out of mind, these establishments were bastions to Victorian care. If you were mentally ill, they put you away. They gave you asylum: hence the name.'

This particular institution, in Coulsdon, Croydon, had once housed Charlie Chaplin's mother and Michael Caine's brother. It had a capacity of more than two thousand patients. After the 1983 Mental Health Act diverted emphasis towards care in the community, Cane Hill fell into decline. It closed for good at the end of 1991, and its buildings were demolished between 2008 and 2010.

'I saw Terry at Cane Hill, too,' comments George Underwood. How nice of him to have been so supportive of his friend by accompanying him to such a place, I remarked. 'No,' replied George, 'I was *in* there. I had a total breakdown. I became an inmate of Cane Hill myself.'

The 'boy most likely to', who had been primed for pop stardom under the tutelage of the world's most prolific and successful record producer, who, compared to his best friend David, was considered to be by far the superior musician, and was being steered towards a glittering career . . . completely lost the plot.

'I don't know why,' George says now. 'I never will know for sure. I was just becoming famous as a singer, and then that happens. I was nineteen years old. I have a very strong suspicion that someone spiked my drink, because the doctors there asked me when did I first start taking LSD. I told them I'd never taken it. I didn't need it: I always had far more imagination than I knew what to do with! I was always painting and drawing, I was looking for images all the time, and my ability to be creative seemed infinite. Anyway, I had a very serious attack. I was a danger to myself and to people around me.

'My mother called the doctor, and I was sectioned. I was in Cane Hill for twenty-eight days, which was the minimum you could be sectioned for. Everything about it was terrifying. I didn't think I'd ever get out. Some surreal and horrible things happened to me in there. I felt like a puppet in a play. At one point, I asked to go into a padded cell, just to get away from all the crazy people about, and to get a bit of peace and quiet. It was a meditative process. When you have hallucinations, they are absolutely real. You don't question it.'

One of the most frightening aspects of the experience was that the specialists there had a file on George already, when he was summoned for his first assessment.

'They had all these photographs of my drawings. They'd been to my home, and raked through my things. It felt terribly intrusive. They were trying to imply that I drew and painted such stuff because I'd taken LSD. Well, I'd smoked a bit of pot, but nothing worse. Then something really odd happened. One of the psychiatrists who seemed fascinated by my drawings, said, "Will you do one of those for me?" I felt really confused by that. It was very upsetting. It didn't seem right that he was asking me to do that. Remember that this was in the days when it was still taboo to talk about mental illness. My family didn't want it to get out. My mum told friends I was staying with her sister. My dad found a private place for me to go to for treatment, in Ticehurst (East Sussex). That was where I had the horrific Electroshock Therapy (EST) in my brain. And when I saw the film *One Flew Over the Cuckoo's Nest* years later, it brought it all back.'[5]

George's treatment, over the two locations, lasted for about three months. On his release, one of the first things he did was tell David all about his experiences.

'And of course it became good fodder for some of his songs,' George laughs. 'All these years, people have been analysing particular lyrics of his, and saying that he must have been writing about his brother Terry, when he was more than likely writing about *me*! Because Terry could be a bit vague, you know? He probably didn't have a lot to say about what went on in the loony bin. But I told David absolutely everything. Every last detail.'

The track 'All the Madmen' on Bowie's 1970 album *The Man Who Sold the World*[6] released in the UK in April 1971, contains references to Electroshock Therapy, lobotomy and the drug Librium: a benzodiazepine prescribed for depression and as a tranquilliser. Although David stated that he wrote the song 'for and about' his brother, the excruciating detail most likely came from George.

His mental illness turned him into 'quite a normal person', George reckons now.

'I'd been quite "out there" before all that happened. After I got out, I just wanted to get back to normal, and to conform. I was together enough while I was inside to know that I didn't *ever* want to go back in that place again. For a long time afterwards I was very straight and really boring. I dressed in clothes that didn't draw any attention, and I no longer had a pop career. Meanwhile, things were really revving up for David. My best friend had gone and created a whole new life, and I was happy for him.'

ENGLISH ECCENTRIC

5

1967–1970

The year 1966 is remembered as the zenith of the Swinging Sixties, when youth culture, music and fashion collided, establishing young teens and emerging adults as demographics in their own right. It is cherished as the year when England won the FIFA World Cup for the first and only time, defeating West Germany 4–2. But in the global scheme, the following year was much more significant. 1967's 'Summer of Love', heralded that January by an unprecedented Human Be-In at San Francisco's Golden Gate Park to a soundtrack by local bands the Grateful Dead, Jefferson Airplane, Quicksilver Messenger Service, and Big Brother and the Holding Company, saw a hundred thousand hippies with flowers in their hair converge on the Northern Californian city. Its Haight–Ashbury district was transformed into the epicentre of the American counterculture, and brought to a head the anti-war stance and radicalism that defined the era. The wider movement focused on 'rights': women's, civil, consumer, sexual. It championed free love, eco-awareness and communal living. It delivered the word 'psychedelia' to the suburban front room.[1]

It was a year of seminal albums: *The Doors*; Hendrix's *Are You Experienced*; the Beatles' *Sgt Pepper's Lonely Hearts Club Band*; the Stones' *Their Satanic Majesties Request*; and *The Velvet Underground and Nico*, a demo copy of which David's besotted new manager Ken Pitt carried home for him from a trip to America (along with the Fugs' *Virgin Fugs*). The love token prompted David to fall head over heels . . . with the avant-garde band.

'Everything I both felt and didn't know about rock music was opened up to me on one unreleased disc,' David said.

It was the tail-end of the Beatles, the year the BBC launched Radio 1 with Tony Blackburn and the Move's 'Flowers in the Rain', and the year of David's debut, eponymous album for Decca.

There is a 'first novel' feel to the album, into which he appears to have poured a phrase, note or sentiment of every kind of music he had ever heard in his young life. Quintessentially, darkly British, it trips up the stairs to the nursery and thunders down into the basement, with its allusions to Victorian nursery rhymes and stiff Edwardian brass made with unmanageable instruments. Here are echoes of the Beatles, Tommy Steele, Anthony Newley and Pink Floyd. Here is a deafening seaside oompah band, and there a whispering waltz of violins.

Either David had no idea what he wanted this LP to be, or he had far too many: he was only twenty when it was released, after all. Perhaps manager Ken Pitt was leaning heavily on him to display his wares as a post-vaudeville all-rounder, instead of as a promising, hip young rock or pop star.

Whatever, he seems to be trying to be all things to all listeners, and not getting any of it quite right. He peers through dusty keyholes into the confounding world of organised religion, and raises an eyebrow at the notion of messianic figures – perhaps asking himself the questions he would attempt to answer just a few years later, on *The Rise and Fall of Ziggy Stardust and the Spiders from Mars*.

He dips a toe into gay, bisexual and androgynous themes, which obviously preoccupy him. 'We Are Hungry Men' has an embryonic 'concept' approach. It scrapes brazenly through science fiction, Nazism, abortion, infanticide and population explosion, and has an earworm of a chorus, beware. 'She's Got Medals' flaunts the androgyny theme full-on, via a female who dresses up as a man in order to join the army, but then legs it when the bombs begin to drop. 'Please Mr Gravedigger' is a worry: delivered in the voice of a child murderer to a backing track of every primitive sound effect and sinister voice that David can drag from his bowels. It is hard to hear, an unpalatable horror story with a noxious aftertaste. It is David at his creepiest and most strange.

He would later dismiss the album – perhaps because it was such a spectacular failure, causing him to be dropped by Deram, the Decca subsidiary label on which it was released.

Not all the ears it fell upon were unappreciative. Chris Welch was then a young record reviewer and feature writer on the *Melody Maker*.

'My job was to discover new talent,' he explains. 'I got hold of David's LP and I played it to the guys who became the Nice.'[2]

'What I liked about it was that, just like Steve Marriott [Small Faces, Humble Pie], David was very *London*. Singing about London. In a London voice. I loved his lyrics: he wasn't trying to be yet another American smart arse. He was writing about things that affected *us*. And he had a great sense of humour. It was all very tongue-in-cheek, and he was sending himself up. He was good-looking, he was a Mod, and he had a huge amount of talent. Sitting around listening to it with the boys in the office, we all agreed that he would go all the way.

'I was living in Catford, South London,' adds Chris, 'and David was a local hero. Nothing quite like one of those. When I interviewed him, he was very charming. He never said what you expected him to say. He had a scattergun approach to conversation, with lots of non sequiturs. Terence Stamp, Michael Caine and Lionel Bart were similar, all handsome Londoners with attitude. David wasn't at all business-like in the beginning; he never expected to be quite as successful as he became. It was more about fashion and art, for him. He was *dabbling* in music: an art student-type who loved the idea of being a rock'n'roll star.'

It was also the year in which one of the most significant producer–artist partnerships in the history of rock was formed. Young American Tony Visconti had already made his mark as a writer and producer in his native New York. An invitation from Decca producer

Denny Cordell, famous for 'Go Now' by the Moody Blues and Procol Harum's 'A Whiter Shade of Pale', was to expand his horizons. Cordell, newly involved with publishers Essex Music, required an assistant. Essex happened also to be publishing David's songs. On a mission to find himself 'the next Beatles', twenty-three-year-old Visconti leapt at the opportunity.

While an astonishing ten albums with Marc Bolan, taking the artist from underground folkie to king of glam, would win him respect and acclaim, it would be the supremely creative musical relationship he forged with David that would cement his reputation as one of the greatest producers in rock.

Another common denominator would be George Underwood. The recovered, retired never-to-be-pop-star had now returned full-time to painting and illustrating, and was no longer a musical threat to his friend. It was George who created the intricate sleeve artwork for Bolan's Tyrannosaurus Rex debut, *My People Were Fair and had Sky in Their Hair ... But Now They're Content to Wear Stars on Their Brows* (released 5 July 1968). George would go on to create inner-sleeve portraits of Marc and Mickey Finn for T. Rex's *Electric Warrior* album, and to illustrate their *Futuristic Dragon* cover. He would also design the artwork for Bowie's *Hunky Dory*, *The Rise and Fall of Ziggy Stardust and the Spiders from Mars*, and Mott the Hoople's *All the Young Dudes*.

At the end of Visconti's first six months in London, he was summoned by Essex boss David Platz.

'You seem to have a talent for working with weird acts, I'd like to play something for you to consider,' Platz said to Tony Visconti, as Tony recalled in his autobiography *Bowie, Bolan and the Brooklyn Boy*. 'This is an album made by a writer I've been working with for some time. We were hoping he'd be right for the musical theatre, but he's become something quite different since he made this record.'

From the speakers emanated a unique and unforgettable voice.

'The phrasing and subtlety was something you'd expect from a seasoned stage or even a cabaret singer. The songs were humorous and dark; the backing was imaginative ... what was this? I listened to half the album and remarked that although it was all over the place, I liked it.'

'His name is David Bowie, and he's nineteen,' said Platz. (He was already twenty). 'Would you like to meet him?'

It was only when Visconti was led into the next room and found David there that he realised he'd been set up.

'I liked him immediately,' Tony said.

The pair became joined at the hip. Both were stupendously ambitious, but neither had much as yet to show for it. David enthused about American music, especially Little Richard. Visconti repaid the compliment, with regard to British acts. They owned the same records. They both loved foreign art films, and took to going to the pictures together. Within days they were collaborating. In a blink, they'd be sharing a roof.

Dana Gillespie had no idea that David was also sleeping with a man while she was still seeing him. The male in question was camp Lindsay Kemp, a Liverpudlian dancer nine years David's senior, who had moved to London to set up his own mime company. David met him during the Summer of Love, when he attended one of Kemp's dance and movement classes at a Covent Garden studio. He also met Natasha Korniloff, a fashion and set designer who would eventually dress Bowie for his 1978 world tour, and who would most memorably create the 'Ashes to Ashes' Pierrot costume. With bi abandon, David became entangled with both – as well as with singer-songwriter Lesley Duncan.[3] He was also still hanging with Dana whenever he could, and within a year would become smitten by ballet student Hermione Farthingale. As everybody found out later, he was fibbing his way blithely from bed to bed.

'It didn't bother me,' shrugs Dana. 'He fell passionately for Hermione, and he was very keen for me to meet her. That was fine, I wasn't possessive. He brought Angie to see me, too, not long after he'd met her. He told me she'd been to finishing school in Switzerland, like me, and that she was bright and funny and sassy. "You'll really like her," he said, and I did. She and I remain great friends to this day. David actually gave me a hard time about it in the Eighties, when he heard that I was still seeing her. That surprised me, but it didn't stop me, of course. No reason at all why I shouldn't remain friends with both of them. Angie came straight here [to Dana's Kensington home] immediately after she left the Big Brother house.[4] As I've mentioned before, an exclusive relationship, for me, was never the goal.'

Kemp was impressed by David's eponymous Deram album, released on 1 June 1967. David, not so much.

'It seemed to have its roots all over the place, in rock and vaude-ville and music hall,' he would later say, not even trying to defend his work. 'I didn't know if I was Max Miller[5] or Elvis Presley.'

Kemp would eventually create a new dance to celebrate their relationship. It was called 'Pierrot in Turquoise', and David played Cloud. It premiered at the Oxford Playhouse that December, and then they took it on the road.

Come 1968, while student riots raged in the news, it was time for David to take stock. The suggestion from manager Ken Pitt was that he was perhaps going in the wrong direction creatively, and should think about jacking in his pop career in favour of cabaret. Tony Visconti would not hear of it, and was keen to try other avenues with his charge. The Beatles' Apple Corps turned David down. He failed auditions for roles in both the nude stage musical *Hair!* and the film *The Virgin Soldiers*, although he did manage a walk-on in the latter.

Close to boracic, and with his anxious father breathing down his neck, he sought work at a London printing and photocopying company. He also moved out of Ken Pitt's Manchester Square flat, and into a flat in Clareville Grove, Kensington with dancer Hermione Farthingale, only minutes from Dana Gillespie's family home. With Hermione and guitarist Tony Hill, he formed the trio Turquoise. A gig later, Hill quit, and was replaced by John Hutchinson, David's old band mate in the Buzz.

They performed David's original compositions, interspersed with tranches of Jacques Brel. Their act also featured him miming, deploying moves he'd picked up while watching Kemp. Further attempts at recordings were made with Tony Visconti. Ken Pitt went cap in hand to Mickie Most, who had once perceived immense promise in George Underwood. By David's album, Most would not be moved. David and Hermione cascaded out of love. David crawled home to Mum and Dad, and Plaistow Grove.

In April 1969 his fortunes turned, when he happened to meet Mancunian Mary Finnigan. With a failed marriage behind her, a record for drug possession for which she had served a short stretch, a parked career as a newspaper journalist and two small children to support, Mary was seeking a fresh start. Having gone to stay with a friend in bourgeois Beckenham in Kent, close to David's home town Bromley, while she searched for a new family home, she found a presentable, affordable garden property on Foxgrove Road. Her upstairs neighbours Christine and Barry were hosting their old friend David one day. Mary lay in the garden, soaking up sunshine, cannabis and David's guitar-strumming from their open window. Within hours, she was offering him lodgings. Within days, he was on her doorstep with his gear.

'This is the first time I hear "Space Oddity",' recounts Mary in her eloquent memoir *Psychedelic Suburbia*, and 'it's my first encounter with a strange instrument called a Stylophone . . . it sounds like a cross between an organ and a jet engine, and absolutely right for a melancholy song about a space mission gone wrong.'

Few know that the Stylophone was a joke present from David's pal Marc Bolan.

David the lodger 'had no money and no gigs', but Mary was not bothered. She blossomed in his presence. Before she had time to think, they were sharing her bed.

'I was spellbound by his charisma, his charm and his talent,' admits this disarming lady, who confesses that, having been celibate for several months, she was simply overcome by the desirable, funny and fascinating creature who had landed in her lap. She felt herself falling in love. They had enough in common. It was David's idea to find a pub and put on folk nights to ease their dire financial situation. On a Sunday evening in May 1969, they launched their folk club in the back room at Beckenham High Street's Three Tuns pub. A fortnight later, he introduced his audience to 'Space Oddity', with Mary's daughter Caroline accompanying him on the Stylophone.

Mary was already exploring Tibetan Buddhism when David announced that he had met the Lama Chime Youngdon Rinpoche[6] – but only on the off-chance, after he dashed into the Buddhist Society library on Ecclestone Square, south-west London, to get out of the rain. Mary had already spotted that David was an all-or-nothing individual. Whatever he did, he did wholeheartedly, with complete concentration. And whenever a thing was over, for him, it was done.

Their affair was short-lived – primarily because David was sleeping with two other people at the same time. In an echo of his triangular relationship with Lindsay Kemp and Natasha Korniloff, David was now involved with Mercury Records A&R guy Calvin Mark Lee, a flamboyant Chinese American, with whom he was sharing Mary Angela Barnett: the coolest chick on earth.

Angie was beautiful, bossy, quirky and clever. She was cunning, accomplished and wild. She was an uninhibited American raised in Cyprus, fluent French-speaking, the daughter of a colonel, the product of Swiss finishing school. At eighteen, she was dispatched to college in America, but was allegedly expelled for having a lesbian relationship. Now a sophisticated student of marketing at Kingston Polytechnic, she was also domesticated, a fine seamstress and a magnificent cook, who could conjure a three-course dinner from a vacant fridge. Exuberant, histrionic and brazenly bisexual, she never took no for an answer. Crucially, she was nineteen, a decade younger than Mary. She lodged in a London flat shared by artist Tim Goffe and DJ Bob Harris, where David often stayed.

The same night that Angie and David were introduced in a club by Calvin Mark Lee, they slept together in one of two places. According to Angie, it was after an evening at the Speakeasy, 'the night King Crimson celebrated their new recording contract, and Donovan got up and sang Buddy Holly songs with them. David came back to my little room above the Nomad Travel Club in Paddington.' But Tony Visconti insists that their carnal debut took place on cushions on the floor of his own one-bedroom flat.

Whichever, Angie and Tony had more in common than they yet knew. Both were to become David's enablers and facilitators. Mary was shocked to discover, years later, that David had been seeing Angie for as long as he'd lived with her. Angie breezed into Mary's home, by now a 'Court of King David' with its constant stream of hippy-ish visitors, and as good as took over.

'He was slim, pale-skinned and a little alien looking,' remembers Angie. 'He was a middle class boy wanting to be a rock star. David had talent but he needed focus. He had lots of girlfriends and even some boyfriends at the time. But when I came along he realized I was someone who could help him reach the next level.'

In an eerie echo of the past behaviour of her future mother-in-law Peggy Jones – who had moved into Hilda Jones's home with her future husband John, David's father, while he was still married to Hilda – Angie became an unshakable fixture. Mary Finnigan hardly knew what had hit her, conceded defeat, and cried herself to sleep for months. Unnerved by David's ruthlessness, but also intrigued, she even allowed Angie to seduce her one night. The earth failed to move.

The experimental Arts Lab movement having taken off around the country, Mary suggested relaunching their folk club as the Beckenham Arts Lab. It rapidly gained traction, luring the likes of Lionel Bart, Rick Wakeman and Peter Frampton. Musician Noel Brown remembers playing there:

'I met David for the first time in Beckenham Recreation Ground, where he put on an outdoor festival with various bands and singers, in which I took part.[7] He said he was running a regular Sunday night shindig at the Three Tuns, and would like to have me play. The Arts Lab was a fantastic scene, where all kinds of people performed, including the Strawbs, Keith Christmas, Marc Bolan,

Mick Ronson and David himself. I ended up playing there quite a lot with a pal on bass guitar. We went down well. One evening, David, Mick, Trevor Bolder and Woody Woodmansey ('Weird and Gilly', the future Spiders) did a killer version of "Heartbreak Hotel" and some other songs I'd never heard David do before. Another time, he showed up with Peter Frampton, both on acoustic guitars, with Andy Bown[8] on double bass. Once again, they stole everything but the furniture, and a great night was had by all.'

When David and Angie moved round the corner that October into turreted Gothic mansion Haddon Hall, Noel became a regular visitor.

'David and I had some interesting chats, which ranged from Stan Laurel to Jean-Paul Sartre to Little Richard and beyond. I even tagged along to a couple of his solo gigs, in Gravesend and Chatham one night, where I saw Angie wade into a fight in the crowd. She walked straight up to the two pugilists and, after shouting at them for interrupting David's performance, she laid the biggest guy flat out with a single punch that none of us saw coming. It had the desired effect, and the rest of the evening went very well.'

Angie, however, remembers the incident differently. 'I'm afraid that story is not true,' she told me in August 2016. 'I may have spoken harshly to some people about throwing cigarettes at the stage. I would never have hit anybody.'

'Later, David and Angie packed his guitar and small public address system into a Fiat 500, and we all trotted off back to Haddon Hall for coffee,' continues Noel.

'The last time I saw David was when he played Wallington Public Halls with the Spiders from Mars, and it was obvious to all that he was heading for much bigger things. My memory of him is that he was always smiling, and that he really was a nice geezer.'

'Our guitarist Mick Wayne told David about our band, Junior's Eyes,' says Tim Renwick,[9] 'and some of us were asked to help out on future recording sessions to be produced by young Tony Visconti, recently arrived from the USA. I ended up playing guitar on a handful of tracks, and the recorder on one, with Tony – who also played the recorder, much to my surprise! Those songs were nothing like "Space Oddity", the subject matter being ex-girl-friends, folk festivals, and so on.'

(They were 'Letter to Hermione'; 'An Occasional Dream'; 'Cygnet Committee' – widely regarded as David's 'first true master-piece'; 'Janine', perhaps in reference to George Underwood's then-girlfriend; the Buddhism-heavy 'Wild Eyed Boy from Freecloud', and 'Memory of a Free Festival', featuring backing vocals by DJ Bob Harris, his first wife Sue, and Marc Bolan.)

'Rather an odd collection, although interesting and different from the norm. I remember that I felt slightly confused by David's diverse musical styles. I couldn't really make him out. I knew his background was a mix of studying mime and running a folk club, and I remembered having seen him on a television show with his former band, Davy Jones and the Manish Boys – a blues-based thing. He must have been about fifteen at the time, and was very pretty.'

Tim got along famously with David, and thoroughly enjoyed the recording process – much of which, he says, was recorded as live:

'I was given a free rein to play whatever came to mind. David seemed quite fragile during those sessions. On one occasion, he was dubbing on some vocals, and he cracked up over some lyrics that were particularly personal to him. He had to take a break and leave the task until later. I was struck by his vulnerability – a rare thing to witness. It turned out that his father had just passed away.'

David's father John had become seriously ill with lobar pneumo-nia in August 1969 while David was away with Ken Pitt, taking part in song contests in Italy and Malta. On his return, he visited his father to show him his awards. Two days later, on 5 August, John died while David was in the studio.

'David later asked Junior's Eyes to back him on some live gigs he had planned,' Tim goes on. 'We were pleased to oblige. I think he wanted to try out his new stage persona in a live situation that would not get too much attention, as the dates were mostly in

Scotland – a rather motley collection of venues, it has to be said. At one place, there was a wire screen across the stage. We were told "if the audience like you, they might throw things at you". I wondered what they might do if they *didn't* like the show! As it happened, the crowd response was fairly mild, really. A burst of interest in "Space Oddity", but not too much else.

'David seemed uneasy and uncomfortable with the whole thing, which was a far cry from his adoring folk club atmosphere. The tour ended up with some BBC radio recordings in London, and a show at the South Bank's Purcell Rooms, which went well. I remember David was very nervous indeed! We parted company after that adventure. Not long after that, my band called it a day. Our leader Mick Wayne had to stop touring for health reasons, and we were all pretty burned out from constant touring, mainly overseas. It had run its course.'

The stars aligned. With the Apollo 11 moon mission came the breakthrough, when David captured the zeitgeist with 'Space Oddity'. Released on 11 July 1969, the single had been recorded on 20 June at Trident Studios in St Anne's Court, Soho, where guitarist Tim Renwick had first met David.

'I was still relatively new to session work, so was probably quite nervous,' says Tim. 'Mick Wayne [now deceased] had been booked to play on the recording of "Space Oddity", which was being produced by Gus Dudgeon' – Tony Visconti having rejected it as a novelty record that was shamelessly cashing in on the impending lunar landings.

'I remember David telling us that it had gone very well, but that he had broken a string while overdubbing the solo. To alert the control room of this annoying thing, he de-tuned his bottom E string – which was enjoyed to the extent that the whole solo was kept, including the de-tuned string!'

The historic record also featured Herbie Flowers on bass and Terry Cox on drums. On Mellotron was the just-turned-twenty-year-old

Rick Wakeman, a gifted Royal College of Music alumnus who was now a full-time session pianist and keyboard player.[10]

Few were more relieved by the success of 'Space Oddity' than *Melody Maker* writer Chris Welch, who had been championing David's cause for years. The interview they did together to celebrate turned into a quaint exchange on the subject of the Arts Lab movement, and culminated in the shock declaration that David didn't, after all, consider himself a performer. That's what he said *then*, anyway:

'I'm a writer . . . I really wouldn't like to make singing a full-time occupation,' he commented in that 1969 *Melody Maker* interview. 'The record is based a lot on the film *2001: A Space Odyssey*. It's a mixture of Salvador Dalí, *2001*, and the Bee Gees. Really, it's just a record which amuses people.'

During the run-up to Christmas 1969, Tony Visconti and his girl-friend Liz Hartley joined David and Angie in their huge, apparently haunted apartment in Haddon Hall. The idea had been to create an artists' commune, inspired by the spirit of the age. But really, it was all about David. Tony and Liz were happy to join the household; the imposing Victorian mansion was a convenient ten-minute jog from Beckenham Junction, which was served by fast, regular trains into the capital. One by one, musicians were drawn as if by magnets to David's eccentric 'Camelot',[11] taking up their positions on mattresses slung around the ornate minstrels' gallery beneath an exquisite elaboration of leaded stained glass.

'I visited David and Angie's home when I was working as a photographer for the *Beckenham Record*,' recalls Hy Money, the mother of my primary-school friend Lisa.

'When I stepped inside, it was just like walking into Aladdin's cave. Everything was brightly coloured. The living room walls were bottle-green, and the chairs had crushed red velvet seat cushions that Angie had made herself. It was warm and fragrant, and felt very Christmassy indeed. There was a fire burning in a grate. I went into David's own room, which had feminine pink walls, and he was there. Very tall. I didn't have flash in those days, so I had to make use of the natural light to photograph him. I remember that the ceilings were painted metallic silver, which made the light bounce oddly.'

By her own admission, Hy was a thirty-something West Wickham housewife in an abusive marriage, with 'different things to worry about from him'. Was she intimidated by David?

'Not in the least. It may sound stupid, but the experience was something of a transformation for me. Suddenly, I didn't feel like a misfit any more. I knew I wasn't "odd", "weird" or "unusual", as I'd been led to believe, especially by my husband and by some of the other mothers at the school gates. I felt at home. David's and Angie's place was just like my house on folk nights. The music, the atmosphere, the colours, the Indian sitar. People sitting around playing guitars, singing, joking, relaxed. Meeting them and their friends that day gave me confidence. It validated my love of impromptu live music, in preference to record players, television and radio. I'd been brought up in India, without such things. We made our own music. What I saw in Haddon Hall was exactly what I'd grown up with.'

What was her lasting impression of David?

'That he was a kindred spirit,' she says softly. 'I don't want that to sound pompous, but it is true. I had played piano for a long time, but I was only just discovering guitar music. What he was doing was something to aspire to. I was just another person who turned up. One of the many. An intruder. I had no real business being there. But he wasn't rude to me. He treated me with respect. I got much more out of the encounter than he did, I'm well aware. But he personally did nothing to make me feel "less than him", not in any way. There is sometimes a frisson between a young man and an older woman. As if they are ridiculing you. I didn't get that from him. He was welcoming and well-mannered. There was an empathy there. I felt it immediately.

'Meeting him changed me. Because of him, I stopped thinking

about the future, and began thinking only about the now. Compared to me, he was just a kid, but he seemed a very old soul: on a mission, with a bigger-picture outlook on life. That's what sets the few apart from the majority, isn't it. I wasn't at all surprised when he became a huge star.'

At the beginning of 1970, David started gigging with a new line-up: Tony Visconti, and Junior's Eyes' drummer John Cambridge and their guitarist Tim Renwick.

'This was Hype, David's next project,' recalls Renwick.

Everyone in the line-up had to dress up.

'Visconti insisted on wearing a Superman costume on stage – rather embarrassing! I only lasted for one show at the Marquee Club. Mick Ronson, a friend of John Cambridge's from his home town, Hull, took over from me. That was the closest I came to becoming a Spider from Mars. I wasn't that sad about it, the theatrical dressing-up thing was not my bag at all, me being an old hippy. I thought it was really uncool! I did get a twinge of jealousy when I saw David and Ronson on the front page of the *Melody Maker* together, but that quickly passed.

'I visited Haddon Hall with my girlfriend at the time, Linda Russell, the sister of photographer Ethan Russell,[12] who I'd stolen from Jackie Lomax, after leaving his band a year before. Haddon Hall was a large, rather gloomy place. We were a little scared off by Angie's interest in Linda, which seemed more than friendly!'

On 20 March 1970, after a threesome the previous night with a mutual female friend in north London, which made them late for their own wedding, David and Angie married at Bromley Register Office (not Beckenham, as often written). It was a quick, humble, sparsely attended affair. No family members had been invited, not even David's mother. Peggy got wind and rocked up anyway – darting to snatch the pen and inscribe the register, uninvited, when came the time.

'I didn't go,' comments George Underwood. 'Although he came

to mine when I married Birgit the following year. I know he did, he's in the wedding photos! I've never understood why he married Angie. There was absolutely nothing conventional about their relationship. But what I must say is how incredibly helpful to David she was during those early years – especially when it came to the creation of Ziggy. She did all the costumes and so much else.

'Basically, David was fucking anything that moved, throughout their marriage – and so was she. But I think she was only doing it because *he* was doing it. If you can't beat 'em, join 'em, kind of thing. She wasn't going to let him humiliate her. It was hard not to be affected by it all. I remember round at Haddon Hall one night, there was a beautiful model I was trying to chat up. David turned to me and said, "Are you staying the night?" It ended up with the four of us in David and Angie's bed – the one and only time I ever slept with him. But I wasn't quite up for that. It wasn't my cup of tea at all. Angie realised soon enough. "The difference between you and David," she said with a great big smile, "is that your balls and your brain are connected." '

For her part, Angie knew that the 'fidelity' vow stood no chance. Using sex 'to get what he wanted' was just what David did.

'Saying he didn't is like saying Picasso wasn't a misogynist,' Angie told the press after quitting Channel 5 TV's *Celebrity Big Brother* house. 'He was, but that doesn't take away from his talent or the value of his art. The same is true of David. He used sex to endear himself to people, so they loved him and did things for him, and worked hard to promote him. It was the pure selfishness of wanting to succeed. You have to use the currency that you have available, and if that is your sexuality, well then, OK.

'David wasn't a good husband. But in those first years, it was sweet and fun.'

In an exclusive interview with my friend Caroline Graham in the U.S. in August 2009, for which she was not paid, Angie admitted the real reason for their marriage:

'I would have been deported otherwise,' she said candidly. 'We got married because I was an American who needed to stay in

London, and he was a weak Brit who needed me to break down doors and turn him into a star.'

Despite the success of 'Space Oddity', it would be more than two years before David scored another UK hit. 'The Prettiest Star' and 'London Bye Ta Ta', recorded in January 1970, were both contenders for the follow-up. The T. Rex frontman on lead guitar on the former, which was favoured for release on 6 March 1970, should have cinched it. (It would be revisited three years later on *Aladdin Sane*, *sans* Marc). On the other hand, Bolan's great if short-lived reign had not yet begun. The rival's first hit, 'Ride a White Swan', would not be released until October that year, and would take eleven weeks to reach Number Two on 23 January 1971. Whatever else they may have taped together, 'The Prettiest Star' was the only Bolan–Bowie recording to be released. It was photographer Mick Rock, now world-famous for his work with Bowie, Syd Barrett, Queen and more, who described Bolan as 'John the Baptist to Bowie's Messiah' It was good, but it was more complex than that.

'The overlap between Bolan and Bowie was quite extraordinary, when you look back,' comments DJ Bob Harris, who was close to both. 'They both recorded at Trident, they were working with the same producer, they sat in on each other's sessions. They were massively interested in each other, regardless of what might have been said and written since.'

Basic but amiable Mick Ronson, an instinctive guitarist formerly of Hull outfit the Rats, was now ensconced as one of the 'mattress minstrels' at Haddon Hall – 'from Hull to heaven,' as he would later jest.[13] Drummer Woody Woodmansey soon followed. Eleven days after his marriage to Angie, David fired his bewildered manager Ken Pitt, who never got over it. Neither David nor Angie had the patience for the time it was taking to become an overnight sensation. They craved a more focused and professional approach. A change in staff structure was required.

On they went, recording and gigging, with Angie as head cook, bottle-washer, shirt-ironer, designer, lighting technician, coordinator, security guard, promoter and interim manager. Most of the tracks laid down for David's new album, *The Man Who Sold the World*, released in November 1970, were written on the fly by a distracted David, while a frustrated Visconti sat yanking out his hair. Things had got complicated. There was a bun in the oven.

Meanwhile, out on the front path at Haddon Hall, lurked two little mates from school.

6

1970–1971

In 1970, David Bowie was just another also-ran. Come the end of 1971, the naysayers would be eating their words. The year was in many ways his turning point, his *annus mirabilis*, during which he made his first, crucial trip to the US, in a dress, to promote his compelling album *The Man Who Sold the World*; became enamoured of America, and aroused by *beaux idéals* Andy Warhol, Lou Reed and Iggy Pop; recorded and released *Hunky Dory*; created *The Rise and Fall of Ziggy Stardust and the Spiders from Mars*; and conjured some of the greatest songs he would ever write. And at just twenty-four years of age, anything but ready, he became a father.

Many remain sold on the notion of Tony Defries as Bowie's point man. The inexorable Londoner of working-class Russo–Iberian parentage, a former solicitor's clerk, had his eye on the big time, and had for ages been seeking his catalyst: some innovative artist through whom to channel his own ambition. Flamboyant, cigar-chomping, bouffant-barneted, larger than life, Defries was just three and a half years older than David, and rather fancied himself as a manager in the Colonel Tom Parker mould.[1] Indeed, he declared his role model to be the Dutch-born chancer who had steered Elvis Presley into the stratosphere.

It's often said that Defries would even carry the 'Colonel''s memoirs around with him as a handy reference guide, but Tom Parker never wrote any. If Defries referred to any book, it was probably the recent, revelatory *Elvis: A Biography*, by American author Jerry Hopkins, which lifted the lid on much Colonel Tom Parker activity. As far as David was concerned, a partnership with an upstart who aspired to emulate the success of the King's head honcho had to be fated.

'Elvis was a major hero of mine,' he would say in 1996. 'And I was probably stupid enough to believe that having the same birthday as him actually meant something. I came over [to New York] for a long weekend. I remember coming straight from the airport and walking into Madison Square Garden very late. I was wearing all my clobber from the Ziggy period, and had great seats near the front. The whole place just turned to look at me, and I felt like a right idiot. I had brilliant red hair, some huge, padded space suit, and those red boots with big black soles. I wished I'd gone for something quiet, because I must have registered with him. He was well into his set.'

Defries decanted his legal aspirations into show business and inveigled himself into a management company called Gem, run by former accountant and lawyer Laurence Myers.

'This was where I came in,' says Anya Wilson.

The sassy house plugger,[2] one of the first females in the job, was a Gem employee. The company worked with producers and writers, including Lionel Bart, Tony Macaulay[3] and Tony Visconti. Their offices were on London's Regent Street, and Paul Raven [the future Gary Glitter, now a convicted paedophile] was the teaboy.

'You established contacts at the BBC – which at the time was the only thing that mattered – and you dealt with producers,' she explains. 'You'd go to weekly meetings to talk them into playing your records. It was all extremely competitive. I was honest. When they asked me if a record had the legs for a hit, I'd say what I really thought. Producers respected my opinion. Tony Visconti and I had become good friends through our connection with Gem. One of the first things I noticed about David was that, when he is with you, he gives you *all* his attention,' Anya remarks, slipping into the present tense. 'It was very special, and he was always like that. He was not one of those who stands staring at you with one eye while the other is over your shoulder, looking for someone much more interesting to walk by. My relationship with him was professional and respectful. But we liked each other.

'I met him the first time at Gem's offices. Laurence Myers had hired me, and he brought in Tony Defries as a partner. David came in with Angela. They looked like a couple of hippies, and they were holding hands. They had not long been married, and seemed incredibly close. We were introduced, and I was told I'd be working with them. It was always "them", not "him". Compared to them, I suppose I was quite corporate-looking; "corporate" in rock-management company terms being platform boots and a short skirt!

'I was assigned to do David's promo, and we did a couple of singles: "Memory of a Free Festival" [released 12 June 1970] and "Holy Holy"[4] [15 January 1971]. I don't think I'd ever met anyone with such a buzz, relating to all kinds of creativity. He knew exactly what he wanted, and he drew inspiration from absolutely everything that came his way. He has widely been accused of plagiarism, of stealing other people's ideas,' agrees Anya.

'If he *did* steal, what he used it for and how he used it was a creative force of its own. It's way far from "ripping off". He was actually very open about it, and thought of himself as a "tasteful thief" of other people's creativity.'

It's a thin line between inspiration and plagiarism. David came clean about his inclination to filch in a celebrated interview with Cameron Crowe for *Playboy* magazine in 1976, during which he commented: 'Mick Jagger, for example, is scared to walk into the same room as me even thinking a new idea. He knows I'll snatch it.'

Musically, David drew on many: Jacques Brel, Kurt Weill, Chuck Berry, Elvis Presley; Little Richard, Andy Warhol, Bob Dylan, Van Morrison; Pink Floyd – especially Syd Barrett; the Velvet Underground, Lou Reed, Iggy Pop. The Move, the Kinks, the Beatles, the Rolling Stones and the Bee Gees were all influences – as were Kraftwerk, Brian Eno, the Chemical Brothers, the Foo

Fighters and Prodigy. Stand-out vocal inspiration came from Anthony Newley and Scott Walker.

Over David's entire career, the thievery was substantial. The examples here are only a few:

'Starman' (1972) is Harold Arlen's 'Over the Rainbow', sung by Judy Garland in the 1939 film *The Wizard of Oz*, blended with T. Rex's 'Telegram Sam' and 'Hot Love', and seasoned with Holland–Dozier–Holland's 'You Keep Me Hangin' On' – this last a hit for the Supremes in 1966, and for Kim Wilde twenty years later.

'Life on Mars?' was written after David had been asked by his music publisher through his then manager Ken Pitt to pen English lyrics to a French number, '*Comme d'habitude*'. David's version, 'Even a Fool Learns to Love', was rejected. 'Quite rightly so,' commented David later. The 1967 song by Claude François, Jacques Revau and Gilles Thibaut was recorded by Claude François and released in 1968. Canadian singer-songwriter Paul Anka heard the song on TV during a trip to the south of France, went to Paris to secure the publishing rights, and reworked the song as 'My Way' specifically for Frank Sinatra in 1969. It became Sinatra's most famous anthem, and is the song most often played at British funerals. Bowie's 'Life on Mars?' deployed virtually the same chords as those of 'My Way'. The sleeve notes on the *Hunky Dory* album, on which it features, state that the song was 'inspired by Frankie'. The song also features the line 'Look at those cavemen go', which references 'Alley Oop', a 1960 hit for US doo-wop outfit the Hollywood Argyles.

As for the lyrics, David explained them as: '. . . a sensitive young girl's reaction to the media . . . I think she finds herself disappointed with reality . . . that although she's living in the doldrums of reality, she's being told that there's a far greater life somewhere, and she's bitterly disappointed that she doesn't have access to it.'

'Life on Mars?' wasn't actually a song about Mars at all, but about the gloom of reality – the drab suburbia in which David himself grew up.

The title of 'The Jean Genie' (1972) is a nod to both the name and the decadent lifestyle of author Jean Genet: a French playwright, novelist, poet and political activist who came to prominence in Paris during the 1940s. A rebellious, make-up-wearing homosexual, a petty thief and a male prostitute (as recounted in *The Thief's Journal*, 1949), he was a favourite of Pablo Picasso, Jean Cocteau and Jean-Paul Sartre. Much of his work contained explicit explorations of homosexuality.

In his 2002 limited-edition book *Moonage Daydream: The Life and Times of Ziggy Stardust* (Genesis Publications), illustrated by Mick Rock, the only official photographer during the Ziggy Stardust period, David admits that the title of 'The Jean Genie' '. . . was a clumsy pun upon Jean Genet.' One promotional video for the track features an edit of Genet's 1950 film *Un Chant d'Amour*. Genet, who contracted throat cancer, died after a fall in April 1986. The song is also clearly informed by the Velvet Underground. David has described it as 'a smorgasbord of imagined Americana', with Iggy Pop as his muse. Its lyric line 'He's so simple minded, he can't drive his module' gave Jim Kerr the idea for his band's name, Simple Minds.

Evelyn Waugh influenced *Aladdin Sane* (1973): David was reading the author's novel *Vile Bodies* (1930) as he sailed home from the US after his first American Ziggy Stardust tour. The film adaptation of the book was *Bright Young Things*, a phrase which features in the song's lyrics. Regarding the book as a reflection of contemporary society, David later remarked, vaguely, that it was 'about young people, just before the two wars, wanting to go and screw girls and kill foreigners'.

The work of George Orwell generated the 1974 concept album *Diamond Dogs*. The post-apocalyptic work had been intended as a musical-theatre adaptation of the novel *Nineteen Eighty-Four*, but Orwell's widow Sonia Brownell refused to grant David the rights. The raw, chaotic, proto-punk album is Rolling Stones-heavy. The track 'Sweet Thing' features David's first attempt at what has widely been referred to as 'William S. Burroughs' cut-up technique'. The practice, which David described as 'a kind of Western Tarot' and which he used as both compositional tool and inspirational device for a quarter of a century, in fact dates back to the Dadaists of the 1920s. Burroughs – Beat Generation stalwart, heroin addict and postmodernist author of paranoid fiction, including *Junkie* (1953) and *Naked Lunch* (1959) – singled out T.S. Eliot's poem 'The Waste Land' (1922) and John Dos Passos's 'USA Trilogy' (1938) as early examples of the technique he merely popularised.

The painter and writer Brion Gysin rediscovered it accidentally in the 1950s, after razoring a pile of newspapers to make a protective table mat. The book *Minutes to Go* resulted from the experiment with words that ensued. Gysin introduced Burroughs to the method at the writer/artist-friendly Beat Hotel on the Rue Git-le-Coeur in Paris's Latin Quarter (itself the inspiration for the late Elaine Kaufman's celebrated Upper East Side, Manhattan restaurant 'Elaine's', 1963–2011). It was Burroughs who said, 'When you cut into the present, the future leaks out' – before taking his place on the cover of the Beatles' *Sgt Pepper's Lonely Hearts Club Band* (1967). Beyond Bowie, the technique would later feature in the songwriting of a succession of artists, including Kurt Cobain and Radiohead's Thom York.

Bowie 'thieved tastefully' right to the end. The track 'You Feel So Lonely (you could die)' on his 2013 album *The Next Day*, for example, is clearly a rip-off of Leiber & Stoller's 'Heartbreak Hotel' ('I get so lonely I could die'), while the flavour of the song is blatantly Leonard Cohen's 'Hallelujah'. He even lifts from his own work in this number: the drums of 'Five Years' and the guitar of 'Rock and Roll Suicide' (both from *The Rise and Fall of Ziggy Stardust and the Spiders from Mars,* 1972) and the vocals of 'The Supermen' (*The Man Who Sold the World,* 1970). Perhaps most startlingly on *The Next Day,* he rips off the artwork of his own *"Heroes"* album, possibly his most revered of all, with his face blocked out by a blank white poster bearing nothing but the album's title. Designer Jonathan Barnbrook, who didn't do overtime that day, explains the rationale behind the cover and why it is symbolic:

'No matter how much we try, we cannot break free from the past. It always looms large, and people will judge you always in relation to your history, no matter how much you try to escape it. The obscuring of an image from the past is also about the wider human condition: we move on relentlessly in our lives to the next day, leaving the past because we have no choice but to.'

Other Bowie influences include William Shakespeare; Friedrich Nietzsche; poet & scholarly mystic Arthur Edward Waite; occultists and authors Dion Fortune and Aleister Crowley; Lewis Carroll; Charles Dickens; William Blake; Jack Kerouac; J.D. Salinger; Salvador Dalí; kabuki dance-drama theatre; Arthur C. Clarke and Stanley Kubrick: (*2001: A Space Odyssey*; also, Kubrick's *A Clockwork Orange*, based on the novel by Anthony Burgess).

'Inspiration' works both ways. Morrissey plundered 'Rock and Roll Suicide' for 'I Know It's Gonna Happen Someday' on his album *Your Arsenal* (1992) – produced and played on by former Bowie guitarist Mick Ronson. (Morrissey also worked with Bowie producer Tony Visconti.) David hit back with a cover of Morrissey's track on his album *Black Tie White Noise* (1993). Blur's Damon Albarn had to grant Bowie and Brian Eno co-writer credits on the band's 1997 song 'M.O.R.' because of striking similarities to 'Boys Keep Swinging' and 'Fantastic Voyage'. Noel Gallagher also pilfered, and was brazen about it. 'I can't understand why David Bowie hasn't sued me,' he said. 'I got three different songs out of "All the Young Dudes".'

When Anya Wilson first heard David's 'Memory of a Free Festival' and 'Holy Holy', she liked them well enough, but says that the tracks 'didn't rock [her] world'.

'His music didn't fit at all into what was going on at the time. But when I got more invested in his drive, heard more new stuff and became infected by his enthusiasm, I couldn't help but share it. He got under my skin. Tony Defries was extremely instrumental in David's eventual success. I don't believe it would have happened without him. He let David do whatever he wanted, and he knew that his own job was to have the world pay attention.

' "David needs to create," Tony would say. "He must have people designing his clothes, he must live in a nice place, he must have help with whatever he needs." Tony was the one who made it all possible. He was a powerful-looking guy, you couldn't ignore him. He'd go around saying, "My guy's going to be as big as the Beatles." That was a very hard thing to achieve with new music.'

Anya was, of course, at the mercy of the BBC.

'I dealt only with them at that time. Unless you got the BBC, you didn't get anything. Producers didn't see David's music fitting their format, but they were all drawn to it, and they liked what he did. There was a guy called John Muir, who had a small weekend show, and he was the very first believer. He knocked my socks off when he played both "Memory of a Free Festival" and "Holy Holy" on air. When David had made it, I made a point of calling him up and saying, "*You* were the first". John Peel and Bob Harris were both there for him in spades, too.'

'I still regard the Seventies as a massive opportunity that we wasted,' mused Bob Harris, during an interview with me for my biography of Marc Bolan, *Ride a White Swan*. 'We were all so idealistic at the end of the Sixties. We were pushing out the boundaries. But we were trying too many new things at once, and so we weren't focused enough. We wound up losing our direction, because life became way too self-indulgent. We opened up a huge opportunity, but then smoked ourselves out of the idealism. By the time we'd begun to wake up, the Eighties were already upon us, and everything was changing yet again.

'I think that's part of the reason why we all still feel so nostalgic about the Seventies. It is unfinished business. It's incredible how much of the music made in the Seventies is still so relevant now. Not just here in the UK, but all over the world. Bowie, Bolan, Elton

John, Cat Stevens, Led Zeppelin: all that amazing music soaked into our DNA. You can't imagine that the singles in the charts today will have that kind of longevity. Play the music, trigger the happy memories. We do see past decades through rose-tinted glasses, it's true. There was actually a lot of social and economic negativity throughout the Seventies. We forget the three-day working week, the miners' strike, the IRA, and that it was all pretty bleak at times.'

For Tony Visconti, their dolled-up Hype gig at the Roundhouse in February 1970, 'all David and Angela's idea', 'will always be the very first night of glam rock. We knew that we had to do something to get noticed. By then, we knew enough to listen to David.'

Marc Bolan was the first upstart to leap for the glitterball and spin it, perhaps inspired by what he'd seen at the Roundhouse that night. Though photos from that gig depict a bemused, denim-clad Marc eyeing the spectacle, he would later deny having been there. But Marc was the first off the block, working the look and scoring the hits. David lay back and thought of Little Richard, his original inspiration, who, at a time when an outrageously flamboyant and trisexual stance could have landed him in jail, had gone right ahead and done it anyway. He had also done it first.

Torn between two superstars in the making, it was time for Visconti to choose. Bowie or Bolan? He was living with the former while focusing musically on the latter – to David's bitter disappointment. Tony also had grave misgivings about both the integrity and the quality of the guidance from Defries. He tried to warn his friend, but David wasn't having it. Oh, anyway. Visconti would be back.

1971 marked the beginning of an emphasis on songwriting. There was good money to be made from cover versions of one's own songs recorded by better-known artists. Visconti knew better than most what was required.

'For me, what makes a great song is something unique and new, coupled with something old and familiar,' Tony said. He might have added to that observation the point that the best songs must be divisible from both the voice and the personality of their creator. Perhaps Paul McCartney's greatest gift is his ability to write songs with universal appeal that can be sung by virtually anybody. David's weakest link, in contrast, may be that his are so idiosyncratic, and such an inseparable extension of himself, that we can barely imagine or warm to the idea of his songs being covered by anybody else.

'Every single song that Bowie has ever written sounds completely different from the next,' points out singer-songwriter-keyboardist Tony Moore, former member of Iron Maiden and Cutting Crew – whose classic 'I (Just) Died in Your Arms Tonight' features one of rock's most recognisable riffs and choruses, and was a universal smash hit that is still played all over the world.

'Bowie's formula is No Formula,' says Tony. 'His lyrics are very personal, and poetically presented. They work on a variety of levels. If you know him and what makes him tick, you learn something about him. But also, you don't have to know anything at all about David to enjoy his songs. The more you do know about him and the many people he interacted with, the more you get from his music. As a writer, he is operatic, eclectic and grand. Even when he's writing a simple folk song. Every single song talks to us about his influences. There's a very appealing humility in this. It's also much more difficult, and uniquely creative, than it looks.'

There came a prime opportunity for interpretation by another artist when David's music publisher selected his composition 'Oh! You Pretty Things' – probably the first song that David composed on piano instead of guitar – as the debut solo single for Herman's Hermits star Peter Noone. (Peter Noone's version was released as 'Oh You Pretty Thing', no exclamation mark, 'Thing' singular.)

David contributed piano on the session: 'I play what is politely called "composer's piano", which means I know enough chords to be able to find my way around a song but not enough to sit down on stage, like Elton John, for instance, who's a wizard pianist,' David commented in Architectural Digest in 1995, in a feature about his

Mustique home. 'I'll have a go at anything and get a screech or an oink out of it, and then think, well that's kind of nice, play it three times and it'll sound like an arrangement. I think that's the secret to half of my success as a composer.'

The 'Pretty Things' cover featured the prolific former Tornado Clem Cattini on drums.

'It was at Kingsway Studios, where I'd worked on all the Lulu[5] stuff,' remembers Clem.[6] 'Mickie Most was the producer, and John Paul Jones [Led Zeppelin] was on bass. I'd met David once before, when I did a show at the Cadogan Hall for Lesley Duncan, and David was there dancing about on stage like Marcel Marceau.[7] We had a bit of chit-chat in the dressing room. He looked very distinctive – blond, and flamboyantly dressed – but he was a really down-to-earth bloke. What you saw was definitely not what you got!

'I've been told that I played on some of his records, down the years – like I did sessions for the Rolling Stones and the Beatles, but I was never allowed to say anything. In any case, you often didn't know what you were playing on, they'd just get you in to record parts without identifying what they were for. We didn't talk about that kind of thing in those days, it was all a big scandal and very hush-hush.

'Session men like me were the rent-a-guys. We were very often called in to re-record inferior parts, even to record entire singles and albums, where the actual band members were found lacking. They could be fine live – or should I say, they *looked* fine when a lot of the time they'd be miming – but recordings were something else . . .'

He digresses. 'The thing I always liked about David, he never made a big deal of himself "out there". Among other musicians, I mean. He didn't oversell it. It seemed important to him to be one of the gang. He was modest and unassuming in the studio, and was a good team player. One of the boys. Polite. Well-mannered. A credit to his mum and dad, as we used to say. We went and had a drink, and we had a laugh. When he went through the roof, it didn't surprise me. He was what I call a true muso. There are one or two who are up their own backsides, but most of us aren't. It's a job, and we just get on with it.'

To be a musician in the UK during the late Sixties, early Seventies was truly a privilege, affirms Clem.

'We were the centre of the earth, and David tapped right into that mood,' he says. 'I next came across him when he did "Sorrow" on his LP *Pin Ups*. I did two versions of that song: the first one for producer Mike Smith[8] with the McCoys [1965], and the one with the Merseys (1966), which was a big hit – and had a fantastic horn arrangement by John Paul Jones, him again. David's version [1973] was a bit ploddy, I thought. He even used that same intro we did, but he slowed it down. Did he improve on the original? No chance!'

David and Angie's son Zowie (masculine of Zoë: Greek for 'life', and pronounced the same way) Duncan Haywood Jones was born on 30 May 1971, courtesy of the National Health Service, in Bromley hospital. The baby was a heavyweight, and his mother suffered. 'David was there the whole time,' Angie told Caroline Graham. 'It was the first and only time I saw David cry.' His arrival inspired David to compose the charming song 'Kooks', which appeared on *Hunky Dory*. By Angie's own admission, David was 'a great dad.' Suzie Frost, a tenant in the basement of Haddon Hall, was engaged as a makeshift *au pair*, while Angie vanished on holiday with Dana Gillespie.

'It was not how it looked,' retorts Dana. 'It has always been written that Angie and I swanned off together on some big lesbian holiday, but it wasn't the case.'

By now, Dana had graduated to a large basement flat in her parents' home. It had a piano, a full drum kit, numerous guitars and an early synthesizer, which attracted a 'growing squad' of musos, including David, Marc Bolan, Jimmy Page, John Paul Jones, Donovan and the photographer Gered Mankowitz.

'Tony Defries had formed his own management company,

MainMan,' she says. 'We now had a captain of the ship, and we were a family, a team. I loved everyone there.

'MainMan signed me as a songwriter and recording artist, and Tony was hugely encouraging of us all, trying to get the best out of us. "In order to become first class," he'd say, "you've got to go through life *being* first class." It was the whole "fake it 'til you make it" ideal. I was having a wild rock life – in London Monday to Friday, and going down to Haddon Hall at weekends. The first time I ever saw black nail polish was when David brought Lou Reed home; he was wearing it. All my mother's family lived in Norfolk, so I did have "normal" to escape to when the rock'n'roll lifestyle got too much.

'It was an idyllic time,' insists Dana. 'There was Angie, queen of the minuscule kitchen, rustling up wonderful food for everyone. Tony Defries and I were together for a while. We "experimented". We adored each other. But he wanted "the woman for him", and that wasn't me. Still, we all went to the first Glastonbury Free Festival together [June 1971] with Angie and David dressed the same. A lot of people were on acid, especially the people on stage. But not David. Nothing like that was around him or me. David was trying desperately to get on stage, but his slot kept getting put back and back. Eventually, he got on at about five a.m., and it was wonderful. As the sun came over the hill to hit the pyramid, he began singing the chorus, "The sun machine is coming down, we're gonna have a party, yeah yeah," from "Memory of a Free Festival".

'Angie had left Zowie at home. The baby was only about three weeks old, but she wasn't coping. She was perhaps heading for post-natal depression, though we didn't really have that in those days. It was David who said to her, "Go on, off you go. Go on holiday with Dana and her mother." Angie and I were, and have always remained, best friends.'

Domestic responsibility neither lessened the work rate nor curbed the Bowies' appetite for nightlife. If anything, it stepped up the pace, as if in defiance of the parental titles their new offspring had conferred. David now took to calling Angie 'Mother' or 'Ma', and sometimes even 'Peg', just as John Lennon addressed his wife Yoko Ono as 'Mother' or 'Madam'.

Meanwhile, remembers pop guru, songwriter and manager Simon Napier-Bell, 'David was out there, all over London, living the life of a gay man to the hilt, and being anything *but* a married father of one.'

Angie soldiered on with her quest to gentrify Haddon Hall, making it 'as grand as can be'. On the antique French walnut bed with marquetry headboard that she found locally, David sat cross-legged to write the lyrics for *Hunky Dory* and *Ziggy Stardust*, strumming the eleven strings on his sweet-toned, twelve-string Harptone guitar. The high ceilings and wood panelling of the house provided great acoustics. Angie also bought him a piano, a Japanese jigsaw desk, Burmese sideboards, Chinese silk drapes and Persian rugs. Much of this eclectic style and blending of different periods and ethnic styles would be reflected in the interior design of Britannia Bay House, the exotic home he would eventually build on Mustique.

'I felt like we were in a magical place,' enthused Angie. 'And the melodies and ideas filled us with resolve to be totally successful. Haddon Hall was always full of people. Musicians, artists and designers all gathered.'

From spring 1971 to New Year 1972, David managed to complete two albums at Trident. Given his penchant for London's nightlife, this was no mean feat. He established a regular presence at the Sombrero on Kensington High Street, the hottest gay disco in the capital, which was run by a pair of Spanish queens. The club's registered name was actually 'Yours or Mine', and was referred to among the regulars as 'the Snake Pit' or 'the Chinese Take-Away', on account of its predominantly oriental clientele. Most of the remainder were ageing, gold-chained, hair-sprayed Middle Eastern fags with leather clutches. The dive had a raised dance floor in the middle, a cross between a boxing ring and the underlit Perspex dance floor in *Saturday Night Fever*. The

Sombrero gained an underground reputation as the HQ of London's carefree swinging sex life during the early Seventies, before the club scene really took off and became mainstream.

Scenester Philip Sallon was a frequent patron, alongside Mick Jagger, Johnny Rotten, Marianne Faithfull, Kit Lambert, Angie and David – although Angie always said she preferred Masquerade on Earls Court Road. They also frequented La Chasse, a private drinking club on Wardour Street, Soho. The Sombrero had its day, but there came the moment 'like someone turning the lights on at the end of the party,' one disciple remarked ruefully. Many of its regulars later died from AIDS.

Who knew where David found the time, let alone the energy, to write for the Arnold Corns, a Dulwich College school band; or to develop material for young Freddie Burrett, a fancy-pants fop they'd picked up on the circuit, who would soon become a fixture, bedmate and co-costume-designer at Haddon Hall. It was Freddie who was selected first to become the mouthpiece, the prototype Ziggy persona, when David decided to appoint him frontman with the Arnold Corns, and stuck an 'i' on the end of his surname. There was a significant drawback, however, in that Freddie couldn't sing. At all. Still, the work in progress continued.

The fairytale gained momentum with each new day and abstract idea. At least Freddie was great at suggesting images and ideas for outfits, many of which he would help stitch, under Angie's supervision. Guitarist Ronson, drummer Woodmansey and newcomer bassist Bolder morphed seamlessly into the as-yet-unnamed Spiders from Mars: a sharp, deadpan backing band for some as-yet-unfound fantastical creature through whom David could channel more excessive, exaggerated and theatrical work than he'd been summoning from his subconscious hitherto. Visconti didn't get it at all, but anyway was committed elsewhere. Into the web slid replacement producer Ken Scott, who had not only engineered David's first two albums, but who had also worked on the Fabs' *Magical Mystery Tour* and *The Beatles* albums, at Abbey Road.

Meanwhile, Defries did the business with RCA Records in America, on the back of the sublime, ever-enduring *Hunky Dory* LP, which was released in the UK in December 1971. As well as featuring some of David's best-loved classics – 'Changes', 'Oh! You Pretty Things', 'Life on Mars?', 'Andy Warhol' and 'Kooks', it is the album of 'The Bewlay Brothers'. Psychedelic and folksy, his 'densest and most impenetrable' song, it might be the most unsettling thing that David ever wrote. It was the only track on *Hunky Dory* that he wrote in the studio, by himself.

The recording is understated; acoustic and electric guitars, a bass, some drums, a bald vocal, lightly twanging and Bob Dylanesque in its inflections. The lyric is plaintive, pain-filled, unbearably sad. Its sinister fade-out Cockney chorus evokes images of starved *misérables* reaching up from the sewers: *Please come away.* The song is most often interpreted as being about David's troubled relationship with his brother Terry. I wonder.

The convoluted and obscure phrases within the lyrics evoke another Dylan from another time, Dylan Thomas from Swansea: . . . *the crust of the sun . . . stalking time for the Moonboys; In our wings that bark; . . . chameleon, comedian, Corinthian and caricature.*

In 2008, David would say this:

'The only pipe I have ever smoked was a cheap Bewlay. It was a common item in the late Sixties, and for this song I used Bewlay as a cognomen in place of my own. This wasn't just a song about brotherhood, so I didn't want to misrepresent it by using my true name. Having said that, I wouldn't know how to interpret the lyric of this song other than suggesting that there are layers of ghosts within it. It's a palimpsest, then.'

Tony Defries secured a contract for David designed to promote him as the natural successor to the artist who had made their label legendary: Elvis Presley. According to Anya Wilson, Bowie had now confirmed his viability with the three vital ingredients of pop superstardom:

'Brilliant songwriting – which I knew as early as "The Man Who Sold the World" was genius, and would always be relevant; his voice – which would evolve down the years, which would strengthen and mature, which many people would try and imitate, but which there would only ever be one of. It's a unique, emotive, emotional, full-range voice that plugs into your core. And his lyrics – which were the masterstroke. I also knew it was only the beginning. That David would only go from strength to strength. It was thrilling.'

On top of all that, and perhaps most importantly, Anya points out, 'he had Angela. No one should be in any doubt about her influence. Haddon Hall was like Mecca, and we'd all congregate there regularly for dinner. I can remember being there the night David got the call from Lou Reed, asking him to produce his album *Transformer*. When that whole scene kicked off, Angela and David had little money. She used some of her allowance to keep them going, but it was quite hand to mouth at first. She turned Haddon Hall into a salon: *the* place to be.

'She was a great hostess. Anyone she and David wanted to meet, they would simply invite them down to Beckenham. Unlikely though it may seem, these people would come; from the other side of London or even the world, if they had to. Suzy Frost, who was sort of Zowie's nanny, helped create the first costumes with Angela. The fabrics for the original catsuits came from Liberty. Angela would literally swoon over fabrics. She was relentless, she never stopped, she was always trying different ideas and coming up with new things. She and David sparked off each other. The chemistry was tangible.

'I knew her well. We've kept in touch, and I've seen her recently,' says Anya, who now runs a hugely successful independent promotions business in Ontario, Canada. In her view, Angie has been as vilified as Yoko Ono or Linda McCartney.

'She's too obvious a target,' she sighs. 'Angela's an extraordinary and lovely person. She's been maligned and misunderstood. There's a very deep love and intelligence about her soul. I feel really sorry for her son Duncan [Zowie], growing up and missing out on that (he and his mother have been estranged for decades). He should know, however, before it really is too late, that aside from her eccentricity, there's real treasure there, too.'

7
1972

Ziggy Stardust was not, after all, the concept it has been cracked up to be: meticulously planned, methodically crafted, and launched as a *fait accompli*. Although David's most enduring fabrication has been much eulogised and scrutinised for forty-five years as both the crystallisation of his creativity and the bridge between hippie-folkie-psychedelic music and punk, there was nothing that designed or contrived about it. Ziggy was, in many ways, David's hit-back: part expression of anger at the music business for not 'getting' him in the first place, and making him toil and wait around for his success; part forlorn declaration of everything he feared would befall the world, the destitution of Western culture, the realisation that over the rainbow lay nothing but doom. No one, least of all those rock critics who ejaculated over it at the time, wanted to hear that Ziggy was no deliberate drawing-board confection, but simply more candyfloss spun from the sweat of his imagination. But the fact is, there was no masterplan.

The Rise and Fall of Ziggy Stardust and the Spiders from Mars has been described as the tale of an oversexed alien rock superstar who achieves fame just as Earth enters the final five years of its existence. Ziggy falls victim to his own success, and becomes a rock'n'roll suicide. This is plausible in hindsight, but not what he set out to record. This was not a minutely plotted *magnum opus*. It was a bunch of disparate songs that somehow gelled around a central figure, who manifested himself gradually as an extreme personification of what David felt about this and that at the time.

In 2004, even David was kidding himself – casting his mind back to Ziggy as 'a concept piece for an album', for which he'd created the characters. But that was rose-tinted wishful thinking, another example of David rewriting history. It wasn't the case. We can overthink things, as David all too often did, through boredom, through mischief or just because he could. Commentators have overthought Ziggy *ad infinitum* for years – perhaps longing for him to have been more than he actually was, because of what he represented *to them* at the time. It is said that the music which awakens us in our early teens is the soundtrack that never fades, the one we dance to for all time. Any wedding disco lends weight to the theory. Says Stevie Wonder, 'Music, at its essence, is what gives us memories. And the longer a song has existed in our lives, the more memories we have of it.'

Likewise, the music's creators take up eternal residence in our hearts. Many who were teenagers during the early Seventies have found themselves unable to part with Ziggy, put him away, or to see him for what he really was, and is: just an illusion.

Had Ziggy Stardust been a racehorse, he would have been by Vince Taylor out of the Legendary Stardust Cowboy; both self-reinventions by chancers with glints in their eyes and an unbridled dream of stardom that got the better of them. The American-idol former was really a Brit, Brian Holden from Isleworth. He became a continental coffee-bar kid with his group the Playboys, had his Warholian fifteen minutes of fame in the early Sixties – 'Brand New Cadillac' was his best-known offering – and wound up as an aircraft mechanic in Switzerland. He died of cancer in 1991, aged fifty-two, and is buried in Lausanne, where David once lived.

The latter, a Chet Atkins-inspired proponent of Sixties psychobilly – a dash of rock, a peppering of punk, a hint of hillbilly, a ripple of rhythm'n'blues – was Norman Carl Odam turned 'The

Ledge', a spaced-out cowboy born in Lubbock, Texas, famous for being the birthplace of Buddy Holly. The Ledge landed on earth the same year as David, who discovered his music when he signed to Mercury Records in America. The Ledge was, David said, 'one of the only other artists they had.' Stardust's *pièce de résistance*, 'I Took a Trip on a Gemini Spaceship', was covered by Bowie on his huge *Heathen* album (released 2002). Credit where it was due, to the character who inspired Ziggy's surname. Now that David's gone, *kerching*: a global tour is said to be in the offing for the San José security guard who still dreams of making it. Come on, folks, cowboys get it where they can.

As for the name Ziggy: was it purloined from the signage of a tailors' shop front that David spotted from a moving train? An adaptation of the moniker of Jim Osterberg's alter ego, Iggy Pop? A twist on model *du jour* Lesley Hornby, aka Twiggy – that's her snuggling up to David on the cover of *Pin Ups* (1973)? All have been suggested. David told *Rolling Stone* magazine it was 'one of the few Christian names I could find beginning with the letter Z' – overlooking his own son's. Maybe it was inspired by Bolan, who had the band-name 'Zinc Alloy' up his sleeve for when he moved on from T. Rex, but was dead before he got the chance. Ziggy could well have been a blend of Zinc and Iggy. Bolan sent up the Ziggy album with his own *Zinc Alloy and the Hidden Riders of Tomorrow* (1974). Well, he would, wouldn't he.

We know that Ziggy Stardust wasn't a concept album because of the work David did with Freddie Burretti and the Arnold Corns that preceded it. On 10 March 1971, they recorded 'Lady Stardust', 'Right on Mother' and 'Moonage Daydream' at Radio Luxembourg's studios. A follow-up session in June, at Trident, added 'Man in the Middle' and 'Looking for a Friend'. 'Moonage Daydream'/'Hang on to Yourself' was released as a single. It died. Both songs later appeared on *Ziggy Stardust* with reworked lyrics. Burretti never sang on any of them. We can't ask him now how he feels about all that. He died of cancer in Paris in 1999.

But the songwriting was sensational.

'Suddenly, everything coalesced,' remembers Tony Moore. 'The record was an aural movie, if we can conceive of such a thing. This was David playing the *role* of Ziggy Stardust. We knew it was him: it says David Bowie on the album cover. And yet it wasn't him. It was this wholly new and almost unbearably thrilling creation. Although there were obviously lead tracks on the album, not one single eclipsed any of the others. Every single one was crazily, masterfully good in its own right. They also all hung together brilliantly so that it could easily be mistaken for a concept album.

'It has always fascinated me that during the period between 1964 and 1970, David's output was evolving slowly, he was not particularly prolific, he was just gently releasing things and seeing where they went. But from the beginning of the 1970s, his output increased dramatically. In the space of seven years, 1973 to 1980, he created a body of work that most artists couldn't hope to make in a lifetime. There is also a definite story arc to his music. You feel that change, across the albums, all the way from glam rock to something much darker and more sophisticated, as he himself matures, and delves even deeper into his heart and into his spirit. What we know with hindsight is that Bowie always created something that was very much in the moment. If it represented what he was feeling right there and then, that's what he put out. There was very much a feel of "publish and be damned" about it. He was so far off the beaten track, so different from everything else that was around at the time, and he dared to keep changing. There have been very few in rock history with the guts to do that.'

On 22 January 1972 came the now-infamous *Melody Maker* interview in which David declared arrogantly to journalist Michael Watts, 'I'm gay and I always have been, even when I was David Jones.'

'And with that, in one fell swoop, he became a kingpin, a figurehead, the salvation of "the only gay in the village",' explains Chris Welch.

'He latched onto the theme of being a misfit, a rebel. In a Britain that could still largely be described as "post-war", that was mutinous and exciting. Back in the early Seventies, it was a *huge* thing to say. David wasn't the first, of course. Quite a number of people at the time were pretending to be gay – like Vivian Stanshall in the Bonzo Dog Doo-Dah Band. It's mostly just a phase young men go through, when they find themselves attractive to, and attracted to, men, women and everything in between. Whatever, there is no denying that this was David's turning point.'

'Even if Bowie's claim that he was bisexual was a fashionable hoax,' said Boy George in his 1995 autobiography *Take It Like a Man*, 'he marginalised himself for a sizeable chunk of his career. He took a risk that nobody else dared, and in the process changed many lives.' Including that of the Culture Club gender-bender, who had started out as plain George O'Dowd. According to David, 'It perfectly mirrored my lifestyle at the time. There was nothing I wasn't willing to try.'

The revelation has haunted Michael Watts ever since. David was, after all, a married father. Besides, homosexuals (even if he was one) did not go around blaring the fact back then. The declaration, however, did nothing to dampen innocent schoolgirl enthusiasm for our local hero. His inceptive hints of all to come were made on 'Starman', released on 28 April 1972. For some, it was a day when life changed forever.

'The first time I ever heard David Bowie was on the radio at my grandparents' house,' recalls Natasha Holloway.[1] 'I sat listening to "Starman" in the back bedroom, going "*That* is *me*."That line from the song, "If we can sparkle he may land tonight": it was like opening up a cocoon, undoing a zip down your back, so that the real you inside could come out. Suddenly, someone *spoke* to me. I was a lonely kid, an only child. I wasn't sure who I was. I was very bookish, with a tendency to lose myself in fantasy: C.S. Lewis's *The Lion, the Witch and the Wardrobe*, the works of Lewis Carroll, Dylan Thomas's *Under Milk Wood*.

'My mum had always been a free spirit. But when she sent me to ballroom dancing classes, saying, "That'll come in handy when you have to go to dinner-dances with your managing-director husband," I felt doomed. Then came Bowie. And I knew, there and then, that just because I'd been brought up in Bromley, I didn't have to be a suburban conformist all my life. I could be anything at all.

'You remember how we all used to watch *Top of the Pops* every Thursday, five past seven. And then we'd all talk about it on Friday. We never actually went to *Top of the Pops* live, but we *always* watched it. And we'd save up and get a few records, and sit there writing out the lyrics laboriously, putting the record player needle back to the beginning over and over again, to get the words down, and even then not always getting them right. Medhurst's music department in the basement, DJ Alan Freeman's record shop on the Market Square, and W.H. Smith with those record bins you could rake through – we could only look at them, we could never afford to buy them. I did violin with Miss Strudwick [a member of the Bromley Symphony Orchestra], but I had to give it up. I so regret that. Music was our life.'

Until David Bowie, Natasha points out, everyone we knew was straight, white and ordinary.

'OK, David was white, but he certainly wasn't straight or ordinary. I took him at face value all the way. I believed in it totally. Thanks to him, we now had choices. You don't have to be "this", or "that", you could instead be *this*. I've always thought that what we experience here isn't everything, and I had long believed that there may be extra-terrestrials. When I first discovered David, it was the words, for me. The lyrics. He opened my eyes to possibilities.

'I went straight out and got a Ziggy haircut at the hairdresser's in Hayes. I took her a picture in. The first night I had it done, I hated it. She'd blow-dried it too much. I cried for a week under the blankets. But it grew into itself, bit by bit, until it was me.'

It didn't go down well at school, where unenlightened others suddenly decided that Natasha was weird, simply for having become a fan of David Bowie.

'I was made to feel like an outcast. But they didn't get it: I'd always felt different from everyone else. I'd never felt at home anywhere. Discovering him changed my life. I can think of nothing else since then that has had that kind of impact. I felt I had so much in common with him. I, too, wanted to break out of the known and the mundane.'

Natasha attended his show at Kilburn Gaumont later on the tour, 13 June 1973, and was startled by Angie Bowie with 'blue/leafy-green hair'.

'I remember talking to her. Goodness knows why. It was the first big, amplified gig I'd ever been to, in a theatre-sized venue, without my mum. It was wonderful. I absolutely loved it, and I loved him. And then I dropped out. Completely. It was David who gave me the courage to do that. It was as if he was saying to me, "You don't have to do what your parents have done, you know, or be what they would like you to be." Only when I went and found a life of my own, and didn't need him any more, did I stop following his music avidly.

'Although I did remain aware. I'd made the final change. I didn't have to carry on re-creating myself any more. There was almost a feeling of disloyalty, that I'd dropped him and gone off on my own. But I'm doing now what I feel I should be doing in my life because of him. Absolutely. I can't say that he was my saviour, but he was certainly my signpost in the road.'

In many ways, Natasha concedes, Bowie was derivative.

'But he took those derivations and made them into something more than they were before. I don't particularly care how you get to the end result in music. You can take all sorts of things and throw them up in the air or stir them around in a bucket. It's what comes out that counts. Show me a rock star who *hasn't* been influenced by musical stars and styles and all kinds of other elements that went before. Plus, he had more imagination than any of them. How do you quantify imagination? You can't. He was extremely savvy. He knew exactly how to appeal to a gauche, frail, young teenage audience. He wasn't so far removed from us in age – not enough to put him in our parents' generation, anyway. And yet he seemed wise beyond his years. He *was* the Ziggy Stardust starman he'd created. He was different. He was a superstar waiting to happen, and it was all such a thrill, having known him as a local hero, to watch him do it. And I did get out of Bromley because of him.'

Nicky Graham's life was changed by Ziggy, too – in more tangible ways. As a young teenager, the South African-born musician had moved with his family to Wimbledon, London at the height of Apartheid, abandoning his school band Nicky Graham and the Cruisers. At Kingston University he studied architecture to please his mother, but the passion endured. Working with a variety of bands during the Sixties, he crossed the radar of Rolling Stone Bill Wyman, who opted to produce Nicky's latest line-up, renaming them the End.

Wyman got them a record deal with the Stones' label Decca, and onto their next tour as the opening act. The band evolved into Tucky Buzzard and cut a couple of albums – the second of which, *Warm Slash*, was recorded at the Château d'Hérouville near Paris, the 'Honky Château' made famous by Elton John's 1972 album of that name, and a mystic place to which David would soon be drawn. Tucky Buzzard's album sleeve featured the cheeky Stones' bassist on the front with his back to camera, obviously relieving himself.

'There was a freedom about the Seventies that meant you could do things like that,' muses Graham. 'We promoted and toured our album for six months. It didn't sell. I returned to England. By this time I'd met my first wife, Diana. She worked for Tony Defries. He decided he wanted to manage Tucky Buzzard, and did a deal with Bill. I was wheelbarrowed in to meet the boss.'

Nicky remembers Tony Defries as an extraordinary character, in skinny flared jeans with an enormous belt buckle, an undone-to-the-waist shirt so tight across his torso that it barely concealed his lunch, and a giant mouth crammed with cigar.

'He wore a massive fur coat when he went out. He looked like a gigolo or a pimp. His catch-phrase was "Leave it to me!" He oozed more confidence than competence. He looked after the affairs of Lionel Bart, for example, and Bart went bankrupt. The next thing you knew, Tony had brought in Bowie. I was looking for something to do, and Di said I should come into the office and help out, as a general all-purpose chap. Then one day, Tony turned around and said to me, "David's going to go out on tour, and I want you to book it." I don't know what to do, I said. "Oh, it's easy," he replied, "you just phone up all the theatres and book 'em." So I got a map of the UK, stabbed it all over with a pin, and started calling up theatres. The tour was just "David Bowie" with his backing band to begin with. He'd shed the dresses and the long hair, which had gone short and red, and he was coming into the office in increasingly eccentric outfits. I loved it! The new image was emerging throughout those spring dates, but it wasn't until 27 May that the Ziggy character and the Spiders were fully realised.

'Despite the fact that biographies and documentaries always quote the Toby Jug, Tolworth gig as "the first", the Ebbisham Hall, Epsom gig, MC'd by DJ Bob Harris, is the one that those of us who were actually there regard as the very first *Ziggy Stardust* gig. David and the band were *not* "Ziggy Stardust and the Spiders from Mars" until that night, I can assure you. It simply hadn't come together until then. David had drawn a "Ziggy" character, and we used it to promote the gigs. I photocopied it onto A4 sheets of paper, and went round with a sheaf of them and a box of drawing pins, and pinned them onto trees. So far, so good. Then we came to do the sound check. No one around. It was all eerily quiet, and we really thought no one was going to turn up. We went off and had a curry, came back, and there were about three hundred people snaking around two blocks. It was the most fantastic gig.'

So efficient did Nicky prove at running the show that responsibility was suddenly piled upon him.

'Out of nowhere, I was now Tony Defries's right-hand man. Taking care of all the transport, the flights – we'd started flying domestically, David had no problem with planes back then – the money, the logistics. David came to rely on me for more or less everything day-to-day, because Angie had taken a big step back for some reason, and there wasn't yet anyone else to do it. I was collecting the takings, dishing out the wages, paying the crew. Peter Gerber was the accountant. I'd go to him and ask for the money for five flights and a car, whatever, and he'd write a cheque, which I then had to go and cash. I was never aware at the time of the bigger picture, which was that Defries was going to RCA on a regular basis for "another half a million quid".'

MainMan set up independently from Gem on Chelsea's Gunter Grove:

'A beautiful old building but a pain in the arse to park at, which was also Defries's home,' says Nicky. 'I was thirty-one years old, and effectively running David's management company while Defries was off swanning about, and spending. Mott the Hoople came on board, and then Iggy Pop. I did all the work, by myself, for those three big acts. And then, for a while, I became a Spider from Mars.'

Lending his finely honed keyboard-playing skills to David's band was an obvious move. It didn't exactly ease Nicky's workload.

'I was fitted for a plum-coloured suit with yellow boots, very *Clockwork Orange*. I sprayed my hair, from cans: silver on one side, gold on the other. Then I'd go and get the money from the Midland Bank on Pall Mall on a Friday morning – there were no cash machines in those days – and do the wages. This involved divvying up notes into brown envelopes and putting some spare in the petty cash. They'd all file in on a Friday afternoon to get their loot. I also had to pay crew and other personnel at the gigs, organise the drinks and food afterwards, drive the minibus to the next town, and get up on stage and play with them as well. I was round-the-clock knackered for the duration. Meanwhile, Defries would be on the phone to the president of RCA Japan or wherever, doing deals, fat cigar in gob, and leaving all the work to me. Yet still I thought he was great. His number one priority was David Bowie. He had to keep his artist happy at all costs.'

Peter Gerber had a heart attack in a tent in Wales, dropped down dead, and things got worse.

'More work for me, but I took it in my stride,' shrugs Nicky. 'I can't say I wasn't enjoying it. I was doing what I did best: playing in a band. Working with one of the greatest artists of all time, as it turned out. I even got to perform as a Spider on that legendary *Top of the Pops* performance of "Starman". But in the end, it all came unstuck – because of Angie.'

It sounds laughable now, but it came close to ruining Nicky's life. Mrs Bowie wanted tickets to an Elton John gig in London that weekend, for herself, Dana Gillespie and a host of other friends. Too late in the day to action the request, no matter how hard he tried, Nicky couldn't rustle up any tickets. Angie also demanded a wodge of readies. Nicky couldn't oblige with that either.

'She came in on a Friday afternoon at around four o'clock, demanding even more money than she'd already picked up. David was getting four hundred a week, which was handsome, while the band were getting fifty quid each. I had Iggy's money and Mott's money in envelopes in the petty cash tin, but nothing more. I wasn't going to give her theirs. The banks were already closed, and I couldn't get any more until the Monday. There was I, working my nuts off, playing and organising and doing absolutely everything for everyone, and I went from that to the sack. I went home. My wife said, "You need to go and sit on a beach somewhere." I got a flight to Ibiza and just sat there.

'What hurt me most was that I didn't get to go to America on the first Ziggy Stardust tour. I'd worked for it, but lost out for a ridiculous, pointless reason. I didn't get over that for a long time.

I'd been very close to David, and I never saw him again after that. When things like that happened, he would always get someone else to do the dirty work. He hung well back. I didn't even get to play the Rainbow. I subsequently spoke to Trevor and Woody, and had lunch with Mick. Much later, after he died, there was a Mick Ronson memorial gig at the Hammersmith Odeon, and I played at that. When they became huge stars, I did feel cheated. But eventually, I got philosophical about it. I came to understand that my life would have been completely different, had I continued as a Spider from Mars. The rejection spurned me on to go and have a proper career.'[2]

Nicky believes that nothing David did post-Ziggy ever lived up to it.

'None of his subsequent music captured the imagination in quite the same way. He had something to prove back then. He never worked quite as hard after that, and it showed.'

'Ziggy really set the pattern for my future work,' commented David, years later. 'Ziggy was my Martian messiah who twanged a guitar. I saw him as very simple . . . fairly like the character Newton I was to do in the film [*The Man Who Fell to Earth*] later on. Someone who was dropped down here, got brought down to our way of thinking, and ended up destroying himself.'

In 1976, he'd rewritten history a little. It was 'I became Ziggy Stardust. David Bowie went totally out the window. Everybody was convincing me that I was a messiah, especially on that first American tour [late 1972]. I got hopelessly lost in the fantasy.'

As for *Top of the Pops*, confirms Nicky Graham, for the record, 'there *was* no big thing at the time. It has all been invented! It's such a cute little pop song, "Starman" – "Over the Rainbow" by another name – and one of the great rip-off songs. But it didn't create any big seismic shift. I was there. I can tell you that for nothing.

'We went down to do *Top of the Pops*, got dressed up in our stage gear, and we went on and mimed and played to the track. There was no hysterical reaction in the studio, nor any great eruption across the media the next day. It was just another night.'

'He was, by then, a curious phenomenon in so many ways,' ponders music writer David Hancock. 'Taking it away from the image and the perception of him: I'm talking David Bowie as a bloke. In many ways, he was effete. He was never the sort of guy who went down the pub with the lads for a pint and a game of darts. He wasn't one of us, and yet he *was*. Everybody who ever spent time with him and then talked about him afterwards said that he was always one of us. And what a really great bloke he was. And how nice. He certainly treated *me* as an equal, and I treated him the same. The weird thing about fame is that you may not think of yourself as any different, once you have it, but other people start treating you differently. They start having different expectations of you. Why? I don't get it, myself.

'I remember being in Brahms & Liszt once [a popular wine bar behind the Royal Opera House, Covent Garden, long gone], with Bob Dylan. He wanted a Guinness, but they didn't have any. I walked across the road to the pub opposite, bought him a pint and brought it back. And everyone was amazed: You can't do that! You can't bring *Bob Dylan* a pint in a wine bar! But why not? That's the trouble with fame: it changes everything. It seems to remove the right to be just a normal person, which is all that any musician or any kind of celebrity still is, inside. And pretty soon, you can't get anywhere near them – and perhaps more to the point, they can't get anywhere near *you*. And then you are both victims of it, the anonymous person as well as the celebrity. So pop does eat itself. David would become more of a victim than most.'

In August 1972, the *Melody Maker*'s Chris Welch saw Ziggy and the Spiders at London's Rainbow Theatre. 'Clad in a suit of silver with matching boots,' Welch wrote, 'he strode out with perfect timing to ankle-deep jets of smoke.

'It would be hard to imagine audiences as long as three weeks ago accepting such a spectacle without recourse to raspberries and maybe even yells of "Get on with it!" But times change rapidly in the rock business ... the triumph was David Bowie's, and he has obviously come a long way since whatever he was doing last year.'

David's ever-swelling entourage now included his erstwhile Andy Warhol Factory friends, former cast members of the outrageous show *Pork*, which had transferred from New York to London, casting them back into his sphere, and putting several of them on the MainMan payroll with not entirely necessary jobs and far-fetched titles. When David set sail for New York on the *QE2* in September, a sizeable number followed on. Elevated to ocean-going status with the main man were George and Birgit Underwood. On arrival, their party checked into the Plaza Hotel, to prepare for a big-spend two months' worth of shows all over the land.

'He wanted someone with him who wasn't in the business, as an impartial friend,' explained George. 'So-called Bowiemania and the whole MainMan thing had exploded, and it was already getting to him. I was his connection to normality. His life was getting increasingly out of hand. He did say to me at one point, "George, the way things are going, we may not see each other for five or ten years. But don't worry. It will always be the same between us." He said I could do some work for him in America as well. We talked a lot on the five-day journey about album covers and stuff. And about life, and when we were kids, and all the other stuff.

'After the first two weeks in America, Tony Defries called a meeting with everyone on the trip. It was about money – expenditure was getting crazily and fantastically out of hand. He said, "The Underwoods haven't cost us anything at all. Why's that?" It was because I took my own money, and paid for everything out of my own pocket, whereas everyone else was charging everything to David. I didn't want to come across as a freeloader: he was my friend. I was asked to stay for the rest of the tour, which I did. I did do some illustrative work for "The Jean Genie". A few sketches and things. But my real job, that trip, was to be David's companion. He liked having me around, keeping him stable. Not that it was all drug-fuelled and mad at that point. That all came later.'

At the end of that US tour, David asked George to come back the following year, and to go on to Japan with him.

'I said, "What would I be doing?" He said, "Vocal back-ups." But I said no. I'd only been married a year [they're still together], Birgit and I had a great flat in Hampstead, and we didn't want to give that up. Besides, I had my own work stuff going on. It's best to be single for that kind of lifestyle, and I wasn't. Geoff MacCormack,[3] who was with David at Burnt Ash School, who was also our old mate from St Mary's church choir, took my place. It was the last time I saw David for quite a long time.'

8

1972–1973

Ziggy Stardust may have made David a star, but the wretch proved Frankensteinian. Eclipsing his creator from the moment he was fully formed, Ziggy subsumed Bowie and might have wound up destroying him, had not David decided to kill him and his arachnids first. Those closest are invariably the last to know.

By 1973, Bowie knew he'd struck gold. Overnight stardom had taken almost ten years, but here he now was, all things to all people: a superstar on both sides of the Atlantic, worshipped as a teen idol, revered as a rock star, lusted after as a bi sex symbol, hailed as some philosophical guiding light. His 'Ziggy as Messiah' stance paralleled John Lennon's 1966 remark 'We're more popular than Jesus now. I don't know which will go first, rock'n'roll or Christianity' – following which John was long regarded as the devil incarnate. Seven years along, the lines were more blurred, the faithful less offended by asinine comparisons. He'd scuppered them all, this ruthless ransacker, this rag-and-bone man, this vampire. Ziggy had sucked the veins of all in his path, and was now gorging on the ultimate resource, his own self.

Out of nowhere, David had a new accomplice: an undelectable, curt New Yorker who had joined the staff at MainMan. Coco came in as if through the bathroom window, a humble dogsbody who rapidly ascended the ranks. She snaffled the job of Nicky Graham's old school chum Hugh Attwooll, the very executive who'd hired her, while he was on annual leave. She was to make herself so completely indispensable to David that her resignation would have been Shankly-esque: no matter of life and death, but infinitely worse. Corinne Schwab was Coco's real name. She remained David's Man Friday for the rest of his life. He credited her on numerous occasions with having saved his. When came the end, he bequeathed her more than £1 million in his will – this has been rumoured to be beribboned with a gagging order. Miss Schwab will never talk or write about her former employer and friend. She has never given an interview. She knows too much. She knows more than David knew himself.

'The funny thing,' comments music journalist Chris Welch, 'is that, in the business today, nobody remembers anything about her. They barely remember her name. She was just a secretary who took over a rock star's life – and relinquished her own in the process. It's a curious way to live.'

A hip throng gathered at Haddon Hall to celebrate David's and Geoff's return from their epic rail adventure. That was where Coco and David met. The welcome-home/house-cooling party was also attended by the long-time-no-see Viscontis; Tony was now married to his Welsh songbird sweetheart Mary Hopkin.[1]

Coco said little that night, preferring to prove her worth within office walls. She was fiercely protective of her private life – probably because she didn't have one, sneered her detractors. Down the years, there would be plenty of those. She had 'Swiss blood'; her father had been a war correspondent and photographer, and it was rumoured that her psychotherapist mother had given birth to her in a linen cupboard in Bloomingdale's. Perhaps someone made that bit up. She was multi-lingual, extensively read, impressively numerate.

She seemed fascinating to David, but 'plain, dull and boring' to everyone else. There are many like her in the music business: I could name a dozen off the top of my head. Freddie Mercury's Mary Austin, for one, who was originally his girlfriend, became his post-gay-confession PA, and who inherited his house and the bulk of his fortune after his death. These women put their own lives on hold to be available round the clock for 'their' artist. They become their bitches, their nurses, their gatekeepers, their Rottweilers, partaking of the rock'n'roll lifestyle to a point, but ever mindful, always awake, more often than not sober.

They are often held in contempt by the rest of an artist's entourage – especially the spouse. They are rarely regarded as more than a mere shadow of their star. Come the day of reckoning, these faithful servants tend to wind up with precious little to show for their devotion, beyond a cache of gifts, a house or maybe a small legacy if they're lucky. Coco would receive £1.4 million from David's estate. There is usually no significant other with whom to share it. Many of them fantasise that their employer is secretly besotted with them, and that they will be together one day – once the rock wives, groupies and doxies have all been spent. The dream is a desolate one. Vapid Coco was no obvious threat to Angie – which was what made her intriguing. Such women, we know, are the ones to watch. Especially when they fall in love.

The Ziggy tour rolled on relentlessly around Britain, a maelstrom of performances, TV appearances, radio, press and fandemonium.

'I went to every single gig, apart from the Earls Court show, which I was really sorry to miss,' says Anya Wilson. 'We'd done so much prep for it. But my own little company, which I'd launched by then, was in such a great place. I had Paul McCartney and Wings as well as David. They had a reception that night, an opener for a Wings tour, and I was obliged to go to it.

'David used to call us every morning after a show the night before and say, "What did you think? Did you like it? What did you make of this line or that move?" We'd have to go over it all with him in the finest detail. He was never satisfied, always trying to improve. He was an absolute perfectionist, and relentless.'

Having written much of the *Aladdin Sane* album on the road in the States, David leapt back into Trident as soon as he could, to fine-tune and record. At the end of January, he set sail again for New York, as the *NME* splashed their headline 'GOODBYE ZIGGY, AND A BIG HELLO TO ALADDIN SANE'. David denied to the rags that he'd created a new concept album – although hindsight, that wonderful thing, would contradict.

So what was with the whole sudden Bowie Doesn't Fly thing? He'd been boarding planes up and down the country and to Europe without protest for some while. But between 1972 and 1977, it was suddenly ships, trains, tour buses, limos, jeeps, cabs, bikes, rickshaws, chairlifts, cable cars and Shanks's pony all the way. On his first major tour, he crossed the Atlantic on a liner, conquered America by road, and sailed the Pacific to take Japan by storm overland. His homeward-bound journey was made by ferry from Yokahama to the Russian port of Nahodka, a connecting train to Vladivostok, and then a ten-thousand-kilometre train ride, most of it on the Trans-Siberian Railway. He traversed the entire breadth of the Soviet Union in one hit, changing in Moscow for the old Moskva-Express (Ost–West Express) that linked the Russian capital with Paris. By the time his locomotive pulled into Gare de l'Est on 3 May, he had notched up his first round-the-world tour. He was twenty-six years old. In 1977, he gave in again to air travel, flying to New York with Iggy Pop. But 2002 would find him back in a deckchair on the *QE2*, Europe-bound, for the Heathen tour.

'David is a lot better at flying these days, and travels by plane when he has to,' said his PR. 'But sometimes he's in no rush, so he decides to take a leisurely cruise across the Atlantic.' Nice work if you can.

Some have dismissed the aviophobia he claimed, intimating that glam ocean-liner travel and the lavish lifestyle that went with it – endless opportunities to dress for dinner, all those brass-clasped, Louis Vuitton steamer trunks – appealed to his inner 1930s Hollywood diva. 'Act special 'til they treat you special,' Defries always said. Others flag up a more prosaic reason: that he developed a fear of flying after a stormy flight home from a visit to the in-laws in Cyprus with Angie. David himself remarked, at the height of his Ziggy fame, 'I won't fly because I've had a premonition I'll be killed in a plane crash if I do. If nothing happens by 1976, I'll start to fly again.' Which he did.

Nothing exceeds like excess. Even ahead of Ziggy's breakthrough, Tony Defries thought big, lived bigger, and spent money like it and fashion had got a divorce. While the 1973 US tour entourage seemed modest in comparison to the previous year's, when at least forty-six individuals were on the list, Dana Gillespie recalls no obvious cap on expenditure.

'Defries was still footing the bills, as far as I knew. I was along for the ride because I'd had to leave *Jesus Christ Superstar* [in which she played the first Mary Magdalene]. I'd got caught in an avalanche in 1964, had buggered my knee, and needed surgery. I was going on stage on painkillers and brandy, and I don't even drink. They were carrying me to and from the stage. David and Angie came to see me in it one night, but left during the interval. I was mortified, but I didn't dare give them a hard time. I probably asked Angie why, but she would have said "*He* wanted to leave". I know they hated the music.

'David's huge fame and apparent fortune didn't affect me. I was with MainMan, I was their artist too, on a trajectory of my own. I was one of them. It all seemed like a perfectly natural progression, the thing he'd been working towards all those years. I was just thrilled that it had come good for him. As for me, I was having a ball. I stayed in the best hotels, limos everywhere, partied like it was 1999, shopped 'til I dropped and charged absolutely everything to the MainMan account. What's not to like? At one point, we were all in the Sherry Netherland, a big old, opulent 1920s place overlooking Central Park, for six months. And every last thing we needed or wanted was going on room service.'

On and on with the show, great cities falling in homage. Kansas

City, New York, Philadelphia – where he boogied with Stevie Wonder and popped new squeezes like spots. The latest was Ava Cherry, wham bam. Nashville, Memphis, Detroit, Hollywood. He played his boogie woogie bugle in a cupboard with Bette Midler *en route*.

Into March, David and Geoff were back on the ocean wave, bound for Canada, then on to Japan, where a manic reception preceded a five-city, nine-show tour, kicking off in Tokyo and taking in Nagoya, Hiroshima, Kobe and Osaka before returning to the capital. The Japanese worshipped him, not least for his homage to their culture. His tour there was even hailed by some as 'the healing of the rift between the Allies and Japan', which might have been egging it. Then again, in 1983 he would star in the movie *Merry Christmas, Mr Lawrence*, playing a conscience-stricken prisoner of war in 1940s Japan. At the very least, the press coverage afforded David an opportunity to remind the West of Japanese culture, traditions and fashion.

Many subsequent artists would follow his lead, including Freddie Mercury, who would wear kimonos on stage; Ultravox; Siouxsie Sioux; and Sparks, who released an album called *Kimono My House* in 1974. The phrase 'Big in Japan' was coined to describe Western acts that had made it there. It also became the name of a 1970s UK punk band. In 1984, German group Alphaville released a song by the same name, which became their only UK hit. Police, Duran Duran and countless other artists would fall for the country's charms. And Simon Napier-Bell, never less than on-trend, cultivated perhaps the best band that never made it globally, but really should have. The most beautiful and esoteric lead singer in rock, David Alan Batt from Beckenham, was hastily renamed David Sylvian. The band was called Japan.

Napier-Bell, the rock manager and impresario who had been offered David on a plate by hapless early manager Ralph Horton, happened also to be in Tokyo in April 1973. He had travelled to Japan ostensibly in pursuit of the cherry blossom – the Who's manager Kit Lambert having enthused to his great friend about its magnificence. But Simon wasn't really there for Hanami – the centuries-old tradition of blossom-viewing and picnicking beneath the boughs.

'I didn't really care about the cherry blossom, it was just an excuse to go to Japan,' Simon admits. 'I travelled continuously throughout the Seventies. I'd reached a moment in life when the excesses of the rock business were boring me. My mind was ready for something new, and in Tokyo I found it. It wasn't just the people or the signboards or the architecture, it was everything. You could feel it in the air. Outwardly, most things looked much the same – the buildings, the clothes, the cars – but this familiar topping was resting on a perversely different cultural base.'

David felt it, too; although in fairness, he'd been developing an interest in Oriental culture, art, fashion, make-up and music for some time. His interest had clearly been sparked by his dalliance with Buddhism during the Sixties. At one point, he said, he even toyed with the idea of donning the aubergine robes and entering a monastery. Hmm. From Buddhism arose his strange fascination with androgyny. He was inspired by representations in ancient Eastern art of the inseparable masculine and feminine energies, the roots of creation. The notion of two opposites co-existing, co-dependent, leading to complete integration of gender roles until they become one, was an underlying theme of his early relationship with Angie.

Japanese culture features a rich variety of androgynous deities, such as Inari: the kami, or spirit, of agriculture and rice, who became a figure of worship in the late fifth century AD, and who is portrayed as both female and male. Japan's complex religious history, a blend of Shinto and Buddhism with seams of diverse, imported elements running through it, intrigued him. Dance and mime tutor Lindsay Kemp had done his share to teach David about Japanese culture in the 1960s, in particular about the onnagata: male kabuki actors who play female roles. It must have been thanks to Kemp that, the second time I met David, pre-fame, at Haddon Hall, he was wearing a lemon silk kimono.

The Japanese word 'kabuki-mono' could have been coined for David: 'a person who attracts attention with strange clothes, hairstyles and eccentric behaviour'. The previous January, working from an image David had torn from a copy of *Harpers & Queen* magazine, Beckenham High Street crimper Suzi Fussey[2] dyed twenty-five-year-old David's with Schwarzkopf Red Hot Red, and cropped it into spikes. It was just the start of his infinite variety. From then on, until he lost the plot, at least, there was the sense that he was laughing at himself and taking none of it seriously:

'When you've had red hair and no eyebrows,' David would say in 1993, 'you've got to have a sense of humour!'

The photo that inspired it, taken by Japanese photographer Masayoshi Sukita, was of a model wearing the flame-red lion kabuki dance wig. The hallmarks of kabuki, or Japanese musical theatre, are elaborate costumes, extreme make-up and eerie music. The model in the image had been coiffed and made-up by Sachiko Shibayama, and was dressed in an outfit created by designer Kansai Yamamoto. David began wearing clothes by Yamamoto ('some cat from Japan' as he would later be referred to, from the lyric line in the song 'Ziggy Stardust'), before the two ever actually met. This was thanks to Yamamoto's own stylist, Yasuko Hayashi, having given David some of Yamamoto's clothes. The pair later met in New York. Yamamoto would go on to create some of David's best stage costumes, which were influenced by hikinuki: the dramatic kabuki technique of switching and altering costumes quickly to denote changes in behaviour, emotion and mood.

'They were everything that I wanted them to be and more,' said David. 'Heavily inspired by kabuki and samurai, they were outrageous, provocative, and unbelievably hot to wear under the stage lights.'

Sukita, who photographed Jimi Hendrix and Marc Bolan before meeting David in London, had shot his first Bowie session during the summer of 1972. It was the beginning of a close forty-year friendship and professional collaboration. The lensman welcomed David to Japan in 1973, and escorted him on many ensuing visits, during which David visited temples and shrines. David began wearing the hachimaki: the red and white bandana, a symbol of perseverance and courage, sported by everyone from sushi chefs to women in labour.

As well as kabuki, he would also become enamoured of Noh: classical Japanese drama dating back to the fourteenth century. In 1977, Sukita shot the iconic cover image for the *"Heroes"* album, his most famous Bowie photo of all time.

From the wings on one of those Tokyo dates, Simon Napier-Bell watched David perform, and was impressed by the extent to which the former London Mod had evolved. He would later describe him as 'probably Britain's most influential solo pop/rock star ever.'

Before he left Japan, David was informed that *Aladdin Sane* had gone gold back home. It hadn't even yet been released. But far from feeling galvanised to continue conquering the world as Ziggy, his mind was made up. Hardly fair on Ronno, was it, to swear him to secrecy that David was planning to retire Ziggy and the Spiders – as Mick Ronson would admit in 1984 that he had known. Bolder and Woodmansey were none the wiser. The circus rolled on.

Another day, another hike, another boat-train. A melodramatic reunion with Angie was staged at the George V off the Champs-Elysées. As David was checking in ahead of his press conference and reception in the hotel's Rouge Room that night, who should he find himself standing next to but the inevitable Simon Napier-Bell. The latter knew the city's charms well.

'I was sent there alone as a schoolboy in 1951,' explains Simon. 'It was one of those family exchange things, but I ended up being the only boy from the school who went on it. When I arrived, the pupil I was swapping with had been sent to summer school, so I was alone in Paris at twelve years old. Bliss. The boy's parents both worked, and left me fifty old francs a day for lunch. I was free to roam around the city alone with my camera. I encountered the cast and crew making *An American in Paris*.[3] I told them my dad was a film director, and spent time with them every day. I've loved Paris ever since, and I go whenever I can. I lived there for three years in the late Seventies, and commuted to London every Tuesday to Friday.

'David adored Paris, too. When I met him in the lobby of the George V that day, he'd just arrived from eight days on the Trans-Siberian Express. "I thought it would be a great adventure," he told me, "but really, it was just a great bore. Which is why I just had to find a couple of days for Paris, without doubt my favourite city in the whole world."'

Just as his latest album was poised to land on the UK chart at Number One, it was back to Haddon Hall for the Homecoming Queen.

The title of David's sixth album, produced by Ken Scott and released in April 1973, was actually a pun: 'A Lad Insane'. That it referred to his brother Terry was a given. As a character, Aladdin Sane was an extension of his predecessor, or 'Ziggy goes to America,' as David described it. The iconic lightning-bolt-face cover, shot by photographer Brian Duffy and snatched up as a totem of the Seventies, blatantly symbolised schizophrenia: both his brother's tragic condition, ever worsening, and the 'torn' state in which David had returned from the States, mesmerised by America but recoiling from its inhabitants – most of whom had fallen considerably short of what he'd imagined as 'Americans'.

Raw, conceited, pretentious, deranged, the record soared. *Aladdin Sane*, featuring the track of the same name, as well as 'Drive-In Saturday' and 'The Jean Genie', became Bowie's biggest album to date, and remains one of his most popular of all time. With Mike Garson on piano and lovely Linda Lewis[4] on backing vocals, the Spiders – Ronson, Bolder and Woodmansey – were all still here, in glorious Technicolor. Unsurprisingly, as they were still on the road with Ziggy. Their days were numbered.

'Be careful what you wish for,' muses Chris Welch. 'I always thought that David was a theatre director at heart, casting himself in the starring role. Underneath it all, he maintained his sense of humour. He never took himself that seriously. I had the feeling that he found stardom uncomfortable when it came. I felt that he found it all too much, too exhausting – and that maybe that's why he started doing drugs. It happens to musicians, Pools winners, Lottery winners; anyone who is suddenly lifted out of their normal milieu and cast into a fantastical, over-privileged realm. David had the inner strength to conquer it eventually. As did Eric Clapton. Finding the strength to cope, and to turn the tables on the music industry, is truly an art.'

David's ongoing obsession with insanity is telling, remarks psychiatrist Cosmo Hallström.

'It suggests that the fear of falling prey to the disease which had claimed his brother probably was his underlying preoccupation. So he turned that to his advantage, and wrote about it. It's compelling material, which after all is one of the primary requisites of the world-class rock star. They also have to have a huge ego, a great deal of energy, and much talent. They have to have the conviction that they can stand alone and achieve where others can't, and they have to be lucky. David was: he emerged from the pile. But it is not a route that any sensible person would choose. It all makes for a confused individual.

'Look at his life. He craved convention on the one hand: getting married young, setting up home, fathering a child. But on the other, he wasn't honouring the commitment. He liked having sex with men, or with several people at once, and hanging with rich theatrical types. He loved the glamorous, decadent lifestyle, but at the same time was desperate for security. David didn't really know what he wanted. He was probably more confused than most.'

Above all, Dr Hallström adds, he was ruthless.

'It's the ingredient that makes all the difference. You need to be ruthless in order to be successful. You have to fuck people in order to achieve your goals. Bowie did so, literally and figuratively. He probably *was* a creative psychopath; never worrying about the people he left behind. Psychopathy is multi-dimensional, and it can get you into all sorts of trouble. You begin to achieve what you've always craved. You become divorced from reality. You are suddenly surrounded by sycophants and yes-men who tell you only what you want to hear, and you start thinking the world revolves around you. Which it does. When people are egotistical, they lose sight of what's right. Ruthless ambition is the name of the game. It's what makes you successful. It's as simple as that.'

Come 3 July, the thriller. The Hammersmith Odeon, west London, the final night of the tour which is now remembered as 'the Retirement Gig' was the only place to be. Ever. It says so in my diary. We were there. This was David's pinnacle, his build-to moment, the culmination of all that he'd slaved to achieve. The place was heaving with three and a half thousand fans. There must have been as many again outside as were crammed within. A film crew was present, and the stars were out: the Jaggers, the Rod Stewarts, the Ringos. David had finally made it into rock's upper echelon. He was now one of them. 'All the Young Dudes'. 'Oh! You Pretty Things'. 'Moonage Daydream'. Freaky costume changes galore.

At one point he emerged with that now legendary astral sphere on his forehead, which we found out later, from the mags we pored over endlessly, had been applied by his make-up artist, Pierre La Roche.[5] 'Let's Spend the Night Together': 'This one's for Mick!' he announced. Ronson or Jagger? Possibly both. Rock royalty graced the line-up, the great Jeff Beck joining them on stage to play along with 'The Jean Genie' and 'Love Me Do'. 'Round and Round' brought David's harmonica out. 'Suffragette City', ever my favourite. 'Land of Hope and Glory' at one point, thank you and goodnight, some upstart leaping daringly onto the stage, a minder chucking him off again. Hammersmith had been heaven. Out of the blue, we went to hell.

'Not only is this the last show of the tour,' cried David, just when it couldn't get any better, 'but it's the last show we'll ever do!'

Say *what*, was somebody, come again, he's only joking right, wait, did he just say, *why*? **NOOOOOOO!**

The whole place was screaming, there was a stampede for the stage, I was small, I hung back, I couldn't find my friend, I needed the toilet. And the band, wide-eyed, it looked as though it was news to them, too, played on. 'Rock'n'roll Suicide'. What the hell? I cried. Many of us did. Hysteria, pandemonium, a throat-cut split-second. However good the show was, and I think it was, I was stunned. I remember only that moment. I recall precious little of the music, not a step of the journey home. I heard later that Kid Jensen had confirmed it on air.

We read later about the after-show, some tasteless, jumped-up luvvie-fest they were referring to as the 'Last Supper', at the Regent Street Café Royal, of all places. I knew it. I'd been there twice with my parents, dressed in the same itchycoo, gold-lamé trouser suit and matching pumps, for this wedding and that bar mitzvah, which says it all. David and Angie apparently lorded it, pressing flesh with ex-Beatles and Barbra and Britt, with Hollywood legends and Cat Stevens and ubiquitous, boisterous Lulu. Even Keith Moon, not known for his fondness for togged-to-the-nines civilisation. Imagine. My schoolgirl mind boggled. This is the way the world ends. Not with a bang, but a whimper.[6] Had David worked so hard for so long for it to all end like this?

'It was fun while it lasted,' David said, post-Ziggy. 'I had a certain idea of what I wanted my rock'n'roll star to be like. I've gone as far with that as I possibly can. The star was created, he worked, and that's all I wanted him to do. Anything he did now would just be repetition, carrying it on to the death.'

But there was a sense of loss in his words only four years later.

'It soured so quickly, you wouldn't believe it,' he lamented. 'And it took me an awful long time to level out. My whole personality was affected. I brought that upon myself ... and it became very dangerous. I really did have doubts about my sanity.'

London's rock community was in mourning. Maybe the world was. We thought so at the time. Chances are, most ordinary folk didn't even notice. David was outta there, on his way back to Paris and then to the Château d'Hérouville – tucked away in the Oise valley on the edge of the village of Auvers, best known as having been the location of Vincent van Gogh's suicide in 1890. The castle had once been the home of Polish pianist and composer Frédéric Chopin, as well as the setting for his covert romance with Amantine-Lucile Dupin, aka novelist George Sand. Tragedy, history, hauntings, intrigue, literature, music: all very David.

I went there, years later, when I was researching my biography of Marc Bolan. I looked into buying the Château in 2013, when it came on the market suddenly, for about the price of an average London family home. Neglected and derelict, it needed a complete, financially prohibitive overhaul. Residential studios had gone out of fashion; musicians can and do record whole albums in their bedrooms on laptops now. Anyway, a group of audio engineers rebuilt the studio in 2015, with the intention of reopening within the year.

The Château was reached via imposing cast-iron gates and up a long, sweeping drive. It had impenetrable-looking, fortress-thick stone walls. The place was adapted as a residential recording facility in the mid-Sixties, and by the Seventies was rock heaven, thanks to its then state-of-the-art, sixteen-track studio. It had two wings, thirty bedrooms, a pool and many outhouses; its own wine, just about edible food, stoked fires and stunning French girls. It had ghosts.

'There was certainly some strange energy in that Château,'

reported Tony Visconti, who worked on the *Low* album there with David and Brian Eno. 'On the first day, David took one look at the master bedroom and said, "I'm not sleeping in there!" He took the room next door.'

It had welcomed the bands of the day into its tranquil midst. Cat Stevens, Pink Floyd, the Grateful Dead, Marc Bolan and Elton John had all recorded there, the latter even naming his fifth studio album after it: *Honky Château*.[7] The Bee Gees, Iggy Pop and Fleetwood Mac would all follow. It was Marc who recommended the Château to David. Not to be outdone by Bolan – ever – he decided to record *Pin Ups* there, with requisite visits from Lulu. He would also return in the not too distant, to relieve himself of *Low*.

Kid Jensen rocked up to interview David for Radio Luxembourg, with the Velvet Underground's Nico on his arm. Ava Cherry dropped in to remind him of what he was missing. It was the start of a beautiful three-year one-night-stand.

How David found time, inclination and sufficient seclusion for extra-maritals was a head-scratcher. Angie was there with him. He was toiling flat-out on his own album as well as Mick Ronson's solo debut. He was often found still working at the piano, having been up all night, when the rest of the household drifted through for breakfast the next day.

'Life on Mars?' from the *Hunky Dory* album, lifted by Rick Wakeman's and Mick Ronson's sublime virtuosity, was out as a single, and went interstellar. By the end of July, all five of David's RCA albums were cleaning up on the UK chart.

AMERICAN MAVERICK

9
1973–1974

Roman holiday, anybody? Nice idea. Incarcerate a self-proclaimed workaholic in a secluded Italian villa for the entire month of August, and expect him to relax and not climb the walls: good luck with that. David went along with it at first, chugging down to Italy with Angie on the sleeper from Paris with a colossal amount of luggage. They installed themselves at the property, set in gorgeous landscaped gardens on the outskirts of the capital, and awaited the rest of their party: their little son, his current child-minder, personal chef Anton Jones, hairdresser Suzi Fussey and her now boyfriend Mick Ronson among them. But the concept of doing nothing was now as alien to David as that quaint old notion of marital fidelity. He was preoccupied with his plans for a musical based on Orwell's *Nineteen Eighty-Four*; a one-act play, *Tragic Moments*; the Ziggy musical that wouldn't go away; recordings with Lulu and Dana, Iggy Pop and Lou Reed, and any number of proposed peripherals.

Before the first week off was out, he threw in the pool towel. He was desperate to return to London and get back to work. His entourage had no choice but to follow suit. Only Suzi and Mick put their foot down and stayed on. Their defiance almost proved their undoing. A fire ignited in the brush around the house, preventing their escape and also destroying the phone lines. It was touch and go for several days, but they emerged unscathed, happy to have had the time to work on Ronno's solo album, *Slaughter on 10th Avenue*,[1] and on their romance.

The primary obsessions were now work and sex. David indulged on both fronts with phenomenal ardour. The consummate narcissist required carnal sustenance on demand, and didn't seem too selective about his suppliers. Workaholic David had become impatient, compulsive, demanding, selfish and driven. He was also well on his way to becoming addicted to cocaine.

'It was such a turnaround,' sighs Anya Wilson. 'When I first knew him and Angela, they were vehemently anti-drugs and they barely drank. They were dead against it all, in fact, and they were both the picture of health and full of energy. But I guess as David got drawn into the celebrity milieu, he was exposed more and more to these things. There comes a point when you have no reason to keep saying no. Everyone else is doing it, which makes it feel safe. I was concerned, of course. But at the same time, I always thought David was immortal. I truly believed that nothing could touch him.'

The period 1973–4 was Tony Defries's heyday, during which he firmly established himself as the quintessential New York music mogul. With offices in London, the original New York premises on East 58th Street, and a fourteen-room suite on Park Avenue, the empire mushroomed like the cloud of an H-bomb. Defries purchased a twenty-room property on an estate in Connecticut, and eight Manhattan apartments. He also had his eye on the ultimate prize for his boy, an Oscar or three, and had therefore opened an extravagant 'West Coast operation' in preparation for David's foray into film. What Elvis had done, Bowie could do better. MainMan staff were under no illusions about their private lives: the job came first.

Where once RCA had squared up to Defries on the subject of profit and loss, forcing the gruff manager to rein things in, produce more meticulous accounts and *sell more fucking product*, Defries now started talking, without irony, about buying out David's record label. Where once new contractual terms had to be negotiated to take care of back debts and eradicate past touring excess, with the sacrifice of a few chauffeurs and cooks here, a handful of maids and babysitters there, for the sake of cleaned-up books, it was now no holds barred.

Defries championed the promotion of every last nowhere-man to Vice President, Agent, Corporate Head and Consultant. He openly approved of the broad-spectrum acquisition of gym memberships, nose jobs, gnashers, boob lifts, hairdressers, holidays and designer wardrobes, all charged to the mother ship. Why not, everyone had to make the best of themselves – and of course it all reflected favourably on The Artist. Angie would be in and out of New York like a dog at a fair, spending literally thousands at a time on shopping sprees, often with Dana in tow. Defries's priority was, in classic mixed metaphor manager-speak, to 'guide his golden goose onto yet another hamster wheel of write-record-tour, making sure he didn't spin his nuts off in the process.' Fake it 'til you make it was still the name of the game. The fans, of course, knew nothing of all this. As far as we were concerned, our local hero had become what Defries had promised. His prettiest star was bigger than the Beatles.

In August 1973, David paid a visit to the New Hampstead theatre in Swiss Cottage to see Marianne Faithfull in a new play, *Mad Dog*. He had his eye on Jagger's ex for a stage show he was putting together: *The 1980 Floor Show* (pardon pun) for America's NBC TV. The major's daughter was a luminescent beauty on the brink of self-destruction. She'd had a Top Ten hit in 1964 with 'As Tears Go By', written for her by Mick and Keith and produced by manager Andrew Loog Oldham. She had been, along with Twiggy, Lulu and Adrienne Posta, one of the 'It Girls' of the Swinging Sixties. But she had lost her Stone to a Nicaraguan actress, and Bianca was now Mrs M.J.

Marianne's starring role in the 1968 flick *The Girl on a Motorcycle* and a few other films had led nowhere. Now she was the falsely rumoured 'Mars Bar Kid' with a cocaine habit about to scroll out of control, and who would soon become a heroin-addicted bag lady. Did David set out to save her while in denial about his own habits? He never said. He certainly didn't let on to Simon Napier-Bell, who just happened to be sitting beside him in the theatre stalls. Him again! It was as if the cosmos was still trying to knock their heads together. It coulda been, shoulda been, a match made on Mars.

The bell tolled for Camelot. The time had come to depart bucolic Beckenham, now beset by little-town blues. It had become a place of both pilgrimage and peril, overrun with fans more aggressive than ourselves. We, the innocent faithful, who had long stood there on the path among the weeds – we *were* the weeds – had competition. Fierce, Ziggy-coiffed and fancy-dressed, the brazen new Bowie-ettes brandished albums and banners. They sang and chanted, and demanded attention. A few even broke in when there was no one home. They snapped each other on David's chaise longue, sitting on his toilet, lying in his bed. One went in and had a scrub in his bath, or so she said. Another claimed to have hidden in Angie's wardrobe, and to have stayed there all night while Mrs Bowie slept. The bowler-hatted schoolgirls slunk away. Three years would elapse before I ran into David again.

Home was no longer his refuge. If anything, it was his personal Cane Hill, but just as hard to retreat into as to escape. David was sad, and reluctant to uproot. He had once harboured hopes of acquiring and renovating Haddon Hall as his principal residence, for life – just as he'd hankered after a cosy seaside bolthole in Margate. But even he could now see the need to move out. While the UK tour cracked on, new lodgings for the Bowies were sought. Angie oversaw the packing of tea chests, the wrapping of relics, the premier-league transfer – while toddler Zowie was holed up with a childminder, watching back-to-back movies in a hotel suite on Park Lane. He grew up to become a film maker. Who'da thought.

By October 1973, they had set up home in a rented flat on Hall Road, Maida Vale, which belonged to *Avengers* actress Diana Rigg. But general household behaviour and timekeeping was not to the taste of other residents, who complained to the management company. 'Sorrow' was out, and the track's title seemed apt.

Angie and David found 89 Oakley Street, Chelsea, a four-storey house just off the King's Road, round the corner from the Jaggers. Angie threw herself into redecorating and refurbishing, working an English Eccentric meets rock'n'roll look. A music room was installed and equipped. Valuable carpets, paintings and art-nouveau *objets* were squandered on and displayed – as was the haunting portrait of David painted by George Underwood, called 'Depth of the Circle', which graced the reverse of the *Space Oddity* album. The third-floor drawing room featured green-and-white fibreglass ball chairs, and a central 'bear pit' containing dozens of cushions where visitors would sleep or get to know each other. Endless dinner parties, all-night jams and lost weekends set in – as well, so it was rumoured, as coke-fuelled orgies. A small coterie of domestic staff acquired the knack for keeping schtum, including chef Anton Jones, secretary Ava Clarke, and the family nanny, Marion Skene.[2]

'Marion had been a secretary at RCA,' says Anya Wilson. 'She then came to work for MainMan, and Angela and David took her on as a nanny for Zowie. She was a lovely Scottish lady, who would take Zowie on little trips up to her parents' house in Scotland, and who kept him on the straight and narrow. She was wonderful with him.'

'We were messed up as a couple,' Angie told writer Caroline Graham in 2009, 'but this little creature came, and David was a great dad. But when the baby was around, our lifestyle just didn't work. David and I were away doing drugs, at first together and then later apart. Marion effectively became Zowie's mother.'

Duncan Jones has agreed, saying that he 'always considered' Miss Skene to be his mother, not Angie.

'What people forget now is that Angie was almost as popular as

David at that time,' points out Anya Wilson, defending her friend. 'They were *the* power couple in the business. It was the yin and yang thing, she was his perfect foil. She was impressive, and lovely, and *American* – which was still so exotic back then. There were David-and-Angie lookalike contests all the time. The media lapped them up. Fans copied her hairstyles and outfits just as much as they copied his. And for every affair and one-night stand that he was indulging in, she was out there matching him. Although I think a lot of that was bravado, getting her own back. It took its toll on Angela, all his affairs.'

Perhaps the most threatening of David's paramours at that time was Amanda Lear. The exotic, staggeringly beautiful blonde had risen to prominence having posed in sprayed-on leather and holding a black panther on a leash, on the cover of Roxy Music's album *For Your Pleasure*. The image was as talked-about as the record. This was Lear's introduction to the music business, and she milked it to the *n*th, determined to achieve fame as a singer in her own right – which MainMan, via David, was supposed to mastermind. She did it, in the end, going on to sell more than fifteen million albums and twenty-five million singles as a disco diva. Marianne Faithfull introduced them. But who *was* she?

Not even Anya Wilson can be sure.

'I knew her well, and yet I didn't know her at all. She was drop-dead gorgeous and super-talented, with a very deep voice – deeper than most men,' Anya says. 'It came from a cavern deep inside. I loved her to death, she was very special. She was the muse of Salvador Dalí, and Bryan Ferry dated her. She was all-woman, I can assure you of that much, but there was always a question mark over her birth gender. I have no idea whether she was this or that. No matter how drunk I got her, she would never divulge.

'Amanda fascinated people. She was very artsy. Dalí used to fly her over to Spain all the time, to do work for him. She used to paint his elaborate backgrounds, and then he'd put his finishing touches on, to make the paintings "his". Quite scandalous, really. She'd get back and I'd say to her, "So what was it like?" and she'd go, "Oh, *boring*. All Salvador wants to do is paint, paint, paint!" She had a long affair with David, for at least a year, and Angela knew all about it. When it was coming to an end, Angela took Amanda out shopping one day, to buy a nightie and some bedding. She told me afterwards that Angela said to her, "Oh, get *this*, Amanda, David absolutely loves this colour!" Amanda said she felt so uncomfortable!'

But who *was* she? She was born in Switzerland, Transylvania, Saigon, French Indochina or British Hong Kong, in 1939, 1946 or 1950; a boy, a girl, a hermaphrodite; an orphan, or the child of British or Russian or French parents. She grew up in the south of France and Switzerland, spoke French, German, Italian, Spanish and English, and became an art student in Paris, where a few still remember her from her nights working in a transvestite revue. She moved to London during the Sixties to enrol at St Martin's School of Art, and became a fashion model. She was Dalí's 'spiritual wife', and introduced David to the artist, after which, for a moment, he became obsessed by him. Lear's music career took off in the mid-Seventies, when she became a massive singing star and gay icon all over Europe and Scandinavia.

During the Eighties she reinvented herself as a TV personality in France and Italy, by which time her own career as an artist was in full swing. Rumours persisted for years that Dalí had paid for her sex change in Casablanca in 1963. She confounded them all by posing inside-out naked for *Playboy*. She once told *Interview* magazine that David Bowie had started the rumours that she'd been born male. In 2011, a copy of a birth certificate surfaced, naming her as Alain Maurice Louis René Tap, born in Saigon on 18 June 1939. Tantalising. But was it genuine?

Who cared? David didn't, at least not at the time. But during an internet chat in 1998, he referred to his former lover as a 'trans-something'. As for Amanda, she was smitten.

'With David it was great, because it was a kind of symbiosis, an exchange, it wasn't just take, take, take,' she would tell the *Melody Maker* in 1978.

'I introduced [David] to Germany, to Expressionism, and to Fritz Lang. I told him about Dalí, and he used *Un Chien Andalou* on his tour.[3] Before I met him, I was reading Tolkein and Herman Hesse. Now, I read Machiavelli.'

David whisked her into his *1980 Floor Show*, an extravagant cabaret filmed at London's Marquee, where for him it had all begun. They duetted on 'Sorrow'. The footage is worst-nightmare territory: so bad, it is actually quite good. The show, which also featured the Troggs, plus Marianne Faithfull performing '20th Century Blues' and duetting on Sonny and Cher's 'I GotYou, Babe' with David, was filmed over a couple of nights in October 1973.

The audience was invite-only, come-as-you're-not, and largely made up of ballot-winning members of the new International David Bowie Fan Club. Tony Visconti and Mary Hopkin, Dana Gillespie and Lionel Bart were all present, as was a frenzy of press, gagging for David's first stage appearance since the shock Ziggy and the Spiders retirement back in July. Angie signed autographs and gossiped loudly during the performances, while David returned to the stage again and again in increasingly eccentric costumes, like some end-of-pier diva building up to a preposterous grand finale.

The *Melody Maker*'s Chris Welch was bemused. 'The rock-and-roll pantomime tinselled on, with another show to complete, 'ere midnight,' was his take. 'It occurred to me that possibly the best way to effect entry to any future such burlesques would be to don the hind legs of the pantomime horse. Or perhaps in view of current trends – the front legs.'

The hour-long special aired in the States on 16 November. It was perhaps best forgotten.

The Bowies' first Christmas party in Oakley Street was celeb-infested and sumptuous. They mixed a dangerous cocktail of sparkling new friends such as Stevie Wonder and Ronnie Wood with edgy pals the likes of Ava Cherry, who was still discussing Uganda with David, and Geoff MacCormack. Their Yuletide caterer had worked for the Prince of Wales, and the house was fripped to the nines, with a gigantic, ballsed-up Christmas tree and exaggerated trimmings. The bash kicked off at around eight p.m. Twelve hours on, most of them were still there. David staggered among the guests armed with a bunch of real mistletoe, snogging everyone in his path. A vast breakfast sizzled by Angie fortified the throng before they lugged their hangovers home. She was not the only one to raise a brow at the amount of Peruvian her husband had ingested that night. Oh dear. The Jaggers would soon be round for Christmas dinner. You can't always get what you want.

On his twenty-seventh birthday a fortnight later, David left her indoors and dragged 'the Lear jet'[4] off to Hampstead on a date with his mate Underwood. George's birthday treat to his old chum was a trip to the flicks. He had tickets to Fritz Lang's Weimar-period sci-fi drama *Metropolis*.[5] The film was silent, and so was the birthday boy . . . who went home buzzing with new ideas for his next album and tour.

Although *1984 the Musical* was doomed, an abandoned project has its uses, and this one was no exception. It inspired David to take greater creative risks than he had ever previously attempted. He was supremely confident, thanks to the two mega-successful years he'd enjoyed since signing to RCA Records. He'd sold more than a million albums, as many singles, and seen six albums grace the charts for a total of nineteen weeks. Outwardly he walked on water, with supreme faith in his own ability. Inside, he was drowning. Now that the thin line between his private and public personas had been rubbed out, he felt more vulnerable than ever.

'I was psychically damaged,' was how he would later describe his state of mind during the mid-Seventies. 'Trying to get what I was understanding expressed in music form.'

David's scarcely disguised disgust for most popular culture was growing. Post-Ziggy, he began to despise his fans for having fallen so guilelessly for the imposter. We clung to him anyway.

For his next trick, he would turn his back on glam, strike out on a limb, and produce something so dangerous, so daring and so utterly unexpected that he risked losing his audience altogether. He couldn't wait. Again, he obsessed, eating little, sleeping less, squalling endlessly among the demons which had tormented him since childhood: isolation, abandonment and anxiety.

When he looked out, all he could see was Armageddon. A Britain on the verge of economic collapse. The miners on strike again. The toppling of Prime Minister Edward Heath and the triumphant return of Harold Wilson, all set to make the country more miserable than it had been under the last guy. Against that backdrop, violent movies, porn and disco soared in popularity. And New York, the centre of the civilised world, was going to the dogs. Little wonder that doom and gloom began to be reflected in music, which grew downbeat, dreary and politically obsessed in response, and which throbbed with the anger of the people. It was the point. Glam rock was out, booted into the gutter by punk nihilism. It was as if David had seen it coming.

'All the little Johnny Rottens and Sid Viciouses, really . . . gangs of squeaky, roller-skating, vicious hoods, with Bowie knives and furs on, and they were all skinny because they hadn't eaten enough, and they all had funny-coloured hair,' David told writer David Buckley. 'In a way, it was a precursor to the punk thing.' He called them the Diamond Dogs.

Now *this* was a concept album. It was set in Hunger City, a forsaken place perhaps suggested by the dregs of grand Old New York and other once pre-eminent metropoles on the downslide. Its theme is almost always described as 'post-apocalyptic': a fractured and fragmented society destroyed by egomania and hedonism, and floundering in the depths of despair.

'Very political,' stated David. 'My protest, more *me* than anything I've done previously.' Halloween Jack, 'a real cool cat', was really souped-up and zonked-out Ziggy. Look at the hairstyle, listen to 'Rebel Rebel'. The music is chopped, the lyrics carved from cut-ups, and the overall flavour is flawed. It is Orwell by any other riff, boasting tracks brazenly entitled 'Big Brother', 'We Are the Dead' and '1984'. It is also Stones-heavy, Spider-free but still Ronson-influenced, despite the fact that David plays a lot of the lead guitar himself, in a Grade IV assault which sounds like a teenager teaching himself, or auditioning for a garage band. But that's precisely what makes this album so bare and compelling.

David insisted on producing the album himself, recording at Olympic Studios, Barnes and Island Studios, Notting Hill, in London; and at Studio L Ludolf, Hilversum, in the Netherlands. Olympic and Studio L Ludolf were chosen because Mick and the boys had worked there, and David was still enamoured – although the latter was primarily for tax reasons. *Diamond Dogs* was also a resurrection of sorts for Visconti. The Young American was welcomed back to create string arrangements. Tony would also mix the tracks in his own studio at his Hammersmith home. This chilling offering, with freak-show art created by Guy Peellaert,[6] would soar effortlessly to Number One in the UK and Number Five in the US. David had pushed the envelope, as if hoping to have gone too far. The hounds heeded the whistle, and rose in droves.

In March 1974, David set off for a meeting in his favourite city. As if sensing that he might not make it back for a while, he abandoned his original travel schedule and descended, Phantom-like, into the sewers of Gay Paree. A week of mayhem and madness ensued, some of it in the company of Geoff MacCormack and Ronnie Wood. Because they were worth it. Time came for a train to Cannes, and a ship bound for Gotham. Don't look back. David never did. Gone for good were the days when London was 'home'.

1975

MainMan might have been mistaken for a prototype *Cirque du Soleil*, a dazzling roadshow of drama and excess that would be considered absurd in the modern music business. Back then, there were Tony Defrieses galore. The Montecristo-munching rock magnate was hardly endangered. Some became as legendary as the artists they nurtured.

Ruthless Peter Grant, an ex-wrestler and bouncer, took on the mighty Led Zeppelin. He became known as 'the most colourful and influential manager in the history of rock'. The Who's Kit Lambert drove Pete Townshend to achievements far greater than mere pop songs. Simon Napier-Bell went the distance for the Yardbirds, Eric Clapton, Jeff Beck and Marc Bolan, and would go on to create the greatest duo of the Eighties: Wham! Malcolm McLaren crouched in the wings, poised to claim notoriety as manager of the Sex Pistols. Forthright Yorkshireman Ed Bicknell conjured careers for Gerry Rafferty, Scott Walker, Bryan Ferry and Dire Straits, whom he guided to glory and ass-wiped for twenty-six years. All were larger-than-life workaholics and flamboyant figures, without whose daredevil antics their artists may well have never hit the heights.

MainMan was taking itself so seriously that the industry was kind of obliged to sit up and listen. By 1974, Defries was taking stock. Major distractions, including the careers of other artists

– Mick Ronson, Iggy Pop, pretty well everyone but Dana Gillespie,[1] for whom Defries retained a soft spot – would be sidelined in favour of the MainMan main man.

Spend, spend, spend. Elevate the artist, force-feed the product, achieve the goal at all costs. It was said that Tony Defries invented the self-fulfilling prophecy. The focus was now the breaking of Bowie in America.

David, bored and restless, had craved a complete change of scenery. Hence New York. He was also somewhat over rock'n'roll, having given it his best. He was now keen to meander down a new musical path; to summon a fresh incarnation. Who would he be? He hadn't decided yet. He was producing a track for Lulu, her again, at the RCA studios in Manhattan, when inspiration ambled through the door – in the shape of a melon-grin Puerto Rican New Yorker with an axe to grind. And what an axe.

Carlos Alomar, a self-taught and intuitive guitarist, would become a mainstay of the Bowie sound for years to come. He sensed what David wanted, and it wasn't white. The pair went to ground arm in arm: exploring clubs and dives, ducking into the Apollo Theater Harlem – the famous music-hall mecca of African-American performers – sampling Marvin Gaye, the Temptations, the Spinners, getting down among the dudes, feasting eyes and ears on every permutation of soul, salsa, funk, R&B and myriad spin-offs, until the next manifestation of David was primed to appear.

Along for the ride was stony-faced Coco Schwab, now elevated to the position of 'personal assistant'. In reality, she was David's chaperone and custodian. How did she do it? Anybody's guess. She managed to intimidate and aggravate just about everyone she came across – a situation that David seemed to relish. Maybe it was just about having one person, exclusively for him, against a set-up that he felt was sucking the life out of him. Where was his wife? Excellent question. As for fatherhood, he had become decisively hands-off.

He was often seen sniggering from behind a cupped hand while Coco was 'going off on one'.

Missing from the line-up was Anya Wilson, the plugger who had worked his records so relentlessly, and to whom David owed so much for his eventual breakthrough. Anya had pulled many more strings than David ever knew, exploiting the most tenuous connections and milking valuable friendships to project him into the company of those who cared.

'When David moved to the US, Angela did ask me if I wanted to go with them,' Anya says. 'They were very attached to their entourages. But things do change, and different people are needed to grab the baton and take it forward. I must admit, I was very nervous of everything that was going on around David at that time. I also had a relationship, and I wanted to give that a chance. I didn't just want to up and leave. Plus, I was working with Mick Ronson and his tour. It was complicated. Anyway, I went over to New York, and I brought some *Diamond Dogs* stuff back for the press. It was nice to see the whole crew again. David was well on his way, he didn't need me so much. It did make me wistful for the days when I was pulling the stunts and doing the deals for him.'

Both the breakthrough *Top of the Pops* performance and his appearance on *The Old Grey Whistle Test* had been flukes, Anya reveals.

'They were cancellations! David would never have got them otherwise! With *Whistle Test*, I had a deal with Jennie Evans, the secretary of the show. She liked David very much. So she and I made an arrangement, just between the two of us. If a cancellation came up, she'd tip me off and then I'd make a casual call to the show's producer, Mike Appleton, to let him know that David was available. We had rehearsed it many times, and it worked! Of course, David was not without ego, so I then had to be extremely careful about how I presented it to *him*. I talked about it with Woody Woodmansey, and he said, "Yeah, David would never have done it if he'd known it was a cancellation!"

'The pivotal parts of my career had my stomach in knots. Navigating all that felt like it could be the death of me at times. I wasn't a plugger, I was a diplomat! It was the same scenario with *Top of the Pops*. I was treading on eggshells all the way there, too. The thing is, I always knew that once Britain saw David, they would be smitten. Because he had IT. And he really did. And now America was about to get him, and I didn't have him any more. Yeah, it hurt. It was like something out of "She's Leaving Home". Like finding you'd lost a beautiful, cherished child.'

The album came out that April. The Year of the Diamond Dogs was underway, heralded by huge hoardings from Sunset Boulevard to Times Square. In terms of publicity campaigns, Defries's speciality, the industry had rarely seen anything like this. The tour itself was a vast undertaking, comprising seventy-three shows across North America, opening in Montreal on 14 June, taking in Toronto, six performances in Detroit, Nashville and Memphis, among others, and seven nights at Radio City Music Hall, New York. It would proceed to Los Angeles, where more than forty thousand fans saw David at the Universal Amphitheater, including sixteen-year-old Michael Jackson and some of his brothers, Diana Ross, and a subdued Marc Bolan, with new girlfriend Gloria Jones. Phoenix, Chicago, three outings in Boston, on to Philadelphia, and concluding eventually in Atlanta on 1 December. Fans were still pitching up to the gigs in full Ziggy regalia. The straddlers augmented the look with Aladdin Sane make-up, just to make sure.

The show started out as a one-man musical featuring David as patch-eyed Halloween Jack, with the choreography of Toni Basil[2] animated by Warren Peace, aka old school-chum Geoff MacCormack, and dancing partner Gui Andrisano. The outrageous set and extraordinary mechanicals were by all accounts jaw-dropping. In trying to conceal his extensive band behind on-stage screens, feeling that to present them as part of the show did not make sense, David lost them one by one along the way. The effect was of a show disintegrating *en route*. It sounds disastrous, but it fitted the theme perfectly:

'It was about a decaying city,' said David, 'so it was quite apropos that it should have fallen down in the middle of the tour.'

Nevertheless, they managed to record David's first live album as they went. Defries champed the Cuban while touting the *Diamond Dogs* film rights. Surprise surprise, the movie never happened.

A lot of other things did happen that summer. Not all of them were edifying. First came David's discovery that the MainMan operation was not, as he had long believed, owned equally by him and Tony Defries. There had been comprehensive wool-pulling. In effect, David himself was footing the bill for the most extravagant and over-manned tour he had ever undertaken. It should not have surprised anybody that the news stopped him in his tracks. Anxiety and insomnia took hold, his coke habit soared, his appetite dried up, and extreme paranoia set in. The guy was in shock.

In an attempt to get a grip of at least a part of himself, he reclaimed 'original him', David Jones, and shoved the imposter Bowie out there, minus a Christian name. Putting the Turn to work seemed the answer: let the upstart do some work for a change. Throughout the tour, David is said to have subsisted on a diet of nothing but milk, hot peppers and copious nose candy. Interviews and footage from the period depict unequivocal self-demolition. David sniffs and honks incessantly. His behaviour is robotic. He spouts bizarre, incongruous responses to the plainest questions. Defries knew all about the coke. He had grave concerns, of course, but he could hardly control it.

Nor could he figure out what else was going on. What was with the revived obsession with UFOs and aliens, for example? Was David delusional, or was this all another act? The BBC's Alan Yentob pitched up to make a documentary, *Cracked Actor*. Its name was taken from a track on *Aladdin Sane*, about a has-been Hollywood star in the arms of a prostitute. In the light of what we know now, was David addressing his mother? The definitive doc stands as proof for all time that David was not pretending to have lost it. He was genuinely, precariously, teetering on the brink. But it was this film – which also featured Coco, travelling with him in LA – that convinced director Nicolas Roeg to cast David as an alien in his picture *The Man Who Fell to Earth*. He would make his feature-film debut the following year.

His salvation was a month-and-a-half-long interlude in the schedule between July and September. David spent it wisely in Philadelphia, booking himself into Sigma Sound studios[3] and reconvening with funky guitarist Carlos Alomar. It was Alomar who cobbled together a band to lift him out of the cesspool, and Tony Visconti who once again took the helm. The recording sessions provided a breakthrough for the young Luther Vandross,[4] a friend whom Alomar had imported for the ride.

'I was always incredibly shy, and my family didn't realise that I sang seriously until one day I went home and said, "Mamma, I met David Bowie, and he likes the way I sing," he told me. "Oh really, baby, that's lovely!" she told me. What happened was, Carlos Alomar and I went to school together. Carlos had gotten the gig playing guitar for David Bowie. I just went to Philadelphia to visit and hang out, and while David was recording out back, I was just sitting there singing along to "Young Americans". I improvised a line, "Young American, Young American, he was the Young American", and David overheard me, and he said, "Oh! That sounds *great!*" Then he asked me if I would like to put it down, on the recording. It was just a knack I had, for vocal arranging. I could always just do it spontaneously like that. Even in school in the hallways, hanging around the stairwells, I used to do that kind of thing when kids were passing the time together, just singing. It came very naturally to me. It has been said to me since that maybe Carlos was helping out a friend, and that he got me to Philadelphia knowing that he would be able to get me in front of David Bowie, and that he would get me a break. Maybe it was. It's the kind of thing that Carlos was always doing, if he got the chance. Helping out a friend.'

Also on backing vocals were Alomar's wife Robin and David's moll, Ava Cherry, who refused to be shaken off. Angie would fly in, tear into combat with David, realise to her horror that she was losing, do nothing about it other than scream a lot and trash things, then flounce off and out again, with nothing resolved. A wife hell-bent on saving her marriage would perhaps have stuck around.

Young Americans would be the album. A departure if ever there was. The phoenix from Bromley was about to rise again: this time as a Gouster.

Say what? It was a style thing. On the South Side of Chicago in the 1960s, boys were either Ivy Leaguers or Gousters. The former were preppies, collegiate wannabes, who swaggered about in straight-legged trousers and button-down-collar shirts with V-neck sweaters thrown over their shoulders. The latter looked more like old-school gangsters, a bit baggy. They swaggered similarly, but in pleat-waisted pants. The Gouster look and stance were what David was going for.

David borrowed the term for the album he was currently work-ing on, and recorded tracks for it that never made it onto what would become *Young Americans*. Some of them continued to kick around, unreleased, until a new '*Gouster* album' was announced in 2016. Back then, the Gouster became John the Baptist for the Thin White Duke.

Back on the road. Cherry, Vandross and Alomar augmented the on-stage line-up. David's look had evolved again: chunky shoulder pads, braces, wide checked tie, a floppy pompadour, even a walking stick. The Hunger City set had been abandoned altogether. David's sound had metamorphosed from white to black, seemed more controlled, felt embroidered with new influences, and was nothing if not the last nail in the coffin for tormented Ziggy.

As for the show, it had now become a starkly thrilling and pared-down soul revue. Which was all very well for the former colony now falling for his charms. Back home, he couldn't give it away. Although the *Diamond Dogs* album proved a huge success, perhaps he'd been away too long. No promoter agreed to stage the tour in the UK, to the devastation of home-grown fans. It really did feel as though we were losing him.

Come the final leg of the make-it-up-as-you-go-along tour, David was suited and booted with glossy soul-boy hair. By Christmas, it was all over. By January, he was as thick as thieves with John Lennon. The pair met in LA, during John's separation from Yoko, on his eighteen-month so-called 'Lost Weekend'. By the time they went home to New York, they were lifelong friends. 'Fame' was a happy accident, a studio interruption that extended into a collaboration; a bit of why-not improv that acquired a life of its own and swirled into a song out of nowhere – much as 'Under Pressure' would erupt from thin mountain air with Queen in Switzerland, a few years down the line.

'Fame' would give David his first American Number One, in July 1975. It has since been picked apart, scrutinised and held up as David's blatant damnation of Tony Defries and his profligate empire. This is what they got for exploiting their chunk of him, for slowly slaughtering their golden goose. That David had had enough, they were left in no doubt.

Michael Lippman was the lawyer who stepped up to the plate, intent on severing the partnership between David and Defries.

'I wanted the whole MainMan thing away from me,' explained David. 'It was circusy. I was never much of an entourage person. I hated all of that.'

At the end of January, David told his record label of his intentions, and then, according to the record, he informed Defries. The madding mogul injuncted. *Young Americans* was placed on ice.

'It wasn't like that,' insists Dana Gillespie. 'I was there, stone-cold sober, and I can tell you exactly what happened. We could all see where things were heading. I went with Tony Defries and his girlfriend Melanie to Mustique, on holiday. While we were there, Tony said, "I don't want to handle him any more." He just couldn't cope with David when he was on cocaine.

'This was the brilliant guy who was going to make David Bowie the new Elvis Presley. He worked tirelessly to achieve that, but then along came the drugs, and it all came unstuck. Mustique was quite a primitive place in those days. It took two days to get a phone call in or out. But Tony had made up his mind. He booked a call, got through to David eventually, and told him, "It's over." After which David was immediately besieged by others, all wanting to assume the role and give him advice. Michael Lippman was one of them. I know for a fact that David was poisoned by others, and of course who are people going to believe?'

Dana was shocked at how rapidly things disintegrated.

'When the collapse came, it all fell apart overnight. Suddenly the offices were gone, the bills weren't being paid, the wages weren't coming in. I had taken a part in a show written by Melvyn Bragg, with P.P. Arnold.[5] I could hardly afford to eat, I had no change to tip the doorman at the theatre, and my fab BMW, which I was unaware was on HP – I didn't even know what HP was – was taken away. I wasn't allowed to record for about five years. Tony Defries shut down on me for half a decade. He simply vanished.

'At one point, I discovered that he was living at the Savoy Hotel in Zurich, working among banking people. He eventually pitched up in LA. I went to see him. We talked and talked, and we resolved. He was out of the business by then. He didn't apologise. I didn't expect him to. We are governed by low-level instincts, humans. I have always said that it's better that I am shat upon than to have to live with having shat on someone else. We have to look for the best in people. As for David, I understood completely what he was going through. He hadn't received love or compassion as a child. As a result, he never knew how to give it. He was ruthless, yes. Of course he was. He had to be.'

Deliberation dragged on well into spring 1975, by which time David was on his knees, defeated, literally. He emerged, blinking, from the conclusive confrontation, during which his lawyers stunned him with the news that he owned nothing. Nothing what-soever. Not only that, but Defries would as good as own *him* for another eight years. He would also clean up on back catalogue, swiping a handsome fifty per cent of all income dating back to *Hunky Dory*. The hideous irony was that, thanks to Defries, David had made it, big-time. Just as his mentor had promised, he was a superstar. A beautiful, bright, broke superstar.

'It is easy to blame the manager,' reasons Simon Napier-Bell today. 'We do get a terrible reputation. The fact is, Defries was a great hustler. I bumped into him a few times, and I liked him. I admire him for having taken risks. He rode roughshod over the record company, and made them do promotion. That first American tour of David's they had no money, yet they made it happen; staying at the Beverly Hills hotel, spending five times what they needed to for everything they wanted, because it all *had* to go on the hotel bill, which RCA were forced to pick up. You have to remember that Bowie was very shrewd at using up managers, spitting them out and moving on to the next. Very sensible, I'd say, why get stuck with one person? The same goes for producers. It's bad enough that this happens in marriage.

'As for "ruthless": it is said pejoratively, and considered to be a bad thing. But it's not. It is far better, in business, to be practical and pragmatic. Why let unnecessary emotion get in the way? Bowie understood this perfectly. Go a bit of distance with Tony Visconti, drop him, go to Nile Rodgers, go back to Visconti years later with a big smile on your face. David had it off pat. Loyalty? He wasn't *dis*loyal. He was simply using the right person for the right thing at the right time. There is talent in that. Everybody has their strengths. You can't continue to be faithful to someone if they cease to be what you want.'

David struck Simon as eminently sensible in everything he did.

'People say he was calculating. But none of us can manage without a calculator. There is a point to them. David understood himself.

He had this total, absolute, obsessional need for an audience. Everyone single one of them [he means rock stars] is like it. He was also very good at predicting what was coming, what was going to be next. He coupled his music with his imagery. He used himself as the essence of his artistic creation. He moulded the self: music and image combined. It's like Laurence Olivier; I never recognised him when he came on stage, he was such a brilliant actor. He walked differently, he'd hold his head differently, he spoke differently. He didn't even know he had it, he was so good at it. You change your whole demeanour, and that's a real actor. Bowie, to some degree, did that. He changed the package every time.'

'David dumped everybody. Literally everybody,' says Dana Gillespie. 'He had to dump everybody, in order to make his next creative move. I understood that. I couldn't see why other people didn't.'

But he retained Coco Schwab.

'Coco? There was nothing *to* dump. She was "The Quiet American".[6] She never said anything about anything. I don't think I ever once heard her express an opinion. When the rest of us were out having a good time – and trust me, MainMan took New York by storm, we were in every bar, every restaurant, every club, and it was jolly good fun – where was Coco? She was making sure that David got the sound checks and to the gigs on time, and that he ate, occasionally. I don't know what else she really did. She squeezed his orange juice. She lit his cigarette for him. She cleaned up his crap. When a few of us sensed that MainMan's house of cards was heading for the big collapse, I don't think she even noticed. She was only an employee.'

She probably did notice. According to George Underwood, 'David couldn't ever get rid of Coco. She knew where all the bodies were buried. She knew everything.'

Young Americans, his self-declared Plastic Soul effort, his blue-eyed homage to God's own country's great soundtrack, consolidated

David's worth in the US but marked the beginning of a decline in popularity back home. Perhaps the music was too normal, too grown-up, too reminiscent of the stuff our parents were listening to. It was the music of adult radio. 'Adult' was not what we were. We didn't get it at the time, but it would eventually make sense: *Young Americans* was David going back to his roots. He'd cut his teeth on R&B. The first instrument he learned to play was a saxophone. This had been where he came in. Not the finest in his catalogue, perhaps, but the album's influence was far-reaching. Where Pied Piper David went, the rats – Robert Palmer, George Michael, Duran Duran, Spandau Ballet and a host of other eager white soul boys – followed.

Meanwhile, David turned his back on New York. He was off to stare at the ocean. The madness had only just begun

II

1975–1976

Paranoid, emaciated, superstar drug addict relocates to the cocaine capital of the world. Nobody says hey wait, perhaps not your best idea, how about we give Amagansett or the Arctic Circle a go? Yes-men never say no. They just keep on banking the pay-cheques.

His defining creation, Ziggy, was a distant memory. His hopeless marriage was heading for the rocks. His relationship with his only child was at best detached, and the empire was in ruins. Disconnected from his mother, his brother and his best friend George, it had all gone west. He might as well head there. So he set off like a latter-day Jim Bowie, in his era a rock star of sorts, who had died at the Alamo with the King of the Wild Frontier, and whose knife had inspired David's stage name. Forging his own Western adventure seemed as good an idea as any.

The soundtrack heaved with reasons to go. 'Blue Jay Way' by the Beatles; Harry Nilsson's 'Fairfax Rag'; the Mamas & the Papas' 'California Dreamin'' and Joni Mitchell's 'California'. Seductive music that made the place sound irresistible. One of the tracks of the decade that perhaps best reflected David's state of mind was a song of 'raging existential angst' depicting a singer between two worlds. It took another Diamond Dog several months to compose. He wrote 'I Am . . . I Said' to find himself.[1]

Two more disparate artists than David Bowie and Neil Diamond are hard to imagine. But during the Seventies, if only psychologically, they were on the same page.

In some ways, it was surprising that David hadn't moved to LA much earlier. For musicians in those days, the lure of Canyons was huge. Just as New York's Brill Building had been the hub of everything from big-band standards to mainstream pop during the Forties, Fifties and Sixties, Laurel Canyon was now the centre of America's music scene. Songwriting talent had migrated towards the Pacific, and the focus was now firmly on albums.

The West Coast was an extreme parallel universe; a hedonistic, narcotic-packed precipice populated by acid freaks, coke heads, occultists, crystal-toting hustlers and groupies of every persuasion. It swarmed with wannabes. Our planet's movie capital was where you went, 'they' said, to make your dreams come true; where everyone wanted to be someone, but where only a relative handful would ever make it. In other words, a mirage. The base notes beneath the eucalyptus on the cloying air were excrement and desperation. David was convinced, thanks to Tony Defries's wildest imaginings, that he had what it took to reinvent himself as a Hollywood superstar.

Some say it was Coco who chose the small, almost windowless late Fifties/early Sixties property at 637 North Doheny Drive, into which they moved during the spring of 1975. Angie claims it was she who found and rented the 'spooky' place (*why?*), a whitewashed cube built around an indoor swimming pool. It sat just a few doors down from where, six years earlier, Charles Manson's followers had murdered eight months' pregnant actress Sharon Tate, wife of film director Roman Polanski. Angie dismissed the house at first, she says, considering it too small for the family's requirements. She was also averse to indoor pools, for all the usual reasons. But this pool was unusual, she explains in her autobiography *Backstage Passes* . . . because Satan lived in it.

'With his own eyes, David said, he'd seen *him* rising up out of the water one night.'

Refusing professional help, David is said to have sat around reading books on witchcraft, snorting his way through Matterhorns of marching powder and sketching pentagrams all over the house.

'I'd stay up for weeks,' he would remember. 'Even people like Keith Richards were floored by it. And there were pieces of me all over the floor. I paid with the worst manic depression of my life. My psyche went through the roof, it just fractured into pieces. I was hallucinating twenty-four hours a day.'

He is also said to have stored his urine, fingernail and toenail clippings in the fridge, and to have sat sentry beside it through the night. Whether or not he truly believed that there were witches 'after his semen', who planned to use it to create a child they could sacrifice to the devil – the very plot, give or take, of Polanski's film *Rosemary's Baby*[2] – you know what they say: when the legend becomes fact, print the legend.[3]

Whatever the truth, it was Coco, not Angie, who was pumping milk, orange juice and eggs into David of a morning, following his monstrous cocaine binges. It was Coco holding a mirror to his face to check that he was still breathing when she'd find him slumped, using the very looking glass on which he'd cut his coke the night before. Whatever they thought of her, and most appear not to have thought much, it was Coco who was keeping David alive. She also, though Angie was loath to admit it, saved his wife's life, when David turned on her in a drug-fuelled rage. The assault happened after Angie happened to lose her temper with Coco. David, she claimed, tried to kill her.

'It was awful,' Angie said. 'David was high. I questioned Corinne rather sharply about the amount of baggage she had assembled for a trip to Jamaica ... she snapped at me, so I snapped back at her, "Don't you dare talk to me like that!" Suddenly, David hurtled across the room. He grabbed my throat with both hands and started squeezing. He was blindly angry, yelling at me as he tightened his grip, and

I started panicking. It didn't feel as if he was going to stop. Corinne pulled him off and saved me. So it's possible that I owe her my life. The fact that she did save me must have pissed her off afterwards. I'm sure she would rather have let him go on and do it, but she must have known she would have to deal with the consequences.'

Angie also describes 'Bo', as she called her husband, performing his own exorcism on the swimming pool, a ritual that led to all manner of terrifying 'paranormal' activity, and which allegedly resulted in a stain appearing on the bottom 'in the shape of a beast of the underworld . . . it was shocking, malevolent; it frightened me'.

No surprise that they moved soon afterwards, settling at 1349 Stone Canyon Road in exclusive Bel Air. David needed new obsessions. 'Making sense of the senseless' is a theme that reoccurs. In the 'Promised Land' of California, he found the California Reich. A documentary made that year really captured his imagination. Focusing on a group of Neo-Nazis based in Los Angeles and San Francisco, it was such a compelling piece that it would not only be nominated a few months later at the 1976 Academy Awards, but would also be screened at that year's Cannes Film Festival.

David's interest in this movement is puzzling, given the far right-wing tenets of Nazi ideology: racism, homophobia and anti-Semitism. But fascinated he became – by Holocaust denial, Nazi symbols, the adoration of Adolf Hitler, even the notion of a 'Fourth Reich'. He soon diversified, as he tended to, this time into Egyptology. Picking up on uncanny parallels between the treatment of the Jews in ancient Egypt and those in Nazi Germany, David identified deeply with the concept of strangers in a strange land.[4]

There was plenty to obsess over in wider America, such as the Watergate sentencing, the Vietnam War ending with the taking of Saigon, and Bill Gates founding Microsoft – the term coined for 'microcomputer software' – in Albuquerque, New Mexico, where David himself would soon head, to begin filming. November saw the country gripped by the headline 'Did a UFO kidnap Navajo

County Man?' Travis Walton, a twenty-two-year-old logger, had been toiling with six co-workers in forestland near Snowflake, Arizona, when he suddenly disappeared. He was found five days later, when he claimed to have been abducted by aliens. His book, *The Walton Experience*, would be adapted for the screen in 1993, as *Fire in the Sky*. David was convinced that Walton's story was true.

What else would he do in LA? He'd have sex. A whole lotta love. He openly admitted to his rampant promiscuity during that period. He indulged in many affairs, primarily with black women, including African American costume designer Ola Hudson,[5] the mother of Guns N' Roses star Slash (Saul Hudson). He knows it happened, says the guitarist, because he found David and Ola together when he was eight years old.

'He was always over,' Slash says. 'They were always together. I caught them naked once. They had a lot of stuff going on, but my perspective was limited. Looking back on it, I know exactly what was going on ... I can only imagine how freaky it was.'

Instant movie stardom didn't quite work out – although David acquitted himself well as Thomas Jerome Newton in *The Man Who Fell to Earth*, a sinister sci-fi picture that has since become a classic, and which led to the creation of one of his best-loved albums, *Station to Station*.

In a cover story for Tina Brown in the *Sunday Times* magazine, David admitted:

'Me and rock and roll have parted company. Don't worry, I'll still make albums with love and with fun, but my effect is finished. I'm very pleased. I think I've caused quite enough rumpus for someone who's not even convinced he's a good musician. Now, I'm going to be a film director.'

There ensued extravagant claims that he had completed nine screenplays, and even that he planned to direct distinguished British actor Terence Stamp in a piece he'd written himself. And he was still banging on about a Ziggy Stardust musical, as well as a film adaptation of *Diamond Dogs*.

'I've always been a screenwriter,' a coked-up David gushed. 'My songs have just been practice for scripts.'

He also came clean, if that's the word, about his generous sexuality.

'I s'pose I do fancy blokes quite a bit, but I spend more time with chicks, particularly black chicks. The only type of chicks I can't stand are New York feminists. Get them into bed, and after five minutes they want you to do something funny with a lightbulb . . .'

Nicolas Roeg's *The Man Who Fell to Earth* was filmed over eleven weeks in the New Mexican desert. David later said that Roeg had 'abused' him and his fragile, drugged-out state, but conceded that the director had paid handsomely for the privilege.

'I really came to believe that Bowie was a man who had come to Earth from another galaxy,' remarked Roeg, during an interview with John Preston for the Daily Telegraph in 2013. 'His actual social behaviour was extraordinary – he hardly mixed with anyone at all. He seemed to be alone – which is what Newton is in the film. Isolated and alone.'

Roeg had also asked David to compose the soundtrack. David made a half-hearted start, but never got round to finishing it. The director attempted to pass on the commission to Papa John Phillips, 'another debauched workaholic'. That too was a non-starter. The ambient music used in the film was created by Kyoto-born keyboardist and percussionist Stomu Yamash'ta.[6]

The music that David *did* come up with, venturing forth into the studio after an absence of six months, was a distillation of his many obsessions while living in LA. *Station to Station*, a curious, experimental album of a handful of tracks, brimmed with Aleister Crowley, Kabbalah – the 'soul of Judaism'– Gnosticism, sci-fi, even references to the Manson family. Metaphor and parable, redemption and salvation framed a witch's brew of themes and influences, the inference being 'there is that which is bigger than I'. It confused the hell out of us.

The title track, at over ten minutes' duration his longest studio recording to date, refers to a devotional enacted by Christians in reflection of the Via Dolorosa or 'Way of Sorrows', believed to be the Old Jerusalem path that Jesus walked to his crucifixion on Mount Calvary.

It was 'very much concerned with the stations of the cross,' David confirmed to Q magazine in February 1997. '. . . I've never read a review that really sussed it. It's an extremely dark album. Miserable time to live through, I must say.'

The album features one of his greatest hits, 'Golden Years', as well as 'TVC15', and was recorded at Cherokee Studios, Los Angeles,[7] during the autumn, with Carlos Alomar and Earl Slick at his side. No Tony Visconti, note. The tragedy was that David would later have virtually no recollection of the time he spent making it.

That December, he travelled to Jamaica, only to find on arrival that his so-called new manager, Michael Lippman, had neglected to make accommodation arrangements. David seized the opportunity to fire him, and promptly moved into Keith Richards' enchanting glass-fronted house, 'Point of View',[8] set into the side of a mountain at Ocho Rios on the island's northern shore. In January, David sued Lippman for a couple of million. Lippman sued him back, and won. David swallowed it, determined to survive. He upped his profile on some of America's biggest TV shows, such as *Soul Train, Dinah Shore*, and the singer Cher's spectacular. He was preparing to take the Thin White Duke, his last great character, out on the road – kicking off in the New Year, 1976.

Which begs a string of questions. Had he been as un-together, out of it and over the edge as received history indicates, how would he have been able to summon the strength, energy and enthusiasm to pull off a major international tour? The suggestion that he was little more than a walking corpse by the time he was ready to go out live again seems to have been part of Bowie mythology, fuelling amazement at, as well as admiration for, his strength of character, determination and self-control. The ability to drag oneself back from the brink implies superhuman qualities. This suited David to the ground. He was ready to floor them yet again, this time with stark raving expressionism. He retrieved his old accomplice Iggy Pop *en route*. The two fell in as bosom buddies in their own road movie for the ensuing eighteen months.

I didn't see the show. I wasn't in the UK at the time. But I was confused by the tour's various names. It was known as the Station to Station tour, the Thin White Duke tour, the White Light tour, and the Isolar, its official name. Why so many? And what on earth was an isolar?

'Isolar . . . "isola" is Italian for island,' David said. ' "Isolation" plus "solar" all equals isolar. If I remember correctly, I was stoned at the time . . .'

Isolar Enterprises was also the name of the new company David launched, effectively run by just Coco and himself, after he dumped the final manager ever to confound his affairs.

The tour opened with a flourish in Vancouver and floored venues across North America. In New York, he seduced Ronnie Spector – perhaps to get one over her record producer ex, Phil. On to Europe, finishing in his favourite city at the Pavillon de Paris on 18 May. At that time the largest concert venue in the capital, the Pavillon was a former slaughterhouse, in a neighbourhood now known as 'les Abattoirs'. What was a rock tour if not a bloodbath, after all?

I read Michael Watts's *Melody Maker* review of the London Wembley Empire Pool outing in May. He found the show and the music funky and ferocious, but lacking in soul. Yet David's new musical approach clearly paved the way for experimentation that the next generation of artists would find supremely liberating. Again, there is no comprehensive footage of this tour, ensuring Ziggy's superiority and longevity among Bowie incarnations. But the Thin White Duke forged a legend of his own that has endured on recordings and in the memory. Reptilian, bitter and cynical, this poker-faced zombie lacked emotion and empathy. He was 1920s silent-movie Dietrich meets 1930s Weimar cabaret. Sharply dressed in black pants, white shirt and waistcoat, with slicked-back hair and cheese-cutter cheekbones, he sang of love with an empty heart.

'A very Aryan, fascist type,' was David's take on him. 'A would-be romantic with absolutely no emotion at all, but who spouted a lot of neo-romance.' He also called him 'a nasty character indeed'.

Fleet Street journalist David Hancock was on hand to witness Bowie's arrival by train at Victoria Station, London in May 1976, when the artist became embroiled in controversy for apparently giving a Nazi salute. The gesture was quickly denied as 'merely a wave'. Following as it did a whole slew of headline-grabbing interviews Bowie had given, in which he extolled the virtues of Adolf Hitler and even described the Führer as 'one of the first rock stars', this seemed disingenuous in the extreme. He and Iggy had already been busted for drugs on the tour, but got away with it. David was also detained in Russia with a stash of Nazi memorabilia in his luggage. And now this.

'I was on the *Evening News*, and was one of the journalists there at the station to greet him after his long absence,' remembers Hancock.

'We splashed the story, and it was billed as a big shock, but obviously he didn't do it. Fleet Street saw this picture, which *sort of* gave the impression of a Nazi salute, and then of course they had to have the story to back it up. It put David on every single front page the next day, even though I can tell you for sure, because I was standing right there, that it *wasn't* a Nazi salute! But we had to run with all his "Europe needs an Adolf / Britain needs a Hitler" crap, because it was such a sensational story. I just saw it as a great throwaway splash, and I had to write it the way it looked. Of course, I realised at the time that the things he said were not what he really meant. They just came out that way. I never did get to discuss it with him, to find out how he felt about all the coverage. I really wish I had. It seems funny now. It was a stupid slip-up, and so easily avoidable. Had he had what he clearly needed – a cracking PR, who would have told him to keep his hands down! – it may never have happened.

'David Bowie was my great hero. He did do wrong. He did make a big mistake. I was simply a journalist on a newspaper who had to make that story sing. That was my job. And every picture sells a story.'

Does Hancock regret it now?

'Not at all. All pop stars do things to recreate themselves within the image that sells them. Was he wrongly maligned? Of course. Did it hurt his career? Not a bit. After the "Nazi thing", he gave a press conference in which he spouted on about all kinds of stuff. He was talking about being really enamoured of Egon Schiele,[10] and there was I, hopping around at the back, going, "Yeah, but your album's shit." Okay, "Wild is the Wind"[11] is an extraordinary piece of music, but I wasn't blown away by the rest of the tracks – and I'm a diehard Bowie fan, remember. We only see art later, I suppose. I understand now the incredible risks he was taking on *Station to Station*. I recognise and appreciate its worth. And I'm in absolutely no doubt today that Bowie was our greatest creative artist ever.'

Whatever else came out of David's extreme preoccupations that gave rise to such controversy, the most abiding effect of the Thin White Duke on his creator was the reminder that he was a European. Bel Air and the California demons were already forgotten. He had taken advice, and heeded the tax warnings. He set up residency in Switzerland in 1976, for tax purposes. It is easy to see why. In California, state plus federal top bracket tax rates were 81 per cent at the time. In the UK, the highest rate was 83 per cent. Switzerland, in contrast, was taxing at 44 per cent, and in 1984 would lower its rates further, to 11.5 per cent.

'If David were to remain a resident of California, he would have to pay a hefty tax bill – $300,000 was the figure I was told – with money he didn't have,' stated Angie. 'These were tax debts accumulated over the previous few years, during which the vast quantities of taxable cash he had generated had vanished into various murky areas.'

His tenacious wife, hanging on by the seams in her fishnets, had packed up Stone Canyon Road and flung back the keys. David would never again live in Los Angeles. Angie travelled ahead to Switzerland with nanny Marion and five-year-old Zowie. There, she found them the 'cuckoo-clock house', Clos des Mésanges, Blonay, above Montreux on Lake Geneva. There, David would paint, read and learn to ski. He would also have a brief fling with Charlie Chaplin's fourth wife, Oona,[12] then fifty-one to David's twenty-nine. The affair meant more to her, close family members say, than it did to her twenty-two-years-younger lover.

It was with a delight bordering on deliverance that David ran into an old friend who was already living in Switzerland. It was none other than the gifted musician who had elevated to the stratosphere, with his own bare hands, 'Space Oddity' and 'Life on Mars?'

EUROPEAN
DECADENT

12
1977–1978

David's old compadre Rick Wakeman had been anything but idle in the intervening years. The former Royal College of Music prodigy who had quit his studies to pursue a career in rock and pop had honed his chops as 'One-Take Wakeman', playing some eighteen sessions a week and contributing to recordings by everyone from Bowie, Black Sabbath and Cat Stevens for whom he created and played the everlasting piano piece on 'Morning has Broken' – to Elton John, Lou Reed and Harry Nilsson. He'd been in and out of Spinning Wheel, and joined the Strawbs; when they released their debut album with Rick in 1970, the *Melody Maker* headlined their review 'Tomorrow's Superstar'.

He'd also married his first wife Roz; become the father of future musicians Oliver and Adam; joined and left Yes; toured America to massive acclaim; made the quintessential prog-rock albums *Fragile* and *Close to the Edge*; and established his solo career with concept pieces *The Six Wives of Henry VIII*, *Journey to the Centre of the Earth* and *The Myths and Legends of King Arthur and the Knights of the Round Table*. This last was as autobiographical as it was Arthurian. He'd also written and arranged the score for Ken Russell's *Lisztomania*, and had appeared in the film as Thor. He'd suffered his first heart attack, rejoined Yes, left his wife and moved to Switzerland. In 1976, when David and family arrived, Rick was living in Montreux with former Mountain Studios receptionist Danielle Corminboeuf.[1]

How did he find David?

'Same old David,' shrugs Rick.

'As far as I'm concerned, he never changed. There was an inner David, a deep volcano of creativity and, you'd have to say, pure genius, that he seemed afraid at times to let out. But it would erupt at regular intervals, engulfing him and driving him, so that he'd be writing and recording as if against his own will. I'd never seen anything like that before, and I haven't witnessed it since. Sometimes he would go quite quiet, and it was as if this other David was taking him over. Not that he'd summon it, it seemed to come randomly, of its own volition. Like he didn't have any say in the matter, so that he was almost a slave to it. I never got round to asking him what that felt like, but I definitely saw it in action. It was mesmerising.

'To have come up with "Space Oddity" at twenty-two and "Life on Mars?" at twenty-six: that is simply magical, it's indescribable. It's Mozart, it's Beethoven. Did we know at the time how important and everlasting those songs were going to be? Oh, yes. But *he* didn't. We all told him. We'd say to him, "Do you realise what you've done here? These songs are absolutely astonishing. They are going to be around forever." He'd just look at you as if to say, "what are you on about?" I told him again when I was round his house, listening to *Hunky Dory* with him.

'I was doing two or three studio sessions a day, every day for three years, for so many different people that I couldn't even tell you who most of them were. This one to the next one to the next, my feet hardly touching the ground for the duration. I might even have been a bit immune to most music at the time. But David's songs stopped me in my tracks. They got under your skin, they haunted you. Trouble was, he'd had so many knocks by then, and success had been such a long time coming, that it was as if he'd lost all his confidence when it came to his songwriting. If anything, he seemed a bit numb, and even reluctant to hear what I had to say. Maybe he thought it would jinx it or something.'

David aged 12 in 1959, taken during his first year at Bromley Technical High School.

40 Stansfield Road, Brixton, London SW9, where David was born, 8 January 1947.

Official copy of David's birth certificate, showing alterations made in 1960.

The Jones Boys. Back: great uncle Bryn, grandfather Emlyn. Front: Bryn, uncle Cliff, father Ken.

Down to Margate … don't forget your buckets and spades and cozzies an' all …

RHYTHM&BLUES

THE CLIFTONVILLE HALL
ST PAUL'S ROAD   CLIFTONVILLE

EVERY THURSDAY
from 12th AUGUST - 13th SEPTEMBER 1965

THE LOWER THIRD

KENT'S R & B FAVOURITES

Admission 3/6   8pm

Printed by TribusTribe

Mod poster for the Lower Third's weekly gigs in Cliftonville, Margate, summer 1965.

Davie Jones and the King Bees performing on BBC TV's *The Beat Room*, 27 July 1964.

Little Richard, David's original inspiration, aged 54 in 1986.

Memory of a Free Festival: David performing on the Victorian bandstand in 'Bec Rec', 16 August 1969.

Man in the chair: David poses in former manager Ralph Horton's Warwick Square, London, flat, 1966.

Dana Gillespic's inescapable teenage assets floored David at the Marquee Club in February 1965.

Hy Money's musical soirées rocked staid suburbia. Front left, the author as a child; third from left, Hy's daughter Lisa.

Hy Money (centre) with her daughter Lisa (left) and the author (right), on the 2014 opening night of Hy's sports photography exhibition.

David at the Amsterdam home of journalist Jojanneke Claassen for *Het Parool* newspaper, 1969.

The author's 1973 diary.

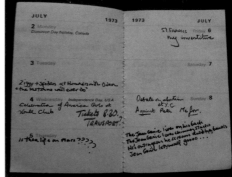

Taking the Mick, (left): David with Mick Ronson on *Lift Off with Ayshea*, ITV, 15 June 1972. Mick 'Woody' Woodmansey drums on.

Amanda Lear and David recording the *1980 Floor Show*, October 1973, Marquee Club.

Vintage glam Bowie backstage during his '72–'73 UK tour, captured by his first official photographer, fellow Londoner Mick Rock 'the man who shot the Seventies'.

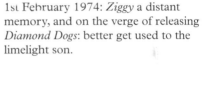

1st February 1974: *Ziggy* a distant memory, and on the verge of releasing *Diamond Dogs*: better get used to the limelight son.

Keeping Mum, looking glum: David in holiday mode with mother Peggy and son Joey, late '70s.

May 1976: David fans the flames over his rumoured obsession with Hitler with an apparent Nazi salute at Victoria station, London.

Striking a pose off-set during filming of *The Man Who Fell to Earth*, New Mexico, 1975.

Taking the Mick, (2): David moves like Jagger in the arms of Stones WAG Bianca, Marbella, 1977.

David guests on the final 'Marc' show, Granada TV, 7 September 1977, 9 days before Bolan's tragic death.

Bowie mourns Bolan at Golders Green Crematorium, 20 September 1977, before vanishing for the night with his friend's estranged wife, June.

Did Rick really expect those songs to last until now?

'The good stuff lasts forever.'

But, he reckons, there was more than a hint of the man David really was in 'Wild Eyed Boy From Freecloud'.[2]

'That's the song I really love. There's a full orchestral arrangement on it by Tony Visconti. I'm convinced that song is the real David, it's him baring his true soul. Listen to it again, and think about it. He never said anything, but I'd swear that was truly him.

'He was quite special, in many respects. We got on really well, and we had a lot in common. Long after we both left London, we were still in regular touch. When we were both living in Switzerland, we'd meet and hang out at the Museum Club in Old Town, Montreux. This was in the late Seventies, when he was drained by all the LA madness and wanted to clean himself up and start again. And he said to me one day, in all earnestness, "I'm not convinced that Capitalism works, you know. I think Communism might be the answer. I'm off to live in Berlin for a bit, to find out." He came back a couple of years later, and we got together again. "Communism's not the answer," he said. We grinned at each other and had another drink.'

David's German sojourn is another period in his complicated life which has been distorted by mythology. In fact, he did not go to the Wall for three years to create 'the Berlin Trilogy', as *Low*, *"Heroes"* and *Lodger* have come to be known. The first of these three albums was recorded partly in France, at the Château d'Hérouville, to honour an existing contractual obligation. David was recording with Iggy Pop at the Château for the latter's album *The Idiot* from May 1976, and the *Low* sessions began there that August. The record was finished at Hansa studios in Berlin. Carlos Alomar was along for the ride, as was Brian Eno.[3] However and wherever the professional and private Davids panned out, his Berlin-based years were symbolic.

'I had approached the brink of drug-induced calamity one too many times, and it was essential to take some kind of positive action,' David told *Uncut*. 'For many years, Berlin had appealed to me as a sort of sanctuary-like situation. It was one of the few cities where I could move around in virtual anonymity. I was going broke; it was cheap to live. For some reason, Berliners just didn't care. Well, not about an English rock singer, anyway.'

'I think David just liked being in Berlin,' is producer Tony Visconti's take. 'There was so much of it, in those days, that was fantastic, fantasy-like, that didn't exist anywhere else in the world. The impending danger of the divided military zones, the bizarre nightlife, the extremely traditional restaurants with aproned servers, reminders of Hitler's not-too-distant presence, a recording studio five hundred yards from the Wall; you could've been on the set of *The Prisoner*.'[4]

Low, according to Visconti, was not such a challenging album to create:

'We were freewheeling, making our own rules. But David was going through a difficult period, professionally and personally. To his credit, he didn't put on a brave face. His music said that he was "low".'

While they lodged temporarily at the Gehrhus Hotel, Coco did the house-hunting. She found them modest living quarters in Schöneberg, a Turkish immigrant neighbourhood notable for having been the birthplace of Marlene Dietrich in 1901. This connection was important to David. Like him, Dietrich had hung on to stardom via constant and compelling self-reinventions. In 1920s Berlin, she found work as an actress in silent films and stage productions. In Thirties Hollywood, she purveyed a brittle glamour and androgyny, which led to her becoming one of the richest and most fascinating movie stars of the age. She entertained the troops during the Second World War, and recast herself as a cabaret act in the Fifties – a role that she would play for twenty years. But in the common consciousness, she was a fixture of the Weimar Republic of the Twenties and early Thirties. It was to this version of Marlene that David was inextricably drawn, perhaps seeing himself in her.

Photographer Helmut Newton was also born in Schöneberg, in 1920. Albert Einstein had lived there, from 1914 until 1933. Christopher Isherwood, author of 'The Berlin Stories' – *Goodbye to Berlin* and *Mr Norris Changes Trains* – had been resident observer and chronicler of the decadent fantasies of pre-Nazi Berlin during the 1930s. His novels inspired the musical *Cabaret* in 1966, with lyrics and music by Kander and Ebb. It was adapted for the screen in 1972, starring Liza Minnelli and Joel Grey, and directed by Bob Fosse. Film director Billy Wilder had lived here in the Twenties, and actor Klaus Kinski in the Thirties. The area around Nollendorfplatz, known as 'Nolli', had been the centre of Berlin's gay community since the early Twenties, and was infamous for its fetish and S&M clubs, its cruising labyrinths, its depraved darkroom bars.

The new apartment at 155 Hauptstrasse, with room for Coco, David and Iggy, was more prosaic, sitting as it did directly above a car parts outlet.[5] Coco stocked up on blank canvases, brushes and oils for David, and would lounge around at arm's length 'reading Nietzsche', while he painted. They lingered often together at the Brücke museum, immersing themselves in early twentieth-century expressionist art. By day, either with Coco and/or Jim, David would wander or cycle about, stopping for coffee, buying groceries, and taking his meals at basic caffs. By night, they would descend into the underworld and amuse themselves among the decadents. David became enamoured of glamorous transsexual club-owner and entertainer Romy Haag. Although they were often photographed together, David would deny their affair when she went public with it. At work, though clearly depressed, he was as driven as ever.

'We had a great time in Berlin,' he would say, looking back. 'None of us had any money then, but we still did crazy things. I remember they all clubbed together once, and got me a rusted 1955 Mercedes. And I remember dropping Iggy [Pop] off at a punk club one night. Maybe it was New Year. They'd made a cake of the Berlin Wall all around the inside of the club, and at midnight, they all jumped in it and ate it.'

While *Low* is a manic-depressive album that was savaged by the critics, it is lifted by the gift of 'Sound and Vision'. The stand-out track, which features Visconti's then wife Mary Hopkin as the doo-doo backing singer, is a light-and-shade blend of upbeat guitar and gloomy vocals. It made Number Three in the UK, and became a Top Ten hit in several other countries including Germany. Not in America, however, where his star was fading rapidly.

As was Angie's. November 1976 fetched a fearful showdown between the Bowies, when the wife pitched up in Berlin to make her stand against her rival. The jumped-up PA, Angie had decided, was exerting too much control over her husband. She intended to patch things up with David and woo him back to Switzerland. She gave him an ultimatum: 'Her, or me.' David demurred. He was hungover, febrile, uncontrollably distressed. He protested that he could not cope without Coco. Angie would later claim that David tried to appeal to her maternal side, suggesting that they try for more children – like that was gonna do it – if only she would retreat to the cuckoo clock and behave like a nice, 'proper' wife. Pot, kettle. Angie was incandescent.

David, overcome, collapsed. He was admitted to a military hospital with a suspected heart attack, which was subsequently dismissed as a false alarm. Angie, demented, flounced off to the airport. When I ran into David at Chartier in Paris about a month later, neither Angie nor Coco was with him. And when David set off with Jim/Iggy, Romy Haag and Coco to celebrate his thirtieth birthday at l'Ange Bleu[6] *boîte de nuit* in Paris on 8 January 1977, Angie's absence said it all.

'Turning thirty is the best thing that ever happened to me,' David would comment. 'Until thirty, I was a dedicated artist. Now I've discovered privacy, I've lost contact. My writing's much better, my music's better, I've played more music in the last year and a half than in all my life.'

David asked Angie for a divorce during a formal meeting at a Berlin hotel, with Coco acting as intermediary.

'We were both drunk,' Angie recalled in press interviews after she left the *Celebrity Big Brother* house in January 2016. 'We had champagne, and then we went home together. We were both relieved it was over. But when we went back to David's apartment, Corinne's suitcases were all over the place. So I did a spot of rearranging, out of the window. I heard the suitcases land on a car outside. We had really good sex, and then I just fucking left.'

Their divorce, like most, was stressful and drawn-out. In the end, Angie's settlement was a relative pittance: a mere half a million pounds, to be paid in instalments over the next decade. According to Dana Gillespie, 'She did not have the wherewithal to fight it. She couldn't afford lawyers, and he could. And the fact that they divorced under Swiss law was very good for David.'

Defeated, Angie was forced to yield custody of Zowie.

'I didn't *not* want custody,' she would tell Nancy Dell'Olio inside the *Celebrity Big Brother* house in 2016, just before David died.

'It was just I was never going to take him away from his father, because they were as tight as can be. It was just one of those things.'

'That was a good thing,' insists George Underwood. 'It was absolutely right that David got custody. In my view, Angie was not a fit mother at that time. She'd probably say it herself.'

Angie had a three-year relationship with punk rocker Andrew Lipka, aka 'Drew Blood'. Their daughter Stacia was born in 1980.

As far as Angie was concerned, it was Corinne Schwab who killed her marriage. When I interviewed her at her London home on 20 May 1987, for a piece which appeared as 'Bitchy over Bowie: How Coco wrecked my marriage, by rock star's bitter ex-wife',[7] she was still spitting blood.

'This is a warning for any woman who lives with or is married to a rock star,' she told me. 'I thought I was being a friend, and I thought she was my friend, too. But she stole my husband, and she wrecked our marriage. She spat it all back in my face. Gradually, she edged closer and closer to David. She started ordering the cars, ironing the shirts, making the breakfast. I suppose I was pursuing other interests, so I was always pressed for time, and glad to let another dogsbody do all the work. That, as far as my marriage was concerned, was my downfall.'

She told me that the then thirty-eight-year-old Corinne – the two women are the same age – was now the most important person in David's life, other than their son.

'Nobody can understand it,' she snarled. 'He's the biggest rock star in the world, he's so good-looking himself, he could have the pick of the world's most beautiful women. To me, Coco is ugly and frumpy. Her skin looks like the inside of a crater, and I think her hair is like string. But there is a reason for all this. David doesn't want good-looking girls. He wants a mother. And Coco is his mother substitute. When we were still married, and when David decided he couldn't write any more, he had a kind of nervous breakdown. But he didn't come to me. He went to Coco. Her mother was a psychiatrist, and I suppose he felt he was getting professional help in an indirect way. When he got heavily into drugs, it was Coco who helped him. When I split from him finally, it was not from the man I knew.'

From then on, for the next four decades, it was Coco who effectively managed David's life and career. It was she who booked every arena, oversaw the stitching of every handmade costume, and paid for every hotel room, meal, bottle of booze and packet of fags. As for David, when I caught up with him in Rotterdam, he defended vigorously the woman he couldn't live without.

'I guess Coco is the one person I could say has been a continual friend to me,' he told me in Rotterdam in May 1987. 'She is my personal assistant and a very good friend. She became the most important person in my life in the mid-Seventies. My whole lifestyle at that time made me quite bonkers, and I had a complete breakdown. Coco was the one person who told me what a fool I was becoming, and she made me snap right out of it, I'm so glad to say.

'Sex is not all there is. There really have to be relationships in your life to make it all truly worthwhile.'

David and Jim hit the road in March, on Iggy's twenty-nine-date Idiot tour. David was on keyboards and backing vocals. They debuted at a hallowed venue, the Friars, Aylesbury, taking in Newcastle, Manchester and Birmingham before landing at the Rainbow in London. During the run-up to the London shows, David spent four days with Marc Bolan, at his flat. Marc later enthused to the press that the pair were making a film together. The tour rumbled on, to the USA and Canada, supported by Blondie from 13 March on. Montreal, Toronto, Boston, New York – where all the Stones except Bill Wyman pitched up. Philadelphia, Chicago and Seattle, among others, San Francisco and LA. For David, the world was no longer a no-fly zone.

'I flew for the first time in five or six years,' he said. 'I think the airplane is really a wonderful invention.'

So what happened to his fear of flying?

'Fear is not a word in my vocabulary any more,' he scoffed. 'I am a man of great inner strength and courage these days.'

Bowie and Iggy flew on to Japan, to flog both *Low* and *The Idiot*. The promotional campaign then swung back to Europe. In Paris, David ran into Jagger's wife Bianca, who was working on a movie, *Flesh Color*.[8] In a heartbeat, the pair absconded to Spain. They were photographed together on the Costa del Sol, where they stayed at the lavish Marbella Club resort.

'That was less about Bianca, more about Mick,' revealed a member of David's entourage at the time, who asked not to be named. 'David had long felt that he was the also-ran, forever trying to catch up with Jagger. Once he'd had Bianca, he felt he had the upper hand. Angie speculated that, in return, Mick had written the Stones' hit "Angie"[9] about her. But it was Keith [Richards] who wrote that song, with a little input from Mick that was supposed to be about his thing with Marianne [Faithfull]. Keith once said he wrote "Angie" for his baby, called Dandelion – I think his daughter's middle name might have been Angela. In his autobiography,[10] Keith took it all back. Rock'n'roll!'

The universally acclaimed ' "Heroes" ', his signature and his best-loved song, made it only to Number Twenty-Four on its release in the UK, October 1977, and failed to make the American Billboard Top 100. It peaked at Number Twelve after his death in January 2016. *"Heroes"* the album reached Number Three in the UK, and Number Thirty-Five in the US. Widely regarded as his masterpiece, it was also the moment he peaked creatively. Not until almost the end of his life, with *The Next Day* and finally *Blackstar*, would David reach such sublime heights again.

The title song was written by Bowie with Brian Eno, produced by Bowie and Tony Visconti, and recorded at Hansa Tonstudio with Robert Fripp's eerie guitar – his contribution was made in a single weekend.

'The song ' "Heroes" ' was about the faceless person, the humble man on the street, who gets his moment of glory,' David said. 'The old Shakespearian quote – "All the world's a stage" [from *As You Like It*, Act II, Scene VII] – I used that. It had been used in every other art form except rock'n'roll.'

Ahead of the single's release, David and Coco flew to the UK on 7 September 1977, where David performed it on the last-ever episode of Granada TV's *Marc* show in Manchester, hosted by his old friend and rival Marc Bolan. But the show turned into a farce. In an attempt to offset difficulties due to a dispute involving the floor manager, who happened also to be the head of the union, Marc instructed his personal assistant and driver, Cliff Wright, to look after David.

'Marc gave David a Fender Strat; a Sunburst with a maple neck,' remembered Wright, when I interviewed him for *Ride a White Swan: The Lives and Death of Marc Bolan*. 'We set up an amp and cab [speaker cabinet] in the studio for him, and they recorded ' "Heroes" ' for the show. This was going to be the first airing of the single on British TV. I thought David could have let Marc play on it with him, to be honest.'

When it came to the recording of Marc's and David's duet to close the show, Bolan was worse for wear, and fell off the stage. The schedule did not allow for the sequence to be shot again. Bolan and Bowie went their separate ways. Tragically, they would never see each other again. In the early hours of 16 September, Marc's jet-lagged girlfriend Gloria Jones crashed the Mini she was driving him home in. She hit a concrete post on a Barnes hump-back bridge. The star was killed outright, by a steel pin which had been holding a chain to the post, and which pierced his temple. Four days later, David attended Marc's funeral at London's Golders Green Crematorium. Tony Visconti for one was angered by proceedings, feeling that fan hysteria made a mockery of the occasion. He was also surprised to see June Bolan there. Marc's estranged wife had been banned from attending, but had managed to smuggle herself in. Cliff Wright saw her, too.

'Outside,' he says. 'She was just standing there afterwards, helpless and alone among the crowd. Then David Bowie came past in his limo. June spotted him, and called out to him: "David! David!" Bowie opened the door, and let her in.'

'I'd travelled there in a limo with Rod [Stewart],' remembers Cockney Rebel's Steve Harley. 'Bowie was sat right in front of me – the only time I ever met him. Rod was staying at the Intercontinental on Park Lane. We were going back there to have our own little wake for Marc. We asked David to join us. He didn't come.'

It has since been confirmed, by a close mutual friend of David's and Marc's, that David and June Bolan slept together on the night of her almost ex-husband's funeral – while Marc's partner and the mother of his son Rolan, Gloria Jones, lay seriously injured in hospital, unaware that he was dead.

It has also been written that David, as Rolan's godfather, took pity on Gloria and the couple's child, and that he took responsibility for paying Rolan's school fees. He did not.

'David Bowie is *not* my godfather,' Rolan told me himself. 'Ringo Starr is. A lot of crazy stuff has been written and said down the years. I can assure you that David Bowie is not, though. Nor did he pay for me to go to school. I've never met him.'

'What happened was, David put some money into a fund for Rolan,' Gloria explained to me. 'Our home was ransacked after Marc's death, and absolutely everything was taken. Even my underwear. I had nothing left. Marc's death left me destitute. David did that for us so that we could live. And he did it without being asked. It was simply that he loved Marc. He wanted to look after us. He didn't say anything, and he didn't have to. It was from his heart.'

David's performance of ' "Heroes" ' at Live Aid on 13 July 1985 is considered to be the best he ever sang it. He also performed it, with the remaining members of Queen, at the Freddie Mercury Tribute Concert on 20 April 1992. At Olympics 2012, it was played over the arrival of Great Britain's team during the Games' opening ceremony. It was repeated for the emotional entrance of our Paralympics team. Shortly after David's death, his loyal American pianist Mike Garson would drop a minor bombshell about the ' "Heroes" ' video.

'This was one of David's great songs – a true anthem,' Garson said. 'You can see me singing back-up at about three minutes in, but, trust me, the microphone was off. I can't sing at all. Almost tone-deaf. That's my confession for the day.'

Also in January 2016, the German Foreign Office thanked David posthumously for helping to bring down *Berliner Mauer*, the Berlin Wall, the barrier that separated West Germany from East for twenty-eight years. 'You are now among Heroes,' they declared. The reference was to a three-day rock concert staged near the Wall in which Bowie took part on 7 June 1987 – about a decade after his departure from West Berlin. Genesis and Eurythmics also starred.

During his performance, Bowie addressed the crowd in German. Just before he sang '"Heroes"', he cried: 'We send our best wishes to all our friends who are on the other side of the wall!' Violent demonstrations broke out among the fans who could hear his performance but not see it. Hundreds were arrested. A week later, US President Ronald Reagan spoke to Soviet Union leader Mikhail Gorbachev about 'tearing down this wall'.

'I'll never forget that,' said Bowie in 2003. 'It was one of the most emotional performances I've ever done. I was in tears. They'd backed up the stage to the Wall itself, so that the Wall was acting as our backdrop . . . there were thousands on the other side . . . it was breaking my heart. I'd never done anything like that in my life, and I guess I never will again . . .

'When we did ' "Heroes" ', it felt really anthemic, almost like a prayer . . . that's the town where it was written, and that's the particular situation that it was written about. It was just extraordinary.'

It seems that David was changed profoundly by his Berlin experience, and by living in such close proximity to the Wall. It stood not only as a metaphor for the state of the world – then living on the knife edge of nuclear war – but as a symbol of his own life, and all that was wrong with it. The superficial calm of the city could have exploded at any moment.

Cycling around town, contemplating the implications of that great, menacing structure and the countless thousands of Soviet troops the other side of it, the fragility of life became clear. He began to think about the plight of the innocents: the ordinary people caught up in a situation that was far from their own making, and now effectively living on the frontline. He listened in on his soul, and was deafened by chaos. The imminence of death woke him up to his life. He began to think and write more deeply, well aware that time was passing. He resolved to reassess, to reshape himself, and to review his priorities. He revisited his dreams.

The song's title (like the album) is always presented in double quotation marks, denoting irony: the heroes in the song are not actual, but notional. The message has been variously interpreted, but appears to be a warning, that those whom we may consider to be our 'heroes', in particular rock'n'roll stars, are in reality nothing of the sort. It is merely our imagination and adoration that make them so. In the words of American author and critic Mary McCarthy, 'We all live in suspense, from day to day, from hour to hour. In other words, we are the hero of our own story.'

Elvis had passed, and Bolan too. Times were a-changin'. In December 1977, David went to see Angie in Switzerland, and informed her of his intention to spend Christmas in Berlin with Zowie. In a rage, she split for New York, where she would go off-radar with friends. At 155 Hauptstrasse, on-off heroin addict Iggy went cold turkey, while Coco quietly cooked a goose. Come New Year's Day, the Bowie marriage was left-overs.

February 1978 kicked off with a confidence trick. David said yes to David Hemmings when he asked him to star in his movie *Just a Gigolo*, because the actor-director assured him he'd get to perform with his idol Marlene Dietrich.[11] In the event, the ageing diva did a Garbo, demanding to be alone. She would face the close-ups for her last-ever screen role in Paris, while David was confined to Berlin, making out with a chair. Dietrich and Bowie never shot so much as a frame together. The ill-fated film, which also co-starred Kim Novak, would receive its world premiere in Berlin that November, only to be summarily trashed. David shrugged it off, remarking that the flick was 'my thirty-two Elvis Presley movies rolled into one'. Paul Newman never lost sleep.

It was a more robust and vigorous, recovering version of David who set off on his most ambitious tour yet – the Isolar II, the Low/ Heroes world tour, or the Stage tour – to promote the *Low* and *"Heroes"* albums. Returning to the West Coast to kick off in San Diego, he played the major venues across North America. The

Rhode Island, Boston and Philadelphia gigs were recorded for the live album *Stage*. He reached Madison Square Garden at the beginning of May. Then they raged across Europe throughout the spring, including two nights at the Pavillon de Paris, and reaching Earls Court, London at the end of June. Between July and November, the tour took time off, during which David repaired to Queen's Mountain Studios in Montreux, to record the final instalment of the so-called Berlin Trilogy, or 'triptych', as he later liked to call it. The last album was *Lodger*.

David's thirteenth studio album, to be completed at the Record Plant in New York, blended themes of travel and civilisation, nuclear war and abusive relationships in a fusion of thought-provoking world-music styles. It spawned the hit 'Boys Keep Swinging', on which guitarist Alomar played drums, and featured both Visconti and Brian Eno as musicians. It was no biggie at the time of its eventual release, in May 1979 – David couldn't win 'em all – but it has grown on people. It is now cherished, rightly, as an example of his growing maturity, and as a dark-horse Bowie best.

The tour swanned on to Australia and New Zealand, for his first concert performances Down Under. In Sydney, David finally learned to swim. He pushed on eastwards to make a triumphant return to Japan, closing at Tokyo's NHK Hall on 12 December. Ziggy was resurrected in all his glory. He rose like a phoenix in blistering form. Still big in Japan, then. Carlos Alomar was band leader on this tour. Natasha Korniloff was back on wardrobe duty, and was thrilled to see her old lover looking so fit.

Rolling Stone summed up the show best, trailing their sparkling review with the tantalising tagline 'David Plays Himself'. There seemed nothing more to do, at least for now. He turned the page, and perhaps even closed the book. He would not give another concert for nearly five years.

He spent Christmas in Tokyo.

GLOBAL ICON

13
1979–1980

David went to ground until *Lodger* came out. We barely noticed. There were plenty of distractions in 1979, despite the 'Winter of Discontent'. Margaret Thatcher became the first female Prime Minister of Great Britain. Phoney Beatlemania had bitten the dust, according to carbon-neutral Joe Strummer. When he and Mick Jones penned 'London Calling', they weren't joking. Punk was dead, its fate sealed by the heroin-induced death of Sid Vicious in New York, after murdering his girlfriend Nancy Spungen at the Hotel Chelsea.

There was the rise and rise of Dire Straits and Kate Bush, of the Police and Michael Jackson. Ian Dury had a hit with a rhythm stick, and the Buggles heralded the MTV age with 'Video Killed the Radio Star'.[1] Elton John became the first Western rocker to perform live in the Soviet Union. Spandau Ballet signed to Chrysalis Records,[2] the best independent label of all, who boasted, among others, the Fabulous Thunderbirds, T-Bone Burnett, Billy Idol, Ultravox, Pat Benatar, Blondie, Leo Sayer, and Huey Lewis & the News. Their subsidiary, 2-Tone, had Madness, Selecter and the Specials. Chrysalis championed the cause of the New Romantic movement into the Eighties, and launched the first-ever music-video album, for Blondie's *Eat to the Beat*. I know. I worked there. It was Christmas every day.

During promo for *Lodger*, David performed his latest, 'Boys

Keep Swinging', on Capital Radio DJ Kenny Everett's TV show, where he met rakish producer David Mallet. The pair fell in. David hired 'Cecil B. de Mallet' to make a video for that single. It was the beginning of a beautiful friendship that would generate some of the most enduring shorts of the music video age.

David moved out of 155 Hauptstrasse in May 1979. He was loath to leave. But Zowie/Joey had enrolled at the Commonwealth American School (now the International School of Lausanne) in Vevey. At eight, he was old enough to go to Gordonstoun in Elgin, Moray, on the far north-eastern coast of Scotland. The brisk, no-nonsense public school which had educated three generations of British Royals, including the Princess Royal and the Prince of Wales – Charles dubbed it 'Colditz in kilts', and (tellingly) didn't send William or Harry there – at least had an excellent drama department. A significant advantage was that nanny Marion Skene's parents lived within visiting distance.

'If I'm honest, it wasn't a great fit for me,' he would say years later, in an interview with freelance writer Martyn Palmer, published in the *Mail on Sunday* in August 2011. 'It was fairly austere, and they still maintained that disciplined regime – the morning runs and the cold showers. I didn't feel comfortable. I was just trying to survive.'

In the end, he was asked to leave after 'sleeping through most of my A levels'. He would eventually take American SATS exams, and study Philosophy at Wooster College, Ohio. Then it would be film school in London, followed by a succession of jobs in production houses, a spell at a special-effects studio, and eventually the advertising industry, making TV commercials. This was all good grounding for what he really wanted to do, which was to make films.

Didn't it ever occur to him to try the classic son-of-rock-star route, and attempt to make a name for himself in the music business? True, there hasn't been a surfeit of success stories. I can't think of a single artist who has eclipsed Mom or Dad, apart from

Miley Cyrus, daughter of Billy Ray. Jakob Dylan had a good go in the Wallflowers. Julian Lennon made inroads, but was never a superstar. Sean Lennon was tipped, but faded fast. Rolan Bolan, son of Marc, had every opportunity, but failed to rise to it. James McCartney, ditto. Brian Wilson's Carnie and Wendy. Bob Marley's Stephen, Ziggy and Damian, and many, many more. Drummers seem to fare better, as Jason Bonham, son of Led Zep's John, and Zak Starkey, son of Ringo, would testify. David tried everything he could think of to encourage his son. It was never going to happen.

'He really, really wanted me to learn an instrument,' Duncan told Martyn Palmer, with whom, during the 1990s, I co-owned a syndication agency.

'He tried to get me to learn the drums, but I didn't want to. The saxophone? No. Piano? No. Guitar – no thanks. Bless him. He kept on trying, and nothing was happening. Nothing would take. I don't know if subconsciously there was some reaction going on; if there was something in me that didn't want to learn an instrument – because I could not have been that incompetent! He'd say, "You have to practise." And I was like, but I don't want to practise. It didn't interest me, so it wasn't going to happen.'

During his son's tenure at Gordonstoun, David spent school half-terms and holidays in Switzerland and otherwise lived in New York, where he'd acquired a downtown loft apartment. With simple décor, Japanese-infused, its edgy location assuaged some of the discomfort induced by this declining hell-raiser's current status as a tax exile, based in a bourgeois Swiss resort. Meanwhile, ensconced in the mountains, what else would David do but learn to ski? In fact, he had already shown interest in the sport, and had taken a few lessons in Aviemore in the Cairngorms during 1976. His instructor there was one Laurence Poole from Lowestoft, an oil rigger who taught absolute beginners on a dry slope at the resort, just over an hour's drive from Gordonstoun.

The experience whetted David's appetite. He would soon seek superior instruction in Zermatt from a legend of the Alps and a pioneer in modern ski instruction, Peter Kronig, who came highly recommended by a string of film stars, movie directors, bankers and musicians. Born in 1937 and ten years David's senior, the pair hit it off from the maiden run. David perfected the art in Zermatt, but his preferred resort was always Gstaad, in the Bernese Oberland region of the Swiss Alps.

In years to come, his music would find its way onto soundtracks for ski films: 'Space Oddity' appeared on Teton Gravity Research's *Tangerine Dream* in 2005, and 'Rebel Rebel' would be heard during the opening of Nimbus Independent's 2008 picture *Hunting Yeti*. There would also be artistic collaborations. Armada Skis commissioned Rick Stultz to create a Bowie graphic for a run of the company's ARGs – a now-classic, reverse-cambered powder ski, released during the 2008–9 season. Armada also did a Bowie graphic for a run in 2005–6. The Park City, Utah company have long been big Bowie fans.

'Artists and athletes who push boundaries have always inspired us to do the same,' commented spokesman Andy Miller. 'So an icon like David Bowie was a perfect fit.'

The new decade would prove a watershed for artists of Bowie's generation. Most didn't die before they got old. The Who minus Moonie, the Stones less Jonesie, the former Beatles, Kinks, Wakeman, Elton, Rod, Ferry, Eno, Ozzy et hoary al were now the elder statesmen of rock, getting eclipsed by the generation below. 'What a drag it is getting old,' Jagger had moaned.[3] Now they knew what he meant. Jim Morrison's end may have been his only friend,[4] Ziggy had yearned for a rock'n'roll suicide. Maybe he'd wait a while.

'Bohemian Rhapsody' is usually credited with having been 'the first rock video'. It wasn't really. The Beatles, the Stones, Bob Dylan and more had been creating credible promotional shorts since the Sixties. But visuals were taking a turn now, in tandem with a new wave in music. Just as the Seventies had revived Fifties rock'n'roll, the Eighties were obsessed with the Sixties. The new pop sound was often over-produced, reverb-y, snare-y, much of it heavy on vocal delays and synths, all thanks to more tech in the game than ever before.

A money-no-object glamour pervaded – even though most were skint. Young London was all about scenes and cults, blag and swag, make-up, mayhem and one-night-a-week clubs, most of them in Soho. In 1978, Billy's was putting on Roxy Music and Bowie Nights – 'A Club for Heroes' for 'freaks and weirdos' – at Gossip's, beneath what was said to have been a brothel on Dean Street. 'It had more to do with decadent pre-war Berlin than reflecting life on a south London council estate,' reflected Boy George in *Take It Like a Man*, his frank 1995 autobiography.

The scene at Billy's evolved into the Blitz, with a Second World War theme. An average wine bar on Great Queen Street became the Style-Central dominion of Caerphilly boy Steve Strange, London-born Rich Kids drummer turned DJ Rusty Egan, Philip Sallon – from Dollis Hill, yet one of the Bromley Contingent – and 'Boy' George O'Dowd from Eltham. George had also once lurked on the garden path at Haddon Hall. Short-lived – it lasted only from February 1979 to October 1980 – the Blitz 'was to the Eighties what Liverpool's Cavern Club was to the Sixties,' said former Rich Kids, Visage and Ultravox singer Midge Ure. 'It helped define a generation.'

In 1980, Sallon, the future Boy George and friends set off on a coach trip to Margate, to poke around a place that Bowie once loved. Rusty Egan opened The Cage, a New Romantic record shop on the King's Road. *The Face* magazine featured Bowie on its cover in November 1980. In 1982, Egan would launch the Camden Palace with Strange. Scenester Robert Elms coined the name for Spandau Ballet, from graffiti he'd seen in a toilet in east Berlin.

In flocked the Bromley Contingent, Derek Jarman, Zandra Rhodes. Up rocked the wannabe bands and local fashion students. The New Romantics movement was born. Kids frequented the

Fridge in Brixton; Greek Street's Le Beat Route and Le Kilt, this last a dive of festering tartan and antlers; there were also Sallon's Mud Club at Busby's on Charing Cross Road, and the unforgettable Wag. The Wardour Street venue had started out as blues hangout the Flamingo, the crucible of mod, metamorphosing into the jazz joint Whiskey A Go-Go.

Whereas the Blitz was no-entry unless you looked more than the part, the shabby, decadent Wag embraced most-comers. At the outset, it showcased new musical styles such as hip hop and house. Its playlist soon throbbed with jazz, Latin, salsa and soul, with rap, reggae and rockabilly, all layered over Seventies funk. Warehouse parties started cropping up in disused depots in Rotherhithe, Southwark and King's Cross. You never knew where they were happening until the night. The Wag became their kind-of HQ. Before the AIDS crisis broke, it got as debauched as it gets. It was welcome to the pleasure dome, all night long.

At what precise moment did David decide to borrow back inspiration from the very kids he'd inspired? He never said. To have been a fly on his wall when that light went on.

He was thirty-three and the father of a nine-year-old. Knocking on. The clubland elite were not enamoured of what he was *now*, but of what he'd been *then*. He'd taught his children well. His fierce instinct for survival told him he must now allow them to teach him. He was dismissive of clones and copycats, and didn't fancy Gary Numan much. He was far more gracious (less threatened?) among the Blitz Kids, who made it up as they went along and wore their hearts on their sleeves. He'd recorded a new album with Visconti at the Power Station studios in New York: *Scary Monsters (and Super Creeps)*. It would not be released until September, when David's contract with RCA was up. He had no plans to renew, having other ideas.

The dazzling jewel in the *Scary Monsters* crown was 'Ashes to Ashes'. A sequel to his own 'Space Oddity' over a decade earlier, the composition is stunning. It's his Pachelbel's 'Canon in D', his

Beethoven's 'Symphony No. 9', his Led Zeppelin's 'Kashmir'. I exaggerate? Go listen. But what the hell is it about?

He had always been reluctant to be a banner-waver for any particular cause, he explained to BBC Radio 1 DJ Andy Peebles in New York in 1980. But he confessed he had seen an alarming amount of heroin abuse in recent years, and the devastating effect it was having on people.

This got him thinking back to one of his original creations, Major Tom in 'Ashes to Ashes'.

He described Major Tom as an individual in a situation he couldn't cope with, and who didn't want to return to Earth. He said that Major Tom still meant a great deal to him; that it was the first time he had succeeded in creating a credible character.

In the song, we return to Major Tom a decade after we first met him, only to learn that the dream has soured: 'Technological ego was what put him up there,' said David. 'The most disastrous thing I could think of was that he found solace in some kind of heroin-like drug. It's also a 1980s nursery rhyme. We're getting round to menacing nursery rhymes again . . . Let's hope I'm wrong. I expect I am.'

Anxious, resonant, vibrating with defiance and doom, the song is musically complex, culturally significant, and was David's kiss goodbye to the Seventies, as well as a love letter to New Romanticism. It also lifted from a precious source: his lifelong friendship with George Underwood.

'We'd had lengthy spells when we didn't see each other – just as he'd warned when we were young,' recalls George. 'So I hadn't spoken to him for a while when I was asked by David Larkin, head of cover designs at Pan Books, to do a portrait of David for the cover of an edition of Walter Tevis's novel, *The Man Who Fell to Earth*. It was to tie in with the film. A "David Bowie stars in" edition. They wanted me to contact him about permission for using his face on the cover. So I said I'd phone him up. They were surprised by that, as they weren't sure that I knew David that well. Anyway, he didn't pick up, so I left a message. I said into the machine, "I'm happy, hope you're happy, too. Give me a ring, when you get a chance." He did call back, and said "What's up?" He obviously stored that message away, in his head or in a notebook or something, and wrote it into the lyrics of "Ashes to Ashes". I'm the Action Man, apparently!

'I went through loads of stills to find the perfect shot for the book cover. I was very pleased with that painting, it was one of my first in oils. I was now a proper grown-up painter.

'When his album *Low* came out, I noticed that they'd gone back to find that very still. It was the same one exactly, they'd just turned it over so he was facing the other way, and given it a red background. Why they didn't just ask me to do it, I don't know. I'd done it already! The thing about David, he always liked to surround himself with whoever was current. The latest trendy person. He'd actually enthuse to me about these new designers he was planning to use, and I'd sit there thinking, What about me?! I never did make a lot of money out of my art. But there is liberation in it.'

When David arrived at the Blitz to cast his video for 'Ashes to Ashes', at the time the most expensive ever made, the Kids were beside themselves.

'If you look at Bowie's career, it's almost as if video was invented for him,' noted broadcaster and writer Robert Elms. 'There is no artist for whom that medium is more perfect.

'A few years after Ziggy and the first shock waves of Bowie, you had a whole scene in London . . . that moved on to this place called the Blitz. Steve Strange on the door, Rusty Egan playing electronic records, but always, always playing Bowie. None of those old-fart rock stars were allowed in the Blitz. Until the night that Bowie comes down. And believe me, I was there. These people, who really were the coolest people on earth, are *so* excited. And then you hear that he's actually looking for people to be in his video. And *everybody* in that room was basically auditioning to be in the Bowie video. I've never seen people preening and prancing and posing as fabulously as they did that night.'

Visage singer Steve Strange was chosen, along with Darla Jane Gilroy, Elise, and Judi Frankland.[5] Boy George was gutted that he was not.

Former Blitz Kid, fashion model, and Blue Rondo à la Turk co-lead singer-turned-artist Christos Tolera has somewhat less romantic memories:

'The making of that video was the death knell for the Blitz, and in my mind, for Bowie as an innovator,' he said. 'It was my first peek beneath the veneer of public perception, and its contrast with reality. Bowie was actually a pilferer and a follower. Stylistically finger on the pulse, but a follower nevertheless. I think that was the day we grew up and left Bowie behind. It was like leaving home.'

' "Ashes to Ashes" was whatever it was,' opines its director David Mallet, obscurely. 'A surreal dream, call it what you want. The video itself was the precursor of the modern Romantics and all that, and was a good way to incorporate this whole Blitz look into a video, which hadn't been done, and was completely new to the public.'

'Mallet's a great person for me to work with,' affirmed David. 'He's incredibly generous in allowing me to do whatever I want.'

Mallet insists that it was a genuine collaboration, '. . . because he knows exactly what he wants. "I want to be a clown, I want to be on the beach, and I want some modern Romantics with me." Then I say, Wouldn't it be great if the sky was black, then he'd say, "Yes, and we can have a burning brazier," and then I would say, Yes, and then we can do the scene from *Quatermass*[6] where you're plugged into a spaceship, and he would say, "Great, and I could hang like this," and I say, Yes, and we'll extend your veins out to the spaceship . . . From an initial concept of his, within an hour, we'd have something fleshed out. And then, thank you very much, Mr Bowie, you've got to work out how to do it. Which would be relatively easy now, but *then* wasn't so easy.'

The hard bit in 'Ashes to Ashes', Mallet explains, was getting the sky to go black without ruining everybody's faces.

'Because there was no such thing as post-production colours in those days. I discovered how to do that by accident.'

In summary, said Robert Elms, 'the New Romantics movement was kids who were actually fifteen, twenty years younger than Bowie. And yet, by bringing them into the video, Bowie manages to co-opt all of that. *He's* suddenly the New Romantic. *He's* the 1980s. He'd been Ziggy in the Seventies, and got it absolutely then. And through that video, he becomes Mr 1980s as well.'

The second single from the *Scary Monsters* album was 'Fashion' – which has been interpreted as everything from a National Front rally-call to a denunciation of the very New Romantic 'style fascists' whose blood David had supped. He explained to Andy Peebles that it was a reaction to the multitude of Ziggy clones who had stalked him since the early Seventies, sporting his haircut and wearing copycat outfits:

'Initially it was very morale-boosting,' he said. 'After a short while, it became quite scary . . . A lot of people who looked like me found out where I lived, and came and sat in my garden. I thought, Well, I've created the damned thing, I've caused this myself.'

David Mallet shot the video in Hurrah, a punk/new wave dance club on West 62nd Street, New York, one of the first clubs to screen music videos on small sets around the venue, at least a year before the birth of MTV. This was where New Order played their celebrated first post-Joy Division, post-Ian Curtis gig in September 1980. Languid, arrogant and bare-chested, David plays it cool in the sequence beside his motley crew of musicians, Carlos Alomar and Robert Fripp among them. The song has a sinister feel: clunky and industrial at the rear, hooky and melodic upfront, and woven through with that pestiferous 'beep beep'. The video features May Pang, John Lennon's former mistress. At David's invitation, Tony Visconti had spent a night in the company of Lennon and Pang in

1974. Visconti and she would marry years later, in 1989. 'Fashion' was released on Pang's thirtieth birthday, 24 October 1980.

That December, Andy Peebles flew to New York to interview John Lennon. A world exclusive and the rock coup of the decade, it would be John's first interview for ten years. Peebles, a star in his own right, was a recognised authority on the Beatles. So nervous was BBC controller Derek Chinnery that something would go wrong and that the team would return empty-handed – the interview was not even confirmed until the day before it took place – that he insisted on an 'insurance policy'. As Britain's public service broadcaster, the BBC was obliged to justify the expense. So Peebles arranged to interview Bowie as well, over the same weekend. The hook was *The Elephant Man*, a play in which David was starring on Broadway.

'I was quite the Bowie fan,' Andy tells me. 'I played most of his records on air when I was on Piccadilly Radio in Manchester, and I'd interviewed him in 1972. Eight years on, and now a superstar, he wasn't exactly dishing out interviews. But he was in the middle of a run at the Booth Theater, playing to sell-out audiences every night, so we had a very good reason to ask him to do it. For the BBC, David was happy to oblige. He got us front-row seats, middle-row, for his play on the Friday night, 5 December. And he guaranteed that he'd be at the RCA studios at three p.m. on the Sunday, to talk to us.'

Andy was stunned by David's portrayal of Joseph Carey Merrick, the monstrously deformed Leicester-born Victorian who was exploited as a freak-show attraction.[7] David had seen Phillip Anglim play Merrick in San Francisco, had succeeded him in the role, and had gone into rehearsals in July. He'd performed warm-ups in Denver and Chicago during the late summer, and had debuted at the Booth Theater, New York on 23 September, with a contract taking him through to 3 January 1981. If David had failed to forge a reputation as a major-league movie star, his command of the theatrical stage in such a demanding acting role more than compensated. The brutal Broadway critics were wowed.

'He was sensational,' affirms Peebles. 'This was David making it clear that he was so much more than just a pop star. Although I had the very odd feeling that, while we were enjoying avant-garde theatre, the majority of the audience were pop fans. They'd come to watch their great idol Bowie perform as a straight actor, and they would have got up screaming if they could have done so without being escorted off the premises. At the end, dozens of them, boys and girls, rushed to the front to pay homage. It was just like a gig.'

David admitted to Andy that his motivation for accepting the role was simply to 'see what it was like, doing a play. That commitment, that discipline.' He acknowledged that it had attracted Bowie fans over theatre fans, but seemed genuinely pleased that they had 'got' it:

'Up until the first night, the biggest worry was what the reaction would be,' he said. 'But we didn't give the fans enough credit. They were interested in the play, and I think the majority enjoyed it.'

He had certainly prepared well for the role, going so far as to visit the London Hospital Museum, where the plaster casts of parts of Merrick's body are kept – along with a little church he had made, and his cap and cloak.

David said that the role came naturally to him. He put it down to the mime-training of his past. He assured Peebles that he didn't have problems with his back despite the many contortions he was required to pull every night, but admitted that his hands got very stiff.

'I find I take a lot of the day on stage with me,' he confessed. 'I incorporate my daily feelings into the role. So if I've had a bad day . . . I keep hold of the idea of the stranger being put into a new environment. And I change the stage every night, in my mind. I play the character exactly as *I* want to do it.'

There were certain aspects to which he had to remain faithful, for the sake of authenticity:

'Merrick's right arm was longer, and the hips were at a particular angle,' he said. But he gave Merrick a London accent and put his own stamp on the role.'

In an interview about the play with lyricist Tim Rice, recorded for television at New York's Carlyle Hotel, David was blokey and jocular, and chain-smoked throughout.

'It's a classic piece of Victorian melodramatic writing, with a slight social subtext,' he said. 'It appealed to me strongly, I thought the structure was very good.

'I have an eclectic thing about freaks and isolationists and alienated people. I gather information on people like that . . . I've learned an awful lot. I hope that I can explore the part even further . . . now things are relaxing, I'd like to stretch out into it more.'

On Saturday night, 6 December, Andy and his production team spent more than three hours with John and Yoko at New York's Hit Factory studios. They emerged late that night, exhausted but exhilarated. For Andy, it was the highlight of a distinguished career. The interview's primary focus had been *Double Fantasy*, the Lennons' new album, with which the majority of critics were not in love. John said that he'd been inspired by David's *"Heroes"*, and 'wanted to make something as good as that'. The pupil leading the teacher: it was happening again. The session concluded in a celebratory dinner at Mr Chow's, the world-renowned Chinese restaurant, hosted by John, who ordered up a feast. The next day, Sunday 7 December, not fully recovered from the intensity of the night before, they made their way to meet Bowie.

'David arrived by himself,' recalls Andy. 'No Coco, no manager, no hangers-on. The first thing he said was, "Have you spoken to John?" Yeah, I said, last night. He gave us three hours and twenty minutes. David laughed. "Sadly, I won't be allotting you that length of time," he grinned. We had exactly an hour. He walked in at one minute to three, and we got down to it. At one minute to four, he got up, gathered his things, shook hands and left. It was all very business-like. I enjoyed him because he wouldn't let me get away with anything. It was a real give-and-take exchange, which is great for radio. Ask the shortest question, extract the longest answer. He said, provocatively, that he was considering leaving the West altogether:

'I'm not quite sure where to go next. The East beckons me – Japan – but I'm a bit worried that I'll get too Zen there, and my writing will dry up.'

'It was clear,' Andy says, 'that he saw this play as something of a sabbatical; take six months off and stand on a stage every night, contorting your body into impossibly painful positions and testing your physical and mental endurance. It's hard to focus on very much else when you are doing something as challenging as that. Intense concentration well outside one's comfort zone is a great way to clear the mind, and I had the impression that he really needed to do that. I was astounded at what he could do with his body. He was a chameleon, a butterfly. And compared to the women in my life, I have to say, he was more skilled than all of them at making himself up. His transformation was extraordinary.'

Andy's acclaimed 'Lennon Interviews' would be broadcast to millions on BBC Radio 1 in January 1981. He could never have imagined at the time he was recording them how they would be made all the more extraordinary by John's murder, two days after the sessions took place.

He and his team spent the following day Christmas shopping, before boarding their return Pan Am flight to Heathrow on the evening of 8 December. When they were halfway across the Atlantic, assassin Mark Chapman pulled the trigger and shot Lennon dead outside his Dakota building home. Only when the plane landed did the DJ receive the appalling news.

Andy was and remains profoundly affected by Lennon's murder. He recognises it as a turning point in the history of popular music. Bound by professional obligations, he kept silent for three and a half decades: about how the interview and John's death were the start of an unlikely friendship with Yoko Ono, and how his feelings of warmth and sympathy towards the Lennons turned gradually to disillusionment.

He now fears that John and Yoko – especially Yoko – manipulated him for commercial gain. He has reached troubling conclusions about Yoko's behaviour in the aftermath of the shooting. He says now that Yoko seemed much happier after John's death; that she paraded her new lover Sam Havadtoy around New York, dressed in John's old clothes; that she appeared to exploit John's memory and legacy; and, perhaps most troubling of all, that the interview was nothing but a sham promotional exercise.

'My blood ran cold when I thought about it,' said Andy. 'Was their "happy couple back together and making their marriage work" stance only for the microphone? Was it all only about the "product", ensuring that they got a hit record out of *Double Fantasy*? I felt sick. I feared I'd been had. This was the ultimate example of a rock star callously using the public for personal gain. And if I *was* duped, they were the finest actors on earth. The only saving grace was that the record was a gigantic hit.'

Perhaps the last thing Andy could have expected was that he and Yoko would become close friends, but he knew it wouldn't last. 'The minute she heard that I'd left the BBC to go elsewhere, the calls dried up. I never heard from her again.'

Yoko, meanwhile, maintained an especially close relationship with David. When Sean Lennon was despatched to boarding school in Switzerland, it was David who had him to stay and who cared for him during school breaks. He would also take them on holiday together. The sons of Lennon and Bowie forged a special bond.

Lennon's assassin had been to see David as the Elephant Man on Broadway. The playbill, with David's name circled in black ink, was later found among his possessions in his room at the Sheraton Hotel. Chapman had taken photographs of David as he exited the stage door. He also allegedly had a hit list, featuring among others the names of Marlon Brando, Elizabeth Taylor, Jackie Kennedy Onassis and David Bowie, underneath Lennon. Chapman had planned, he later said, to hang around for John to return to the Dakota building on West 72nd, where he would shoot him dead. If John failed to show, he was going to dash down Central Park West to the intersection with Broadway at the New York Coliseum, cab the remaining dozen or so blocks to West 45th at Times Square, apprehend David as he left the theatre, and kill him instead.[8]

The quotes that David is said to have given after John's murder are impossible to verify, and may well not be genuine. What we do know is that, shocked to the core by the loss of his dear friend John and also fearful for his own safety, he declined an extension to his *Elephant Man* run; that he left New York, retreated to Switzerland, and kept a low profile for the next two years. Under pressure was an understatement.

14
1981–1984

There are days we don't forget. The morning after Lennon's murder, staff congregated in shock in the lobby of Stratford Place, the Chrysalis Records' HQ off Oxford Street, waiting for George Martin to arrive. The so-called 'Fifth Beatle', the man who had inspired Tony Visconti to become a record producer in the first place, had a suite of offices on the ground floor there, from which he and John Burgess ran AIR Studios.

George had weathered with dignity endless vitriol from John throughout the Seventies. He belittled their producer's 'influence' and input, while Paul, George and Ringo were, George insisted, 'always sweet'. Implacably loyal, he was of course beside himself at the news of John's death, and cried with the rest of us as we stood huddled. Perhaps we'd hoped that George would take the lead. He had no words. After a while, he left for Montserrat,[1] where he had opened his dream residential recording studios the year before. When he came back, George said he'd sat staring at the ocean, listening to Lennon in his head.

There was no funeral. A week later, on 14 December, a global ten-minute silence was held in John's name. Millions of people formed a ring around the world. Thirty thousand in Liverpool, a quarter of a million in Central Park, every radio station in New York off-air for the duration. Compounding the fracture came the pointless suicides of fans unable to cope with the loss.

David called John 'my greatest mentor':

'I guess he defined, for me at any rate, how one could twist and turn the fabric of pop and imbue it with elements from other art forms, often producing something extremely beautiful, very powerful, and imbued with strangeness. Also, uninvited, John would wax on endlessly about any topic under the sun, and was over-endowed with opinions. I immediately felt empathy with that.'[2]

Just as George Martin had gone off to sit and stare at the sea, David did the same on Lac Léman, as Lake Geneva is known locally. He withdrew into his unloved cuckoo-clock house beneath the jagged Alps, which, Freddie Mercury was always saying, guarded lost treasure, stashed by Nazis during the War. David could take or leave the picturesque retreat that Mercury adored, but he based himself there for several more years. He couldn't think straight. He hadn't yet made up his mind where he wanted to live permanently.

He'd considered purchasing an elegant apartment on the Île Saint-Louis near Notre Dame, and had pondered the idea of a mansion in the Bois de Boulogne. He had also visited the eighteenth-century Moulin de la Tuilerie south of Versailles, the country retreat of the Duke and Duchess of Windsor. The Moulin was the primary residence of Edward and Mrs Simpson after the former King's abdication in 1936. The duke, known as David, had welcomed Elizabeth Taylor and Marlene Dietrich as guests, and had been famously sympathetic towards Adolf Hitler.

But Paris was impossible, now that David was mobbed there wherever he went. Hordes of fans would stake out hotels he wasn't even staying at, whenever they heard he was in town. Kyoto and Tokyo were magnets, but not a practical option while his son was still at school in Scotland. Europe it had to be for now. He'd had enough of London, and at least Montreux had history. Mary and Percy Shelley once spent holidays at the lake with Lord Byron, and wrote ghost stories there – one of which evolved into the novel

Frankenstein. Its chocolate-box beauty and tranquillity had attracted many celebrities down the years, including Audrey Hepburn, Noel Coward, Richard Burton, Peter Ustinov and Phil Collins.

As for rock'n'roll connections, the Stones kept a mobile studio there, parked up beside the casino on the edge of the lake, which was famed as much for drug-taking and debauchery as for anything recorded in it. Deep Purple put the town on the map when they made *Machine Head* there in 1971, one of the greatest rock albums of all time. Its track 'Smoke on the Water' was written after a fan misfired a flare at a Frank Zappa gig in the casino, and the place burned down. Watching fumes billowing out across the lake from his hotel room window, Roger Glover reached for his bass guitar. Multi-track Mountain Studios were created in the new complex. When Queen purchased the facility in 1978, a new era was born. Rockers formed a disorderly queue to record there.

'It had a magic, the place,' one high-profile rock manager told me. 'Almost any artist, of any genre, could get a sound there in the good old days that was almost spookily, brilliantly, a cut above everything they'd done before.'

Having recorded his album *Lodger* there the previous year, David acquiesced. There would be more Bowie-in-Montreux albums to come: *Never Let Me Down* in 1987, *Black Tie White Noise*, and *The Buddha of Suburbia* soundtrack, in 1993, and *1.Outside* in 1995. Yes, Rick Wakeman, AC/DC, Chris Rea, Iggy Pop and a host of others recorded at Mountain, as of course did Queen, who achieved their finest work there. In 1981, they convened in Montreux to begin their album *Hot Space*.

'I was living above Montreux at around the time Queen bought Mountain Studios,' says Rick Wakeman. 'Switzerland is a very staid country, but there was always an element of acceptance for what you were. The locals were thrilled that Queen owned the studios. Nobody gave a monkey's toss what you did behind closed doors. The press in Switzerland didn't give a toss either. So it was a great place for rock musicians to live and work.'

There was one pub on the main street called the White Horse, at Grand Rue 28, known to musicians as the Blanc GiGi. It is now sadly closed.

'It was the place where everybody working at Mountain Studios would congregate,' says Rick. 'If a couple of bands overlapped, or if Queen were in, the Blanc GiGi was where we'd end up. I'd hang out there mainly with Roger and Brian, but Freddie would often turn up. Invariably with a young French boy, but so what. He wasn't openly out, of course, but nobody said anything. Those were different times. Queen loved Montreux. To have their own studios made good business sense. Plus, they got to go and stay there whenever they wanted.'

Artists in those days were essentially bone-idle, he admits.

'You'd rock up at the studio costing thousands a day. One would be off skiing, one would be in bed pissed from the night before. Jon [Anderson] and I might turn up, write a bit of a song, toddle off down the pub, and then finally get down to it at about seven p.m. It was rare for anyone ever to do a full day's work. What should have taken five or six weeks was taking five or six months. The studios were making a fortune. You couldn't record like that now.'

David was Rick's neighbour.

'It was on one particular night when he wandered into the pub, had dinner with the Queen lads and then went back with them to the studio, that things kind of turned into history.'

Mountain Studios' engineer, the late David Richards, who was working with Rick and the rest of Yes, had assisted Tony Visconti on David's 1977 album *"Heroes"* in Berlin. Bowie was booked in at Mountain to record the track 'Cat People (Putting Out the Fire)', which he had written with producer Giorgio Moroder for the film *Cat People*.[3] When David wandered into the studio after leaving the pub, he found Queen mid-session.

'An extremely long night,' said Brian May.

'We were all drunk and in the studio, and we were, just for fun, playing all sorts of other people's songs, old songs, just jamming,' said Roger Taylor. 'It was whatever came into our heads.'

Freddie Mercury had recently seen David in *The Elephant Man* on Broadway, considered him 'a remarkable talent', and was up for it. In the end, David said, 'This is stupid, why don't we just write one of our own?'

What came out was a song they called 'People on Streets', which evolved more or less instantly into 'Under Pressure'.

Brian remembers the recording as 'very hard. You already had four precocious boys, and David, who was precocious enough for all of us. Passions ran very high . . . I got so little of my own way. But David had a real vision, and he took over the song lyrically.'

As David would later recall:

'The song was written from the ground up, on the night I visited their studio. I believe the riff had already been written by Freddie and the others, so then we jointly put together the different chord sections to make it a cohesive piece of music. Then Freddie and I came up with our individual top line melodies. So when you hear Freddie sing, that's what he wrote, and when you hear me sing, that was mine. Then we worked on the lyrics together. I still cannot believe that we had the whole thing written and recorded in one evening flat. Quite a feat for what is actually a fairly complicated song.'

Every member of Queen, and David, has subsequently given conflicting accounts of how the song happened. Time and alcohol notwithstanding, none of them could remember for sure. But they also had visitors that night. Capital Radio DJ Roger Scott and I were in town.[4] Roger was recording an interview with Rick Wakeman, who informed us that Queen were at Mountain. We, too, had supper in the White Horse, and wandered over towards the studio on our way back to the Montreux Palace hotel.

It was late. Outside, the night was tranquil, the air pine-scented. In the studio, they were smoking up a fug. Spirits were high, and the fun was infectious. Roger captured some chat with Brian, Freddie, Roger and David on his Uher, a weighty but portable reel-to-reel machine with a hand-held mic, that he carried everywhere with him in a shoulder bag. The recordings he made with the Uher were of broadcast quality. Roger and producer John Pidgeon would later include segments of these talks in Roger's coast-to-coast interview shows for Westwood One.[5] The session was as silly and as haphazard as they've all implied, collectively and individually. A kind of magic.

Two weeks after that drunken session, Freddie, Roger, Queen producer Reinhold Mack and David reconvened at New York's PowerStation studios, to remix the track. Brian May, still miffed, had backed out of the project, and did not attend. 'Under Pressure' turned out to be one of the most challenging recordings any of them would ever make. The mixing desk collapsed, David insisted on remaking the track from scratch, he didn't get his way, and everything came to a head. At one point, David refused to sanction release, but in the end gave in ... under pressure. He was glad when it was all over.

The October 1981 single, David's first released recording with another artist, reached Number Twenty-Nine in the US and became Queen's second UK Number One, David's third – after 'Space Oddity' and 'Ashes to Ashes'. The hit was not the only thing to celebrate. David was at last free of his contract with Defries, who would receive not a penny more of his 'new' income. He celebrated by off-loading the 'hideously twee' house that Angie had found for them, and got himself a new gaff: the majestic Château du Signal on the edge of the Sauvabelin forest, built in 1900 for a Russian prince. He had reasons to dance, and he wrote about them. The first thing he began, he said, under his fancy new roof, was a song to define an album destined to recast him – in a guise that people of all ages, creeds, tastes and persuasions could embrace.

Still starved of real recognition as a screen actor, David tested the water with Brecht for the BBC. He made *The Hunger* ('sexy and bloody!') with Susan Sarandon, and started a secret three-year affair with her. And he departed for Raratonga and New Zealand, to make his Oscar bid (he wished: 'It's the best piece of work I've done yet,' he said, hopefully), in *Merry Christmas, Mr Lawrence*. He gave it his best shot. It was still far from enough to bag a gold-plated doorstop.

Why didn't the cine-camera love David? It has long been pondered. Both the video and the photo lens adored him. He projected well, and effervesced with presentational and chameleonic talents, as evident in his many videos and countless live performances. It has been said that pre-digital film couldn't capture his luminescence, and that modern technology might have done him more favours. From as early as 1967, he'd longed to be a movie star, putting himself about in quirky, experimental pieces such as *The Image, The Pistol Shot* and *Pierrot in Turquoise*, and had his blink-and-you'll-miss-it moment in *The Virgin Soldiers*. But most of his feature films fell short.

Perhaps he should have been more amenable towards screen goddess Elizabeth Taylor, and taken her up on her 1974 offer of co-stardom in an update of 1940 picture *The Bluebird*. But David 'hated the script'. He missed a trick: basking in forty-two-year-old Hollywood veteran Liz's reflected limelight would have done the callow twenty-seven-year-old pop star no harm at all. The actress was single at the time, and on last-ditch heat. Terry O'Neill took some provocative shots of them together, which were snapped up by picture editors around the world. This somehow led to gossip in the rags that Bowie would play Sinatra in a biopic. Acerbic Ol' Blue Eyes was predictably 'underwhelmed' by 'the guy with one of each'. He was in no rush to be immortalised on celluloid by 'some faggot'.

His 1976 movie *The Man Who Fell to Earth*, which garnered some gush, was neither the 'cosmic mystery' nor the 'mind-stretching experience' it was whipped up to be. David is wooden, seems always conscious of the camera, and is too aware of himself and of the impression he's making. His movements are jerky, and his speech is stilted and unnatural. *Just a Gigolo* two years later, in which he was billed as 'one of the few true originals of our time' and in which he overacts *ad astra*, was a raving flop. Films like *The Hunger* (1983) and *Absolute Beginners* (1986) were comprehensively panned – although his title track for the latter was a winner. *Labyrinth*, in which he plays Jared the Goblin King, was quite a hit. But it wasn't really *him*. Yet in his cameo performances, in which he plays himself, he is magnetic, confident, commanding, chillingly sexy. You can't take your eyes off him.

As he always said, even the act was an act . . . in other words, Bowie was already a performance. He was David Jones pretending to be someone else. To layer another character on top of that was to over-egg the brulée and to become indigestible. Being the rock star, just himself, and not impersonating anyone else, was David at his most powerful. Up at the mic in 1981's *Christiane F.*, he is the personification of cool.

Just as writers often discover their true opinion on a subject only when they sit down and force themselves to write about it, David surprised himself constantly when he was performing. He found, time after time, that he could peel away layers of himself to reveal something entirely new, something he might have been unaware of. He was a bottomless pit of strange fascination. Still, the majority of movie critics – frustrated screenwriters, many of them – never really rated him. The more grudging among them may even have felt that he should stick to what he was good at, quell his greed, and settle for international rock superstardom. Some people are never satisfied.

There are snippets to cherish; some precious moments when film succeeds in recording a little of the real David. Eric Idle's 1983 comedy *Yellowbeard* features him in a literal walk-on that raises a titter. Julien Temple's 1984 short about *Screamin' Lord Byron*, an extended play of the video for the single 'Blue Jean', is gauche and a notch overworked, but nicely Michael Caine-esque. The knife fight with King of Rockabilly Carl Perkins in John Landis's 1985 comedy *Into the Night*, starring Michelle Pfeiffer and Jeff Goldblum, is a killer. I'm fond of his bartender in *The Linguine Incident* (1991), and of his Warhol in the 1996 biopic *Basquiat*. Most of his TV bites, not least *Arthur and the Invisibles* and *Sponge Bob Squarepants*, I can live without. Ricky Gervais's 2005 *Extras* featuring Bowie is worth a squint. But see for yourself. Everything's out there.

'I continue to read scripts and look at parts,' he told me in 1983. 'And I do the parts I consider to be worth doing. But I suppose the singing thing is a lot more under my control. That's what I've always done, and I'm not going to give it up.'

He was free of RCA, had a new recording contract with EMI America, and it was time to get back in the studio.

Tony Visconti was bewildered by what happened next. Bewildered, confused, and then downright angry. He had every right to be. One minute they were asking him to book out time, arrange his tickets and await scheduling instructions regarding the new album that David was about to start recording. The next, nothing. Zilch. Nada. *Why?* Yet again, David got Coco to do his dirty work. Tony received a brief, desultory call from the gatekeeper, informing him that David had 'met someone else', and that his services were no longer required. They would not work together again for the next twenty-two years.

Nile Rodgers was lying naked on a nudist beach, the first time he ever heard Bowie. He was on a retainer at a Miami Beach night-club, and hanging with the club's female staff photographer. The pair decided to spend a cheeky night together among the sand dunes, and the sexy snapper turned up with a tape of *Ziggy Stardust and the Spiders from Mars*. Nile had no idea who Bowie was – the music had unfathomably passed him by. Nevertheless, he found it instantly intoxicating.

When the Chic[6] co-founder and guitarist finally got to meet Ziggy's creator, it was on a bender in a bar some months later, with Billy Idol as the go-between. David was alone, and on the orange juice. Nile chatted him up. Within a week, they were collaborating, on the album that would become the biggest-selling of David's career.

They began their research, Nile would later recall, by playing dozens of records from across the genres, and quizzing each other about what the album 'should say'. Then one day, David pitched up with a photo of a scarlet-suited Little Richard climbing into a red Cadillac convertible, and told his new co-producer that this was what he wanted it to sound like.

'How do you translate that!' exclaimed Nile in an article for the *Guardian* in 2016. 'But in actual fact, I knew exactly what he meant, and that was the point I realised that David Bowie was the Picasso of rock'n'roll. He got uncomfortable with me calling him that, but I did it anyway. Because I realised he saw the world in an abstract way, as well as in the way we all see it. And what that picture meant was not that he wanted a retro record, or something based on Little Richard's music, but that he wanted something that would always look modern. He showed me the future and the past, and it was evergreen.'

Rodgers was an old hand at the hit-making process. David wanted some of Nile's funky magic in the mix.

'I thought about my songs, and how they all start with the hook, because in the black world we don't have many stations or chances to get a hit, you have to feed people dessert before the main course,' explained Nile. 'So I said, let's put the hooks at the beginning. Let's have the first words out of your mouth be "Let's Dance!" He fought it for a little while, and then he understood why. Years later, at an awards ceremony, he was presenting me a prize, and he said, "Ladies and gentlemen, I am honoured to give this to Nile Rodgers, the only man on earth who could get me to start a song with the chorus!" '

'Let's Dance' became the fourth of David's five Number Ones. The album also spawned singles 'Modern Love' and 'China Girl', the latter written by Iggy Pop.[7] David Mallet created the videos for 'Let's Dance' and 'China Girl', both of which, Bowie said, were his 'simple and direct' statements against racism and oppression.

'David hadn't been in the public eye for two or three years when we made the video for "Let's Dance",' recalls Mallet. 'He'd been writing and being a bit of a recluse. So it wasn't a comeback, but the first thing people had seen for quite a while. "Let's Dance" was a total change, musically, for Bowie, and a total change for all of us, making videos . . . because it was one of the earliest videos that was made on film. At the time, none of us had any idea that it would be that big a hit.'

'These videos were loaded with symbolism,' opined Robert Elms. 'The red shoes, for example, that appear in "Let's Dance": are they the red shows of Hollywood and the Yellow Brick Road, or are they the red shoes of the shiny new capitalism that is taking over everything? These are the kind of debates that you have with Bowie.'[8]

'It's something that somebody else had already created as a symbol, and it seemed apropos for this particular video,' explained David himself. 'They are the sinfulness of the capitalist society, a pair of luxury goods, red leather shoes, and also they are striding for success. In black music, it was always, "put on your red shoes, baby".'

As Robert Elms pointed out, David was not known, hitherto, for being an overtly political artist:

'He doesn't make political statements, *per se*. But I think he often puts hints – perhaps sort of quasi-political ideas, particularly in the videos. He very overtly makes a song called "China Girl", about a relationship with a Chinese girl. And I think he does that in this period an awful lot. He looks forwards, to a globalised corporate world . . . even if he doesn't quite know he's doing it.'

David Mallet still rolls his eyes at what he calls the 'dreadful hoo-hah' over 'China Girl', the original incarnation of which was considered offensively sexual, and came a cropper with the censors.

'Complete rubbish about nothing!' he scoffs. 'In fact, the version that everybody now sees is the expurgated version. There was a slightly more X-rated version. All it was, was that the scene [from the film *From Here to Eternity*]⁹ with Burt Lancaster and Deborah Kerr on the beach, redone, with the waves washing over them, and they're at it like snakes, and that's the point. We cleaned it up after the initial fuss. I wish I could find a copy of the uncleaned-up one, because it's actually rather beautiful.'

It was. David ignored the 'hoo-hah', picked up his naked co-star, Geeling Ng, and went off and had an affair with her.¹⁰

'There was always pressure to make something that MTV would play,' sighed Mallet. 'Plenty of people tried to do things that MTV *wouldn't* play. And indeed they didn't play them, and therefore the money got wasted. I think, when we made "Let's Dance" and "China Girl", the record labels had got much more involved in the making of music videos. But they didn't have much chance with us, because we were in Australia!'

The 1983 Serious Moonlight tour acquired its name from a line in the lyrics of 'Let's Dance': *... under the moonlight, the serious moonlight.*

The rationale? Well, some of it would be under moonlight, David explained, probably tongue-in-cheek, adding that he had written a 'desperate love song' which had that quality to it.

It would be bigger and better than anything he'd done before. The longest outing yet: on the road for the best part of a year; rehearsals in New York and Dallas, warm-ups in Belgium, Germany and France, a quick nip to California, back to London and Birmingham, wassailing across Europe, flipping back to the Milton Keynes Bowl, a jaunt to Canada and the US, and then on to Japan. By November they'd be playing Australia and New Zealand, and would hit Singapore and Thailand just before Christmas.

He couldn't extend it any more, he insisted, even though demand to take it even further was high, as he wanted to get back to writing in 1984. It was by far his most ambitious tour to date; reaching boldly into brand-new territories, a total of ninety-six shows in fifteen countries, playing to more than two and a half million people around the world. It was the most expensive, pared-down, in-your-face rock spectacular, and the pinnacle of his career. It was the tour that established Bowie's status as the greatest-ever solo rock artist.

Now a music writer working primarily for the *Daily Mail*, I was along for the ride. I was one of seventy-five international journalists invited to attend the Claridge's Hotel London press conference on 17 March 1983, at which David himself, fresh in from Australia, announced the tour. I interviewed him backstage at the Birmingham NEC (National Exhibition Centre) on 6 June, and I was present at his first New York concert in five years that July.

Even he had not been expecting such riotous acclaim, he said.

His largely misspent past was apparently behind him. At thirty-six, he looked like an athlete filming an ad for organic breakfast cereal. We could barely believe our eyes.

Nowadays, we call them 'extreme makeovers'. This was a whole new person. Gone was all the cowering behind garish and ghoulish alter egos, the skeletal, the peculiar, the bizarre. He was hardly recognisable. The snow-white tan had bronzed up fetchingly. You could even say he glowed. The hair was blond and perfectly styled, and he was dressed in bespoke baby-blue. What brought this on?

'I was tired of the idea of being a cult figure,' he said. 'I no longer wanted to be so icy and cold. I wanted to do something friendly, having more empathy with the audience. But I didn't even know if they'd bother to come. Then, having got them there, I didn't know whether we'd like each other any more. We did – we do! But in fact it's more than that – yes, it's a kind of love. The response from the audience is magic. Tours haven't been that popular of late, even for bands who are continually in the limelight. I certainly didn't expect this much limelight. I can't explain it, and I don't understand it. That wave of feeling – it's tremendous. Pretty tiring, but it's a joy to me. I've never performed like this before.'

And when David Thomas asked him, for *The Face* magazine, whether he'd had any idea during childhood of the fate that awaited him, he said this:

'I had every inkling. I knew from when I was about my son's age now [Joe was then eleven] what would be happening to me; that I was going to do something very important. I didn't quite know what. At the time I thought I was going to be a great painter, but that changed in my teens. I never told anybody . . . there was one other person in my class at school I thought was going to be more important than me. His name is George Underwood, and I think indeed he is more important, but he hasn't been recognised as such. But I really thought that it was my task to do something important and make a statement about something or other.'

Perhaps the guilt that he felt over George was weighing heavily on his mind.

Backstage at the NEC, hovering hungrily over the buffet, I had my first close-up with Corinne Schwab. While David was cucumber-cool and relaxed, Coco came on like a woman who had eaten too many egg sandwiches. Anxious. Ruffled. Holding it all in. While not exactly ravishing, I found her not unattractive. Looking in need of a good wash and a whole night's sleep, she kept shoving her pale, lank hair behind her ears, dragging the back of one hand across her forehead, disappearing and reappearing without obvious purpose. She didn't smile. She didn't say a thing.

'She's mild today,' murmured one of the band. 'She can be really tough at times. He just sits back and lets her do everything. And I mean, everything.'

The gossip was that David was sleeping with her. I didn't dare ask him if it was true. I guessed that it was, and of course, there were rumours.

As for his new music, he was contemplative:

'My material with this band is an interesting combination of R&B and a more modified European soul. At least that's what I am, vocally. I'm not a soul singer. I don't pretend to be. But I like this combination. There are influences from the past. "Let's Dance" has obvious roots in "Young Americans". I feel more at ease as a singer-songwriter now.

I'm closer to it in my own heart. It's not so detached. I'm more one-to-one with my audience, and with the new material. It's true to say that I've gone full circle. This is as near as one can get to me, I suppose. Singing in the front room, almost! Mentally reducing the audience to ten or fifteen people. Bringing it all nearer.'

He was thoroughly enjoying being 'just him', then.

'Exactly. I'm absolutely loving this tour. I'm not carting a character round the country any longer. I have the confidence to interpret myself as myself now. My real stuff is actually a lot more emotional than I thought it would be, which surprises me.'

When I asked him about his influence over other musicians, he flashed an old-fashioned look.

'I wonder if they *are* so influenced by what I've done. I mean, if you look at the whole electronic rock thing, it can't *all* be down to me. You have to credit bands like Roxy Music and Kraftwerk as well. But of course, I'm very flattered if people think that.'

On stage, he was elegant and laid-back. All the frenzy of yesteryear had evaporated. Sporting a pale, classy suit, an un-bowed bow tie hanging faux-carelessly at his collar, he could have been an Antony Price catwalk model. As he strode out to meet his fans, the audience erupted. It had been the longest wait for the loyal family, but more than worth it. If he no longer hit the high notes with all-out vigour, he was paying the right backing singers to fill the gaps. His performance was high-camp-macho theatrical, yet somehow natural. The paradox was him all over.

He larked with his audience when introducing his band: 'And on trombone . . .' (*wild applause*) '. . . we haven't got a trombone!' Earl Slick and Carlos Alomar cracking up behind him. Then, as he took up his guitar to resurrect Major Tom: 'How about "Ride a White Swan"?!' A moment for lost, lamented Bolan. Six years on, he didn't mind admitting, David still thought about Marc every day.

On 30 June 1983 he was back at Hammersmith Odeon, almost ten years to the day since he'd retired Ziggy and the Spiders, for a charity event in aid of the Brixton Neighbourhood Community Association. And in Toronto on 4 September, David welcomed a VIP to the stage. Seizing Earl Slick's guitar to join the main man in 'The Jean Genie', ladies and gentlemen, Mr Mick Ronson.

On every tour, a *pièce de résistance*. Not Grade II-listed 'Hammy-O'. Not Ronno, this time, though how exquisite. Not Madison Square Garden, 25 July, although that was a trip and a half. Polished, controlled but still shaking a leg, blue-draped David utterly owned the place. But the moment to treasure forever came at the Hong Kong Coliseum in Hung Hom, the last night of the tour. The 8 December show happened to coincide with the third anniversary of John Lennon's death. David and Earl Slick had decided to perform 'Across the Universe' in homage. But then David thought, what the hell. 'If we're going to do it at all, we should really do "Imagine".' They rehearsed the song in Bangkok, and performed it in Kowloon.

Above them, only sky.

15
1984–1985

There persists an impression that it was all downhill for Bowie from then on. His classic hits, the songs we all know and love, were well behind him. There would be a handful more albums, three of which would make Number One: *Black Tie White Noise* (1993), *The Next Day* (2013) and David's parting gift, *Blackstar* (2016); a video jig with Jagger, and their chart-topping hit, 'Dancing in the Street'; a moment at Live Aid; another best-forgotten film, *Absolute Beginners*; two further excursions: the Glass Spider tour, something of a bafflement, and the fond farewell, A Reality Tour, cut short by a medical emergency. After that, a whole decade of not much at all. But it wasn't quite like that. The final thirty years were in many ways the most creative and most personally fulfilling of David's life.

Tonight may have been a UK Number One hit album, coming as it did on the heels of such a successful tour. But it didn't review well. It was never clear who liked it the least, the rock critics or David himself. He would later remark that he could 'kick himself' for the LP on which he played no instruments at all for a change, and on which there was considerable input by Iggy Pop.

Widely damned as a lazy attempt at retaining the new audience he'd attracted with the *Let's Dance* album and Serious Moonlight tour, it produced three singles. 'Tonight' featured vocals by Tina Turner, and aligned the passionate pair for a sizzling dalliance.

Tina, a Zurich resident, was virtually a neighbour, after all. At thirty-seven to his date's forty-five, David was yet again indulging his penchant for the older woman and the duskier maiden. 'Blue Jean', released ahead of the album, was inspired, David said, by American self-taught blues guitarist Eddie Cochran, who died in a car crash in Wiltshire during his first and only UK tour, aged just twenty-one.[1]

'Loving the Alien' was the showpiece. David had demoed it in Montreux, recorded it with the rest of the album under the stewardship of Hugh Padgham[2] in Quebec, and released it in May 1985. The song arose out of negative feelings about organised religion generated by conspiracy-theory literature he'd read, but didn't fully understand. David had always been a sucker for a bit of scandal and propaganda. He'd become sold on the theory that much theological teaching, tradition and culture could have been misconstrued, as the result of the inaccurate translation of Christian, Islamic and Jewish scriptures.

While it is always right to challenge, he was waylaid by sensationalist views. He didn't know enough about Christian doctrine to form sustainable opinions, but wrote about it anyway, all the while wearing the cross and chain that his father had given him. He dismissed it as a 'good luck charm'. He was not devout, describing himself as 'C of E' rather than 'Christian'. That is to say, his religious status was for form-filling purposes only. Non-theistic for most of his life, he would turn back to Buddhist ritual in extremis.

' "Alien" came about because of my feeling that so much history is wrong – as is being discovered all the time – and that we base so much on the wrong knowledge that we've gleaned,' he said. It was just one of many hazy statements made in a string of strange and inconclusive interviews, which as usual were received on bended knee. Hype reported, specifics unquestioned. Same old, same old.

Live Aid was the world's first 'global jukebox', a concert staged in two vast venues in London and Philadelphia on 13 July 1985.

Between four hundred million and 1.9 billion viewers (depending on where you read it) across a hundred and fifty nations tuned in, to witness more than seventy acts perform live to feed the world. Horrified by television news bulletins highlighting the plight of Ethiopians in an unprecedented famine, Boomtown Rat Bob Geldof and Ultravox frontman Midge Ure conceived a fund-raising single, 'Do They Know It's Christmas', in December 1984. It was recorded by a stellar line-up including the Durans, the Spands, Boy George, Paul Weller, George Michael, Status Quo and Phil Collins. Bowie and McCartney, who were otherwise committed, made their contributions remotely, which were dubbed on later. Sir Peter Blake, who had created the iconic artwork for the Beatles' *Sgt Pepper's Lonely Hearts Club Band* album cover, designed the sleeve. Band Aid was born, its name a pun on a common brand of sticking plaster. This would be a 'band' that would 'aid' the world. The single became the UK's fastest-selling single since the chart's inception in 1952. It sold more than three and a half million copies.

America responded with the supergroup USA for Africa, and Michael Jackson and Lionel Richie co-wrote 'We Are the World'. It trumped our effort by seventeen million copies, America's fastest-selling pop single ever. There was more to this, as Geldof twigged. He ran with the ball, announcing his ambitious intention to stage the greatest rock extravaganza of all time. Without so much as a fax machine, let alone a computer or a mobile phone, none of which yet existed, Bob and promoter Harvey Goldsmith mounted a miracle. Where governments around the world had failed to act, the rock and pop community took the lead. The result was extraordinary.

Needless to say, Her Britannic Majesty's press corps and the international media community were out in force. I'd stayed with the Who's John Entwistle and his girlfriend Maxene Harlow in Roehampton the night before, and had arrived at Wembley in their Harrods-green Rolls-Royce convertible. In the boot, with the dog, a giant Irish wolfhound called Fits Perfectly. There are times when it is better to arrive.

PR Bernard Doherty masterminded publicity for the event, taking care of all the media on the day.

'We knew we had to keep the press sweet, to ensure maximum coverage,' he said, in an interview for my book *Freddie Mercury: The Definitive Biography*. 'I had only eight triple-A laminate passes, but hundreds of press. We had to share them around. One by one I said to everyone, Right, you've got forty-five minutes in there, get what you can, get back out. See you in the Hard Rock Café, of which there was a branch backstage.'

Backstage was a wagon-train-style scenario, with all the artists' Portakabins pointing inwards, and Elton John cooking up a barbecue in the thick of it all because he didn't fancy the offerings of the Hard Rock.

'David Bailey set his photo studio up in a stinky little corner, he wasn't proud,' remembers Doherty. 'Nobody's conditions were ideal. It was all thrown together on the fly. But somehow it happened. Everyone got into the spirit of the thing, most people left their egos at home, and it worked.'

At the time, Doherty had David Bowie as a client, and was looking out for his needs, too.

'Always a little nerve-wracking when you are doing two jobs at once. In my case, that day, about eighteen jobs. There wasn't much love lost between David and Elton – they'd obviously fallen out. David came out of his performance OK. He was genuinely pleased to see Freddie Mercury. They really were delighted to be together again. They stood chatting as if they'd only seen each other yesterday. The affection between them was tangible. David was wearing an amazing blue suit, and looked incredibly sharp and healthy. Just before he went on, Freddie winked at him and said, "If I didn't know you better, dear, I'd have to eat you." No wonder David went out on stage with such a big smile on his face.'

While Queen are generally reckoned to have stolen the show on the night, in a quintessential performance that reignited their career, David's set remains the most memorable.

The original plan had been to sing a duet with his one-time bedfellow and long-time adversary, Mick Jagger.

'We were going to do a live satellite thing, where Mick would sing in New York [he may have meant Philadelphia] and I would sing in England,' David explained. Then we found out that the half-second time-delay thing really screwed it up. There was no way that we could technically overcome that, so that we could both sing together. There was no way around it. So we decided to do a video together instead.'

The song they chose to cover was Martha and the Vandellas' 'Dancing in the Street'. Re-enter David Mallet, who would shoot the video in London's Docklands.

'They'd turned up in a studio in the afternoon, and recorded the song, so none of us had ever heard it until they rocked up,' remembers Mallet. 'They just gave me the tape and we literally made something up as we went along. I think the entire British film industry was there. We had about nine feature-film crews. Everybody turned up for nothing to do it, for a bit of a laugh.

'Jagger and Bowie worked well off each other and with each other. It was like two members of the same band. Everybody chucked ideas in. There's one scene with people coming out of a door and someone popping up from under the camera, which was conceived by Bowie, of course. Another bit, which was Jagger, was when he was walking up the empty street, doing rather good choreography, I thought. It was all joined together with bits shot in sheer desperation. Before the dawn!'

Broadcaster Robert Elms described the video as 'Bowie and his old sparring partner, these two kids from Swinging London. It's as close as you'll get to a completely off-the-cuff, unguarded Bowie.'

'We finished filming at about five a.m.,' says Mallet. 'In fact, the very last shot you can see has some cars in the distance, with their headlights on. And that was because it was actually getting lighter. To give the impression that it was still dark, I had to get all these cars facing us with their headlights on, full-beam. I think the video worked as much because they made such a good record as anything else.'

BBC Radio 1 DJ Andy Peebles, one of the comperes at Live Aid, had the privilege of introducing David on the day.

'The whole day was extraordinary. Up at six a.m., BBC car to Wembley, get briefed on our tasks and schedule only once we'd arrived. I remember there had been quite a debate as to who would be involved and who would do what. I worked a lot with Jeff Griffin, who produced the radio side of Live Aid (Michael Appleton took charge of the TV broadcast). Only when I arrived did I discover it had been decided that the two on-stage announcers would be Tommy Vance and me. There were other famous names lined up to host proceedings, such as Noel Edmonds, Paul Gambaccini, Mel Smith and Griff Rhys Jones, and Billy Connolly.

'Tommy Vance and I sat like two schoolboys on high stools on the stage, just behind the curtain. We had a microphone each, on booms, and the running order. We went down the list, deciding who each of us would like to introduce. I said, would it be all right if I introduced David Bowie? Tommy said, "Of course, can I do Queen?" David came up to us just before he went on at 7.22 p.m., and said hello. I then introduced him live, and off they went. His image on the day was perfect. He was into his booted-and-suited rock superstar look, and it suited him well. And his performance, of course, was terrific.'

He leapt on and off stage in the pale blue suit designed by Freddie Burretti for the Diamond Dogs tour in 1974, which still fitted him perfectly. Shoulder-padded, cropped jacket, wide pants teamed with crisp white shirt and tie: David was every inch the rock star. Floppy-haired, sneering and suave, he barely broke a sweat. He had the power, and was mesmerising. Tessa Niles witnessed it at point-blank range. She was one of David's two backing singers.

'I was on holiday at my parents-in-law's house in Spain when I got the call,' Tessa remembers.

'I was a huge Bowie fan. Well, not so much of the music. I came in at the 'Fame' / 'Golden Years' stage. It was more his iconic image and status that I fell for, which I think was the case for a lot of people my age: twenty-four, while he was then getting on for forty. I'd never sung any of his songs before.'

She had sung just about everybody else's. A professional backing vocalist since the age of eighteen, Tessa had been in big demand for years by Clapton, the Stones, Police, Tina Turner, McCartney, Quo, Dusty Springfield and dozens of others, on hundreds of albums, singles and live tours.

'I was sent the lyrics by post – no email back then! It was a selection of a few of his songs, as they weren't sure which ones they were going to do yet. In the end, it boiled down to "TVC15", "Rebel Rebel", "Modern Love" and ' "Heroes" '. It was straight into rehearsals at NOMIS Studios in Shepherd's Bush, as there was hardly any time. This was literally the week preceding the show. Thomas Dolby[3] was the bandleader, and he rehearsed us all. When everybody was up to scratch, in came David.

'I remember clearly that first time he walked in. I'd worked with a lot of globally famous artists, and I wasn't usually fazed by celebrity. But David Bowie was different. I had told myself to be cool, and not to go to pieces. But, of course, he was devastatingly handsome. He had the light tan and the swagger – which he wore comfortably, it was not the frantic, look-at-me Jagger swagger. He was gracious, relaxed and very charming. So engaging. But when he looked at you: Oh, my God! I had not been expecting the eyes to have such an effect. It felt as though he was looking right into my soul. I was young, trying to maintain some decorum – I was very aware of my professional reputation, and conscious of the fact that I had to preserve that at all costs – but it wasn't working!'

Beautiful blonde Tessa was also under the eagle eye of Coco Schwab.

'Oh yes, she was there. She was always there. At every single rehearsal. She was *very* intimidating and controlling. It seemed sometimes that David didn't dare move, for fear of what she might say. All rock managers are bullies, of course. They have to be. It's always down to them to steam in and do the unpleasant stuff. But what struck me about Coco was that she seemed to really enjoy that aspect of the job. That was what unnerved me about her. When I think about it, it still does.'

David took time to talk to every member of his band, one to one.

'He listened to each of us individually, and he told me he liked my vocals very much. He had the miraculous ability to put everyone at ease, and to make us all feel extraordinarily special.'

But the longest conversation Tessa had with him was not about music. It concerned what they were going to wear on the day.

'He sat down with Helena Springs (the other backing vocalist) and me, and he was almost girlfriend-y about it! It was intimate and natural, but so surprising, when I look back. We told him what we were thinking of wearing, and he approved. I chose a diaphanous blue shirt, leggings and black heels, and teamed it with just the one glove, in homage to Michael Jackson.'

On the day, the band members rendezvous'd at Battersea heliport.

'We flew in over Wembley and landed in an adjacent field. Until that moment, we'd had no idea how big this was going to be. Even so, there would be no sound check. Everyone was just winging it, and taking things as they came. I feared the sound would be dreadful, but in fact it was brilliant. As we walked from our Portakabin up to the side of the stage, David turned to us, smiled, and said, "*Go* for it, everybody!" He wanted us to feel as fantastic as he did.

'And he smashed it. He empowered us all to give a great show. Because, of course, that would make *him* look good. I was under no illusions. I shared a mic with him at one point, in front of about a third of humanity. I knew exactly what he was about. I was slightly jealous when he danced with Helena on stage instead of me. Black girls have a very easy way about them, and Helena was very sassy, a bit pushy, determined to make it in her own right. I was just a little white girl from Essex. And he *was* rather drawn to ladies of colour, as we all know!'

Before taking to the intro of ' "Heroes" ', David dedicated the song 'to my son, to all our children, and to all the children of the world'.

'When he introduced us to the audience at the end of his set, he got my name wrong and called me "Theresa",' Tessa laughs. She shrugged it off. 'During the grand finale, when everyone was on stage together, Helena was right up front, grabbing the mic off Bono for "Feed the World". I was quite happy four rows back, next to McCartney.'

There were after-show parties all over town, that night. Many of us wound up at Legend's on Bond Street in the early hours. Not Tessa. She packed her bags and made her way straight home.

'I never saw David again. Nor did I ever hear from him. A personal message would have been lovely. It never came. But I was much more aware of Bowie after Live Aid. He intellectualised music. He had empathy, he had class. He personally made the day an unforgettable experience.'

Live Aid was David's first performance since the end of the Serious Moonlight tour in Hong Kong, more than eighteen months earlier. *Rolling Stone* would later call it 'his last triumph of the 1980s'. As it happened, they were not far wrong. Meanwhile, he could fly over mountains. He could laugh at the ocean. But he could never stop thinking about Terry.

16
1986–1987

David wasn't the only one who'd been neglecting his half-brother. When their mother Peggy saw her elder son at Cane Hill on Bonfire Night 1984, Terry's forty-seventh birthday, it was her first visit to the asylum for more than seven months. She told him that David was in the process of buying her a new flat. Terry must have wondered why his rich, world-famous brother wasn't helping *him*. A private psychiatric hospital would have made all the difference, and David could easily have afforded it. The Cane Hill environment would have filled anyone with despair – which is probably why they all stayed away, every bit as afraid of their own mental frailty as they were of Terry's.

The last family member to see him alive was his Aunt Pat, his mother's younger sister, ten days or so before Christmas – a challenging enough time for mentally stable people, many of whom torment themselves with unrealistic expectations, extreme self-reflection, and regrets about the past at that time of year, more so than any other. For someone as psychologically damaged as Terry, with a failed marriage behind him, and no family member willing to support him, the despair would have been unbearable. The day after Boxing Day, he walked out of Cane Hill, made his way to Coulsdon South railway station and jumped down onto the track.

He must have lost his nerve when he heard a train approaching, somehow managing to shrink within the rails. The train didn't hit him. He was found shortly afterwards by British Rail workers and was returned to Cane Hill, where they discarded the key. It wasn't his first suicide attempt. Terry had hurled himself through a window in 1982. It seems likely that there would have been other, unrecorded incidents. A week after his long-absent younger brother David's thirty-eighth birthday, on 16 January 1985, Terry escaped. He went back to Coulsdon South, got down in front of the oncoming Littlehampton to London express train, and was killed. At his funeral, the only family members were mother Peggy and Auntie Pat, who didn't exchange a word. No David. His pink-and-yellow floral tribute to the elder brother he had hero-worshipped as a child bore a card with an obscure and perplexing message:

'You've seen more things than we could imagine, but all these moments will be lost, like tears washed away by the rain. God bless you. David.'

In fact, David had purloined and paraphrased a line of dialogue from the movie *Blade Runner*,[1] 'I've seen things you people wouldn't believe . . . all those moments will be lost in time, like tears in rain.'

David clearly warmed to the 'tears in rain' theme. He deployed it again, in the lyrics of 'Girls', a song he wrote for Tina Turner, who recorded it for her 1986 album *Break Every Rule*:

My heart, suspended in time
Like you, vanish like tears in the rain.

He also recorded the song himself, during the sessions for his *Never Let Me Down* album: two versions, one in English, the other in Japanese. Both appeared as B-sides of the 'Time Will Crawl' single in 1987. Waste not, want not.

The tabloids were unforgiving, their fire fuelled by the tongue-lashings of Auntie Pat. David was vilified, and accused of neglect. He refrained from defending himself, and kept schtum. Not for eight more years would he address his brother's suicide publicly. He did so eventually in a song, 'Jump They Say', on his album

Black Tie White Noise, which was released as a single in March 1993.

'I invented this hero-worship to discharge my guilt and failure, and to set myself free of my own hang-ups,' he tried to explain. He also implied that he'd never really known his half-brother:

'I think I unconsciously exaggerated his importance,' he said – compounding the fracture.

It was David himself who was now the lost child. 'Jump' was his last ever British Top Ten hit.

The more he tried to distance himself from his brother's suicide, the more David was confronted by the fragility and ultimate futility of life. He took stock. He had restored his health, with Coco's help. He was chain-smoking, but could 'quit any time he wanted'. He was still using cocaine, but 'recreationally'. He was drinking heavily, but 'only socially'. He had forged a solid and mutually supportive relationship with his son, spending as much time with Duncan as possible. He was in command professionally, his focus the kind of music he truly wanted to make, as opposed to product against the clock of contractual obligations. He was a global celebrity who could have anyone he wanted, and did. But only for the obvious.

It wasn't that he lacked companionship: Coco was hardly ever further than the next room. He even talked about marrying her, at one point – she'd sure put her ten thousand hours in. He must have gone off the idea. He never said. He was rarely alone, but he was niggled by loneliness. He spent time with his old school-friend George Underwood; observed him playing happy families with his beautiful Danish wife Birgit and their children, and wanted some of that. He longed for a proper home life, a woman to wake up to, and a future.

'I saw a bit more of him in 1986,' says George. 'Yeah, he was a superstar by then, but he was always the same person with me. The thing about David, he can change, whenever he wants to [the first-person tense again]. It's a nifty skill to have. I'd be with him sometimes, going into a club or something, and he'd slip on a mask, if you like, when he didn't want to be talked to. He would become very aloof, and that really wasn't him. He was acting it. Putting it on. So he didn't have to communicate with anyone. That's when I realised that the fame thing is a double-edged sword. You can get a good table in a restaurant and all that, but you have paparazzi sharing your life night and day. That's how it was for David during the Eighties. I couldn't have stood it myself.'

He started craving the things not even his money could buy. Meanwhile, his would-be singer ex-wife Angie was practically destitute.

When I went round to see her at her rented terraced house in London's Battersea on 2 March 1986, her phone had just been cut off because she couldn't pay the bill. She had painted some of her wallpaper black, to give the place an artsy feel, but nothing could disguise the shabbiness of her furniture. The only clue that the occupant had once commanded international attention were framed photographs depicting a platinum-haired female on stage. For a decade, she had lived in thousand-pounds-a-night hotels, flown first class, and cavorted with A-listers. Now, she was facing bankruptcy. She had already spent half her divorce settlement, in less than six years. While David was skiing in Gstaad, Angie was slumming it, and fretting about her creditors.

'I have several cash-flow problems at the moment,' she admitted to me, during an interview that was published in the *Daily Mail* in March 1986. 'I am financially embarrassed. I am doing my best to sort out all these debts. I've always believed in my own talent, but setting myself up as a singer cost much more than I thought. People ask me, "Won't David help you out?" You must be kidding. It wouldn't occur to him, and I certainly wouldn't ask him. I am not really bitter, but I do have every right to be. I haven't seen David in seven years, and nor do I want to. I don't miss him at all. The person I do miss is our son. He is fifteen now, and at Gordonstoun. Sadly, he now returns my letters unopened. He's made it clear he thinks it best we don't meet.'

Meanwhile, David was pressing flesh with Haves and Have Yachts. She was called 'Deneb' when he took possession of her, remembers George. A one hundred and twenty-five-foot luxury motor yacht, built in 1977 in Viareggio, Northern Tuscany, by boat-makers Benetti, one of the oldest luxury yacht makers in the world. Gleaming white and exquisitely appointed, she had five suites for ten guests and accommodated a crew of seven.[2]

'We went down to the south of France to meet him for the christening of the boat,' says George.

It was an unusual name, but oh-so-David. Deneb is the brightest star in the constellation Cygnus, one of the vertices of the summer Triangle, and forms the 'head' of the Northern Cross. It is also the nineteenth brightest star in the night sky, a blue-white supergiant brighter than the sun.[3]

'What's in a name,' laughs George. 'Anyway, it was a very big yacht, and we were staying on it. On one of the days we were down there, he was having some people over for lunch. The staff had done this great big buffet. The guests all started arriving, and they were all superstars except us. There was Robin Williams, with a Russian girlfriend. Eric Idle. Steve Martin. Michael Caine – he actually did say to me, "Allo, my name is Michael Caine" when he came aboard. So I was there videoing all of this. My daughter was doing some water-skiing around the boat, and I was filming her. I just happened to swing the camera around a bit. Robin Williams clocked what I was doing, and played to it. He took over the show.

'It was quite a performance, and I had all that on film. At the end of the day, once everyone had left, David asked me to give it to him. He confiscated it! When *Dirty Rotten Scoundrels* came out, which was the film Michael Caine and Steve Martin were making on the Riviera, we had such a laugh about it.'

Just before Christmas 1986, the Jaggers invited David, Duncan and Coco to spend the holidays with them on Mustique.

Born of an eccentric young aristocrat's dream and a wistful

princess's taste for fantasy, Mustique – whose name derives from the Creole word for mosquito – sits south of St Lucia, about a hundred miles west of Barbados. Part of the chain of some six hundred islands known as St Vincent and the Grenadines, the island is just one and a half miles wide by three miles long. It was colonised by European plantocracy during the eighteenth century, who commandeered it to grow sugar cane. All that remains of its original seven plantations are a mill and 'Cotton House', which in 1969 opened its doors as a twenty-room colonial-style hotel.

When the eccentric young aristocrat in question, twenty-eight-year-old Colin Tennant, 3rd Baron Glenconner, came across it in 1958, he was immediately struck by the island's potential as a winter retreat for his chums. He purchased the island for less than £35,000, renovated its infrastructure, created a new village for the existing inhabitants, planted coconut palms, fruit trees and vegetables, developed its fisheries, and paused to ponder how to put the place on the map while preserving it as an exclusive jet-set haunt. His Eureka moment arrived with the royal yacht *Britannia* in May 1960, with a pair of high-profile honeymooners on board.

It was HRH Princess Margaret's[4] second sojourn in the Caribbean. She had first visited British colonies there in an official capacity in 1955. As a glamorous symbol of post-war Britain, so great was Margaret's popularity that her tour created a sensation throughout the West Indies. Margaret was treated like the Queen. Little wonder that the beautiful twenty-nine-year-old found the region irresistible, with unspoiled islands, islets, reefs, cays and calypsos being dedicated to her. She chose it for her honeymoon after marrying society photographer Antony Armstrong-Jones in London.

Waiting on Mustique with the wedding present to eclipse all others was her bosom pal Colin Tennant, whose wife, the suggestively named Lady Anne Coke, was one of Margaret's ladies-in-waiting. Tennant's forward-thinking gift was a ten-acre parcel of land upon which the princess might do whatever she pleased. He knew that she would build a palace in paradise, and that the rich and famous would follow. Within the walls of Les Jolies Eaux, the house designed by an uncle of her husband Lord Snowdon, Margaret threw house parties of such eye-popping excess (allegedly once discussing Uganda with Mick Jagger) that Her Majesty was scandalised.

The world's press were enthralled. The coverage drew more celebrities to the island, in search of their own exclusive holiday homes. Mustique's rolling hills and bleached beaches captivated the beautiful people and made it the ultimate destination during the Sixties and Seventies. The home-owners were an eclectic mix of tycoons, creatives and aristocrats, who would welcome each other to wild dinner parties at their English Country and Caribbean gingerbread-house homes.

Jagger had built his own house there, on Macaroni Beach. As Mick had one, David had better get one, too.

'I got stranded one day when the boat due to pick me up lost its propeller,' he later said, explaining how he came to build a house there. 'I wandered off, poked around, and came across a bit of free land. I talked to the owner, and I thought, why not? Then there was the question of what to do with it. I wanted something as unlike the Caribbean as possible, because it's a *fantasy* island. It had to be impressive. Because on Mustique, all the rich people get together and see the same people they see all the year round, but in a holiday setting. It's a tropical version of Gatsby's East Egg, where everyone goes to be rich together. How crazy is that!'

Surrounded by a proliferation of architectural styles, he was spoilt for choice. French château or plantation manor house? Replica Taj Mahal, Oriental temple with ornamental gardens, or your basic Georgian mansion? He didn't fancy any of those. But rock theatre it had to be, come what may. He would have, 'in a vaguely Indonesian style, a potpourri of all the islands of Indonesia, running the whole gamut, the ring of fire'. In the end, with the help of Swedish architect Arne Hasselqvist and New York designer Robert J. Litwiller, he plumped for a clutch of Balinese pavilions on the hill above Britannia Bay, with *trompe-l'oeil* swimming pools and Japanese koi carp ponds.

The property took five years and fourteen containers of cargo to complete. There was a hexagonal Javanese dining room made of coconut palm trunks – of course it was – its chairs copied from those used at Raffles colonial hotel in Singapore. The master bedroom suite and its wide veranda – David's own, and in which I slept when I stayed there – had a beautiful set of Egyptian Revival furniture and antique lacquered rattan flooring, and looked out over the ocean to the west and south-west, and across to St Vincent and Bequia to the north and north-west. Even the mosquito nets were silk-screened with palm fronds.

'I think Mustique is Duchampian,' David told *Architectural Digest*. 'It will always provide an endless source of delight. The house is such a tranquil place that I have absolutely no motivation to write a thing when I'm there.' He would spend five or six weeks there over Christmas and New Year, and return sometimes in June or July, for a top-up. He would invite the smallest group of close friends to accompany him.

'I throw one big party a year,' he said. In 1992, when the theme for his New Year's bash was the Seventies, 'I put on a disco, and Iman brought down a mirrored ball with her, an electric one. We had dinner for fifty but then invited people in for dancing afterwards. They all go down to Basil's [the rickety bar on the beach, run by Vincentian Basil Charles, the 'King of Mustique'] when they've had enough. I'm up on the hill, which keeps me away from the odd tourist boat.

'My ambition is to make music so incredibly uncompromised that I will have absolutely no audience left whatsoever, and then I'll be able to spend the entire year on the island.'

'Once it was finished, we went down there for New Year,' says George. 'It was the New Year's tradition that everyone would gather on Macaroni Beach at dawn to greet the rising sun. I remember on New Year's Eve, quite early on in the evening, David was desperately trying to find Mick Jagger. We went round looking for him together, in every haunt we could think of. Which on Mustique, didn't amount to many; Basil's on the beach, the bar at the Cotton House hotel, three or four friends' houses. No luck. David said, "He must be at home, then." So we went round to Mick's.

'There he was with Jerry, watching *Lawrence of Arabia*. "Are we interrupting?" we said. "No!" Mick said, "Come in and have a drink." David sat there drawling back at Jerry in her Texan accent, which would have been funny, had he been a bit less drunk. I had to apologise to Mick that David was so out of it. Mick had said to me, "'Ere, your mate's a bit leery tonight, innee? Let's leave 'em to it. Fancy a game of pool?" I'm not very good, I said to him. "Neither am I," he laughed. I thought he must be bluffing; all those years on the road, on tour, with far too much time on his hands. Surely he must have learned to play a decent game of pool by now. But he was right. He really *was* rubbish!

'David was with Melissa, that Christmas and New Year,' George says, referring to actress and dancer Melissa Hurley, twenty years David's junior, whom he'd met during his Glass Spider tour.

'He told me he was going to marry her. He had it all planned out. The specific church in Italy, everything. But in the end, she told him she couldn't go through with it. *She* chucked David. It's been written everywhere that he ended it with her, but as far as I know, that was not the case. She told him she was still too young to settle down. She had her career to think about. So that was that. But you don't chuck David Bowie! Imagine doing that! He took it incredibly badly. He was drinking pretty heavily at the time, and when he drank, he was truly awful. I found out later from Coco that he'd been having blackouts. He was not what you'd call a nice drunk.'

Coco and George had always got on well, until the night they fell out in Mustique.

'It was hideous really,' says George. 'There we all were, in the music room. There was a bunch of us: David's son, Marion the nanny, David, me, a few others. It was a full house. We'd had a few, and we were telling jokes, and falling about all over the place laughing. David was lying on the sofa, and he fell asleep. In came Coco. She saw him lying there, and said to me, "We've got to get David to bed." I said that he seemed all right where he was. But then she gave me the look. So I tried to rouse him. "Come on, David," I coaxed him, "Coco wants you to get up." It was the wrong thing to say, apparently. She did get him up, and took him out and dealt with him. And then she came back. "George!" she thundered. "I don't need that from *you!*" I was standing there trying to figure out what on earth I'd done wrong. I didn't understand. She took it completely the wrong way.'

The next day, David quizzed his friend about what had gone on the night before.

'I didn't hold back. I said to him, "What *is* it she's got on you?" and he groaned and went, "Oh *no*, you're just like all the rest!" I found out later that he was prone to falling in the pools when he was pissed, and Coco was worried he might drown. I didn't get much support from anyone else at the time, I have to say, which did annoy me. David was angry, but he didn't hold it against me for too long.

'The wedding which David had planned with Melissa in Florence would eventually take place with Iman, albeit much more high-profile than what he'd originally had in mind.'

I know what George meant. A glittering celeb-fest splashed across the pages of *Hello!* was not what anyone would have expected of David Bowie.

David spent his fortieth birthday skiing in Switzerland with his son, and relaxing before the onslaught. He had no idea that a major sponsorship and marketing deal was going on behind his back. He was supposedly going to accept sponsorship from the makers of Babycham – the sparkling perry which had been hugely popular in the UK during the Sixties and Seventies, and the first alcoholic drink to be advertised on British TV.

'The sponsorship deal was for the 1987 Glass Spider tour,' recounts Nick Fitzherbert, a former public relations expert who now offers training in presentation skills.

'The client was Showerings, and I was working on their PR. Francis Showering was the Shepton Mallet, Somerset brewer who invented the drink. Babycham was still a big brand in those days, but they were looking to reinvent it. They thought that David Bowie would be a sure-fire, fast-track way to do this. This all went on for about four months.

'They talked to David Bowie's people. It got as far as Concorde flights going backwards and forwards to New York. A comprehensive video was made to explain why it was all such a brilliant idea. I didn't personally believe that it would ever happen. But I knew more about music than anyone else on the team, so I got dragged to all these important meetings with lawyers for both sides. All the contracts were drawn up in both names – David Bowie and David Jones.

'The idea was that he would promote the product during his live performances on the forthcoming tour. We hadn't got as far as deciding exactly how we were going to brand it, but an enormous amount of money had already been spent. I was planning to start with an outrageous idea, such as, David was going to perform with a microphone shaped like a Babycham bottle, and he'd have it in his face all the time, during every concert! Perfect! Then somebody thought, finally, that perhaps it might be a good idea to mention it to David himself. Needless to say, his horrified reaction was "absolutely no way!" You'd think that someone might have thought to ask him first!'

Come March 1987, he was up to his neck in press and promo for the Glass Spider tour – *sans* Babycham bottle. In April came the album that the outing was founded on, written and recorded in Lausanne and Montreux: *Never Let Me Down*. He wrote the title track for Coco, a loving tribute to the woman who had always been there for him; who had indeed, never once, let him down. She thought it 'better than a wedding ring', insiders said. Despite the fact that the first two singles were Top Ten hits around the world, and that the album sold well – to begin with, at least – it was less than a life-changer. The fans admired it a good deal less than the critics . . . but of course they bought it in droves, because it was the latest by David Bowie.

The show was baffling. Between the end of May and the last day of November, it was seen by six million fans over eighty-six shows from Rotterdam to Auckland, many of whom found it unsatisfying. The tour itself was cursed by accidents, mishaps, fan and crew-member deaths, even lawsuits. One woman scorned accused David of having infected her with AIDS (he hadn't). Carlos Alomar surpassed himself, suspended on ropes while doing a Hendrix from the roof of the stage. How did he keep a straight face? Dancers wafted through flames, choreographed (she was back) by Toni Basil. David dropped in on a swing, he was hurled about, he got spun to high heck, it looked agonising. I might have believed a man could fly, at one point. As the PR bumph had it, this was no ordinary rock show, this was a veritable voyage through life. In your nightmares, possibly.

What inspired the arachnoid concept? A documentary about sexual cannibalism in the genus Latrodectus, the so-called widow spiders. Very David, I suppose. I still think about it sometimes. And I still don't get it. He was the highest-profile rock superstar on earth, we'd spent months sucking up to his PRs, buying them drinks, picking up the tab at four-hour, five-star lunches, going out of our way to crowbar items about lesser artists on their roster into the paper, bagging ourselves a place on the tour. Such effort. We weren't about to let either David or ourselves down with a bad review, because then we wouldn't get invited on the next one. This is how it was. It was our *job* to like it. So we wrote that we did.

'Bowie is back!' I gushed in the *Daily Mail* on 1 June 1987.

'Back in captivating action, back in sensational style, back in an orgy of show-stoppers, live on stage for the first time in four long years. This is the Last Tango in Rotterdam – the swansong of the only rock superstar brave enough to continually reinvent himself, appearing in his latest and possibly last persona: the rock star on a farewell tour. When forty-year-old Bowie brings his European tour to a climax in Britain twenty days from now, it will be the end of his touring days, he says.'

I lavished on about the 'fast-moving, edge-of-the-seat' extrava-ganza. I drooled over his delectable scarlet silk suit made by Diana Moseley, a favourite designer of Freddie Mercury's. Even David's red-and-black suede boots tipped with steel got a mention. I raved about the sixty-foot-high mechanical spider – what was it *for?* – and about the sixty thousand Dutch fans 'caught in his musical web'. Oh, my.

It gets better.

'Speaking to me exclusively before stepping on stage ... a relaxed, confident Bowie said:

'"This tour is a coming together of all the performances and theatrical elements that have fascinated me and amused me all my working life. Hell," he smiled, with a jaunty toss of his head, "it's only rock and roll – but it makes *my* head spin."'

Gawd, what was I like. He'd said nothing of the sort to my face. I must have pulled that quote from a Rogers & Cowan press release. I *did* interview him backstage at Rotterdam's Feyenoord Stadium before he went on. 'Tis true, there's magic in the web of it.[5] But there wasn't a lot of chat about the show. I hadn't even seen it yet. He recognised me, which was nice, despite the fact that our paths hadn't crossed for ages. I was nearly six months pregnant, and bulging. I had hamster cheeks, thighs like tugboats, and mismatched contact lenses in.

We had a laugh about it. Within minutes we were back in Bromley and Beckenham, raking through yesterdays. The weedy path to Haddon Hall. The day we had tea with him and he was out of milk, when he was painting his nails black with a cocktail stick. Hanging around with guitars in the Bromley Library Gardens, shaking a leg in the old Beckenham ballroom, flipping through the records in Medhurst's. We talked about his old art teacher, Owen Frampton, whose son Peter was playing for David on this tour. We talked about Freddie Mercury and the AIDS rumours already circulating, which would be resolutely denied until the eve of Freddie's death.

'Off the record? It's no big thing,' scoffed David. 'He'll be absolutely fine, you'll see. Even if he does have it. There's always a shot for these things. They always come up with a cure. Melina will be all right, because the world can't live without her.' 'Melina' being Freddie's nickname among the rock'n'roll in-crowd, after Melina Mercouri, the late Greek actress and politician. (Freddie would taunt David with 'Zoë', the feminine version of his son's original name). I asked him whether he'd ever had an AIDS scare himself.

'Not so far.' He smiled thinly. 'Always a first time, I s'pose. Let's hope not, eh. I was treated for syphilis once, a long time ago. I think I got away with it.' Ironically, he would be tested a few months later for AIDS, when a woman scorned accused him of infecting her.

We recalled another Jones boy, long-gone. A Welshman called Emlyn, a wizard with the ball. The other players called him 'Mickey'. He'd been a hero to thousands at Everton F.C. and at Southend United; an even bigger one to the kids on Margate beach. Remember him by there, on the putting green, my grandad? David did, he said.

It was a whisper of time on the back of a new tomorrow. He was giving up touring, he revealed. Funny, so was I. With my first baby due in a matter of weeks, my days on the road with bands were numbered.

'Look me up whenever you're in Switzerland,' he said.

Oh, sure!

'Or in New York, eh? Always nice to have a chat about the old days. Not many of us left. Better stick together. Let's have a bit of munch.'

It was the rub. David was severed from his roots, detached from his family, divorced from the mother of his child. He had distanced himself from his beginnings, and he'd gone off and conquered the world. Now, there was nowhere else to go – except maybe into space – and definitely nothing left to prove. There was no going back, he knew that for sure. But his past still mattered to him. It always had, deep down. So what if he'd parked it for a while. Most of us do. He never let it go completely, which was evident from our conversations.

It was the reason he clung to George Underwood and Geoff MacCormack, who had as good as replaced Terry and were virtual brothers to him. Coco was his mother substitute, caring for him with more love, affection and devotion than Peggy Jones had ever been capable of. And then there were the peripheral people: we who dipped in and out of his life and who supported the cause – because every superstar needs pet journalists on his side – and who provoked just about the right amount of poignant memories. Those who were a conduit and a connection to the past. We who had been there.

I wasn't really his 'friend'. It would be preposterous to presume so. Adult friendships tend to depend on equal footing and mutual respect. He could become friends with, say, a Gary Oldman or an Eric Idle, because shared status and equivalent fortune permitted it. Other musicians were a given, though there was often rivalry involved. There usually is. As for me, I knew my place. He was never about to become bosom buddies with a hack. He was a planet, I was a satellite, and that was that. But we did share history. We went way back. The cul-de-sacs of his heart and the top shelf of his memory were places I knew.

After my daughter Mia was born that August, I was hired as a feature writer by Nick Gordon, editor of YOU magazine, the *Mail on Sunday* colour supplement. A few months later, I was back on the beat. Manhattan was a frequent port of call, with coordinator and stylist Sandy Williams and photographer Geoff

Wilkinson. We were a team, bagging the cover stories: Richard Gere; Bruce Willis; Liza Minnelli; Donna Rice – the girl who brought down senator and potential president Gary Hart; LaToya Jackson; Cyndi Lauper; The Donald's first wife, Ivana Trump. It was New York every other week in the late Eighties. It sounds mad when I think of it now, but that's how it was. I didn't forget my promise to David. We did have a bit of munch.

1988–1991

The moment the media bestows nicknames, be it honorific or derogatory, musicians know they've arrived. Bruce Springsteen, 'the Boss', Whitney Houston, 'the Voice', James Brown, 'Mr Dynamite', Madonna, 'the Queen of Pop'. Otherwise known as 'Madge'. One of the reasons she quit England, the 'Material Girl' moaned, was that she could no longer bear that awful name.

But there's usually a reason behind an alias. Frank Sinatra, 'Ol' Blue Eyes', wasn't green-eyed, and was also the 'Chairman of the Board' – in reference to his alleged Mafia connections. John Bonham was 'Bonzo', a hell-raiser, Ozzy Osbourne was 'the Prince of Darkness', and Eric Clapton was never swifter than a 'Slowhand'. Paul Weller became 'the Modfather' for having resurrected the Mod movement with the Jam. Morrissey, 'Mozzer', 'Moz', as was, is still the 'Pope of Mope'. *Nul points.*

A gleeful music press, never slow to send up an icon, retired 'The Thin White Duke' handle during the late Eighties height of Bowie's fame, and dubbed him 'The Dame'. It stuck. There ain't nothing like a Dame.

But why? It was never explained. The consensus is that it started as an insult which over time acquired a glaze of fun and affection. The Pantomime Dame, a comedic character usually played around Christmas by famous-ish male thesps, remains one of Britain's best-loved entertainment figures. David didn't mind it. He was never backward in coming forward when it came to blurring the furring. Down the years, he'd been everything. His gent was bent, his feminine side was fabled, his androgyne was anodyne, he was non-binary in his finery. Underneath, he was still a bloke. But that's oke. It's why the ladyboy is a tramp.

The Glass Spider tour drained him dry, physically and emotionally. He seriously considered jacking it in, during its aftermath, and retiring to his easel and paints. But he was still contracted, expensively, to EMI. Such are the dilemmas. After the failure, as he couldn't help seeing it, of *Never Let Me Down*, and the Glass Spider rout, he neither knew whether he could write hits any more, nor whether he wanted to. He withdrew into his new winter routine: Mustique for Christmas and New Year, followed by skiing with his son in Gstaad.

After several months based in the mountains, zipping back and forth to New York, summer 1988 brought a chance benefit at London's Dominion Theatre, for the Institute of Contemporary Arts. Thrown together with guitarist Reeves Gabrels, something gelled. David invited Reeves to spend a weekend with him at his home in Lausanne. A month later, he was still there. Montreux may be boring, but it's irresistibly serene. The thirty-minute drive from Lausanne along the shore of Lake Geneva is one of the most beautiful journeys to work on the planet. The pair took to pitching up at Mountain Studios every day. Back at the house, they'd trawl through David's records, seeking inspiration. Before long, it dawned on David that what he really wanted to do was retire solo superstar Bowie, and get back to where he once belonged. He needed to be in a band again.

Tin Machine are so often described as having been doomed from the start, because David was a solo superstar, and therefore could never be just one of the boys in a group. There could be no democracy between its members, because one was so rich and famous, while the others were, how can I put this, not. There would always be disparity in the focus of attention; indeed, Tin Machine would only be deemed worthy of any recognition at all because David Bowie was one of them. They'd never have commanded column inches otherwise. He wasn't going to let trifling matters such as these compromise giving it a go. It was a challenge to say the least.

'Tin Machine was David's unrealistic fantasy,' affirms former Cutting Crew star Tony Moore. ' "I'm just the singer in the band": it was never going to work. The number one rule, of course, is that you still have to make hit records. It was a niche market. If only he'd been able to do what the Foo Fighters did. Dave Grohl was very successful previously, with Nirvana, before starting his new band. But he always understood that you've still got to write hit songs.

'What makes a hit song? Traditionally, I would have said, very beautiful, finely constructed, puzzlingly intriguing but never corny lyrics. But the literary value of lyrics today is debatable. Pop lyrics have been dumbed right down. The modern consensus is that if the melody is strong enough, the lyrics don't matter. In truth, it *all* matters. It certainly did back then. And Tin Machine just didn't get it right.'

'I interviewed him for Tin Machine,' remembers music journalist Chris Welch. 'He seemed quite nervous about it all in a way. "Our fans are called the Tinnies," he told me, enthusiastically. I got the distinct impression that he was trying to re-create the Bowie of the Sixties. As if he were still back in Beckenham, doing the Arts Lab, and that he still had his whole life to come. The way he talked to me about this new group was exactly the same way as he'd talked about the Arts Lab movement way back then. As if it were the answer to everything. There was something very mournful about it; as if he knew, deep down, that those innocent, hopeful, everything-to-play-for days were gone, never to return. He knew that, of course he did, but it still didn't stop him trying. My heart did go out to him. I actually felt sorry for him. But Tin Machine were never really my thing.'

The other essential band members would be the Sales brothers, bass player Tony and drummer Hunt, whom Iggy Pop had unfathomably dumped. Tony had survived a near-fatal car crash in LA, and David had been one of the few who visited him. Some have speculated that the creation of Tin Machine was David's way of helping a friend back on his feet. Whatever it was, the boys congregated, with guitarist Kevin Armstrong, at Mountain, with hope in their hearts. Their producer was Tim Palmer. As a precocious assistant engineer at London's Utopia, Tim had already worked with Mark Knopfler and Dead or Alive when, at the age of twenty-one, he scored his first Number One single, mixing the Cutting Crew perennial '(I Just) Died In Your Arms'. As a producer, he achieved prominence with the Mighty Lemon Drops, Gene Loves Jezebel, and Robert Plant.[1]

The project moved to Compass Point in the Bahamas. David's girlfriend Melissa, his son Joey and John's son Sean Lennon came on down. Coco, for once, was absent, so the atmosphere was cool. It was rumoured that she'd fallen for some type in LA, but where was the proof?

The Tin Machine sound, mostly a punky, hard rock, frantic squall, was always intended to be as far removed from late-Eighties Bowie as it was possible to get. In this, it mostly succeeded. Their debut album, released in May 1989, was received with excitement. This was Bowie, after all. Anxious to get out on the road and show the world what he'd been up to, David decided to put a club tour together. It would kick off in New York in June 1989. The fans were beside themselves. The great stadium superstar was coming back down to their level. They'd get to see him point-blank. They queued for tickets for days. There were even a few riots, mini-ones.

Chris Poole was Bowie's publicist throughout the Tin Machine pageant. We go back. He was Head of Press at Chrysalis Records when I was assistant to Art Director John Pasche.[2] Poole Edwards, the company he ran with Alan Edwards,[3] were working out of offices in London's Charlotte Street.

'Alan had Bowie when he worked at Rogers & Cowan,' recalls Chris. 'He also had the Stones. Somehow, the Stones fired him, and they went to Bernard Doherty. Alan kept Bowie. When Alan and I went in together, Alan was Bowie's main guy, but we split the work.

'Many people who worked with David down the years maintain that he was just an ordinary bloke. But he wasn't,' insists Chris, 'he was different. He was tall, for a start – lots of pop stars are short, which must say something about what drives them to become pop stars. There was an aura about him, something other-worldly, that was hard to put your finger on. From Serious Moonlight onwards, with the yellow hair and the tan, he was luminescent. He'd become the opposite of how he was in his Thin White Duke days.

'By the time we got him, he'd stopped drinking – he did Alcoholics Anonymous for a long time. He and Coco were always going to meetings together, every week if they could. So I never once saw him drunk. He was always together and in control, and his work ethic was impressive. He was incredibly motivated. He wasn't spending a lot of time in London in those days. To be honest, he wasn't really living anywhere. He had the house in Switzerland, and he was back and forth all the time to New York.'

One of Alan Edwards's functions was to keep David up-to-date musically and culturally.

'Every week, wherever David was, Alan would send him a package of the latest CDs, books, music and art magazines and so on. Alan became his eyes and ears in Europe, and especially in the UK. David was insatiable, relentless. The only other person I ever worked with who was similar to Bowie was Prince. They were both regarded as aloof and detached, and that is absolutely how they were. They were driven to surpass themselves with every new project.'

Surprising, then, that Tin Machine, both artistically and in terms of sales, was the lowest point of Bowie's career.

'It was weird,' agrees Chris. 'He wasn't prepared for that. Everything he did, he approached in a very organised and obsessive way. It was all very drilled, meticulously planned, and quite fascinating to observe. The Bowie machine went into action for Tin Machine, and we all had to be cogs in the wheel. David wanted to be back in a rock band – like Prince, who did the same thing. But you can't make those drastic changes out of the blue. The fans won't let you. And among rock journalists, I seem to remember that Tin Machine had only one fan. We got loads of coverage because it was David Bowie, of course, but that went completely against the philosophy and point of the band, who were very much all for one and one for all.'

On the road, Chris found David demanding, and his regime gruelling.

'He'd get up *really* early – like about five or six a.m. He'd read and do God knows what. And if he hadn't heard from me by about eight a.m., he'd wake me up, and say, "Have you got the reviews yet?" I had to go and get all the papers, and get some chambermaid or equivalent to translate them, when we were in Denmark, Germany, Holland and France. I mostly did go and get them, got them translated, did all that – but sometimes I pretended I hadn't, because the reviews were so bad. I'm sure he knew I was hiding them from him. David questioned everything, and he had to be in charge of everything. He was an absolute control freak. He had the band all in black suits, for example, which he'd paid for! Not exactly democracy, is it. Not a lot of equality going on, as far as I could see.'

Did he like David?

'He could be enormously charming,' Chris concedes. 'But he was distant. Never one of the lads. I got on much better with Coco. I became good friends with her. She was really good to me, always down to earth, always nice. On my fortieth birthday, she gave me a volume of W. B Yeats's poetry and some photos of Ireland. The book was signed: "To Chris from David and Coco". The inscription was written by her.

'She really *was* devoted to him. Their relationship was incredibly close, but there was nothing romantic about it – at least, not on his side. I always wondered if she might really have been in love with him, but it wasn't reciprocated. Not in that way. It was like an adult having a nanny. I didn't feel sorry for her, though. She wouldn't have wanted that. We had some really good times. We went to art galleries together, all over Europe, whenever we had a day off. I hung out with Coco a lot more than Alan did, and we got on very well. She wasn't someone you could read easily. I think that the media and fan reaction to Tin Machine really shook David, and that Coco might even have been secretly a bit glad about that. Because it gave her the upper hand again. She had David back where she wanted him: a little vulnerable, deferring to her, dependent on her to make him feel better.'

After a dozen shows in six countries, during which they performed the entire debut Tin Machine album, David might have called it a day. He had plenty on his plate. His RCA catalogue was being remastered in preparation for release on compact disc, the groundbreaking new 'digital optical disc data storage format' set to replace vinyl records, and to revolutionise the music industry. Being Bowie, his albums were handled in something akin to a military operation, by only the best in the business. Having been mastered by Rykodisc, who would release them across Europe, David's albums would be licensed to EMI for release in the US. Being Bowie, they would be better than any other artists': beautifully designed, with special additions, and covetable-extra oddities and rarities.

His special 'Sound + Vision' presentation package prompted musings about a Greatest Hits tour. For an artist who was all about 'pushing boundaries', 'breaking down barriers' and 'reinventing' his image and music constantly – who was all about the future – it was the ultimate paradox. It went ahead, nevertheless, kicking off on 4 March 1990 in Quebec, concluding on 29 September in Buenos Aires, delivering one hundred and eight performances in twenty-seven countries across five continents, and eclipsing both the Serious Moonlight and the Glass Spider to become his biggest yet. It would be, David said, the last time he would ever perform his back catalogue. Who could believe him? The fickle fiend had retired songs, incarnations and formats before, only to dust them down and parade them again, whenever he felt like it.

He spent the first couple of months of 1990 rehearsing a modest band in a West Side, New York hall. The set list was decided by phone poll and postal ballots. The stand-out feature of the live show was a huge gauze screen, used to create shadow puppet theatre, and onto which videos and images were projected. The show was recorded in Tokyo, Milton Keynes, Brazil and Chile, for later broadcast. There were ten shows in the UK. I saw it at the London Arena on the Isle of Dogs on Monday 26 March 1990, the first of three nights, as a guest of the guy who owned the place: boxing promoter Frank Warren, my youngest child's godfather. A lot of rock'n'roll mouthwash went down that night. So memorable, and yet so not.

Melissa Hurley vanished, towards the end of that tour. David told everyone he'd called it off.[1] A superstar must save face. Whatever, David was now forty-three years old, mega-rich, thin, handsome, and still had hair. He also had a gobful of crowded, unaligned, nicotine-stained canines. He'd told me a few times that he liked them that way. As did I. His imperfect smile made him look down to earth and real, I thought . . . not to mention British. I felt oddly proud of him for not having sought and bought the standard Hollywood grin. David had always championed the cause of the misfit, had given courage to the many who feel different. To have submitted to cosmetic dentistry in order to 'improve' his mouth would have been to relinquish integrity. When he did succumb, eventually, I felt stupidly sad.

How did it feel to be one of the world's most eligible bachelors? You're having a laugh.

'Yeah, well. I can pull anyone I want,' he said. 'But try getting someone to want you for the right reasons when you are me.' It was a moment of vulnerability that made me feel sorry for him.

Nah.

We talked. No subject was taboo. He would sometimes let me buy lunch: 'As long as Rothermere [Viscount, proprietor of Associated Newspapers, my ultimate boss] is paying!' I probably did slip one or two lunch bills onto expenses, if I'm honest, but it was more often than not on him. He was generous. We talked kids, his and mine, and compared pictures. He was a single parent, finally mindful of the responsibility. He said he felt remorseful that Joey – Duncan – didn't have the most idyllic childhood, and wished now that he hadn't sent him away to boarding school. It 'didn't really work out,' he admitted.

He couldn't take politics. Current affairs, he could leave. He liked travel talk, always wanting to know about where you'd been lately. A lot of the time it was literature, occasionally sport. He wouldn't have won Trivial Pursuit on the latter. He loved the 'flair' of martial arts, he said, and he did like boxing. He was fascinated by pugilists, particularly Ali. He wanted to know about the decade my father spent on the road with the Greatest. He said that he would like to meet my dad. It never happened.

It was Richard Lord, an American coach in Austin, Texas, who taught David how to box. He'd been a fan of the sport since school, in fact, where his art teacher Mr Frampton also taught boxing. On the Diamond Dogs tour in 1974, he yanked on a pair of red boxing gloves, ever so fetching with his blue eye make-up. After recording the album *Let's Dance* with Nile Rodgers, the cover of which featured David in the same gloves, he was preparing for the 1983 tour to promote it in Dallas when he decided to have another go, and get fit for the road. Eyebrows were raised. David had always professed to loathe the gym. Any exercise other than skiing was anathema to him.

One of his team in Dallas recommended local coach Richard Lord, something of a legend in the state. He had been both an amateur and a professional, and his self-training regime consisted of running up and down the steps of the stadium at his alma mater, the University of Texas, like some scene out of *Rocky*. David approached him, and the trainer agreed to take him on. Lord soon had the star legging the steps, and banging the bags at an ancient downtown sweat palace. David progressed to sparring, and was doing OK, but then off he went on the road, and never saw Lord again. He remained partial to a few rounds from time to time for the next twenty years.

We talked about Wales, the land of our fathers. I'd often stayed there, growing up, while David barely knew it. It fascinated him that there is no 'J' in the Welsh alphabet, but that Jones is its most common surname. Our Joneses originated in Llanfihangel-y-Creuddyn, West Wales, where my family's names dating back to the 1700s are inscribed in the parish register at St Michael's church.

My great-grandfather, grandfather and father were born in Merthyr Tydfil, at the top of the Taff valley. Several family members played football for Merthyr Town before being snapped up by English clubs. They migrated to the Midlands to make shells and bullets in the munitions factories there during the Second World War. Post-war, industry in the Valleys fell into decline. Some returned home, some stayed in Birmingham and others moved south to the coast, where they settled in Margate.

David's Joneses were said to have hailed from both the Rhondda and the Llynfi valleys, specifically from Llangynwyd, forty miles south-west of Merthyr.[5] It is one of the most ancient villages in South Wales, a seat of the thirteenth-century bards of Tir Iarll. The thatched Old House Inn, one of the oldest pubs in the land, had once or twice welcomed Pontrhydyfen-born Richard Burton and his wife Elizabeth Taylor. During the first week of September 1992, only four months after his wedding to Iman, David and Coco would drop in for fish and chips and a ploughman's while in Wales seeking clues to David's ancestry.

His family had migrated earlier and further north than mine. The growth of the iron industry in the Valleys from the mid-eighteenth century, and the later development of the South Wales coalfield, had created a reserve of skilled metalworkers, foundrymen and miners who could find employment easily in other rapidly expanding industrial areas. Many Welsh families relocated to Yorkshire.

During the early twentieth century, Doncaster would become one of the largest coalmining areas in the country.[6] David had little to go on, he had to admit, but was determined to unearth his roots. He was certainly blessed with what is said to be the primary attribute of the Cymric race: an energetic and expansive character. He also had more than his share of Celtic gloom. He loved Dylan Thomas and his 'lubricated command of language', especially *Under Milk Wood*, from which he would quote lines:

> . . . *spring, moonless night in the small town, starless and bible-black, the cobblestreets silent . . . the sloeblack, slow black, crowblack, fishing-boat-bobbing sea . . . From where you are, you can hear their dreams.*

It is a common preoccupation among the middle-aged, who have lived more of their lives than they have left to live. The artist who'd made a fortune out of forging ever forwards was now ready and even yearning to go back. It was about coming full circle. He'd found his life partner, and felt settled with his mate. This new quest was the metaphorical coming home. It was about knowing where 'home' was.

Once, long after the furore had died down, we talked about his brother Terry's funeral.

'They didn't understand,' he said. 'The Terry he was, wasn't the Terry he was, if you get me. It was meaningless to me to rock up and stand to attention at the funeral of this tortured person who bore no resemblance to the lad I knew when I was a kid. He became someone else. I'd become someone else. The Terry I'd lived with, that wasn't him. I invented someone I could look up to, for all kinds of reasons, and I projected onto him some things that he really wasn't. That was my fault. The person I wanted him to be never actually existed. The real Terry had faded from my life long ago, and I from his.'

So why did he send flowers?

'It's expected,' he shrugged. 'I was damned if I did, and damned if I didn't. I wasn't going to turn up to have my picture taken at a media circus that was supposed to be someone's solemn laying to rest, just for the sake of making myself look good in the papers. It wasn't for me to go hogging the limelight, which is the way a lot of people would have perceived it.'

You showed up at Marc Bolan's, I said.

'Completely different. At least half the people there were so-called celebrities. Marc himself was famous, he lived his short life in the public eye. He wanted that, he loved it, he went after it. Terry wasn't, and he didn't. It didn't seem right. No one else understood. We'd let each other go, long before Terry died. The Terry I grew up with had passed away years ago. Anyway, funerals are all about the people left behind. I had nothing to say to my aunt or my mother, at that point.'

Legend holds that celebrity hairstylist Teddy Antolin, a mutual friend who had toured regularly with David, set him up on a blind date with Iman at his own birthday dinner party in Los Angeles, on 4 October 1990. They had in fact met already, backstage at this and that gig, but why let the truth intrude. The attraction between them on this occasion was as filings to a magnet. David famously remarked that he started naming their children that first night.

'My attraction to her was immediate and all-encompassing,' he told *Hello!* magazine in 2000. 'That she would be my wife, in my head, was a done deal. I'd never gone after anything in my life with such passion . . . I just knew she was the one.'

'David arrived in a white Mustang sports car, wearing white jeans and a white jacket, all denim,' Antolin remembered. 'Iman showed up in a black Mercedes wearing all black leather. And I thought, what could be more perfect. The minute she walked in, all the attention went to her, she just claimed the room. She had a big smile, and her and David looked at each other, and it was love at first sight. You could feel the electricity. Something went off. They spent the night talking to each other like they had known each other forever. They were looking at each other like, now what, shall we just skip dessert and go home? There was no one else in their lives but those two from then on.'

Publicist Chris Poole is almost gleeful at the memory.

'When David fell for Iman, Alan Edwards and I looked at each other and went, "*Coco!* Oooh, this could be interesting! What's going to happen now!" Coco hated Angie with a vengeance, she made no secret of that. How on earth was she going to handle this one? A staggeringly beautiful, stunningly black, rich, world-famous supermodel? You'd give up. There were a few months off, during which we saw little of them, and then everything went back into overdrive, ready for Tin Machine to go out on the road again.

'The band rehearsed in Dublin,' Chris remembers. 'This was 1991. Ireland was still practically third-world in those days. Shoeless street urchins, horses and carts. We'd taken a gated studio, Factory in Ringsend, for them to rehearse and do warm-ups in. We had a few interesting visitors: Marianne Faithfull came down to Dublin to see David, while they were rehearsing. And then I was doing paperwork in the office one day, and the band were at it, when I got a call from one of the producers of *Far and Away*, the Tom Cruise and Nicole Kidman film with them doing cod-Irish accents that came out the following year. It was directed by Ron Howard.[7]

'The guy on the phone goes, "Hi. I'm assistant producer on so-and-so. Tom Cruise heard that Bowie is in town, and he would like to come and hang out with David." *Hang out!* I'm sitting in the office, waiting for them to knock off, and I can hardly conceal my mirth. David and the band finished what they were doing, and they wandered into the room. "Er, David." I tried not to smirk. "I've just had a call from Tom Cruise. He wants to come down. What do you think?" David didn't miss a beat. "Um, I don't know," he deadpanned. "Guys, what do *you* think?" "Yeah, OK, then," they said, not really interested.

'Where Tom and Nicole were shooting that day was only about ten, fifteen minutes down the road. I let them know. Shortly afterwards, a limo pulls into the courtyard, the door flies open, and out falls Tom Cruise – who marches straight up to me and introduces himself vigorously, before introducing me to Nicole. I took them into the rehearsal studio. And there they sat, cross-legged on the floor, right in front of the band, for half an hour. Without opening their mouths. Just watching David and the guys rehearse. And then they buggered off!

'I've met virtually every big star in the music industry. It's like meeting anybody else. *But*, I've always found it a little difficult meeting movie stars. They are larger than life on screen, and they are larger than life in their own heads. The reason they're different from everybody else is because they *think* they are.'

Tin Machine were back in business for another seven months from that August, beginning their It's My Life tour with warm-up gigs at the Factory, and wrapping at the Budokan Tokyo in February 1992. Come October, Iman was David's fiancée and a fragrant permanent fixture. Coco would just have to get used to it. EMI, meanwhile, weren't that keen on the idea of a second Tin Machine album, given the reception afforded the first.

'So David signed a very precise deal for the band with Phil Carson at Victory Records,'[8] says Chris. 'He knew what he wanted, both professionally and personally. He always did. It occurred to me then that he really wasn't a human being like the rest of us. He was obsessive about everything. He was almost arrogant at times about his own music, yet at the same time he was wracked with insecurity. His life now seemed consumed with tracking all that was going on out there, musically and culturally – almost as though he was desperate not to be left behind. He was extraordinarily private in his private life, and yet he sold his wedding to *Hello!* magazine. That kind of thing. The contradictions baffled me.

'Did anyone really know him? I'm not sure anyone did. Coco? Only to an extent. Iman? They were husband and wife, and they lived together, so that's a different dimension. Outside their marriage, which was strong and unique, I don't think anyone else came even close to knowing him. That would have been exactly what he wanted, too.'

During the Tin Machine dates in Germany, Chris got to see for himself, unexpectedly, that the most intimate rumour about Bowie was not apochryphal.

'It was down-time, we were back at the hotel, and I went to the gym and for a swim. I wanted a sunbed, but there was only one there, and it was occupied. I sat down to wait. After what seemed like ages I was about to bugger off, when the lid came up and out got David, stark naked. It was like Apollo, rising from the sea at daybreak. He radiated light. And I saw for myself, at point-blank range, that everything I'd heard about the most infamous append-age in rock was true.'

In November 1991, David's longstanding buddy and fellow Montreux rebel-rouser Freddie Mercury lost his life to bronchial pneumonia, but really to AIDS. To mark his passing, Queen's magnum opus 'Bohemian Rhapsody' was re-released as a Christmas single. It soared to Number One, raising over a million pounds for the Terence Higgins Trust AIDS charity. The following April, the other side of grief, the great Queen frontman got his big send-off.

The Wembley stadium concert staged in his honour before seventy thousand fans would be described as the greatest live rock event of the Nineties. Almost everyone who took part performed a Queen song. The show was broadcast to about a billion people in seventy-six countries, and filmed by David Mallet for a future documentary. Favourite moments were Elizabeth Taylor's blousy AIDS prevention speech; Robert Plant's renditions of 'Crazy Little Thing Called Love', and 'Innuendo'; Roger Daltrey's 'I Want It All'; Liza Minnelli singing 'We Are the Champions', George Michael doing Freddie's mother's favourite, 'Somebody to Love', and David with Annie Lennox, obvs, on 'Under Pressure'.

Whoever decided that Queen, Joe Elliott and Slash should perform 'Tie Your Mother Down' was inspired. Picture Slash silently eyeballing Bowie backstage: 'You shagged my mom!' Poignant, too, the sound and vision of David and Mick Ronson reunited, augmented by Roger Taylor, Brian May and an acutely shorn John Deacon. It would be John's last-ever live performance with his old band mates. He never did get over Freddie's death.

David paid tribute to all the musicians of the Sixties and Seventies who had left us: 'We played the same dancehalls, slept with a lot of the same people . . . ,' and he name-checked T. Rex and the Stones. They performed David's gift to Mott the Hoople, 'All the Young Dudes', with singer Ian Hunter on lead vocals. Then he and Ronson took, inevitably, to ' "Heroes" '.

David, just days ahead of his civil wedding, was a portrait of health: lightly tanned, slim, immaculately coiffed, dressed in a boxy spearmint-green suit, striped blue shirt and green-and-yellow tie. Ronson, in contrast, looked wan in a casual white open-necked shirt, hanging loose over his emaciated frame. He was desperately ill with liver cancer. Who could have known that, with cruel irony, the same disease would claim David's life twenty-three years later. Mick performed incomparably for the final time. He looked elated to be there. But when famously 'non-Christian' David dropped to his knees to recite the Lord's Prayer right in front of him as the song concluded, there was puzzlement.

'I decided to do it about five minutes before I went on stage,' David explained to the late *Arena* magazine the following year. 'Coco and I had a friend called Craig who was dying of AIDS. He was just dropping into a coma that day. And just before I went on stage, something just told me to say the Lord's Prayer.'

What he said next was a turn-up for the books.

'In rock music . . . there is no room for prayer, but I think that so many of the songs people write are prayers. A lot of my songs seem to be prayers for unity within myself. On a personal level, I have an undying belief in God's existence. For me, it is unquestionable.

'. . . Looking at what I have done in my life, in retrospect so much of what I thought was adventurism was searching for my tenuous connection with God. I was always investigating, always looking into why religions worked and what it was people found in them. And I was always fluctuating from one set of beliefs to another until a very low point in the mid-Seventies, where I developed a fascination with black magic . . . And although I'm sure there was a satanic lead pulling me towards it, it wasn't a search for evil. It was in the hope that the signs might lead me somewhere.'

Four days later, David and thirty-six-year-old Iman Abdulmajid were married by the civil registrar at the City Hall of Lausanne. With three divorces between them, and given that Iman is a Muslim, they could not legally be married in a Christian church. There were two witnesses but no guests at the brief civil ceremony. To his 'queer', 'bisexual' and 'freak' tags, David could now add the rather more uplifting distinction 'miscegenationist'. It fascinated him to note that, within a century, interracial marriage had evolved from being illegal in many parts of the world to being distinctly taboo, then merely frowned upon, and by the time he joined the party himself, still relatively unusual. During his lifetime, it would become commonplace, a welcome realisation of the prediction of Blue Mink's 'Melting Pot'.

It would be followed several weeks later by a full-blown religious service, re-affirmation of vows and blessing at the Gothic revival St James Episcopal American church in Florence, Tuscany. Where else but the art capital of the Renaissance world, the place where opera was invented, where Galileo pioneered astronomy, where Giotto, Botticelli, Michelangelo and Leonardo da Vinci created the great works of the era, where Dante, Petrarch and Boccaccio wrote history, where . . . well honestly, where else for Bowie? Like every choice he'd ever made, it was a statement. Florence is enchanting, mysterious and eternal. So would this marriage be. Once he got her up the aisle.

Iman and her bridal party arrived in Florence several days in advance, to prepare for the wedding. David and his son, having spent the previous weekend on Mustique for Joe/Duncan's twenty-first birthday, checked in the day before.

'There were a few logistical hiccups, and a particularly fraught episode the night before,' remembers publicist Chris Poole.

'It could have been all off! We'd done a deal with [photographer] Brian Aris to do all the pictures for *Hello!* On the eve of the ceremony, the wedding party were all at dinner in the hotel, Villa La Massa' – a gorgeous sixteenth-century Medici estate in the Tuscan hills beside the Arno, about ten miles from the church, with a terrace overlooking the river.

'David had taken the whole place, and the entire party was staying there. All of a sudden, hell broke loose. Brian started making this terrible fuss because the steak tartare he'd ordered had not been done to his liking. He created such a stink that management lost it, a massive argument blew up, and David's party nearly got thrown out – meaning that there would have been nowhere to stay, and no wedding reception the next day! It was pandemonium for a bit, the Italian temperament having got the better of everybody. I didn't think David would ever forgive Brian. But Brian did still shoot the wedding photos the next day, as arranged; and David would have him back eight years later to do the baby pictures in New York, when Alexandria was born. So all's well that ends.' David and Iman spent Friday night in separate rooms.

The wedding was set for 4 p.m. the next day, Saturday, 6 June 1992. It was a significant date, being the twentieth anniversary of the release of *The Rise and Fall of Ziggy Stardust and the Spiders from Mars*. The helicopter which had been circling above the church all morning alerted locals and tourists to the fact that something special was about to happen. How the Italians love a drama. By early afternoon, a wildly enthusiastic throng had gathered around the church, who had to be restrained by police and security guards. The bride and groom arrived in separate motorcades, escorted by carabinieri and outriders. Sirens, flashing lights, squalling mobs, traffic jams, the whole nine yards. Tiny Yoko Ono was nearly swept away in the maelstrom as she stepped down from the hotel mini bus outside the church. It rained, but the star-gazers reassured one another that this was lucky: a wet wedding day is said to signify the cleansing of the past, renewal, unity and fertility, and to symbolise the last tears a bride will shed until death.

'It *was* grey and rainy,' affirmed photographer Brian Aris. 'But in true storybook fashion, the sky began to clear as the magic hour approached – and when they emerged from the church after their wedding, the sun was shining brightly.'

Classical music performed by a group of Italian musicians played the guests in – all except U2's Bono, who had missed his flight from Dublin. At least he made it in time for the photos and the reception. During the service, further music played that David had composed himself.[1] Six ushers led by publicist Alan Edwards seated the guests. The bride processed to the altar on the arm of her father Mohamed, to the Bulgarian folk song 'Kalimankou Denkou' ('The Evening Gathering') sung by Bulgarian folk choir Le Mystère des Voix Bulgares. Her maid of honour was her best friend Bethann Hardison.[2] David's suave son was his best man. With identical haircuts and tans, they could have been brothers.

Before its imposing white marble altar, under stunning stained glass more than a glint reminiscent of the majestic window back at Haddon Hall, they knelt before Reverend Mario Marziale during the fifty-minute service. Iman was gorgeous in oyster silk Hervé Léger, with drop-dead diamonds and pearls in her ears and carrying white lilies. Dapper David, kitted out by his chum Thierry Mugler, also present, sported black tux and white tie. Both looked overwhelmed during the service, with David on the verge of tears.

The sixty-eight attendants, a multi-coloured swap shop of family and friends, included old chums Birgit and George Underwood, and Geoff MacCormack, who read Psalm 121; Coco Schwab; Brian and Anthea Eno, Eric and Tanya Idle, Bono, Yoko Ono; David's cousin Kristina Amadeus, who read from Corinthians; Iman's parents, her mother Maryan Baadi[3] resplendent in traditional red and gold African dress – contrasting fantastically with David's mother Peggy in her long-sleeved, button-through black and white frock, very Beckenham High Street charity-shop. Iman's fourteen-year-old daughter Zulekha Haywood by her second husband, and brothers Elias and Feisal, made it. Sadly her sister,

Nadia, did not, her visa having failed to come through in time. The nuptials were splashed for posterity across the pages of a bumper edition of *Hello!* magazine, which was the A-list-marriage thing to do. The so-called 'curse of *Hello!*' has since put paid to much of that kind of thing. The publication features more wannabes these days than has-beens or ares. A fee north of £2 million was paid for the exclusive coverage.

Did the church service confirm a spiritual change of heart on David's part, just as his unscripted Lord's Prayer recitation at the Freddie tribute had indicated? Was it prompted by tradition – many non-believers marry in church? Or did David want something formal and photogenic that would lay to rest the ghost of Angie, while eradicating for good the memory of that loose-change Seventies wedding and its sordid threesome prelude the night before?

'I know the forms were signed,' David told *Hello!*, 'but at the back of our minds, our real marriage, sanctified by God, had to happen in a church in Florence.'

'Getting married did not convert me from a Muslim into a Christian,' insisted Iman.

But the message from David seemed unequivocal. Although he would question it over and over in his songwriting to come, and clearly still felt queasy and unsure of his views on 'organised religion', his moving introduction to his wife's 2001 book *I Am Iman* – primarily a stylish, coffee-table pictorial augmented by pointed criticism of racism and sexism in the fashion and beauty industries – appeared to confirm a genuine spiritual awakening. In the foreword, he identifies as a Christian.

Anyone in doubt might listen again to the lyrics of 'Lazarus' on his final album, *Blackstar*, released in January 2016. In his last-ever photographs, he was gravely ill but beaming with joy, controlling how the world saw him to the end. Iman's heartbreaking tweet at the point of her husband's death read: 'The struggle is real, but so is God.'

The lyrics of 'Word on a Wing' come again to mind, from his 1975 *Station to Station* album, the closing track on side one:

Lord, I kneel and offer you my word on a wing,
And I'm trying hard to fit among your scheme of things.

He would later remark that, if he had to choose between his marriage and his career, his marriage would win hands down.

David and Iman left the service together, in a dark blue Mercedes Benz saloon. Their reception was an opulent banquet back at the calm-again Villa La Massa. The guests were seated on eight tables for dinner, which was followed by a fireworks display over the river, announcing a traditional wedding disco. Stylist Teddy Antolin, who did both David's and Iman's hair for the ceremony, lapped up every minute.

'David was very happy,' he enthused. 'He never looked better, he was so sharp. He did make a speech, and after dinner we went to dance. David had put together a really great tape, disco and dance music, and a few of his own but not too much. It was a fun party.'

There was no keeping up with these Joneses. They vanished to the Far East on their honeymoon, sailing off into the sunset towards a blissfully happy-ever-after. And that was that. We who had wandered into David's orbit, who'd overlapped with him on the circuit, touched base, hung out, felt the heat of his limelight and been grazed first-hand by his magic, were now the past.

It was nothing to do with me, of course. But it felt as though a door had slammed. When one closes without prospect of ever being opened again, we are inclined to pine for whatever is no longer reachable on the other side. I found myself thinking more and more in those days, weeks and months about the old David, or should I say the young David, the desperate-to-make-it boy I'd met in Beckenham all those years ago. The cocky twenty-two-year-old gangler I'd felt instantly able to say anything at all to, who would chortle childishly at the same things as me, who made fun of the same things, who was rude and irreverent about the same people. Where was he now? Ah, but isn't marriage just like the past. A foreign country. They do things differently there.[4] With a minuscule population and impenetrable territory, it abides by its own rules and has an exclusive code of conduct. It ties its own knots, and wallows in its own miseries. It is reluctant to welcome interlopers. It is a mission on a bicycle made for two.

Absurdly, I became quite depressed for a while. I know now that I felt sad for my life. For all it had been, and for what it would soon no longer be. I, too, was about to re-marry, and would have two more children. Imagine the vagabond rock chick chained to a kitchen sink, an acquiescent mother of three. It was time to vacate the Neverwood forest, to loll out of the lagoon, to grow up. I didn't want to. I did a good impression of being in control, but I was ripped between identities underneath. I heard the echoes of Neverland fading, watched the pirate ship putting to sea. A recurring dream brought the Jolly Roger in a violent squall, in which the hero was being dragged down to Davy Jones's locker.[5] The David he no longer was.

Or was that me? They began revisiting in my head at night, the Lost Boys: brothers, cousins, innumerable male chums, colleagues and acquaintances from the past, who had married, settled and gone before. Where were they now? Perhaps a wife cannot be blamed for pulling the blinds on the once-upon-a-time females in her spouse's life. Because that was then. How Coco had managed to cling on all these years was nothing short of a miracle. Then again, since he refused to own one, she had an essential role – as David's mobile phone. Or was there more to it? Always, more?

Maturity is reckoned to fetch the veritable self to the fore, however strenuously we resist it. Maybe I was simply a victim of myself. We can't help mourning our fading youth. We can ignore it or deal with it. I set myself a task. I resolved to pull things into perspective. I made a huge effort to see rock stars for what they truly were: an extreme version of the rest of us, with much more money. As people who can indulge their wildest whim and fancy, leap at will onto trains, boats and planes bound for far-flung provinces, buy and build fantasy homes, buy other people, even, to do whatever their bidding may be this week. I forced myself to think of them in actual terms, as confections of childhood dysfunction, need and insecurity; as well as in the abstract, as marvellous whirlwinds of mankind-uplifting talent and creativity.

In the end, I came to regard them as I see them today: as perhaps the strangest strain of the human race ever conceived. And yet, how to detach oneself completely from their wonderful out-of-nowhere choruses and verses, their magical melodies and lyrics, their bizarre, un-unravellable personalities and insane, addictive lifestyles – all the qualities which rendered me 'normal' compared to them? Not gonna happen. I'd started writing about this extraordinary breed in the first place precisely because I never had a hope of becoming one of them. But I still wanted to understand. I'd started because of David, because of some switch he didn't realise he'd flicked, which had tripped me, sent me tumbling down the rabbit hole, and which had landed me here, an imposter in their impossible wonderland. The trouble was, I wasn't bored yet.

Not long after their marriage, on the advice of a new and highly astute financial adviser with broad experience across the media and entertainment, and with whom I have recently worked, David acquired a six hundred and fifty-acre estate outside Dublin, Ireland. Since 1969, the Irish tax code had exempted the royalty earnings of musicians, writers and other artists from income tax. When Ireland began capping the annual exemption in 2007, some artists such as U2 relocated their music publishing companies to the Netherlands. Also during the early 1990s, David invested heavily in a new ski resort. When he began pitching up to party at Marcus Bratter's Farm Club nightclub in his Hotel Nevaï, the gossips went into overdrive.

I'd bump into him briefly a few times more, out and about in New York, when I was there for work. A couple more years down the line, when we were having a cup of coffee in a bar in his old-favourite Caffè Reggio on MacDougal Street, he happened to mention that he was planning to put Château du Signal on the market. Iman was never wild about Switzerland, he said. She found it chilly and remote, even in summer, and there was nothing much there for her to do. Mustique was not without its problems, either; I could well appreciate why his wife would have issues with the fact that all the domestic staff were black.

'I wouldn't have thought she would want to live there,' agrees George Underwood. 'For a start, there's not a lot there. It's a holiday destination, nothing more. David talked about putting new technology in and writing albums down there, but who was going to fix it when it went wrong? Nice idea, but just not practical. It's also terribly racist, the place.

'One time when I was down there, Arne Hasselqvist,[6] the Swedish architect who did the house, came round for dinner and treated the servants like shit. I didn't like that. Another time, when we were out and about, we passed by the places where the servants lived, and it was these grotty, rotting shanty towns. I don't think Iman was being at all unreasonable about getting him to offload it – although he did sell it well short of what it was worth, I thought, considering the amount of work he'd put into it. Importing all that Indonesian wood and antiques from Bali.'

She would be known, hitherto, as Mrs David Jones. She had fallen in love with a person, Iman declared, not a persona. Bowie was a creation who came to life only under the spotlight. She intended to have a full private life with the man behind the mask.

Yet who was she, behind her own mask? Some of the world knew her as the Tia Maria girl in the telly ads. There were rumours, but where had she come from? Could her story really be as exotic as her looks, or was her mythology as manufactured as David's?

Yep.

Iman Mohamed Abdulmajid was born in Mogadishu, Somalia on 25 July 1955. She never set out to be a model, she said: in her country, it wasn't even a profession. 'Modelling didn't exist where I come from, so I never aspired to be a model. I always intended to approach modelling as a business move, as a stepping stone to something else.'

When celebrated American artist, wildlife photographer and author Peter Beard spotted her in Kenya, she was a married teenage student of political science at the University of Nairobi. She let Beard take some pictures of her, which he presented to the Wilhelmina Modelling Agency while he was back in New York. They invited Iman over for an interview. By the time she landed in America, she was already a sensation, thanks to a carefully contrived, strategically placed piece in a New York tabloid. Beard and Iman concocted it together, to project a myth. It claimed she was a simple, illiterate, animal-herding tribeswoman from the bush (they said 'cattle', the mischievous tabloids upped it to 'goats'), who had landed her big break.

As PR spin, it was hard to beat. Iman was in fact the daughter of a diplomat and a doctor, fluent in five languages, and had been educated at elite boarding schools.

'My mother was an activist, so was my father,' Iman would remember in an interview with Carol Cadwalladr published in the *Guardian* in June 2014 entitled 'I am the face of a refugee'. 'They came from a generation of young Somalis who were actively involved in getting independence for Somalis in 1960. So I remember when I was five, how busy our house was. People would come in the middle of the night, meetings after meetings, and protests and all that . . . and she instilled in me the fact that nobody can take your self-worth unless you give your consent.'

She was the most sophisticated goatherd in history, then. But the fakery did the trick, just as they'd known it would.

'A lot of people have the notion that Peter Beard independently victimised me, but that's not true,' she insisted, of the artist once married to supermodel Cheryl Tiegs. Conniving from the outset, her international career began. Her marriage to a Somalian businessman ended. In 1977, she became the girlfriend of movie star Warren Beatty. Later that year, she married basketball player Spencer Haywood, gave birth to their daughter the following year, and divorced him within the decade. At the peak of her game, she was raking in millions. She eventually quit while she was ahead, before the cut-throat fashion and beauty industries inevitably put her out to grass. She had already retired by the time she met David.

Immediately after her honeymoon, she took a BBC film crew to Somalia to make her harrowing *Somalia Diary* documentary, raising awareness of war, drought and famine in her homeland. In the mid-Nineties, she would launch Iman cosmetics for women of colour; and in 2000, the year the couple's longed-for and years-awaited baby Alexandria-Zahra Jones was born, she would present her new line, I-Iman Make-Up.

'The whole Iman thing, I didn't buy it,' says independent entertainment producer and accredited psychotherapist Richard Hughes, who has made countless studies of celebrities for film and television.

'Obviously they fell for each other, but their relationship seemed too good to be true, almost like a PR stunt. A lot of us were sceptical, and clearly we were all proved wrong. But I do still wonder about it. He seemed to change personality completely. It was as though he'd drawn a line under his past, everything he'd strived so hard to become, and now allowed her to take control. He let her sell his homes – places he'd invested a huge amount of time, money and emotion in, places he cared about – so that they could begin a whole new life together, free from any hangover of the past. That was classic behaviour. That was her, pissing in the corners, establishing her own territory with him, putting her mark on things.

'And then they went off the grid. Just like that. They had their new life, their private realm, their fabulous New York apartment, they were cocooned. There was no way in any more. It was those two against the world. I'm surprised the fans never held it against him. Because from that point on, he never created any more *great* music. There'd be an album every couple of years, but they kind of came and went. By the time it got to what turned out to be the farewell tour, his megastar days were over.'

Richard, along with millions of others, couldn't help feeling let down by Bowie.

'I definitely felt that. And then I started to look back over all the other times down the years when I'd felt short-changed by him. I was at a boys' boarding school when I became aware of him originally. I came in at *Aladdin Sane*. I grew up knowing that he was "gay" or "bisexual", yet there was something inauthentic about it – like it was stance, rather than genuine. At least with Freddie Mercury, you always knew where you stood. However much he tried to conceal it, you just knew he was gay. When David hit his *Let's Dance* period, I went for the look. I copied his whole preppy, slouchy, linen-suited, dropped-lapelled, big shoulder-padded, floppy-haired image. People said I looked just like him. But it was around that time that I realised there was a sadness running through Bowie. A melancholy that the bounce in his music couldn't conceal.'

Richard hated in particular the Live Aid recording that David made with Mick Jagger.

'It epitomised the overblown, trashy, uninteresting, middle-of-the-roadness of the Eighties. We'd all heard the rumours about Bowie and Jagger sleeping together, but I never believed them. To me, they were like two horny public schoolboys getting pissed and fiddling around with each other, but really wanting to poke a girl. I felt quite depressed about music and what it represented, at that point. The late Seventies and early Eighties were about people trying too hard to be open-minded.

'Then along came AIDS, and we all put our knickers back on and went into reverse. David Bowie became conservative. Once again, he let me down. In the Nineties, he went all Britpoppy in a parka, with fring-ey hair. It was not that interesting. Yet again, it didn't feel genuine. The music lost me, then. Nothing he released moved me for years. And then suddenly, out of nowhere, two massive swansong albums. Work that one out!'

He says that he still can't help wondering, to this day: what did David *do* for twenty-odd years with Iman?

'They holed up together. They tried and tried for a child together, they had IVF, they were even talking about adoption, and then under the wire they got one of their own. Then he did the John Lennon thing, tucked away in New York, "baking bread and bringing up baby". And he doted on his daughter: dads do have this incredible connection with their baby girls. Freud is still weirdly relevant.'

However disappointed many of his fans felt, this was a fresh, spruced-up, settled down, composed, organic Renaissance Bowie for the Nineties. Would the music live up to it? To begin with, it did. The so-called 'wedding album', *Black Tie White Noise*, was produced by Nile Rodgers and created at Mountain. It appeared on a new record label, Savage, and debuted at Number One. Both LP and label were short-lived. There was a crowded-corkboard feel about this sequence of songs; too many pictures, not enough drawing pins, an overkill of themes and thoughts and influences. It was the one with songs for tragic Terry, in particular the startling 'Jump They Say'. Here was more nostalgia, yet more looking back, when he had everything to look forward to.

Mick Ronson guest-guitared on the record, now that David and he were involved again. But Ronson was heading for the shadows, literally fading before their eyes. The completion of circles, the reach for closure, the last big gasp. That final, sad contribution by the Spider with the platinum hair was just as they knew it would be. He was leaving them on a high. Within weeks of the album's release, Mick Ronson was dead.

REAL NEW YORKER

19

1993–1997

What was his normal life like, during the mid-Nineties? He was just an old married man, he would tell you. When he was not on stage, he spent most of his time working – both in the studio and at home. He conducted interviews for a British arts magazine he was involved with. He wrote songs. He found that he had more time than ever for family and friends. Where once he had been 'terrible' at keeping in touch with people, he was now very good at it. His friends were mostly writers, painters and musicians, though he steered clear of the music industry. He had grown very fond of downtown New York, which he loved for its bohemian nature. He had simplified his life, and maintained just the one home. He and Iman travelled a good deal – often to Indonesia. He didn't understand that country, he said, which was why he liked it so much.

What did he find himself looking for, during those days?

'Glimmers of hope. I personally have to feel hope. I want my family to live joyful and fulfilled lives.'

If the wider perception was that David simply 'went off the grid' and faded away musically after his marriage to Iman, that was not his experience, nor that of his true fans. While other so-called 'dinosaur rock' heritage acts were being ridiculed for rehashing the past, cleaning up on 'safe' comeback tours, 'one last' outings and yet more compilations of greatest hits – come on, Tina, Rod, Macca,

Elton et al, and what on earth of worth had the Stones composed since 1972's *Exile on Main Street*? – at least David was doing his best to keep abreast of the current. He would absorb something of all of it, just as so many of them had gorged on him.

Madonna, Michael Jackson, Spice Girls, Backstreet Boys and all the other girls and boys aside, the Nineties were about alternative rock and independently recorded music, which crossed success-fully into the commercial arena when serviced by new indie labels. The scene throbbed with sub-genres, all to the beat of punk, includ-ing Britpop, indie pop, indie rock, gothic and grunge. As it evolved, 'alternative' became the umbrella under which such music achieved mainstream significance, thus contradicting the term. All over the US, college rock rolled. It was all really history repeating itself to the chords of the late Sixties, when the Velvet Underground and Iggy and the Stooges were the 'alternative', and when Bowie, T. Rex, Can, Neu, Kraftwerk, the New York Dolls and their ilk caught the baton and ran. What goes around, comes around.

Give, and take. To be fair, where would Gary Numan or the Smiths have been without Bowie? The Seventies glam-infused songwriting of die-hard David disciples Morrissey and Marr would not have been the same. What about U2? When the band ran dry after *Rattle & Hum*, they sloped off to Hansa in Berlin to rework their sound, just as David had done for his 'trilogy'. Joy Division, likewise, who were originally called Warsaw after the Bowie song 'Warszawa', and who were heavily influenced by David's Berlin albums. Minimalist composer Philip Glass created symphonies in homage to two of them, 'Low' and 'Heroes'. Nirvana, the Killers, Vanilla Ice – who sampled 'Under Pressure' on his hit 'Ice Ice Baby'. To come, Kanye West, with the all-action multi-discipline approach; and Lady Gaga. We should have known.

Flicking back through the CDs, R.E.M. were the big thing then, with *Automatic for the People* their major crossover and most of their albums (at least in this house) acquired retrospectively. They pioneered the genre and paved the way for Nirvana, the Pixies, Pearl Jam, They

Might be Giants. We saw the rise of Nine Inch Nails, the Smashing Pumpkin and Hole. We became obsessed with Bowie-influenced Radiohead. Cool Britannia ruled the airwaves, with Oasis, Blur, Pulp and Suede dominant. The latter's Bret Anderson candidly admitted: 'Bowie gave me a strong sense of ambition for the band.'

Who else? No Doubt; the Red Hot Chili Peppers, who were superstars by the Nineties; Alice in Chains, Green Day, Foo Fighters – formed in 1994 by drummer Dave Grohl after the suicide of his band Nirvana's frontman Kurt Cobain. 'Punk Rot!' screamed the tabloids. What did they know. Nihilistic, grindy and bleak was the message. The more the miserable-er. Shredded guitars, hard-core metal, with shades of prog, goth and psychedelia chucked in. David got stuck in, to all of it.

1. Outside marked his unsentimental return to Brian Eno and pianist Mike Garson as collaborators, on another concept album. David revisited the dystopian concepts which had preoccupied him in the past, this time set on the brink of a true-to-life new century. It was recorded at Mountain, Montreux, and at New York's Hit Factory. Inspired by all they had read about a ground-breaking Austrian mental hospital, David and Brian visited the Maria Gugging Psychiatric Clinic on the outskirts of Vienna, in January 1994. It had an international reputation on account of the 'outsider' art created by some of its patients, known as the Gugging Artists.

It was the psychiatrist Leo Navratil who first hit on the idea of getting patients to draw for him, so that he could use the drawings in his diagnosis. A year later, he recognised that a number of his patients were extremely talented artistically. The French painter, sculptor and champion of 'low art', Jean Dubuffet, confirmed this, coining the term Art Brut, or Outsider Art. Navratil published his first book on the subject, *Schizophrenia and Art*, in 1965, after which many Viennese artists were attracted to the Gugging. The patient-artists were given their first exhibition in 1970, and their works were presented in shows often thereafter. The Centre for Art and Psychotherapy was then founded, in 1981. The house of artists is today regarded as 'the model for psychiatric reforms based on art therapy as a means to reintegrate clients into society.'

It begs all the questions. And it seems the doctors at Cane Hill asylum who invited George Underwood to draw and paint for them all those years ago were not so suspect after all. If only tragic Terry Burns had been offered such ground-breaking therapy. If only David had discovered Gugging sooner, and had felt able to sponsor treatment for his brother in that amazing place.

1. Outside was experimental in the extreme. Not a stave had been pencilled prior to the band convening in the studio. Eno re-introduced his Oblique Strategies idea-generating flash cards, and David even deployed a new programme called the 'Verbasizer' on his Mac computer, to imitate the old cut-up technique for lyric writing. He was making a statement, thus, that technology would be a dominant force in his music going forwards, and about his intention to keep pace with hi-tech development and breakthroughs. He was making starkly clear that he would not be left behind.

The result is overridingly dark and sinister, it's quite a worrying album in places. Reflective, eccentric and sad, with blurts and drones of vocals and peculiar noises, it evokes the sound effects on some seaside Ghost Train ride as it edges ever closer to the dimension of the disturbed and the deranged. David later added niggly spoken excerpts of a murder mystery he'd penned for *Q* magazine towards the end of 1994. The album's track 'The Hearts Filthy Lesson', no apostrophe, is industrial, confrontational and grim, and is a pejorative Bowie take on developments in the world of art. It was released as a single, with a controversial video, but didn't do much.

The closing track, 'Strangers When We Meet', was first recorded for his 1993 *The Buddha of Suburbia* soundtrack. This new version was also released as a single, together with a studio reworking by Eno of 'The Man Who Sold the World'. It barely dented the chart.

You, you, you, how those lyrics haunted me. Not to mention the title. It's how I felt when I saw him in the street.

The Outside tour opened on 14 September 1995, in Hartford, Connecticut, with glam and new wave-influenced industrial rock band Prick supporting the first show. An unusual move, beginning the tour to promote the album before the album was actually out, but hey. It was released by Virgin America, by now a division of EMI, on 25 September, by which time the tour was well underway. Presentation was non-theatrical, pared-down, half-cocked; more like a building site than a stage set. David's look leaned towards grunge, but at least featured a trio of exquisite jackets by Alexander McQueen.[1] Across America, he and his backing band, which featured stalwarts Carlos Alomar, Reeves Gabrels, Gail Ann Dorsey, Mike Garson and more, were supported by Trent Reznor's Nine Inch Nails. Bowie's first tour since the consignment of his classic hits to the vaults on the 1990 Sound + Vision tour, he chose also to deliver some obscure and previously unperformed songs.

Morrissey was selected as support act for the European dates, commencing with four nights at Wembley, but stepped down after his first nine, with the hump. Something to do with feeling miffed by the proposal that his and David's sets should segue, thus depriving Morrissey of proper bows and encores only for him, as Morrissey explains in *Mozipedia: The Encyclopedia of Morrissey and the Smiths* by Simon Goddard. Another love affair over. The Gyres, Placebo and a few local bands joined the tour at different stages. The 13 December show at Birmingham's NEC featured Alanis Morissette, the Lightning Seeds and Echobelly. They wrapped at the Palais Omnisports de Paris-Bercy on 19 February 1996, after which David took the shortest break before retreating, sleeves up, to the Philip Glass studio in New York.

Nothing goes away. David would continue to innovate, elevate, self-renovate, even exterminate. If there was a theme to his next album, *Earthling* – the one featuring rear-view Bowie in the stunning Lee McQueen Union Jack frock coat, surveying England's green and pleasant land – and recorded at Philip Glass's, and at Mountain, David summed it up as this:

'I guess the common ground with all the songs is this abiding need in me to vacillate between atheism or a kind of gnosticism. I keep going backwards and forwards between the two things, because they mean a lot in my life. I mean, the church doesn't enter into my writing, or my thought; I have no empathy with any organised religions. What I need is to find a balance, spiritually, with the way I live and my demise. And that period of time – from today until my demise – is the only thing that fascinates me.'

Sonically, and everyone said so, this one really *was* the best thing since *Scary Monsters*. Aggressive, distorted, robotic and tense, an assault of industrial, electronic, drum & bass sounds and much else, David produced it all himself. It featured a Tin Machine song, 'Baby Universal', which stood out better here, and the hooky 'Little Wonder': a 'stream of consciousness' number in which he'd taken Snow White and the Seven Dwarfs (of all fairytale characters) as his starting point, re-imagined every dwarf in succession, and had made up a line for each of them. When he ran out of dwarfs, he simply invented more.

It would return to haunt me a year later, when my son was born, and I took him in his Rockatot one chucking-down evening to attend an interview for my daughter at a posh London school. Only after her one-to-one session with the colour-coordinated Head did I hear that she had enquired about Mia's baby brother, and had asked whether we had any nicknames for him.

'Oh yeah,' said Mia, blithely, 'we call him after all his bad habits, like the Seven Dwarfs: Fatty, Stinky, Farty, Burpy, Pukey, Porky, Wailer.' I can still hear myself, gnashing all the way home: 'You said *FARTY* to a *HEADMISTRESS*???' She didn't want to go there, anyway.

Come June 1996, they were back on the road, for a short Outside Summer Festivals tour beginning in Tokyo. The short, twenty-seven-date tour was due to push on into Russia and Iceland, and conclude with a series of European festival appearances, ending in Switzerland on 21 July.

Also on the road in the Far East were Danielz and T. Rextasy, the world's only official tribute band to Marc Bolan and T. Rex, who were hugely popular in Japan. Neither David nor Danielz could have known that they were destined to meet there. David had just played the Sun Palace, Fukuoka, on the north shore of Kyushu island. T. Rextasy had performed at the Crossing Hall in the same city. For David, it must have been a spectral double-take: not only is Danielz exactly the same height and build as Bolan, and even owns and wears some of his clothes and shoes, but he sports Marc's corkscrew hairstyle. To this day, he is Marc's dead ringer, and makes even diehard fans gawp in amazement.

'We were travelling back to Tokyo on the bullet train, just before midday on 17 June 1996,' remembers Danielz. 'It was a warm, clear day on the brink of summer. We had missed the notorious crush of the Japanese rush hour, and the train station wasn't very crowded. Even so, there were plenty of people about. But being a very polite race, none of the Japanese people there would have dreamed of approaching the instantly recognisable individual standing a little way down the platform.

'I didn't spot him at first. We were standing there waiting for our chaperone to bring our tickets when our guitarist Leo said, "David Bowie just walked past!" I looked, and sure enough, it was him – with his manager, Coco, and one of his musicians. I didn't notice any of them with any luggage, so I guess it had all been sent ahead by the promoters, just as ours was. I instinctively went up to him with my hand out, and he shook it willingly. He was on his way to Russia to perform at the Kremlin Palace Concert Hall the next day. They had planned to fly to Tokyo and catch a connecting flight. But the local airport he was due to fly out from had had a serious fire, so they were having to take the bullet train like us.

'I don't know what made me do it,' Danielz says, 'but I thought, what the hell. I wanted to talk to him about Marc, and thought I'd probably never get another opportunity [which turned out to be correct]. So I went over to him and said, my name's Danielz. "I know who you are," he said. "I've been reading about you in the press, and I've seen your photos." I asked him what he was doing catching a train, and he explained to me about their convoluted journey to Russia. After that, I just came out with it. Do you still miss Marc? I said. Without a flinch, he looked at me and said, "I miss him every day. Every day." He repeated it. I could tell he really, genuinely, missed his friend.

'We had a brief chat. I told him about our tour, and what a huge fan of Marc's I'd been. We barely talked about his own music at all! I didn't want to come across as a starstruck fan. I'd been a massive Bowie nut in my youth, of course: I got into him slightly after T. Rex, during his *Aladdin Sane* period. "Drive-In Saturday" is still one of my favourite songs of all time. Also, from what Visconti has told me about him [Danielz and Tony later worked together, and became friends], I knew that he didn't like talking too much about himself. I then asked him if he'd mind being in a couple of photos with me. When my wife Caron took the first one, Coco walked right in front of us so that she interrupted the shot. This was obviously a pre-arranged ruse they had between them. "No! No!" David said to her, "These guys are cool." Caron took another one of David and me. When we got home, we found that in fact both of them had come out.

'The train arrived. We wished each other luck, and all got on. He went to the right. So as not to seem like pests, we went to the left. During the journey, when one of us got up to go to the dining carriage, and passed by, we waved to the other. It was an extraordinary journey in so many ways. The bullet trains are the most fantastic I've ever been on. Some of the seats are made of soft leather that can be spun around a hundred and eighty degrees, so that you can take in the sights while travelling. They move at tremendous speed with Rolls-Royce smoothness, and there's a speedometer in every carriage so that you can check how fast you are going. The conductors all bowed before entering each carriage. They wore white gloves, and showed the utmost respect for all passengers alike. The

March, 1975: David, Yoko Ono and John Lennon at the 17th Annual Grammy Awards, Uris Theater, Broadway, NYC.

C'est Chic ... with Nile Rodgers at the Frankie Crocker Urban Contemporary Awards, Savoy Ballroom, NYC, 21 January 1983.

Taking the Mick, (3): with Jagger and Tina Turner at the Prince's Trust 10th Annual Rock Gala, Wembley Arena, 23 June 1986.

Ready for his close-up on the Serious Moonlight world tour, 1983.

The dubious delights of the Glass Spider world tour, 1987.

George Underwood marries Birgit in Bromley, 12th May 1971. Angie is only 3 weeks off giving birth to Zowie.

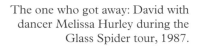

The one who got away: David with dancer Melissa Hurley during the Glass Spider tour, 1987.

David marries former supermodel Iman, Florence, June 1992. Front, fourth from left, George Underwood. Seated, David's mother Peggy Jones; David's son and best man Duncan; maid of honour Bethann Hardison; Iman; David; Iman's parents; Coco Schwab; hairdresser Teddy Antolin.

The author's first-born Mia in David's drawing room,
Britannia Bay House, Mustique, 1992.

Humble scribe relaxes
in infinity-pool pavilion
of multi-millionaire rock
superstar's Caribbean
hideaway.

Mummy, can we live here forever?

David's hexagonal Japanese
dining room made of
coconut palm trunks.

Mia co-pilots a 6-seater
Merlyn Commander from
Barbados to Mustique.

David double-takes with Danielz, frontman of Bolan tribute band T.Rextasy, as they await the bullet train in Tokyo, summer 1996.

Bowie/Bolan producer Tony Visconti, captured by the author during Q&A at *Born to Boogie: The Motion Picture,* BFI, Southbank, 20 May 2016.

Rick Wakeman performs during An Evening With Russ Ballard, Leicester Square Theatre, London, 20th January 2016.

Spooky Ghost: Bowie guitarist Gerry Leonard in an acclaimed solo gig at London's Water Rats, Gray's Inn Road, 5th May 2016.

George Underwood and David on Bowie's yacht, Deneb, cruising the French/Italian Riviera, summer 1988.

Jumping tracks, changing towns ... David and Coco Schwab (to his left) at Waterloo station, London, 30 June 2002.

One eye sees …
November 1995.

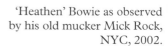
'Heathen' Bowie as observed
by his old mucker Mick Rock,
NYC, 2002.

Fans leave touching tributes
to David on the pavement in
Beckenham, January 2016.

The Three Tuns pub,
157 Beckenham High Street,
where the die-hards bid
him a fond farewell.

passengers in turn were very respectful towards them. It was busy, but not over-crowded: bullet train tickets are expensive.

'Of all the musicians I've ever met during my career, David was by far the biggest star. All the other musicians I've worked with who were hugely popular in their day – Boy George, Marc Almond, Slade, Suzi Quatro – paled in comparison. He was a global superstar. And yet there was nothing at all starry about him. He came across as a really normal and very nice guy. He wasn't hiding himself away, and he wasn't in disguise. He was just one of us. Just another musician out on the road who was catching a train.'

Someone else who got a snapshot of what David Bowie was really like during the mid-Nineties was society photographer Fergus Greer. David had designed a range of wallpapers for home interiors retailers Laura Ashley, of all cool and minimalist outlets, and was being interviewed by the Review section of the UK *Sunday Times* to promote them. Fergus and he met in London to shoot portraits to accompany the piece.

'Candice Temple was the picture editor back then, and she commissioned me,' Fergus recalls. 'As always with such things, her perspective of the shoot and what happened was very different from my experience of it. We commonly make assumptions about what people are thinking, which is not the case. Probably I know more about that now than I did in those days.' With some sixty to eighty pictures of his owned and regularly displayed by the National Portrait Gallery, Fergus is now a full-time professional psychotherapist.

'I was on the cusp of leaving the UK to live in Los Angeles. I had a contract with the *Sunday Times* magazine to do covers and features, and I worked for the Review section quite a lot. It was all arts-related. Candice rang me one day and said, "I've got a really interesting person for you to photograph: it's David Bowie." I went, *Waoh!* I'd grown up at school listening to *Hunky Dory*, *"Heroes"*, *Ziggy Stardust* and so on. I was a huge fan, and he was a big star. A legend. I'm not usually starstruck, but this was amazing.

'He was forty-nine years old – younger than I am today. That whole main, mad period of his career had already passed. So he was a mature, successful, iconic musician. The classic hits were history, and I wasn't quite sure where he was up to with his music. You never were sure with Bowie, what he was, who he was, what he was up to, or what his presentation was going to be. This would be the first time I'd ever met him. I was a little intimidated, you could say that. The age difference was significant: I would have been twenty-five to his almost-fifty.'

He was in awe of him?

'Oh, totally. I'm always in awe of people I photograph, to a certain extent. I don't mean that I'm in awe of "celebrity" per se, but people who have done something extraordinary, whether it be culturally, literary, politically, sportingly, whatever. Achievers. Culty film-makers. Major Hollywood film directors. This was the man who had set the pace for a very long time in terms of sexuality, creativity, art, music, photography – an entire milieu of things. Someone who'd had a massive effect upon us all. He was highly ambitious, and had an extremely competitive edge. He had it first with Marc Bolan, and then with Mick Jagger. It was one of the many things that made him fascinating.

'Candice the picture editor was going to be there at the shoot, which was unusual. But she wanted to meet him, too. We arranged to do it at his agent's house in Fulham – what I now understand to have been Coco's place. Only she wasn't there. The story was to promote the designs he'd done for Laura Ashley wallpapers. And I thought, how *weird*. I really can't see David Bowie doing Laura Ashley wallpapers, but anyway. It was all to do with reinventing himself yet again, I suppose. So it was odd, but we all got on with it. His wallpaper had a minotaur design, for which he'd used Photoshop and collaging. He was using the computer to create new art. This was a fresh medium, and one that he was really excited about.

'We arrived at this bog-standard terraced house – I can't remember which street it was in – and I was preoccupied with various plans. We used huge amounts of equipment in those days, and I had a lot of stuff to deal with and coordinate. I suspected that his boredom threshold would be very short. And, you know, the time that we'd have together, that his capacity would be limited. So to keep him engaged in it, the shoot needed to be well-organised so that we could move from A to B to C very quickly, and get a lot of different images in a very short space of time.

'I usually worked like that, in most of my photography. If the budget allowed for it. And if it didn't, I would pay for it anyway. I'd do a number of set-ups, all set and lit separately, and a few scenarios which could be lit differently, turn one off, turn another on, so that you'd get a series of completely different looks without him having to hang around while I changed everything. That way, you get a big body of work in a very short period of time.

'And that's what I did. But we had the added restriction of it being a relatively small terraced house, with lots of furniture and ornaments in it. We weren't working in a studio. It was quite a lot to work around, and not really the right setting in which to do an in-situ shot with such a major and unique artist. Plus, it wasn't *his* house, which I could have made use of, but a residential house anyway, which is always quite personal and cluttered. On top of that, it was quite a *female* house. For me, taking a portrait of him in that setting was saying things that he didn't necessarily want to say. I think the use of that house was for convenience, more than anything else. I knew where he was going on to, a private viewing at the Saatchi Gallery.'

David was particularly interested in where Fergus was going to shoot him, and what kind of poses he was going to be asked to make.

'It was an early summer's evening, and David arrived alone, with a huge smile on his face. "Hey," he said, "I'm David." He was very relaxed, he asked what was going on, he was very chatty. We got straight down to it, and I got him into the first set-up, which was a backdrop with his wallpaper. Candice later recounted, in a piece she wrote, that he then started talking about German expressionist art and all that. I have no recollection of it. She wrote that I knew a lot about it, and that David did, too, and so that's what we talked about for the next two hours. I don't quite remember it like that! But we did talk a lot. Mostly about art school. I'd gone to St Martin's, where I studied sculpture initially, and he said he went to Ravensbourne College of Art [he didn't]. And he told me something quite disarming, that he realised very quickly that he was never going to make much money from being an artist, and that was why he went into music. "It was very clear to me, very early on, that this was the way to do it," he said.'

Fergus had set up a nine-foot-wide white backdrop in the back garden, ready for the next shot.

'We talked a bit about photography, and he said, "The one thing I really don't like is white backgrounds . . ." I gulped. I was about to take him outside to the biggest white background we could fit in the place! We got out there, and he smiled. "OK," he said, "white background!" We laughed about it, he did the picture without complaint, and that was that. He had every reason and right to refuse, but he didn't.

'David had this big energy. It filled the room. So did the fug; he did smoke rather a lot during the shoot. He was in good shape, very slim, and comfortably smart-casual. His jacket, shirt and pants were very good clothes. It looked like Armani of the period.'

Was Fergus thrown by the reality of his eyes?

'Not initially, when we were doing the wider shots, and I wasn't going tight on him. But obviously it became more apparent as I worked more close-up. One's a dilated pupil and the other's not. It's a specific peculiarity. I tried to behave well, and not to stare! It's like if someone has a scar on their face. If they invite you to peer at it, great, but otherwise you can't say, Stop a minute, I just want to look at that scar of yours! It's the elephant in the room.

'Portraits have always interested me. Because they are simple. There is no clutter. People go, "Oh, that's boring," but actually it's not boring, because it's all about the person. Their nakedness. What you see is what you get. It's about them presenting themselves as nothing other than what they really are. You can go back and revisit a portrait, and it has a certain calmness to it, a unique quality. Every time you look again, you find new things. The white all around is equally as important as the subject in the centre, really, in terms of getting the balance and rhythm exactly right. How much impact or effect are the background and light having? Space and positioning play a huge part.

'But of course I was distracted from all that by the eyes. They were extraordinary, and incredibly striking. People's eyes always are . . . even dead eyes. All the emotion is in the eyes, and if that's not there, viewers are not going to connect to the picture. David's eyes were obviously hugely important to the whole concept of who David Bowie was. The other thing was his left-handedness. We discussed it. He used his left hand to write with, he said, but did most other things right-handed. That was fascinating.

'David was a very easy sitter. Very comfortable with who he was. His manner of relating to people was really personable. Had I been expecting that? You hear rumours, you speculate, you make assumptions. But when the person turns up, you have no idea how they are going to be. You are suddenly in a very intense relationship with them for a very short time. I found him highly professional, and great at getting everybody else to relax. He made everyone feel included, from the assistant to the art director. He treated us all as equals. That's an art in itself. Also, he didn't try to stage-manage me. He gave himself up to the process. He was cool, he engaged with it, he did exactly as I asked. And he didn't ask to see the Polaroids.

'Terence Donovan, the famous photographer with whom I did my apprenticeship, once said that only really intelligent people can handle fame. Because it's hard to manage huge amounts of wealth and great fame. From my limited exposure to David Bowie, I was convinced that he was managing it extremely well. Behave like a normal person and you get treated like one. It's not rocket science.'

David received an inordinate amount of stick for the acts he chose to share the spotlight with him at his fiftieth-birthday Madison

Square Garden celebration on 9 January 1997. Why so? Wasn't it up to him who he fancied going out and playing with on his birthday? Where were the Spiders, crowed the old-timers, while others bleated in defence of Konrads, King Bees and Margate's finest. Shouldn't it have been a major retrospective? Couldn't he have got up there with his superstar equals, inviting Elton, Jagger, Tina and Macca to the stage? He did not go gentle, and he did just as he pleased. Lou Reed gave it a go, as did more light-footed artists such as the Smashing Pumpkins, Black Francis of the Pixies, the Cure's Robert Smith, Dave Grohl of the Foos. The songs that David performed were mostly from his recent two albums. He saved the classics until last, giving the crowd what they craved: ' "Heroes" ', 'Under Pressure' and a most moving 'Space Oddity'.

'It's wise not to get too euphoric or too melancholic,' he would tell Jarvis Cocker in an interview that year. 'A balance in between for me has always given me a much wider and easier passage through life. I find it such a disillusionment to get incredibly excited and happy about things, and that will not maintain. Also, it's quite psychotic to become like that. I mean, it's really depressed schizophrenic, when you go from these incredible heights to lows. I've done all of those, and it really serves one badly.'

Just under a month later, on 3 February 1997, *Earthling* was released. The tour to promote it would stretch from June until November, and would take him all the way from Lübeck, Germany, across Europe, North America and down into South America, calling it a day in Buenos Aires after eighty-three shows. Lee McQueen[2] was once again on wardrobe duty. I didn't get to see the August shows at Shepherd's Bush Empire. A small matter of being a week away from giving birth. David would look forward to taking most of the following year off. He wasn't the only one.

★

20

1997–2004

Were it possible to teleport back to any Bowie era and incarnation, I'd go looking for quaint fifty-something David, who could be found pottering around the streets of Manhattan early in the morning and late at night during the final years of the twentieth century. Rocked-out, been-there Bowie was now Hip Dad Keeping Up with the Kids. It was touching. One minute the hair was a blond flop, the next a foxy bath brush. The angular chin would get goatee'd, then shaved. The Eighties perma-tan had faded back to his pallid Celtic hue. A skin cancer-awareness stance? After so many years spent bronzing himself in the tropics and on UV tanning beds, he was now going natural. He was cutting down on his life-threatening sixty to eighty cigarettes a day – at least he'd downgraded from Gitanes through Marlboro to Marlboro Lights – and would soon quit for good. He had resumed boxing training at a local gym. He was wearing comfortable shoes. This was Green-Card-carrying, low-key Englishman in New York David, keeping it real.

The World Trade Center still stood, Mayor Rudy Giuliani had cleaned up the city's act, and the economy was back on track. The desirable downtown SoHo/NoLIta neighbourhoods which he'd shortly be scouring for a fab apartment were a bustle of kooky galleries and boutiques, cranky record stores and bookshops. There was an abundance of small, credible live music venues, somewhere different for every night. McSorley's Old Ale House on East 7th, the Leo Castelli Gallery at 420 West Broadway, the Alternative Museum, the Rizzoli Bookstore and Caffè Reggio were some kicky places to hang. Bleecker Bob's Records at 118 West 3rd Street, once the Night Owl Café of Lovin' Spoonful and James Taylor fame, was still trading vintage vinyl. David loved to hang there at odd times of day and night. The staff would stick 'The Laughing Gnome' on the turntable when he walked in, just to annoy him. (When the beloved scruffy store closed eventually in April 2013, many mourned the end of an era.)

New York still felt like the centre of the world. Just as John Lennon had done, David relished the freedom the place afforded him. He could come and go without anyone bothering him, which no celebrity could do in Pap-Central London any more. He was left alone as he stalked the avenues, side streets and parks in contemplation, pleasing himself. There was neither reason nor inclination to ever leave.

'I've become quietly domesticated, which is a major change to me,' he told writer Richard Wallace in 2002. 'I used to like living in different countries. But I enjoy our life together so much now that it doesn't really matter. New York's fine.'

He stopped short of calling himself a 'native New Yorker'.

'You had to have been born in one of the five boroughs to qualify, or on a plane about to land at JFK or something, so they tell me,' he said to me one day during lunch. 'But I also heard that it's not enough to have been born here. You have to live here for donkey's years, and you have to die here, too. So maybe I'll do that at some point in the future, when I'll finally be regarded as a real New Yorker and not some upstart infiltrator, like Dylan Thomas – who of course was born in Swansea but died the classic New York death, practically drowning himself in whisky at the White Horse Tavern on Hudson. Where a lot of other writers have tried very hard to die, I should think. It's that kind of place. I've often thought I would have had a lot in common with Dylan Thomas. Never short of an opinion. Always right about everything. At least I used to be, until I got married!'

In February 1997, together with flamboyant American banker David Pullman, he launched the much-lauded Bowie Bonds, or 'Pullman Bonds': an asset-backed security which used current and future revenue from twenty-five of his own albums as collateral. The two hundred and eighty-seven songs used as the underlying assets of these bonds were recorded prior to 1990. What did he need the $55 million for? To buy back songs that were owned by former manager Tony Defries. He forfeited his royalties for the ten-year life of the bond. They had an interest rate of 7.9 per cent.

This scheme was unusual in that it was one of the first ever to use intellectual property, 'I.P', as collateral. The bonds' shelf-life was finite, and began to decline with the growth of online music and file-sharing that led to the inevitable decline in album sales. They were liquidated in 2007, as originally planned, and the rights to the income from his songs reverted to him. The advent of legal online music retail revived interest in these and similar securities towards the end of the decade.

Spring 1998 delivered an opportunity for mischief, when David became involved in a literary hoax conceived by the novelist William Boyd. The book's subject was an obscure, abstract expressionist painter, and was called *Nat Tate: An American Artist 1928–1960*. But Tate never existed. Boyd imagined him as a depressed and dissatisfied soul at odds with the world, in despair at the quality of his own work, who leapt to his death from the Staten Island ferry. His body was never recovered. Several luminaries were in on the act, including writer Gore Vidal and David, who was at the time on the board of the magazine *Modern Painters* and a director of 21 Publishing, the house behind the book. The character's name was inspired by two of London's most popular art galleries, the National and the Tate.

On the evening of April Fool's Day, 1998 – maybe the date should have rung a few bells – David hosted a glamorous launch party in the studio of American artist Jeff Koons at the junction of Broadway and East Houston. The majority of the guests at this event of the season were art critics, dealers and collectors, mingling with a handful of celebrities: writers Paul Auster and Siri Hustvedt, and artist Julian Schnabel among them. David got up to read aloud from the book, while Picasso's biographer gave an address about Tate's very special relationship with both Picasso and Georges Braque.

The hoax, which 'fooled some of the biggest names in the art world', was exposed by the London *Independent* about a week later. It was a classic Emperor's New Clothes wheeze, a ripe bit of mischief that caught the cool lot with their boxers down. They were all in the altogether. David clearly just couldn't resist. It was, wrote David Lister in the *Independent*, 'one of the best literary scams in years'. Boyd would later deploy Tate in a supporting role in his novel *Any Human Heart*, and in its television adaptation. Far be it from an author to waste a perfectly good fake.

'In 1998 we were at the height of the Young British Artists' delirium,' Boyd later commented to the *Daily Telegraph* in November 2011. 'The air was full of Hirst and Emin, Lucas, Hume, Chapman, Harvey, Ofili, Quinn and Turk. My own feeling was that some of these artists – who were never out of the media, and who were achieving record prices for their artworks – were, to put it bluntly, not very good.'

The story flashed around the globe, and left its magic mark. In 2011, a drawing signed by 'Nat Tate' was sold for a significant sum at Sotheby's. It was by William Boyd.

In September 1998, to great fanfare, David launched BowieNet, his own internet service provider, offering subscription-based, hi-speed dial-up access to the emerging online world. The ISP was made available first in the US, then right across the world. Users were provided with the internet, their own customisable home page – creativity was expected – and had access to unreleased tracks, software and other benefits.

'I wanted to create an environment where not just my fans, but all music fans, could be part of a single community where vast archives of music and information could be accessed, views stated and ideas exchanged,' David said. He'd seen the future, and the future was YouTube. The venture would win him a Guinness World Record: as first musician to create an internet service provider.

Philip Norman, the internationally acclaimed journalist and biographer, was invited to interview David exclusively for the *Sunday Times*, to promote another of David's forays into the worldwide web. Surprisingly, given that both were amiable and easygoing men, it was loathe at first sight.

'Bowie asked for me to interview him after reading a piece I'd written about Bob Marley,' Philip tells me. 'I was flown to New York in the care of a PR who resembled the young Erich von Stroheim.[1] The peg was the launch of bowieart.com, the internet service provider set up to market Bowie's own paintings [which make Ronnie Wood's brown buffalo portraits look like Van Goghs]. We talked for barely an hour at the studio where Bowie was working; he blew cigarette smoke in my face throughout, and there were continual interruptions. I found him rather dull and over-reliant on quotations from Monty Python ("No one expects the Spanish Inquisition!"), though he did volunteer the surprising statement that he hated performing live, and wouldn't care if he never had to again. I had been warned in advance that "David cares only about the future, and isn't interested in the past"; and that, in particular, his half-brother Terry was a no-go area. However, he brought up the subject, and spoke about Terry in detail and with real feeling.'

At the end of the session, Philip was informed by the PR that he'd had all the interview time he was going to get.

'I said I needed more, or there would be no *Sunday Times* piece. There was some humming and hawing, then young von Stroheim said, "David wonders if you like his new album." "Yes, I do," I said. "But you didn't tell him so," was the reply. In fact, I'd been saving the subject of the new album for the second interview. I've run up against many superstar egos, but none so absurdly fragile. In the end, I was granted another forty-five minutes the following day. It consisted mostly of an unfavourable review by Bowie of our previous conversation when, he said, I'd harped on the subject of his half-brother, despite knowing that he was only interested in the future. My protest that he had brought up the subject of Terry, and talked quite obsessively about him, was met with icy denial.

'I've interviewed many tricky subjects, from James Brown and Little Richard to Elizabeth Taylor and Richard Burton, and hit it off with all of them; only Bowie lives in my memory as a total prick.'

Late in 1999, to no great fanfare, David took his internet exploration a leap further with the launch of Bowiebanc, his own online banking facility, through USABancShares.com. It was envisaged, declared his spokespeople, as being 'one more way to create online community'.

'David has always prided himself on being first,' said Ron Roy, one of Bowie's partners in the online company Ultra Star, which ran his official website and internet service provider. Users of bowiebanc.com received ATM cards, cheque books and other banking materials featuring David's name and image, together with a year's worth of BowieNet service. He and his partners predicted that fans would clamour to use the bank to express their loyalty to the ever-changing Bowie brand. They got that one wrong. It was a megalomaniacal move too far. Bowiebanc evaporated into the ether in no time.

I never got the chance to ask him about his last album of the century, the best he'd made in years. I could barely remember the last time I'd been moved to tears by a Bowie record. I'm not ashamed to say that I wept when 'hours . . .' arrived. To be fair, I was postpartum hormonal and tearful 24/7, thanks to baby number three. But I wasn't by any means the only one to fall upon *'hours ...'* as *Hunky Dory* for the new millennium. Many were the fans of this bewitching meld of past triumphs and tribulations, a return to the fresh, uncluttered form of David's twenty-something songwriting.

This was a riotous cake left out in the rain, proof that music was still his first love. An all-American yet resolutely British Pie, sprinkled with gaiety and grief. This was gritty, grinding, cute, optimistic, resigned, considered, and wise. His voice sounded cavernous and bloodstained. There was a vaulted, churchy stillness behind the mania. A *soupçon* of bitterness, too, did I detect? He seemed to be holding nothing back. The whole was tenebrous, and underpinned with mountainous confidence. You could almost hear his tummy rumbling, the creak of his thoughts.

A great many much younger Bowie fans quote this as the album they came in on. Hardly surprising, it's that good. The initial songs were written by David with Reeves Gabrels as a soundtrack for a computer game produced by Eidos – '*Omrikon – the Nomad Soul*' – in which David also played a character, 'Boz'. The collection was soon a respiring entity in its own right. 'Thursday's Child', the opener, 'The Pretty Things are Going to Hell', and 'The Dreamers', its kiss goodbye, are as good as he gets. 'Seven' is epic, dreamy and mournful. Just an acoustic guitar, a little country twang in the backup, and a London boy's flat-vowelled, never-leave-me vocal. David's so close to the mic, he's almost whispering in your ear. I was enchanted. This was just like listening to him back at the Arts Lab on Beckenham High Street all those moons ago. It sounded like a metaphor for his life. I played it over and over, as if possessed.

Released on 4 October 1999, on Virgin for EMI, it was the first full album by a mainstream artist available for download via the internet – a fortnight before the CD could be bought in the shops. This was yet further confirmation of David's growing fascination with advanced technology. He found thrilling the infinite possibilities of the internet. He once said he wished that he'd been born with 'a more scientific mind', and lamented his inability to understand challenging subjects such as quantum mechanics and physics. You and me both. What if the neurobiologists engaged in reading an individual's brain patterns could find a way to transmit them into the brain of someone else? What other avenues would be opened up by engineers developing materials able to bend the light of an object out of view, rendering it invisible?

And what about 'the new magic', teleportation: the ability to arrive at a destination without travelling? One minute pushing through the Market Square, or listening to the rubber band playing out of tune in the Library Gardens; the next, regarding Earth from Chryse Planitia on Mars: no god-awful small affair. How about the first steps being taken into Human Exploration Telerobotics, allowing man to navigate space vicariously, via a Mars rover, say, or using mechanical arms to touch some far-flung asteroid? It was, he said, the fantastical future of communication, real-life *Star Trek* meets *Doctor Who*, edging ever closer. Who wouldn't time-travel, if they got the chance? Then again, as H.G. Wells said, 'We all have our time machines, don't we. Those that take us back are memories. And those that carry us forward are dreams.'

He toured the *'hours . . .'* album briefly, and without loyal compadre Reeves Gabrels, their friendship and chemistry having flared but been snuffed out. There were just eight live shows in North America and Europe, beginning at Wembley, and augmented by many TV appearances. The 14 October 1999 performance at the cherished old Elysée Montmartre, Paris, was filmed and recorded. The Vienna gig was played on the same date as the launch of BowieNet Europe, and so was also relayed, thrillingly, as a live webcast. His 19 November New York outing was also made available as a webcast, transmitted on 7 December 1999 – the date of the final show of the tour, in Copenhagen. On Christmas Eve, he presented for 'interview' over the internet by some twenty thousand pinching-themselves fans.

'I don't think it's an over-estimation to say that David Bowie has been the most influential artist of the entire second half of the twentieth century,' commented broadcaster Robert Elms. 'And I say the word "artist". I don't just mean "singer". I mean designer, stylist, videos, fashion. Wherever you look, if you scratch the surface, you can see the influence of David Bowie. Pretty much every band now will have grown up listening to him, whether it's *Ziggy Stardust* or it's *"Heroes"*, or it's *Young Americans*. Go through your generations and you can hear echoes of Bowie everywhere. He's touched pretty much every creative artist, I think, working in Britain today, in one way or another. Because he's that important.'

All had been quiet on the domestic front. Not for much longer. Prayers were answered, soon into the New Millennium, with a gift for which David and his wife had longed for years. The announcement of Iman's pregnancy made headlines around the world. At forty-five, the mother of a twenty-two-year-old daughter and twenty-nine-year-old stepson, she must have despaired that her moment had passed. She was hardly at the peak of fertility: by the age of forty, the chance of getting pregnant in any given month is just five per cent. David's former heavy alcohol intake, drug abuse, excessive smoking and relatively advanced age – fifty-three – couldn't have helped.

After eight years on the project and several failed bouts of IVF treatment, they had just begun to weigh up the fors and againsts of adoption when their 'miracle' occurred. It's a common phenomenon, the years and years of trying, the medical intervention, the resignation and the eventual giving up, only to find oneself naturally with child once the 'need' to conceive is let go. The couple were beyond joyous. But within weeks, David was burying his eighty-eight-year-old mother Peggy, whose 'unexpected' death was announced on 2 April. It is often said that a baby is born when a family member dies. Many regard this as symbolic in the 'circle of life', or as karma: replacing an existence extinguished with a new life begun. Whether reincarnation, mere coincidence or nothing but a wives' tale, who cared. They were over the moon as were David's son Duncan and his wife Rodene, when their own bundle of joy, baby Stenton David Jones, arrived on 10 July 2016. Stenton for his great-grandfather, David for his grandfather: 'Exactly six months after his grandad made room for him,' wrote Duncan, on Twitter. 'All my love and awe to the incredible @rodeneronquillo, who made a human being in her belly. Warrior woman and every day, my hero.'

Alexandria Zahra Jones was born at Mount Sinai Hospital, New York, on 15 August 2000.

'Prepared?' David tittered. 'Are you joking? We did all the breathing things, and the counting. But nothing prepares you. We raced there in the car, and I got to cut the umbilical cord. And then the fun started.'

Just seventeen days after her birth, *Hello!* magazine was preparing its colourful world exclusive, with pictures by Brian Aris shot in the Jones abode overlooking Central Park. Iman looked model-chic in satin, while David was casual and dad-like in an untucked shirt. Lexi, lying fast asleep in a Moses basket on the carpet, poppered into a fingernail-pink Babygro, knew nothing of any of it. Their baby's arrival was, said Iman, 'the happiest of times in my life'.

'We've always been very close, but if it's possible, we've been drawn even closer. There's a joy or a contentment that's almost palpable to both of us. Overnight, our lives have been enriched beyond belief.'

Tony Visconti was working with over-the-top, hard-rock outfit D-Generation towards the end of the year when he received the phone call that would turn back time. It had been fourteen years since he and David had last spoken. There is everything and nothing to say in such a moment; a profound awkwardness offset by familiarity, longing and regret. Tony's eyes filled spontaneously with tears, he later said. If he'd missed his friend and shipmate dreadfully, he'd perhaps never allowed himself to acknowledge the void.

'I'm not sure what the silence was really all about, except that we never spoke after I told him that I wasn't able to mix the sound for his Serious Moonlight tour,' Tony says in his book, *Bowie, Bolan and the Brooklyn Boy*. 'It was all water under the bridge anyway, and we made a date for coffee.'

No other producer had ever reached, to the extent that Tony had, into the furthest recesses of David's soul: to drag out of him, and capture honestly, his most fundamental and natural musicality. It is no exaggeration to call their unique bond a thing of wonder. The stars were at it again.

The album they convened to work on in early spring 2001 was *Toy*, a scrapbook of new and old, including 'Let Me Sleep Beside You' and 'Conversation Piece', tracks that Tony had originally produced for David way back in the Sixties. Even though there were hundreds more where those came from, David was also writing afresh. The album began veering off, becoming something other than David had at first imagined. In the end, perhaps as the result of in-house record company politics or some other issue, but 'for reasons that are not entirely clear to me,' said Tony, the record was shelved. It was never released in its own right.

Virtually every song, however, has been deployed as a bonus track or B-side on subsequent singles and albums. What mattered, to Tony, was that he and David were reunited, creating music together again. They had survived rock's killing fields. It was business as usual. In the cramped loft studio at the modest house Tony shared with his girlfriend in West Nyack, Rockland County, New York State, about eighteen miles north of the city, their comeback album first stirred. They were soon back to their old give and take, chop and change, brushing and scraping off each other routine, as if they'd never been away.

The only difference was that they were now working on computers. As the sun went down on their first day back, they sauntered out for sushi. The following day, Tony took David to visit a very special studio: Allaire, outside Woodstock in the Catskills, overlooking the vast Shokan reservoir. Secluded in the mountains and immersed in nature, neither could imagine a more peaceful or creatively promising place. 'Remote, silent and inspirational,' David called it. They would record *Heathen* there.

Lulled by a gorgeous summer upstate, blissed out by the progress that he and Tony had made on the new album and having just celebrated the first birthday of his cherished baby girl, David could not have been less prepared for what came next. On 11 September, as on any other day, he flicked on the TV set in his quarters to catch up with the news before heading across to the studio to crack on with the day's work. He was confronted by repeat footage of American Airlines Flight 11 crashing into the North Tower of New York's World Trade Center. David called Tony, interrupting his morning work-out, and the producer rushed in to witness United Airlines Flight 175 hitting the South Tower. The latter collapsed at 9.59 a.m., after burning for fifty-six minutes. By 10.28 a.m., the North Tower was down, too. All domestic aircraft were grounded immediately. Every inbound international flight was redirected or turned back, with nothing allowed to land in US territory for the next three days. Mobile phone networks were suspended, and landlines were constantly engaged. America was at war.

'It was incredibly traumatic, one of the nastiest days of my life, especially for the family,' David told my friend Richard Wallace, in his piece for the *Daily Mirror*.

It was, said David, as if the world had gone mad. He managed to get through immediately on the phone to his wife, who told him that she was standing at the window, feeding their baby and watching the tragedy unfold. She didn't see the first plane hit, but was watching the aftermath. The Twin Towers stood right in front of their apartment building. While they were speaking on the phone, the second plane struck, at which point David yelled at Iman to "Get the fuck out of there!"

Iman tore around the apartment, shoving Lexi and necessities into the pram. Then Iman, an incredibly fit woman, ran uptown with her baby for twenty blocks, to the home of a friend. 'But the worst thing was, the phones just went down, and we lost contact,' said David. The police put barricades around the city. Nobody could get in or out, and it was just a horrendous feeling of being cut off. I didn't speak to her until the night time. I was in a right state. I had no idea if she and Lexi had got out. It was so, so horrifying.'[2]

A new star flickered in the aftermath. Gerry Leonard,[3] an offbeat, gentle Irishman from Clontarf, a coastal suburb of northern Dublin, had relocated to the East Village during the mid-Nineties in response to his calling. When he and David crossed paths in a favourite NoHo studio, a reaction occurred which would lead to collaboration over three albums and two tours.

'I was working as a guitar player in New York, just hanging out, seeing what was what, and I met a lot of people in the business,' Gerry says. 'One day I happened to be producing a little record in Looking Glass studios.[4] I was in the small room, and David Bowie was up in the big studio with producer Mark Plati.[5] Mark came down and gave me this track they were working on. They wanted me to do some ambient guitar work on it, which I did, and which they loved. I asked to meet David, and he was very gracious. Our relationship grew. Over time, they called me to do more and more work. And then they shelved the *Toy* record. They were still working on *Heathen*, and they asked me to come in and do some overdubs.

'Then I had a night at the Living Room,[6] doing one of my little gigs with my friends. There were about fifty people there. It was all very improvisational and fun, and David came down. I guess he wanted to see, "Can Gerry *rock*?" He can be very low-key when he wants, which he was that night, and it's New York City, ya know? People are cool, they don't get too clamouring. He joined in the fray, but there was definitely a buzz. A lot of whispering and mumbling that *David Bowie* was in. He heckled me during the gig, which was good. He said, "We need to get a priest in here!" at one point. We bantered back and forth, which broke the ice. After that, he asked me whether I wanted to join his band for the Heathen tour. Mark Plati was the MD of the band for that tour, but he had to leave. He called me to say that he'd put my name forward to replace him, and that I should do it.'

Despite the fifteen-year age gap between David and Gerry, they quickly fell in and became friends.

'David was above so-called constraints such as age barriers,' Gerry remembers. 'I think that his many years in the music business, being a Buddhist, practising meditation – all these experiences had brought him to a point at which he was brilliant at getting to the essence of things. He did things for the right reasons. I never pandered to or yes-manned him. He liked that. I get along with everyone, and he respected that, too. He knew we could speak directly and candidly to each other, which was something he appreciated. He didn't like people fawning over him. I guess in his position, with people agreeing with everything he did and said and never saying no to him all those years, he must have been wondering half the time who he could really trust to be honest with him.'

Gerry focused on the work, he says, and not the glory of the work.

'David got that. Having made mistakes over the years, I wanted to make it very clear as to what my role was, and to focus on getting the job done. We would have some conversations about stuff that was not to do with music, but on the whole he was a very private person. I'm like that myself, so it worked. He came back for me a few times, so he was clearly comfortable. We had a layer of friendship and trust, which was something I cultivated with him. The more I got to know him, the more I respected him. There were a lot of layers to David. I hadn't realised quite what an actor-comedian he was. He could do a perfect Elvis, a brilliant Bob Dylan, a spot-on Neil Young. He'd have you in fits. It was really an honour to meet him, work with him, and to have that continue. He'd really got it, in spades. He was a real rock star. There aren't too many of those. Overall, the band he put together was very happy, and we played well. It gelled.'

On 6 June 2002, David and Iman celebrated their tenth wedding anniversary.

'She gave me a 1957 original Little Richard stage jacket,' David revealed. 'He was my idol, and I wanted to play the sax just because of the Little Richard band. Why was he called "Little" Richard, is what I want to know; he was *huge*! He must have had a big torso and little legs. I got her a subscription to a very good yachting magazine. Oh, and some jewels.'

His last-ever in-depth press interview was with the New York *Daily News*. It was published on 9 June, and contained a telling confession:

'I'm frighteningly happy,' he said. 'I don't see ever wanting to change things in my personal life. Iman and I are very happy, and we have the most fabulous baby.'

But as a consequence, he did admit, he had lost what younger men still have:

'A sense of becoming. At a certain age, you realise you are no longer becoming. You are being. I like knowing what's up. But I do miss the excitement of not knowing quite what's around the next corner.'

He also said that the questions that preoccupied him were now of the existential variety:

'I'm approaching those questions in the new songs. At first, I thought, well, if I write about this, I won't have anything left to write about. But then I realised that what life is about is quite a subject to take on. And at the moment, I feel like I've only scratched the surface.'

Gerry Leonard's first live appearance with David was at the Roseland Ballroom in New York on 11 June 2002 – the official release date of the *Heathen* album – when they performed *Low* and *Heathen* in their entirety. David 'saw an affinity between the two albums', said Tony Visconti. Although David insisted that every track on *Heathen* had been written prior to 9/11 – production had begun well before the terrorist attacks occurred – many fans read deeply into the lyrics, desperate for answers, and assumed that his songs were Bowie's reaction to the tragedy. David denied this, although he did acknowledge that they reflected his growing anxiety about living in America in modern times. Looking back, he would say this:

'It was written as a deeply questioning album,' he told American author and music critic Anthony DeCurtis in June 2003. 'Of course, it had one foot astride that awful event in September [2001]. So that was quite a traumatic album to finish . . . it did affect me and my family very much. We live down here.'

Heathen came to be regarded as a soundtrack for the tragedy. David's reticence about it, of course, derived from the fact that he would not, could not be seen to be 'cashing in'. But it did have a prescience that was heart-stopping. Tony Visconti called it David's 'magnum opus', and assured his friend that it was 'more like a symphony'. It echoed the disillusionment of *Ziggy Stardust*, particularly with its shades of 'Five Years'. 'Slip Away' is wistful and radiates 'Space Oddity', especially in the Stylophone. 'Sunday' is reminiscent of *Low*. The covers – 'Cactus' by the Pixies, and 'I've Been Waiting' by Neil Young, are haunting; 'I Took a Trip on a Gemini Spaceship', the old Legendary Stardust Cowboy number, reveals a continuing preoccupation with whatever's out there. There was a sense here of David confronting mortality, baring his teeth at it, while accepting that there was not a lot he could do about it. 'Heathen (the Rays)' is the closest of all its tracks to being about the destruction of the Twin Towers, even though it was penned before they fell.

The Who's Pete Townshend played lead guitar on 'Slow Burn'. This was not the first time he had contributed to a Bowie album:

Pete also played on *Scary Monsters (and Super Creeps)*. Foo Fighter Dave Grohl took the lead on 'I've Been Waiting'. David himself contributes drums on 'Cactus', and also played more instruments on this album than on any other, including synthesizers and some piano. But never bass. It's Tony Visconti on bass.

The listener is left with an overwhelming sense of the writer's awareness that time was running out. For him, or for the world? Both? When we hit that point is when we begin to look back. The album is obviously loaded with nostalgia. Brilliant, melancholic, spine-chilling, ghostly, it cleaned up, earning him some of the finest reviews of his career. It soon went platinum.

But who was the Heathen?

'He cannot feel any of God's presence in his life,' explained David. 'He is the twenty-first-century man.'

The Roseland show was the official opening of the Heathen mini concert tour. It was interrupted by David's lengthy trip to London, where he had accepted the post of Artistic Director at that summer's South Bank Meltdown Festival.

In a return to his anti-aircraft stance of old, he took a five-day voyage on the *QE2* from New York to Southampton, catching up on his reading and on a stash of old black-and-white European and Japanese films on DVD, which he watched in his sumptuous Grand Suite while taking a bath with a sea view.

'Right now, at this moment, I've got my phobia about flying back again,' he confessed. 'I'm coping with it to a certain extent. I flew the whole of Europe [during his tours] but I just can't face that transatlantic trip. I don't want to be on a plane going over the Atlantic. I got my phobia before 11 September. It started when my baby was born.'

On 27 June, David recorded a special edition of *Friday Night with Jonathan Ross*, for transmission on 5 July. Between live performances with his band of hits such as 'Fashion' and 'Ziggy Stardust', interspersed with tracks from *Heathen* including 'Slip Away' (for which he produced his trusty Stylophone), David looked some-what on edge during Ross's inimitable interrogation. He spoke of '. . . a sense of mystery, that I'll never be able to fully confront, you know, there's a need to escape from certain things . . .'

His new teeth were clearly uncomfortable, and seemed too numer-ous for his mouth. He raised his hand to his face a good deal, exactly as Freddie Mercury used to do, and could be seen munching his gums – especially when Ross raised the question of sexuality.

'What was the deal there, because you were gay for a while, and then you were not gay . . .'

'I was just happy,' grinned David.

'Were you bisexual, were you pansexual, were you trisexual?' persisted Ross, with great cheek and charm. ''Cause I thought that being gay was a bit like the Foreign Legion. Once you joined, I didn't think you were allowed back.'

'I was just very, you know. I got my leg over a lot,' laughed David, helplessly.

'Did you have relationships with these people as well?'

'Not if I could help it . . . I was incredibly promiscuous, and I think we'll leave it at that!'

When Ross asked David whether he thought that Jonathan should sample 'the man-love', David politely declined to answer, and retreated back into silly voices and baby talk.

'There is no doubt that David Bowie reneged on the gay commu-nity, when he denied having been gay after all,' says Simon Napier-Bell. 'People were angry about that. But his honesty on the Ross show redeemed him. So from my point of view, all was forgiven.'

David arrived back in New York on 26 July, and the tour resumed two days later. Ziggy-zagging henceforth between the US and Europe, it reached a favoured old haunt on 2 October: the Hammersmith Odeon in west London, restyled for now as the Carling Apollo. It was good to be back. His trek terminated in Boston twenty-one days later.

David had now relinquished all drugs, cigarettes and alcohol – the days on which he had given up being the best of his life, he said, after meeting Iman. But his workaholism was back with a vengeance. After only a few weeks' holiday with his family, spanning Christmas and New Year, he was ensconced with his loyal handful of musicians in tiny Studio B at Looking Glass in January 2003, to begin recording the Reality album. Tony Visconti would co-produce. They would also record at David and Iman's SoHo apartment, and at pianist Mike Garson's place out in Bell Canyon, Ventura County, California; a scenic, densely forested sanctuary populated by deer, coyote and many unusual birds. It was a nod to the Allaire experience.

But *Reality* is loaded with clues that the record was mostly created in relative confinement, deep in the city. The broad spectrum and space of its predecessor is certainly absent. But what it lacks in extent, it makes up for in humour, detail and thought provoking despondency. In his attempts to explain the *Reality* album, David talked about the notion of reality as having become 'an abstract for so many people over the last twenty years.

'Things that they regarded as truths seem to have just melted away, and it's almost as if we're thinking post-philosophically now. There's nothing to rely on any more.'

Two tracks aside – George Harrison's 'Try Some, Buy Some' and 'Pablo Picasso' by Jonathan Richman – all songs are David's. A raw honesty runs through them, they are deceptively simple and ponderous. 'The Loneliest Guy' is almost too perfect to listen to, and didn't please everyone. The supreme, inevitable sweep of Visconti's production hems a tapestry of magnificence, making an album to listen to over and over, and then some. The critics were charmed.

'There's a part of David Bowie that definitely does not want to repeat himself,' said Tony Visconti. 'So we were committed to avoiding the *Heathen* formula.'

'I was looking for something that had a slightly more urgent kind of sound than *Heathen,*' David explained. 'I think the mainstay of the album is that I was writing and recording it here in downtown New York. It's very much inspired by where I live and how I live, and the day-to-day life down here.

'These days', he would also say, 'it's great to be able to record more frequently and clear the decks of the songs I'm writing. For me, this is a far more preferable way to go. I think I find an album a year very comfortable. It doesn't faze me at all, and it tends to follow the pattern and the rhythm at which I write.'

He was also dipping a toe into the literary pool, and had begun work on a novel.

'It needs about a hundred years of research,' he told Paul Du Noyer for *The Word* magazine.

'It'll never be completed in my lifetime, but I'm having a ball.' David explained how he planned to start with the first female trade unionists in the 1890s in London's East End, and trace the story all the way through to Indonesia and the South China Seas. He was amazed, he said, by how easy it was to research his subject on the internet. 'It's something I've been writing for the last eighteen months, and it's hideously hard.'

It was so 'epic', he went on, that he didn't believe he'd ever finish it, and even wondered whether his notes might be of interest to a publisher after his death.

As for his personal life, he was a contented man, and didn't mind sharing it.

He admitted that he had stabilised his life over the past decade. He said he felt very at ease, and that he liked it. 'I never thought I would be such a family-oriented guy. I didn't think that was part of my make-up. But somebody said that as you get older, you become the person you always should have been; and I feel that's happening to me. I'm rather surprised at who I am, because I'm actually like my dad!'

By 2003, he couldn't imagine living anywhere other than New York. He had lived there longer than he had lived anywhere else. He felt like a New Yorker. It was as if he at last felt that he had earned the right to say it. His daily routine, when he was not in the studio, was often an early morning walk around Washington Square Park, a coffee or a bite of breakfast at one of his favourite local haunts, and a poke around a bookshop – McNally Jackson on Prince Street and the Strand Bookstore on Broadway were favourites. He came and went untroubled. That year, we both became founder members of Soho House New York, on Ninth Avenue in the Meatpacking District. Members are drawn from the media, the arts and fashion. It's the one that featured in Season Six of television series *Sex and the City*. Real New Yorkers at last.

He took *Reality* out on the road in the autumn, debuting in Denmark on 7 October. It soon turned into another tour beset with problems. The signs were not good. Gigs were cancelled and dates put back as David struggled with a series of relatively minor but nagging illnesses, including laryngitis and 'flu. There was tragedy: the 6 May 2004 concert was cancelled after a lighting technician dropped from the rig to his death. And there was catastrophe: on 18 June in Oslo, a fan lobbed a lollipop at the stage, which somehow became lodged in David's eye socket. More ominous was his abandonment of the 23 June Prague show, when he staggered from the stage in agony with a suspected trapped nerve in his shoulder. Two days later, while performing in Hamburg, he suffered the first in a series of heart attacks, and was airlifted to hospital for emergency angioplasty.

'The tour was full-on to begin with, without all that,' reflects guitarist Gerry Leonard. 'With rehearsals, it was thirteen months, all go. I thought it was too much for him. We had a few hiccups when he missed a string of shows, and there was the added pressure when we had to make up the gigs that we'd missed. We never had more than four or five days off on any given stretch. He was doing a three-hour show every night. And he really gives, ya know? David never short-changes. The scope of the tour was monstrous. Easy to say afterwards, but I always thought it would take its toll.'

Even so, Gerry couldn't bring himself to believe the worst, that David thought this would be his last-ever world tour.

'It was only when he became very ill that he thought twice, reconsidered and allowed the remainder to be cancelled,' he says. 'I have always said that touring is pretty gruelling. It's just slog. You miss your friends and your family. You're always away for the big things. Until he got sick, David had been talking enthusiastically about making a record every year, and about touring regularly. There's no doubt in my mind that he wanted to work as much as he could. His performances were tremendous, he was at the top of his game. Sound-wise and visually, the Reality tour was everything he'd ever wanted. He was happy to wheel out the jukebox and play most of the popular songs, too, he'd got over that whole thing of "I don't play the ancient hits any more". He knew the fans wanted to hear them. Probably more than the new stuff, some of them. And that was OK with him.'

Finally, David was comfortable enough to concede.

'At one point,' adds Gerry, 'we had sixty-four songs ready to go, of which we would play thirty every single night. He's nothing if not an all-or-nothing kind of guy. He was enjoying it so much, until he was rushed off for surgery for the blocked artery, and they put the stent in. And that's the kind of thing that shakes us to our core. A real wake-up call. You think, "Maybe I don't *have* to do this." David took a long breath. And then he said, "Touring is done. I'm not going to wheel myself around any more." '

21

2005–2014

It's easy to disregard the reality of our heroes ageing. Rock's Peter Pans represent nothing if not our own stubborn resistance to growing old. Look, there's hope: they lived fast, they didn't all die young. Those who did – Hendrix, Morrison, Joplin, Jacko, Lennon, Amy, Mercury, Cobain, Prince et al – will forever be remembered as they were when they checked out. Never older. Meanwhile, the groovers go marching on.

'Yeah, you're getting older, but what the hell can you do about it?' was Grace Slick of Jefferson Airplane's take. 'Nothing. So you may as well ignore it as best you can, and just be who you are, be who you were, be who you continue to be.'

Maybe David, *comme d'habitude*, was ahead of the game. Perhaps he'd resolved to quit while he was ahead, to retreat into the nest of family and grow decrepit in obscurity. It made sense – even though we'd somehow come to expect that he would rage, rage against the dying of the light, when the time came. Because he was Bowie.[1] Maybe he'd made up his mind that he was never going to disintegrate into a seventy-something rocker, of which there are many, and which has become the most delicious oxymoron. On the one hand, why shouldn't they keep doing it? On the other, it's the freakiest show. Mick'n'Keef, Pete'n'Rog, Macca, Dylan, Bruce, Clapton, Brian Wilson, Rod Stewart, Elton John; Steven Tyler, Tom Petty, Iggy; Joni, Stevie, Diana, Debbie: all caricatures and official tribute acts of their own once glorious selves.

When we fork out fortunes to experience them live, it's not the artists they are now that we rock up for. It's for who they used to be, before the mainstream subsumed them: the risk-takers, the rule-breakers, the anarchists, the eccentrics, the supple sex-gods and goddesses who wrote the songs that made the whole world sing. The songs that taught us how to think, to love, to make sense of it all. To try to. It's a nostalgia trip. And there's nothing wrong with that. It's why Simon Napier-Bell's *Raiding the Rock Vaults* classic hits extravaganza cleaned up in Vegas and then went strutting across God's own country. It's why new jukebox musicals sell out within half an hour. Anyone who saw Freddie Mercury perform live would have cringed at *We Will Rock You*. But for those not yet born when Queen were on their valedictory lap in 1986, how else to experience his magic? The promoters weren't slow to latch on to the irony: that nostalgia never gets old.

'Old men do it better,' Robert Plant retorts. Who's to argue? The heritage acts have bequeathed an outstanding soundtrack, but many now seem to be hanging on by threads. With vocal chords slacker than last summer's thong, they croak notes that don't even aim, let alone get high. One more for the road, for posterity, for the old days, for the brothers who didn't make it? One last fray? They could keep on cranking, if that was their schtick. Never too old if you're still breathing, or if you can lie on the floor without holding on. Meanwhile, David was done.

Or *was* he? Ever the promise, never the goods. Hooked for much of the time to the internet, he'd be in and out of the chatrooms on BowieNet, hinting tantalisingly at creations to come. He'd use the handle 'Sailor', and at least some of the time it was really him. Why Sailor? Many a sophisticated theory has been propounded, often propagated (it is said) by Bowie himself.

David said, ooops, Sailor said, 'I think it's something to do with solitude, freedom, and travelling the uncharted waters ...' or something.

It happened to be an anagram of Isolar, his own company. But its genesis was simpler, and more obvious:

Sailors fighting in the dancehall,
Oh man, look at those cavemen go . . .
(from 'Life on Mars?')

He was back, in this arena, to his glib, schoolboy humour, every pun intended. His default was smart-arse:

'That's a very personal question. Let's keep the bedroom out of this! Aren't you a Catholic? This really is Hallowe'en, isn't it?'

And in response to the query, 'What do you think of single sex education?':

'Do you mean teaching one person at a time? This would take ages and ages. The population may dry up by then.'

He had refused hands down to become 'Establishment', declining a CBE, Commander of the Order of the British Empire,[2] in 2000.

'I seriously don't know what it's for,' he commented. In 2003 he said no again, this time to the big one, a knighthood.

'I would never have any intention of accepting anything like that,' the reluctant Sir David Bowie declared – despite the fact that the title attached to his adopted name would have bestowed a deliciously Arthurian ring. 'It's not what I spent my life working for.'

Curiously, he had accepted the French Légion d'Honneur in 1999. Perhaps he'd reviewed its implications, and had handed it back.

True to his word, he and the road were through. He accepted the odd forgettable movie role, nothing Oscar-worthy. He played a couple more benefit gigs. In September 2005 he contributed memorably to Fashion Rocks at Radio City Music Hall, and performed at SummerStage in Central Park, with Arcade Fire. And in November 2006 he troubadoured for jewellery-rattling New

Yorkers at the third annual Black Ball benefit, held at the fittingly named Hammersmith Ballroom, co-hosted by his wife.

And that was it. What do you mean, a charity fundraiser in front of a bunch of social X-rays was Bowie's last-ever gig? Well, it was. He may not have known so on the night, but then again, have a look at the footage on YouTube, which somebody captured on their phone. Accompanied by Mike Garson on piano, he gives 'Wild is the Wind' and 'Fantastic Voyage' his bewitching best shot, but he looks . . . only half there. He performs 'Changes' as a duet with Alicia Keys, beams winningly at the audience, takes a bow, retreats from the stage hand in hand with her, and will never sing another note in public. Mr Bowie has left the building, ladies and gentlemen. Thank you and goodnight.

He turned sixty a few weeks later, in January 2007. He did so privately. Best way. That May, he curated a major arts and music festival in New York, and bagged a couple more awards. A year later, the grapevine buzzed with news that the London Boy was on his way home. Someone leaked that he'd purchased a property back in Blighty. But the beautiful Old Rectory on Gilston Road, Kensington/Chelsea remained mostly unoccupied. The Joneses barely spent the night there, let alone moved in. Less than three years later, it was on the market again.

The gossip gained momentum, given that David was hardly ever seen, on any continent. There were rumoured to have been at least half a dozen heart attacks, a series of surgical procedures, and even the Big Scare. Once or twice, I even heard said that he was dead. Say it ain't so. The right people usually know the truth.

'We would occasionally have lunch or meet for a coffee, and I always knew he was healthy,' said Tony Visconti. 'I don't know why he's been quiet. People would say to me, "He's dying, isn't he," with a tremble in their voice. I'd say, if he's dying, he's the best-looking dying man I've ever seen in my life.'

In January 2009, David was snapped at the Sundance Film

Festival in Utah, which he attended to support Duncan, his film director son, who was presenting his movie *Moon*, starring Sam Rockwell. Made on a shoestring £3 million budget, it told the nightmare tale of an astronaut during the last days of a mining mission. It would land him a BAFTA award.

When Duncan's mother went to see the film independently, she wept:

'I boo-hoo'd like an absolute child,' Angie confessed to Jan Moir in the *Daily Mail* in January 2016 . 'Because the film was all about abandonment, and I got it. I thought, that is what David told him. David said I abandoned them. And I got it, and boy, was I mad. I didn't abandon Zowie, but at some point I couldn't take any more humiliation from David, so I took my dignity and got up off my arse and left, to start another life.'

The success of *Moon* led to a commission for Duncan to direct the sci-fi thriller *Source Code*, starring Jake Gyllenhaal, at a cost of £19 million. The film grossed more than £75 million worldwide. Son of Ziggy was on his way. The slightly scruffy, jeans, T-shirts and stubble-wearing figure, who looks more like a hungover roadie than a world-class movie director, looked distinctly like his mother when he was a toddler. He bears no resemblance to either parent now.

That April, David lent his celebrity to the Tribeca Filmfest in New York, looking exhausted and strained. He was barely heard of again for the next three years. When he emerged, in October 2012, he was seen shuffling by himself along Lafayette Street, stubble-faced, dressed in a baseball cap, sun specs, plain blue hoodie and baggy jeans. Lurking paps captured him leaving a lunch date with Coco Schwab, shortly afterwards. They went home in separate cabs.

Only a handful knew that Tony Visconti and David were recording together again by 2010. The session guys, the staff at SoHo's Magic Shop studios and everyone else involved were obliged to sign non-disclosure agreements. David's chosen musicians knew better than to risk their contracts by discussing publicly a project that may never see the light. Everybody kept their head down. The magicians were at work.

'It was amazing how I got involved in *The Next Day*,' reflects guitarist Gerry Leonard.

'I heard that David was coming up to Woodstock with his family, where I live with mine, and I thought I'd invite them over for coffee. It seemed like a decent thing to do. And while they were round, he just turned to me and said, "Do you have a drum machine? Let's write a song." And so we did. He came back on two more occasions, and we wrote some more songs. In the space of two hours, we'd have one – just like we all used to work, back in the day. Just bashing around. In the end, to my great surprise, he wanted to include one of the songs we did together, "Boss of Me", on his new album. I was blown away.'

There were precious moments. One was when David arrived with a Fender Stratocaster for Gerry to play on *The Next Day*. A late Sixties Sunburst model, with a maple neck. The very guitar that Marc Bolan had gifted his superstar friend in the Granada TV studios in Manchester back in the summer of 1977, three and a half decades earlier. The day he fell off the stage, leaving David in fits of laughter. The day they ran out of time. The last performance that Marc would ever give.

Contrary to internet rumour and gossip, David did not return the Sunburst Strat to the family after Marc's tragic death. He had treasured it for decades. Tony Visconti has it now.

'Working with David *does* change your life,' says Gerry. 'I don't mean the royalties. God, no. In this day and age, all of that is not the same as it once was. The reality of Spotify: you get two hundred thousand plays, and you're lucky if you walk away with something like eleven cents. You're not going to be buying a house nor even a car on it. But the experience of something like that is immense. You can't put a price on it. You couldn't try.'

In January 2012, it was the big Six-Five. In the real world, a mile-stone age. He'd be facing retirement, his pension, perhaps a part-ing-gift gold watch. He might be contemplating a move to the seaside. Maybe Margate, at last. He'd be fretting over flourishing nose hair, the odd bald patch, his thickening waistline. He'd be preoccupied with senior citizen discounts, travel passes, two-for-ones and subsidised eye checks. But in the rarefied realm of rock superstars, such considerations barely compute. Did it cross his mind that Ziggy was now an old coot? We'd have known better than to ask. But you can bet your bottom dime he must have thought about it.

We grow old. We shall wear the bottoms of our trousers rolled.[3] The passing years become more significant the longer we live. Most people don't feel much change between forty and fifty. At sixty-five, we had better face facts: that we're heading for the abyss. The majority of sexagenarians are not so much fearful of dying as terri-fied of never having lived. David could scare the faces off people with some of the things he'd experienced in his lifetime. He'd lived for us all.

A few weeks later, on 27 March, he was notably absent from the official unveiling of the Crown Estate blue plaque at 23 Heddon Street, off London's Regent Street, to commemorate the fortieth anniversary of the *Ziggy Stardust* LP. The location was where the album's front cover photo was shot. The brief ceremony was followed by a VIP breakfast attended by original Spiders from Mars Trevor Bolder and Woody Woodmansey, Spandau Ballet's Gary Kemp (who had stepped up to pull the curtains, and to give a wee speech), co-producer of the artwork Terry Pastor, and record producer Ken Scott. Where was Nicky Graham, the original key-pounding Spider? Where, for that matter, was Mike Garson? Where, too, was George Underwood, who played a significant part in the sleeve design? Not a single family representative was present. There was something 'Eleanor Rigby' about it. The throng came and went.

Another month on saw David and Iman celebrating their twentieth wedding anniversary. Not that we did see them. There had been no summons to steak tartare-munching Brian Aris for an official shoot, no lucrative world-exclusive with *Hello!*

If we felt disappointed by their low profile, we were placated by what happened next: an announcement that the David Bowie Archive had given unprecedented and exclusive access to the prestigious Victoria and Albert Museum, the V&A, in London, to create a major retrospective of David's life and work. This was the first time that any museum anywhere in the world had been granted admission to David's extensive, hermetically sealed and, yes, temperature-controlled personal collection. This was like Howard Carter entering the tomb of Tutankhamun. For the man who never looked back, this was now the way forward.

On 7 November, David's forty-one-year-old son Duncan Jones (where did *that* go?) married his fiancée Rodene Ronquillo in Los Angeles. There was no gown, no glamour, no church, no guests, no coverage. They decided only on the day itself to tie the knot. Three days earlier, on 4 November, Duncan had noticed a lump in his thirty-two-year-old photographer girlfriend's breast. The emergency biopsy revealed stage two cancer.

'We were a little overwhelmed by the news,' Duncan said. 'Cancer and Election Day, so we decided to make it a set, ran down to the Court House and got married! . . . Two days later, Ro was in surgery.'

The couple shaved their heads together in preparation for her gruelling chemotherapy, and posted pictures on Twitter. They began campaigning immediately to raise awareness of the disease, and made a point of stressing the importance of early diagnosis. Duncan and his father had always been close, never failing to Skype each other every weekend, and often hooking up in New York. It was disappointing to have to get married without him present.

'He's just a wonderful guy and father,' said the director of 2016's *Warcraft*. 'I think he understands that I'm a creative person in my own right. He gave me the time and the support to find my feet, and the confidence to do what I do.'

On 8 January 2013 it was David's sixty-sixth birthday. No one beyond his dearest could have anticipated what he would do to acknowledge this one, having ignored the significant Big One the year before. Typical David. Do the unexpected and keep them guessing, even in apparent retirement. There was no press, no promotion, no photographs, no inkling that anything new could possibly be due.

'I had a meeting with him in New York, and he played me this album, which was great,' Alan Edwards, his PR since 1982, told the *Independent* in January 2016.

'Then he said, "I want to put it out on Tuesday." He knew more about the job than I did. He had such a feel for what was going on. He had gone from being the coolest cult act in the world to the biggest superstar in the world.' He had also become vehemently anti-hype.

Alan was then charged with having to let the media know something was going on, without giving the game away, and without being able to offer a single interview.

His press release went live at 5.30 a.m. The disturbing video for 'Where Are We Now' was posted on David's website. BBC Radio 4 gave the debut single its first airplay, which then became available immediately on iTunes in a hundred and nineteen countries. In many of them, it flashed straight to Number One. Within the hour, the track had become a global sensation, with social media in meltdown. Little wonder: this was Bowie's first new release in a decade.

'It was a ground-breaking campaign,' Alan Edwards conceded. 'At the end of the day, it was his master plan, his concept. That's the confidence of a great artist.'

Two months later, on 8 March, *The Next Day* album was released on ISO Records/Columbia. Produced, like the single lifted from it, by Tony Visconti, it became David's first UK Number One album for twenty years. It would be nominated for that year's Mercury Prize. It would also be named in the category Best Rock Album at the 2014 Grammy awards; and for Mastercard British Album of the Year at the 2014 BRIT Awards. It didn't win. But it did.

What a moving piece it is. Described as 'art rock', a melting pot of his life to date, you couldn't help but regard this as the last hurrah, one final burst. 'Bowie's twilight masterpiece,' the *New York Times* called it; although Tony Visconti, charged with handing all the international media interviews as David himself wasn't doing any, hinted at plenty more where that came from. He even suggested at one point that, while David had left his musicians in no doubt that there would be no tour to promote this album, there may well be a one-off performance at some point. There never was.

There didn't need to be. I have used the word 'inevitable' before, about the special chemistry between David and Tony. Now here it was again. A boyish joy can be heard bouncing between the notes, which hints at the exuberance they must have felt when they first discovered each other; when they tinkered on that first album together, a lifetime ago in 1970, *The Man Who Sold the World.* 'Where Are We Now?' is an introspective ballad, littered with references to David's past, confetti-ing down like shreds of paper on a wet Berlin street.

The moment you know you know, you know.

What an aphorism. The song's disturbing video was surreal and Dalí-esque. 'The Stars (Are Out Tonight)' is a giant rock number. It throttles, and is strange. 'Love Is Lost' is addictive, it throbs and moans with controlled anguish and a quavering vocal. So menacing. Gerry Leonard's co-write, 'Boss of Me', is funky yet sedate. It's a broad canvas, this album, with a lucky dip for everyone. Whichever Bowie you were looking for, and we all had one, you were sure to find him here.

'David Bowie Is' opened at the V&A, London, at the end of March 2013. It was immense. You had to go three times to take it in. It presented stage costumes, videos, photography, artwork, instruments, sheet music, artefacts, technological gadgets, live performance footage, let's not forget music, in a soundly curated and interactive setting, its emphasis on style and design. Together with its accompanying book, it charted the significance of David's impact on the world, and underlined the importance of the audience in his evolution. It was captured on film, as the *David Bowie Is* movie, a documentary of the exhibition of the life, and would be re-released in cinemas in July 2016. This ground-breaking retrospective probably did help, as it set out to do, to establish David in the wider cultural consciousness as one of the most important artists on the planet of the last fifty years. The Bromley boyo done good.

'The next time I saw him, after *The Next Day* came out, was for Tony Visconti's seventieth birthday party in New York,' recalls Gerry Leonard. 'This would have been April 2014. Tony's son Morgan asked me to play in the house band. I ran into David at the party, and he said to me, "I'm going to be doing something else – but don't worry." He wanted me to know that he was working on another album, but that I wasn't going to be part of it this time. I wanted to be, of course! But what he was telling me was that he needed freedom to do something new now. I respected that.

'He knew he was ill. I guess we all knew too. It wasn't something we talked about. David always liked to keep his personal life private. Everyone involved with him on a project was expected to button their lip. It was what I did.'

That summer, though none of us knew it at the time, David made one last visit to London. Accompanied by his wife and daughter Lexi, he arrived at Luton airport on a private jet, no doubt chuckling to himself at the memory of Lorraine Chase being wafted somewhere from paradise, Campari and orange in hand. The family transferred discreetly to a suite at the Jumeirah Carlton

Tower in Knightsbridge, a short stroll from Harrods. They spent a week seeing the sights, including the Tower of London and the London Eye.

They moved unrecognised among the tourists, dressed casually like everyone else, and wearing trainers, flat caps and sunglasses. A single bodyguard tailed them, but wasn't needed. They took Lexi to see the house on Stansfield Road, Brixton, where her father was born. On Plaistow Grove, she photographed him standing outside the house he had lived in as a child. They drove all over Bromley, refreshing David's memories of his youth, and visited Foxgrove Road, Beckenham, where he had lived with Mary Finnigan in 1969.

Iman wore a commendably brave face throughout. In a rare interview with the *Guardian* that same year, she made a convincing excuse for her husband's waning visibility.

'David is even more of a homebody than I am,' she said. 'At least I go to parties once in a while!'

She insisted, however, that he had simply grown fond of his own company: 'I also think,' she added, 'there is nothing that he hasn't seen.'

22

2015–2016

'Truth is stranger than fiction,' said Samuel Langhorne Clemens, the father of American literature better known as Mark Twain. 'But it is because fiction is obliged to stick to possibilities. Truth isn't.'

You couldn't make it up: David only went and caught us unawares again. We'd watched assiduously for signs as each subsequent Bowie birthday approached, hoping to second guess him. No chance. For almost three years, deafening silence. Then, just as disappointment subsided, as resignation sank in, and when we were beginning to think we'd probably heard the last of him – he did it again. On 19 November 2015, a new single dropped out of the blue. Entitled 'Blackstar' and almost ten minutes in length, it was released as a digital download and was accompanied by a macabre video. The film features Bowie as a surreal blind man who somehow regains his sight. Demons, angels, crucified scarecrows. An apparently deceased spaceman – Major Tom? – with a jewel-encrusted skull inside his helmet. The smiley-face pin on the astronaut's taped-up suit is the face of Gerty, the robot companion in *Moon*, the first major feature directed by David's son. Beautiful touch. Rituals are danced on terra incognita which for all we know is Mars. What to make of it? It generated all manner of conflicting interpretations at the time of release. To me, it seems somehow loaded with redemption and awakening. The tantalising single it served to illustrate simply came and went, barely troubling the charts.

A month later, on 17 December, he delivered the follow-up, a Christmas-present: 'Lazarus'. It would be his last-ever single, and his first Top Forty hit on the Billboard Hot 100 for more than twenty-eight years. It didn't even limp past Number Forty-Five in the UK.

Look up here, I'm in heaven.
I've got drama, can't be stolen.
I've got nothing left to lose.

A parting lament? Lazarus of Bethany in the Gospel according to John in the Christian Bible was resurrected four days after his death: an event revered as an endorsement of the power of Jesus over mankind's inexorable enemy. Something to celebrate, then. Yet David sounds angry and inconsolable in this song, almost to the end, when, lyrically at least, he becomes a bluebird: a universal symbol of angels, and of joy and peace. In the video, stark images of the ailing artist alone in an infirmary echo the plight of tragic brother Terry, over whom he may still be feeling guilt-ridden. Bandaged and tormented, with buttons sewn to the binding across his eyes, he is a dead man raging: finally! He retreats into an armoire, the doors closing on him, as if backing into a coffin. It begged the question. It proffered the answer. What we didn't know was when.

'There are no atheists in the battlefield,' remarked David to a close friend, during the final months of 2015. It seems obvious now, from his parting music, that he 'got God' during the last year of his life – albeit in his own idiosyncratic way. When it boils down to fundamentals – the miracle of birth; the inevitability of death; the hope for life everlasting, because we know it's not going to end well, and no one wants to believe that all this was all for nothing – it is to the church, whatever church, that most people lean. The alternative, atheism, is an empty realm, offering no comfort whatsoever when comfort most matters. David had been on a quest for spiritual enlightenment since teenagehood, dipping in and out of Tibetan Buddhism, the Kabbalah, Christianity, the occult, pseudo-religious Nazism, Ariosophy, Theosophy and more. But in 'Lazarus', he appears to be spelling it out, with the sanguine lyric:

Look up here, I'm in heaven.

And the eyes of them that see shall not be dim.[1]

On 8 January 2016, his sixty-ninth birthday, a splice of these two disturbing videos appeared on British commercial television during ad-breaks, proclaiming the release of a new album without a name. Its packaging bore no words, merely a symbol: a simple five-pointed black star.

Speculation as to the meaning of this random little regular concave decagon roared into overdrive. Was it a reference to the nature of celebrity, a visual quip on the ephemerality of stardom? Could it be a poke at the brassy pink terrazzo twinklers on the Hollywood Walk of Fame? Might it be a religious reference? If so, where the hell to start? As a Muslim symbol, it represents the Five Pillars of Islam. In Christianity, the Star of Bethlehem, alluding to Jesus's birth and incarnation, and also the Epiphany star. It features in Mormonism. As a pentagram or pentangle, drawn in a single manoeuvre, it is a symbol of the occult and of Satanism. It represents the human body, and also the five senses. It may even indicate the five 'wits' of Elizabethan sensibility: common wit, imagination, fantasy, estimation (instinct) and memory.

A black star is a cancer lesion, usually of the breast; the name of a hidden planet supposed to be on a collision course with Earth; another name for Saturn; in physics, the term for the transitional state between a collapsed star and a singularity, a state of infinite value. It is also the title of an obscure Elvis Presley number, which was a song about death.

And when a man sees his black star, he knows his time, his time has come.

Was it any, all or even none of these?

'This was a man who was facing his own mortality,' said sleeve designer Jonathan Barnbrook, long-time Bowie collaborator, who first worked with David in 2002, on *Heathen*. 'The Blackstar symbol, rather than writing "Blackstar", has as sort of finality, a darkness, a simplicity, which is a representation of the music.'

It was 'the biggest work of death-art ever to hit the internet,' proclaimed the *Guardian*. It was also, said many, the first-ever Bowie album not to feature his image on the front cover – there is a photo of him looking forlorn and every minute of his age, on the inside instead. In fact, the original cover of *The Buddha of Suburbia* album did not feature a picture of David on the front either. But as that recording is generally categorised as a 'soundtrack album' rather than a 'studio album', it probably doesn't count. There are plenty of Bowie fans who will argue otherwise.

But what was he telling us about his feelings pertaining to the end of life?

'I can't think of a time when I didn't think about death,' David had said, in 1997. 'I'm fairly easy-going about the length of life in a way . . . it'll happen when it happens.'

Just before the release of *Blackstar*, David contacted Tony Visconti to let him know that he wanted and intended to make one more album. He said that he had written and even demoed five further songs, and was keen to get back in the studio as soon as possible. Tony revealed to *Rolling Stone* that he knew David's cancer was terminal. When that conversation about the new songs took place, Tony had no idea how close David was to the end.

'At that late stage, he was planning the follow-up to *Blackstar*,' Tony said. 'And I was thrilled. And I thought, and *he* thought, that he'd have a few months, at least. Obviously, if he's excited about doing this next album, he must've thought he had a few more months. So the end must've been very rapid. I'm not privy to it. I don't know exactly, but he must have taken ill very quickly after that phone call.'

Visconti also revealed that, when David pitched up at the recording studio for the first *Blackstar* sessions, he arrived straight from a chemo session. His eyebrows had vanished, and his head was bald.

'There was no way he could keep it a secret from the band,' said Tony. 'But he told me privately, and I really got choked up when we sat face to face talking about it.'

Mid-2015, his health had apparently improved, and he began to feel optimistic about his condition. The treatment was working. David seemed to be in remission. But come November, the cancer returned with a vengeance. His entire body was riddled with it. Despite his courage and astonishing energy, he was losing the war. In December he collapsed with exhaustion in New York, at the American premiere of his musical, *Lazarus*.[2]

'Sometimes I would look at him and I'd be silent for a moment and I'd see tears,' said the director, Ivo van Hove. 'Not in his eyes, but directly behind his eyes. He was really, truly suffering. He was suffering because he did not want to die. I knew it was coming, but still you never know when it will happen. It was an emotional blow.'

Perhaps the I-word is over-used. It is all too common a cliché, for which we can thank the modern media. I don't think I ever once described anyone as an 'icon' when I was a showbiz writer. Nor as a 'genius'. But such words are everywhere now, and have lately become synonymous with the name David Bowie. Is he really these things? If Michelangelo, original Renaissance Man and the greatest of all artists was a genius, how could Bowie be?[3] David, for all his immense charisma, music and artistry, not to mention the unique manner in which he performed his compositions live and on film, was probably not in Michelangelo's league.

'Icon' always puts me in mind, obscurely, of that maddening

phrase 'the new black'. *Private Eye* magazine had a field day with that one, listing the best references to it in the media each week. And yet. No one could say that David has not cemented his place in the pantheon of contemporary songwriters, composers and performers whose names and creativity have rendered them legends. He remains a defining figure because of his vast output and influence. Countless younger musicians defer to him, who speak of having cut their teeth on his records, and of how they seek to emulate his style and sound.

If David Bowie *is* a modern icon, *why* is he?

Because his images and reputation have survived his death. Because he is known throughout the world. Because his music is unique, and instantly recognisable. Because he is notorious for his complicated personal life and many infamous liaisons, which make him as fascinating as an individual as he is compelling as an artist. And because of the sudden, surprising and seemingly controlled manner of his death.

My father once said that the truest test of iconic status is to carry your subject's photograph into a remote village in the bush where English is not spoken, to see whether the image can be recognised. The list is obviously debatable, and by definition brief. Here's mine:

Her Majesty Queen Elizabeth II
Michael Jackson
Muhammad Ali
Marilyn Monroe
James Dean
Madonna
John Lennon
David Bowie

When fame, reputation and influence transcend geographical, linguistic, religious and cultural barriers, and when one has touched the lives of ordinary people all over the world, one may fairly and reasonably deserve to be described as an 'icon'. Perhaps David Bowie is one after all.

Dr Julia Jones, 'Doc of Rock' and a culture, media and sport specialist, spent several years of her PhD research analysing two decades' worth of the UK music sales data published annually by the British music industry. She observed a clear trend, which shows that the musical tastes formed during our youth generally last for our entire lifetime. Our connection to the music and artists we grew up with leaves an indelible imprint in terms of emotional resonance and memories.

'The generation who grew up with rock'n'roll are now entering their seventies,' Dr Jones observes. 'And they are markedly different from previous generations of seventy year olds. They grew up with the rebellious rock genre that was despised by their parents. They have common interests, because they all consumed the same music in the same way. There were just a handful of TV channels, radio stations and magazines when they were young, so most of their generation's experiences were the same. This created a very powerful connection among those who grew up during the Fifties, Sixties, Seventies and Eighties.

'I recently revisited Elvis Presley's home, Graceland, in Memphis. No matter what time of year I return, it is always packed. In fact, compared to my first visit ten years ago, the city has now embraced and deliberately leveraged its music heritage in order to attract visitors. Sun Studios and Beale Street downtown are also crowded with tourists of all ages: the generation who grew up with Elvis, Little Richard, Jerry Lee Lewis, plus their children, and sometimes even their grandchildren, too. The power of this preoccupation with music heritage appears to be growing, not declining. Liverpool is experiencing the same effect, with endless streams of visitors arriving in the city to visit the Cavern Club (not that it's even the original!), and to soak up anything to do with the Beatles.'

These 'music generations' segment the market, Dr Jones affirms.

In other words, those who grew up with Elvis and his contemporaries in the 1950s maintain a very strong connection to the music of that era. Those who grew up with the Beatles and their ilk during the 1960s retain a strong connection to the music of that era, too.

'The second part of my research consisted of a three-year period of interviews and a closer examination of the effects of music from their youth on today's forty- to sixty-five-year-olds. I asked participants to name an artist or artists whom they considered to be "iconic". I did not define the term for them, so their answers were based on their own interpretation. Bowie was regularly cited. Others named were Freddie Mercury, Pink Floyd, Led Zeppelin, the Who, the Rolling Stones, the Beatles and Prince.'

Bowie is a fascinating example of the power of youthful formation of lifelong musical taste, she says, because those who grew up during the 1970s connect with his Ziggy Stardust, Aladdin Sane and Thin White Duke incarnations; while those who were teenagers during the 1980s adhere to his *Let's Dance* era. The two are almost entirely disconnected, beyond the fact that the same artist was responsible for them.

'The music we are exposed to later in life doesn't seem to have such a strong effect,' Dr Jones reveals. 'The "Youth Music Effect" is now being deployed in dementia care, because of its deep-rooted emotional effects. Even patients who can't talk and who never walk have been observed as being able to sing along and dance to a song from their youth.

'In terms of the longevity of artists, we have no idea whether this legacy will continue after the original cohort who grew up with those genres and artists are no longer with us. Although we can identify several generations within the same family enjoying this music catalogue together right now, it does not necessarily mean that the younger generations will continue to connect with it once their parents and grandparents have passed away. They grew up with their own music catalogue in the 1990s and onwards. So if the trend we have identified continues, it will be *that* music that they will have the lifelong emotional connection with, not the catalogue that their parents grew up with.

'We can safely say, however, that David Bowie will be very much "alive" for several more decades – at least until his original audience expires. Elvis is likely to endure for longer, because Graceland as a rock and nostalgia destination is growing bigger by the year. But Bowie doesn't have a dedicated destination. Not even his Beckenham home, Haddon Hall, still stands. I travelled to Hansa Studios in Berlin last year, and was interested to note the Bowie Tours have grown in popularity in recent years, attended by people in their fifties and sixties who grew up with him through his 1970s era. However, the Berlin Bowie Tours are nowhere near in the same league as the Graceland experience.'

Elvis Presley has consequently become mythical in music legend – as have the Beatles. Neverland might well have achieved the same effect if things hadn't gone so wrong for Michael Jackson. Paisley Park may become the new Graceland for those who grew up on the music of Prince in the 1980s. Freddie Mercury fans still make the annual pilgrimage to Montreux. But Bowie doesn't have a Graceland, a Neverland, a Paisley Park or a Cavern Club. It is the real-estate assets which go the distance towards embedding legendary musicians even more firmly in history and in the public consciousness. The Who, the Rolling Stones, Pink Floyd, Led Zeppelin and their ilk are similarly without such literal foundations. Location, location, location: they should cement their real-estate legacy while they still can.

'Another interesting aspect arising from research relates to cultural capital,' adds Dr Jones. 'We have a vast body of academic research dating back over the past fifty years which examined cultural capital and social stratification. During that time, music had very clear links with social class. Classical music was traditionally considered the only genre which could deliver social and cultural capital – while popular music was deemed low-brow, for the masses, and not a true art form. People in positions of seniority or blessed with great wealth were inclined to boast about their visits to the opera, and sought to impress their clients and peers with expensive, covetable seats for productions at the Royal Opera House. This has all changed.

'Today's chief executives and high-net-worth individuals now boast about having tickets to sold-out shows at the O2, the Royal Albert Hall or Glastonbury. They treat their clients to concerts by the Rolling Stones, Adele or Peter Gabriel. This represents the clearest indication yet that popular music has finally achieved legitimacy in terms of cultural capital. It has acquired the same if not greater status and credibility as opera, and is now clearly viewed as a legitimate art form.

'This has largely been driven by the generation who grew up in the 1960s and 1970s, as they enter their fifties and sixties and as their careers reach the executive pinnacle. They are *proud* to champion the music they grew up with. They don't need to attend the opera or buy classical music to demonstrate cultural capital. They can now do so by wearing a Pink Floyd T-shirt. This generational shift in taste is massively significant. The upper classes are now driving the VIP ticketing sector in the pop rock genre, with premium-priced tickets often selling out within hours or even minutes.

'We see several social classes mixing together at these live events: the super-wealthy rubbing shoulders with the workers, who will have had to save hard from meagre salaries to see their idol up close and in concert. Physical products are also feeding the increasing consumer appetite, with high-priced "premium box sets" presenting additional exclusive content. Innumerable merchandise articles have become collectibles, with their value increasing year on year.'

Bowie, Dr Jones agrees, is a prime example of the way in which the hugely popular rock and pop genre has achieved greater artistic credibility than its rivals in other categories. He crossed a variety of artistic boundaries, experimenting in music, fashion and art. There is great depth to his work. The 'David Bowie Is' exhibition at the

V&A was an unprecedented success, showcasing his work across a variety of disciplines.

'So in that sense,' she concludes, 'it might turn out to be this ability to deliver cultural capital that results in Bowie's longevity. Because just as we were taught at school about Bach and Beethoven as history's most notable musicians, there is now justification for contemporary artists to be lauded in the same way. Elvis, the Beatles, Freddie Mercury, David Bowie are the new "classics". They will go down in history as artists who truly helped the popular music genre to attain credibility as a valid art form. While classical music continues to recede further, appealing to a decreasing niche audience, popular music will continue to expand until it becomes an entire universe of its own.'

'He always knew what he was doing, even when he was smacked out of his head, so none of the above would have been news to him,' comments former promotions executive Allan James, who worked for EMI during the Seventies before becoming one of the industry's most celebrated pluggers, representing Elton John, Rick Wakeman, Kim Wilde, Alice Cooper, Eurythmics and more.

'The thing about Bowie, he was always that step ahead. None of what they are saying about him now would have surprised the man in the slightest. He was always on it. Never off. He was absolutely iconic – in the same way that Lennon was iconic. He kept ahead by taking chances. Many of his ideas failed, and made him look a bit ridiculous, but he would keep taking the chances regardless, until something stuck. Wear a dress on an album cover, wow, shock, that worked, what's next? Push the boat out, rock 'em in the aisles. Tell the world you're gay, that'll get a reaction; not sure if you're a boy or a girl, but you're married with a kid? *Blimey.* EMI was full of gays, so I was used to all that. As a good East End boy, I confess I was slightly shocked by its overtones at first, but then I thought, *brilliant.*

'We can see, with hindsight, how calculating and *designed* it all was. He had more front than Selfridges, more neck than a giraffe, he was a glittering, sparkling presence in a dull and largely has-been game. All musicians have this dreaded fear of being found out. It follows them around like a bad smell. But not David. You never heard him say any such thing. He was super-confident. And even if he wasn't, he gave the supreme impression that he was, and that nothing could touch him. He never over-sold himself. He didn't have to. He just came out with "new" and "different" every time, to the point that you wondered where it was all coming from. And then he waited for the rest to catch up.

'He wasn't always available, and people want what they can't get. He was his own best marketing man. His own most deft puppeteer: he knew exactly how to pull all the strings. And perhaps most importantly, he had a different sort of relationship with his fans than almost any other rock star I can think of. He could come out, after a spell away, and deliver an entirely new act – risky to say the least – and the reaction would be, "Ah! He's taking us with him." Bowie fans have always felt privileged. They know their hero was an innovator, never an imitator. Every time he got on stage, it was something new. He was David Bowie. He could have just stood there and it would have been enough.'

'I didn't know he had cancer until after he died,' admits George Underwood, David's closest friend since they were eight years old. 'And I'm glad I didn't know. It saved me from worrying. He knew what it would do to me, which is why he didn't tell me. He did me a favour, really. If you know your best friend has a year to live, what are you going to do about it? It knocks you for six. I'd have just sat there moping, and he knew that.

'I heard about it in a text, at about seven in the morning. "Sorry to hear about David," it said. *What?* I put the radio on. The next call I got was from a news reporter. I knew, then, that it was true. That was the only interview I did. After that, I said, no more.

'There was such an outpouring. I don't mean of grief, but of music he'd created, in such a wonderful way. He was prolific, right to the end. He was saying something about his life, and even his death, until the moment he died. He'd found a spirituality he never knew he had. He'd been a Buddhist one minute, an atheist the next, but he could never settle on anything. Now, it seemed, he'd found the answer. Mix them all up, fling a bit of jazz in, and wow! Get a load of that! Maybe he'd found the meaning of life. What a kick if he did. *Blackstar* is an album we will listen to for years and years to come. I didn't like the video, it disturbed me a lot. But after he was dead, it all made sense.

'His daughter Lexi was at his bedside when he died. I was glad about that. She did get that closure. You see them die right in front of you, that's something that brings you closer together. It binds you in death, in a way that can't quite happen in life. I can't explain it, but I know it's true. We do tend to fear death in our society. Some people handle it better than others. If you've lived a full life, it's not so bad. David probably felt that himself.'

The best way to learn about David Bowie is to listen to his last album, insists journalist and Bowie devotee David Hancock.

'Listen to it once and you won't understand anything. After four or five plays, you will know that it's absolutely beyond anything that any other artist is capable of in terms of popular music. And that's what makes it David Bowie. The secret is that he's always that little bit ahead of everyone else. It may be a trite thing to say, but it's true. As an album, an entity, this is the most incredible thing he ever did. He saved the best 'til last.

'Because until "Blackstar", there had been no definitive turning-point song. Everyone says "Space Oddity" or "Life on Mars?" or ' "Heroes" '. But they are missing the point. With "Like a Rolling Stone", Bob Dylan changed public perception as to why lyrics are so much more important than melody. When people come to look back, Bob Dylan will be seen as the turning point in popular music, not the Beatles. Until they met Bob, they were still going "Love,

love me do". Dylan changed *all* musical writing in the twentieth century. Once you understand that, you can understand David Bowie's lyrics, and why he matters in the scheme.'

The great thing about David was that he never aspired to *be* Bob Dylan, nor anybody else, explains Hancock.

'He perceived, at a very young age, that the only thing to aspire to be is yourself. He knew that to strive to be something else, to attempt to climb the capitalist tower and become famous and rich for the sake of it, was not the answer. Take this from a gay man: you have to be who you are, who you really want to be, in spite of how difficult it's going to make your life. David got that. It's all there, on "Blackstar".'

It was the triumph of his career. A fierce, soaring cacophony of seven songs produced by Tony Visconti, of course, and played by a bunch of jazz musicians who sound as though they've been out all night at a rave. Every musical genre and style is paid homage to here. He throws everything in, from hip hop to electronic, from opera to funk, from the requisite chunk of rock'n'roll to what sounds like cutlery in the kitchen sink, keeping it quintessentially and unmistakably Bowie. The gems, for me, are the heart-rending farewell 'I Can't Give Everything Away' – I had to stop the car, the first time I listened to it – and the breathtaking 'Girl Loves Me'. The language of the latter has been described as a blend of argots, a mash-up of Polari – an old cant slang or dialect used exclusively by actors, fairground folk, criminals and Soho gays – and Nadsat – the fictional jargon spoken by teenagers in *A Clockwork Orange*. Its author Anthony Burgess was also a linguist, and that Russian-overtoned, unintelligible English was his own creation.

But guess what the obscure parlance on 'Girl Loves Me' really is. I'll have to sit down, here. This was David harking back some sixty years, to the genesis of the first meaningful relationship outside his family that he ever had, and which would last his entire lifetime. To when he and George Underwood would communicate secretly using their own schoolboy lingo, 'K Cab G-Nals' – baCKslaNG – which not another soul in their midst could comprehend. This one's for you, George, it's as if he was saying. I've never forgotten. I never could. It was always us, and it has always been us. Just you and me, kid. You and me against the world.

Having succeeded in maintaining musical relevance across an incredible five decades, and having delivered his parting-shot album, the *sine qua non*, David was done. Two days later, he was dead.

'I'd had a warning from a friend at BBC News about a year before,' recalls former Spider from Mars, Nicky Graham. 'She rang me up and said, "Do you know anything about David Bowie's illness? We've had a big tip-off, and we need to update our bios. He is said to be very ill." But I couldn't tell her anything. Even if I'd known, I wouldn't have said a word. There was always an incredible loyalty towards David. People did tend to keep his secrets. Any illness he might have been suffering from was nobody's business but his, unless or until he chose to tell.

'The song that goes round and round in my head to this day is "Life on Mars?" I remember hearing it on the radio for the first time, and thinking, My God, what an unbelievably well-crafted song this is – coming as it did out of a rock musician. It should have been in a West End show! Yes, I was very sad indeed when he died. But in a philosophical way. David lived out what I'm incredibly glad and thankful that Marc Bolan didn't.

'It was a blessing that Marc died before he got old, as the song goes, because he is perfectly preserved for the rest of time at the age of twenty-nine. His fans will always remember him as that young, vibrant upstart with the world as his oyster. Had he lived, Marc would have wound up a short, fat, balding ex-pop star, no question. That would have made him deeply disappointed and bitter. He wasn't going to come up with any further genius. His star was in the descendent, he was written out, and on the verge of being written off. With David, on the other hand, it seems likely that he would have gone on creating forever.'

'I was a bit stunned when I heard the news,' admitted David's former publicist, Chris Poole. 'I felt very sad. It was really odd, because I'd got up that day to go to someone else's funeral – Brad's[4] – at Golders Green crematorium. Sitting on the train from Norwich to London, lots of things were running through my mind. I'd been such a big fan of Bowie's in my youth. I saw him on the original Spiders tour. I was nineteen years old and already a father, but moonlighting as a rock fan by night. I saw him perform in Norwich, and I was at the last gig of the tour at Hammersmith Odeon. It was the biggest-ever indoor gig in the UK then. Bad sound, awful staging, violence in the aisles. But I loved it. I sat there by myself on the train, reliving those early gigs.

'It was very strange to find myself at a funeral where everyone was going, "What about David Bowie, then?" instead of talking about the deceased we were there to pay tribute to. I can understand why people were so upset about it. Your own mortality comes to the fore. What I didn't get was the god-like status – which I have to say, David did cultivate. He did rather enjoy holding court, and having people come up to him, paying homage – as demonstrated by that whole Tom Cruise episode in Dublin. It is and always has been surprising to me, the blind devotion that people felt for him.

'In his early days, he did have something original to say. Most artists are not just singers, they are actors, too. They take on personas when they go on stage, and sometimes the two become indivisible. It happened to David, but he managed to shake it off, and took back control. He then took that into dance, film, painting and other areas. He would have loved to be taken seriously as a definitive Renaissance Man. That was his dream, but I have to say, it never quite happened.'

'If I had been able to speak to him one last time, I wouldn't have had anything to say,' admitted Angie Bowie. 'But I have no regrets. I will remember David now as a passionate talent. The two of us, we set out to change the world with his music. And that's what we did.'

'Most of the eulogies heaped on him seemed hugely overblown,' comments author Philip Norman. 'Yes, he "pushed the sexual boundaries", but so did many others in the Glam Rock era. Was there ever anything camper than Rod Stewart singing "Georgie"? Self-reinvention wasn't his invention; it's what every major performer must do to survive. And what Bowie lyric can anyone quote beyond "Ground control to Major Tom", and "Ch-ch-changes"?'

'I'm still suffering from shock that he's gone,' says former BBC Radio 1 DJ Andy Peebles. 'It has been a year of extraordinary loss in entertainment. In January, Robert Stigwood, Paul Kantner of Jefferson Airplane, Alan Rickman, Glenn Frey of the Eagles, David, Ed Stewart, Terry Wogan. In February, Maurice White of Earth, Wind and Fire. In March, Tony Warren, the father of *Coronation Street*, Paul Daniels, Ronnie Corbett, Keith Emerson, Sir George Martin. In April, Merle Haggard, Billy Paul, Prince. All these people, whom I loved and admired so much, are shuffling off this mortal coil at a rate of knots. It has been horrendous.

'Seemingly, David Bowie stage-managed his own demise. Two singles released so closely together, the biggest album of his career launched on his sixty-ninth birthday, and then, two days later, he dies. I don't know about you, but I can't see that as coincidental. It has been suggested to me in quite a number of phone calls that his death was the result of assisted suicide. Who might have assisted him, and exactly how they did so, we will never know. To protect them, I am sure he won't have involved his family or his close friends. But when you think about it, David stage-managed absolutely everything else, throughout his entire career. Why would his death be any different? I don't see that as a bad thing, by the way. If he was able to do it on his own terms, good for him. It's what we'd all wish for.

'I consider it remarkable, the way he organised his ending.

Supremely creative *ad mortem*. That's how he was. You can say this about so few pop stars: that you never once willed him to quit. Because he never allowed himself to reach his sell-by date. On a regular basis, he looked at himself in the mirror, no longer liked what he saw, so he just took the bull by the horns, and he changed it. It takes enormous courage to do such a thing even once. But he did it time after time.

'He was blessed with such authority and power, command of imagery, musical majesty. I always knew I was watching a consummate professional. He was discerning and intellectual. He'd started at the bottom, and had travelled the length of the M1 and the M6 in order to play the sweaty clubs, learn his craft, pay his dues. He'd put in his ten thousand hours, and he never forgot how it felt to be an absolute beginner. He was able to respect and work with younger, breaking musicians, because he remembered what it was like to be in their shoes.'

'They like to call him a rock star,' comments Tony Hatch, one of David's earliest producers. 'I prefer to think of him as a pop artist. Will he and his music always be remembered? I'm afraid that I don't see his music as having the longevity of a Mozart or a Beethoven. Although anything's possible. Elvis Presley and Michael Jackson seem to have transcended their roots. Presley didn't write, of course, while Michael wrote with Quincy Jones, Rod Temperton, musicians like that. And you'd think to yourself, were those Michael's riffs, or *theirs*? I think the McCartney music will go on forever and ever. He and Lennon didn't in fact write very much together, to begin with. Although they had an agreement, and everything was credited to Lennon and McCartney down the line. But it's absolutely clear to me that Paul wrote most of the songs. I can tell, simply by listening to them.

'So no, David is not up there in that league. When he died, the media, the DJs, the commentators, his contemporaries, went way over the top, in my opinion. The grief was out of all proportion to the loss. What they were mourning was their *own* loss. The death of their own teenagehood. That's what David Bowie represented to them.'

'We remember only songs,' reckons rock manager and producer Simon Napier-Bell. 'In the end, we won't remember *him*. Because he wasn't a consistent force. He changed all the time. There are exceptions to the rule: we will remember Maria Callas much more than any of the arias she sang, because she was so unusual, and her life was so tragic. We will remember Diana Ross. But Bowie going forward will be all about the music. So in some ways, that diminishes him as an artist. It's the way it is.

'But for as long as those of us who knew him have left to live, we will admire his act. Because it was *all* an act. Every moment of it. A day or so before he died, he was photographed outside his apartment building in a beautifully cut charcoal suit, tie and a fedora, wearing a big broad smile and looking fabulous. It was a deliberate *act*. As was everything he did. He knew that he was dying; he'd known for about eighteen months. And that's how he wanted to be remembered: upbeat and happy. He controlled his image to the last. There's nothing wrong with that.'

'It was the death of an immortal,' says David's former record plugger Anya Wilson. 'It shook me to the core, I don't know why. He was bigger than life. I mean, he was very human, obviously. But there was so much more to him. I don't think I've met anyone since with such a buzz about him, to do with all kinds of creativity. As people pass away, what I miss most is their intelligence and their knowledge. The thought that I can never again have a conversation with David breaks my heart.'

'One day, generations will look at Bowie's work with the same insight and wonder as they do with Picasso or Mozart,' commented his one-time guitarist, Reeves Gabrels. 'It's art for the ages.'

'He always wanted to turn off all the lights and listen to the record in the dark, so that emotionally you can just be taken on this journey,' reflected another cherished Bowie guitarist, Carlos Alomar.

'Our friendship lasted all those years to the end because whatever he wanted, he got it. It's very rare to be able to go to one person or one place and always be able to find something new. So in the same way that his bands found that about him, I think that he found that about me. We were able to adapt. Also, I knew there's only one chief on that stage: David Bowie. And as long as you understand that, you honour that, I think anyone would get along with David Bowie.

'Lately I've been seeing news of David's cremation . . . no funeral etc. Hmmm. David *hated* goodbyes. Many times when tours would end, who would not be around? David.'

'I felt a sense of guilt when he died,' confesses former Bromley schoolgirl Natasha Holloway. 'I'd abandoned him long ago. So I didn't have a right to feel grief, as I hadn't been attached to him for a long, long time. But the fifteen-year-old me grieved very much. I was cast right back. It made me nostalgic and wistful, and desperate to go back there and do it all again. We will never see Ziggy Stardust on stage again, more's the pity. But we still have the music. He was my lightbulb moment. I'll always owe him for that.'

'As soon as I heard the news, I jumped in my car without stopping to grab my coat, and I drove all the way from home in Sussex to the Three Tuns on Beckenham High Street,' says Hy Money. Well into her eighties, she is still a fixture at Crystal Palace F.C., still taking pictures, still painting, still playing her guitar.

'I just had the impulse to go there. It tied things up. It completed the circle, it was the beginning and the end. I felt heartbroken. I hadn't set eyes on David for many years, and he would no longer have known me from Adam. But I had to go. Because when I met him, he awakened something in me that dictated how I lived the rest of my life. I needed to be there for him. After paying my respects at the pub, where I stood shivering on the pavement reliving the memories and what it was like back then, I drove round the corner to his old home, Haddon Hall. My heart came out of my mouth when I saw it had gone. Vanished. That beautiful house where it had all started for him had been knocked down, and there was a block of flats in its place. I couldn't believe it. It was the end of an era. I got back in my car and cried.'

Those final images of David in his bespoke suit and fedora were taken by his long-serving photographer Jimmy King, to herald the release of *Blackstar*. The accompanying caption could not have been more upbeat, nor less indicative of what was happening.

'Why is this man so happy? Is it because it's his 69th birthday, or that he has released his 28th studio album today, and it's a corker? Who knows, but we're sure you'll want to join us in congratulating him on both. Many happy returns of the day to David Bowie.'

On the back cover of the *Blackstar* insert lies an eight-pointed star. A symbol of regeneration across cultures and religions, it also said to represent the eternal intelligent order that underpins manifest reality. It is synonymous with salvation, resurrection and infinity. It denotes harmony and communion at the heart of all creation. And it reminded me of somewhere: a place I'd first visited as a little girl.

The magical Shell Grotto on Margate Hill is reached by a narrow chalk stairway descending to a winding, vaulted corridor and a small rectangular chamber. Its walls and ceilings are covered with mosaics made from the best part of five million shells, most of them local: cockles and mussels, limpets and scallops, oysters, winkles and whelks. It was discovered by accident in 1835, and its secrets remain intact. Whether prehistoric astronomical calendar, ancient temple or hidden meeting place of the Knights Templar in the

Middle Ages, it has never been dated with any accuracy. The chamber contains what is presumed to be an altar with an ogival arch, its central feature a beautiful eight-pointed star.

David visited the Shell Grotto while he was hanging around at the seaside, half a century ago. He could barely believe what he'd seen there, he said. So many shells, such intricate patterns, for no explicable reason: it was amazing. The maritime equivalent of Stonehenge. He'd always loved a mystery. Perhaps it was that particular star on the grotto wall which had lodged in his memory. I hope it was. Its appearance here, on the *Blackstar* artwork, hints at a gate to the cosmos, a portal to space, maybe even a crack at eternity.

'I'll be right here,' he seems to be saying. 'Out there – but also still here. In your ear. In your heart. I haven't gone far.'

Chapter Notes

BOWIE IS DEAD

1 William Shakespeare, *King Richard II*, Act II Scene I – David's 'favourite Shakespeare play'.

'Shakespeare is said to have misrepresented Richard II,' he said, in conversation with the author, 'but nevertheless, the play is completely intriguing. The speeches are magnificent. Exceptional language. It's so ambivalent: he's gay, of course. Bisexual, at least. He is portrayed as white-faced and quite feminine, though a good six foot tall. He was crowned at the age of ten, but his uncle was put in charge, which led to all kinds of shenanigans, and ultimately to his death. He definitely had a personality disorder of some kind, and some modern scholars have said it was likely that he suffered from schizophrenia. He ran an opulent court, was a great patron of the arts, especially literature, and Chaucer was his diplomat . . . writing poetry as he went. An early rock star! Richard had always known his place, it seems, but then he came to question it. It's an irresistible story line, and I identify with him a lot. His death was the end of an era.'

2 Future presentations of the exhibition were subsequently planned.

LOCAL HERO

1 'Song of the Margate Boatmen' from *The Minstrel Melodies*, 1839.

2 Mike Leigh's Oscar and BAFTA-nominated *Mr Turner*, 2014, starring Timothy Spall as the artist and our friend Marion Bailey as his landlady and mistress Mrs Booth, was shot on location in Margate.

3 The Cockney rhyming slang for hair – from Barnet Fair, an annual livestock and fun fair in north-west London, dating from the reign of Elizabeth I – was also the maiden name of David's first wife Angie.

4 Jan Cox, twentieth-century American mystic, was said to have transformed the understanding of mysticism in the Western world. His talks can be found online. His achievements were largely overlooked during his lifetime. He died in 2005.

Jan Cox, abstract and figurative painter, suffered from acute depression, and committed suicide in 1980. He is buried in Antwerp. *A Painter's Odyssey*, 1988, tells his story on film.

CHAPTER TWO: 1953–1961

1 *Sgt Pepper's Lonely Hearts Club Band* by the Beatles was released on 1 June 1967. Created after the group retired from touring, the alter-ego line-up they invented allowed them freedom to experiment musically – just as Bowie's alter ego Ziggy Stardust would extend him the same opportunity during the early Seventies. Ironically, David's debut solo studio album – music hall meets end-of-pier – was released on the same day as *Sgt Pepper*.

2 Compulsory military call-up ended in Great Britain in 1960, so there was no National Service for David or George.

3 Later attended by one of the author's best-friends-to-be, Karen French, and her sister Maggie, whose mother 'Auntie Mon' became their school dinner lady.

4 'Time to jive on the old Six-Five' was DJ presenter Pete

Murray's catch-phrase, a reference to the time that the show went out.

5 Granada TV's first transmission of 'Corrie', the kitchen-sink drama series that would become the world's longest-running soap, was on 9 December 1960.

6 Antimacassars were washable cloths placed over furnishings to prevent stains on fabrics. Macassar oil was used as a hair dressing from the early nineteenth century. A paper version is still used today on trains.

7 Owen Frampton was the father of future rock star Peter Frampton, who achieved massive solo success beyond his bands Humble Pie and the Herd. He is best-known for his hits 'Show Me the Way' and 'Baby I Love Your Way'. Three years younger than David and George, he also attended Bromley Technical High School, where his father was head of the art department. Peter began playing in his first local band the Little Ravens when he was twelve years old. He would later appear as a guest guitarist with David on his Glass Spider tour, 1987. Owen died in 2005.

CHAPTER THREE: 1962–1965

1 Altman's hits include Diana Ross's *Christmas Album*, Björk's 'Oh So Quiet', George Michael's 'Kissing a Fool' and Aled Jones's 'Walking in the Air'. As an arranger, he is perhaps best known for 'Always Look on the Bright Side of Life' from *Monty Python's Life of Brian*, and as a composer for the Oscar-nominated period music for James Cameron's *Titanic*. John scored *Just a Gigolo*, the 1978 film starring Bowie and Kim Novak, about a war hero who returns to Berlin jobless, and becomes the escort of lonely, loaded broads. On Goldie's 1998 drum & bass album *Saturnz Return*, John arranged the song 'Mother'. On the same album, Bowie featured in the song 'Truth'.

2 The Beckenham Ballroom metamorphosed into the Mistrale

Club during the late 1960s, where Peter Frampton and the Yardbirds performed. In 1968 alone the club showcased Manfred Mann, the Alan Price Set, Ike & Tina Turner, the Bonzo Dog Doo Dah Band, Marmalade, P.P. Arnold, T. Rex, the Pretty Things, Black Sabbath and the Isley Brothers. By 1971, they were hosting Mott the Hoople and Fleetwood Mac. In the late 1970s, the club transformed into Tites, which is where we came in – dancing at discos presented by BBC Radio 1 DJs Emperor Rosko, Johnnie Walker and Tony Blackburn. Tites had a make-over in the 1980s, and re-emerged as Lautrec's, before becoming the Bridge.

3 The venue for many a local wedding reception.

4 David had written to wealthy Bloom, imploring him to become the King Bees' Brian Epstein. Bloom did not respond, but he did tell his friend Leslie Conn about them.

5 The first Welsh emigrants to the New World, Prince Madog and a band of supporters, are said to have arrived as early as the twelfth century, pre-dating Columbus. Howell Powell, who left Brecon for Virginia in 1642, was the first official Welsh settler in America. Welsh people began emigrating *en masse* during the 1600s, to the Americas, Australasia and South Africa.

A significant number settled and assimilated in Pennsylvania's 'Welsh tract' in the early 1680s, setting sail in wooden ships from Cardiff and landing some seven weeks later in Philadelphia via the Delaware river, having endured a treacherous passage across the North Atlantic. Most left their homeland because of poverty or oppression. Others went to trade, or to set up military and naval outposts. In America was the promise of cheap land, religious freedom and opportunities for betterment. Sixteen of the fifty-six signatories of the Declaration of Independence in 1776 were of Welsh descent.

6 At one point the most successful record producer in the world, Mickie Most was legendary in the business, having produced hits for Herman's Hermits, the Animals, Donovan, Lulu, Suzi Quatro,

Hot Chocolate, Kim Wilde and many others. He started out as a singing waiter in the 2i's coffee bar on Soho's Old Compton Street. His own group Mickie Most and the Playboys were huge in South Africa. Drawing on his extensive production expertise, he became a panellist on TV talent show *New Faces*: a role model for future mogul Simon Cowell. Mickie died from cancer aged 64 in 1995. His 'little boy', Calvin Hayes, a classical pianist, keyboard player and drummer, was part of the Eighties new-wave band Johnny Hates Jazz, before becoming a successful producer.

7 The Marquee became known as 'the most important venue in the history of modern pop music'. Opened in 1958 on Oxford Street, it presented jazz and R&B, and featured the Stones, the Yardbirds and the Animals in the early Sixties. In March 1964, it relocated to 90 Wardour Sreet, Soho, hosting Jimi Hendrix, Bowie, Cream, Pink Floyd, Manfred Mann, the Who, Led Zeppelin, and many more. It became a key venue during the development of punk rock, and during the prog-rock revival of the early Eighties. The premises were sold in 1988.

8 Dana began writing and recording music as a young teenager, and has worked on more than sixty-five albums. She played Mary Magdalene in the original *Jesus Christ Superstar* by Tim Rice and Andrew Lloyd Webber, which opened at the Palace Theatre London in 1972. She rose to fame as a blues singer. Jimmy Page played guitar on all the tracks of her 1965 Decca album *Foolish Seasons,* and produced the track 'You Just Gotta Know My Mind', which was written for Dana by Donovan. She performed backing vocals on 'It Ain't Easy' on *The Rise and Fall of Ziggy Stardust* ... Her album *Weren't Born a Man* was produced by Mick Ronson in 1973. David wrote the song 'Andy Warhol' for her, on this album, and sang backing vocals and played his twelve-string guitar on that track. Dana went on to become the organiser of and a performer at the annual Mustique Blues Festival.

CHAPTER FOUR: 1965–1967

1 Tony Hatch, a prolific songwriter, producer, arranger and pianist, had made his name working with Chubby Checker, Connie Francis and Pat Boone. Under the pseudonym Fred Nightingale, he composed and produced the Searchers' hit 'Sugar & Spice'. At Pye, he also produced Benny Hill, Bruce Forsyth, Buddy Greco, Sacha Distel and many others. In 1964 he made his first trip to New York, and wrote *Downtown* with the Drifters in mind. It became Petula Clark's most enduring hit, created an everlasting partnership between him and the popular singer, and is now the inspiration for a new musical. Tony also composed TV soap themes including *Crossroads*, *Emmerdale* and *Neighbours*. In the Seventies, he became a star on TV's *New Faces* – yet another role model for Simon Cowell. He produced songs for David on which other producers were credited.

2 Vince Taylor was born Brian Maurice Holden in Isleworth in 1939. His family moved to the American east coast when he was a child. On a chance visit back to London, he formed his first band, the Playboys, at the 2i's coffee bar, where he also adopted his new name. He became a huge star on the continent, especially in France. But his career was thwarted by drug addiction and ill-health. By June 1972, the month that *Ziggy Stardust* ... was released, Taylor had turned himself around, and released an album, *Vince is Alive, Well and Rocking in Paris*. It had little impact. Having spent much of his life in correctional establishments and asylums, he died in Switzerland in 1991, aged 52.

3 The Doors' late frontman was interred at Père Lachaise in 1971, having died on 3 July. Two years later to the day, David retired the Spiders at the London Hammersmith Odeon.

4 According to David's and Iman's mutual hair stylist and friend Teddy Antolin, who had engineered their first meeting and who died a month after David, aged 68, 'David took her out to the

Adriatic Sea on his yacht, and proposed in the Bosphorus Strait: so very romantic.'

5 Based on the 1962 novel by Ken Kesey, the distressing 1975 film starred Jack Nicholson, Louise Fletcher and Danny DeVito, and won the 'Big Five' Academy Awards. It is still considered by both the industry and movie fans to be one of the greatest films ever made. The 'cuckoo's nest' in the title refers to the mental-hospital setting. The title itself is a line from an old American nursery rhyme, about three geese leaving a flock: 'One flew east, one flew west, one flew over the cuckoo's nest.' Author Kesey disagreed vehemently with the adaptation, successfully sued the production, and never saw the film.

6 The 1970 US cover of Bowie's *The Man Who Sold the World* album featured a cartoon by his friend Michael J. Weller, with a John Wayne style cowboy in front of one of the dreary Cane Hill buildings. Weller had also apparently been a patient there. The alternative cover, released in the UK, featured Bowie posing on a chaise longue at Haddon Hall, in his Michael Fish finery. He would wear the same Mr Fish dress on his first promotional tour to America in 1971.

CHAPTER FIVE: 1967–1970

1 In the UK, 1967 was also the year that homosexual acts between two males over the age of 21 was decriminalised. Things were rather different in the US. Illinois had become the first state to eliminate penalties for 'consensual sodomy' from its criminal code, in 1962. The rest of the States would have to wait almost ten years to catch up. In 1969, the Stonewall Riots were staged by the LGBT community in New York City, a turning point for the gay liberation movement. By 2002, thirty-six of fifty states had repealed their sodomy laws. Louisiana's statutes still include laws against same-sex copulation.

2 Keith Emerson's first successful group, categorised as 'English progressive rock', was formed to back soul singer P.P. Arnold,

famous for her hits 'The First Cut Is the Deepest' (a Cat Stevens composition) and a cover of Chip Taylor's 'Angel of the Morning'. Pat's version of the latter was produced by Stones' manager/producer Andrew Loog Oldham. The lyrics of this song prompted a celebrated mondegreen: 'Just call me angel of the morning, angel/Just smash my teeth before you leave me, baby . . .' Keith Emerson left the Nice in early 1970, to form Emerson, Lake & Palmer. Tragically, he took his own life in March 2016.

3 The reclusive Duncan was best known for her composition 'Love Song', which more than 150 artists covered, including Bowie. She worked extensively with Elton John, and with Scott Walker. Her backing vocals are a famous element of Pink Floyd's 1973 album *The Dark Side of the Moon*. Drawing a line under her musical past in 1997, she moved to Mull, Scotland, and became a gardener. She died of cerebrovascular disease in March 2010, aged 66. David was expected at her funeral in Scotland, but didn't turn up.

4 Angie was a housemate in Channel 5's *Celebrity Big Brother* in January 2016. During her stay, she learned that her ex-husband David Bowie had died of cancer. Other housemates mistook her declaration 'David's dead!' to mean that fellow housemate producer and impresario David Gest had died. There was an outcry when it was discovered that Gest was merely ill in bed. Angie quit the house days later, forfeiting her £200,000 fee. A cruel twist of fate brought Gest's own death outside the house, a few weeks later, on 12 April 2016. He was 62.

5 Max Miller was a 'Cheeky Chappie' comedian who dominated British stand-up from the Thirties to the Fifties.

6 Chime (rhymes with 'Jimmy') became David's meditation teacher, mentor and close friend. He also befriended Tony Visconti, and kept up with David's progress through him.

7 Beckenham Free Festival, Saturday 16 August 1969, at which Angie manned the barbecue.

8 The Herd, Judas Jump, Status Quo.

9 Renowned session guitarist associated with Junior's Eyes, the Sutherland Brothers and Quiver, Elton John, Al Stewart and Pink Floyd – with whom he went to school.

10 Rick Wakeman also recorded sessions for Junior's Eyes, T. Rex, Elton John and Cat Stevens: he famously composed and played the beautiful piano parts on 'Morning Has Broken'. He would go on to achieve fame with prog-rock band Yes.

11 Originally the mythological castle and court of King Arthur, from which he presided over his realm, and the meeting place of the knights of the Round Table. Also famously used in reference to the brief early-Sixties US Presidency of John F. Kennedy.

12 American photographer and music-video director Ethan Russell was the only rock photographer to have shot album covers for the Beatles, the Stones and the Who. On the Stones' US tour in 1969, he became part of their entourage and captured stills that have become classics. He shot the portraits for the Beatles' *Let It Be* album; with the *Daily Mirror*'s Monty Fresco (longtime colleague of the author's father) and Beatles assistant Mal Evans, he was one of only three photographers allowed at the last formal Beatles photo session in August 1969. For the Who, he shot the cover of *Who's Next* (1971) and images for the book that accompanied *Quadrophenia* (1973). He produced and directed films for many artists, including Joni Mitchell, John Lennon & Yoko Ono and Paul Simon.

13 *Heaven and Hull* was to become the title of 'Ronno''s final solo album, released posthumously in 1994. It featured Bowie, Mott the Hoople's Ian Hunter, John Mellencamp and Chrissie Hynde. The 'All the Young Dudes' track was taken from the live recording of the Freddie Mercury Tribute Concert at Wembley Stadium in 1992, which Ronson played despite being terminally ill with cancer. Broadcast to some seventy-six countries and an audience estimated at more than a billion, it was Ronson's last-ever gig. He died in 1993.

CHAPTER SIX: 1970–1971

1 Tom Parker's real name was Andreas Cornelis van Kuijk. His style of management, which assumed control of every aspect of a client's life and career, was the prototype of the modern talent manager. He demanded, and got, twenty-five per cent of Elvis's earnings, a share which had risen to fifty per cent by the end of the artist's life. He was eventually exposed as a conman. He falsely claimed to have been born in the US, but was in fact a former carnival barker from the Netherlands, who may have run away to America to escape punishment for murder. He entered the US illegally, conned his way into the military, was listed as a deserter, suffered a breakdown, and became a music promoter in 1938. He signed Presley in 1956, and masterminded his first RCA/Victor release, Jerry Leiber's and Mike Stoller's 'Heartbreak Hotel'. That Elvis's beloved mother Gladys never liked nor trusted 'the Colonel' spoke volumes. Parker denied his charge the opportunity to tour the world in the Seventies, citing 'security issues' as the reason. Perhaps the Colonel's dark secret precluded a return to Europe. He died in 1997, aged 87.

2 Promotional agent who represents an artist's records to radio producers and DJs.

3 Tony Macaulay wrote, among many other songs, 'Love Grows (Where my Rosemary Goes)' for Edison Lighthouse, and is a nine-times Ivor Novello Award-winner. He was Anya Wilson's former boyfriend.

4 'Holy Holy' became the B-side of the 'Diamond Dogs' single in 1974. It was also later adopted as the name of a band fronted by Tony Visconti, featuring drummer Woody Woodmansey, 'the last man standing'; singer Glenn Gregory, former frontman of Heaven 17; backing vocalists Lisa Ronson, daughter of Mick Ronson, and Jessica Lee Morgan, daughter of Tony Visconti and singer Mary Hopkin. Visconti himself plays bass. The group toured the UK in September 2014. On the road through 2015 and 2016, performing the entire *The Man Who Sold the*

World album and other early Bowie classics, they became much in demand after David's death.

5 Lulu's real name is Marie McDonald McLaughlin Lawrie. The diminutive Scot scored her first hit at fifteen with a cover of the Isley Brothers' 'Shout'. She won the Eurovision Contest 1969 with Peter Warne's and Alan Moorehouse's 'Boom Bang-a-Bang'; married Bee Gee Maurice Gibb, and later internationally acclaimed hairdresser John Frieda; and had affairs with TWO Davy Joneses: the Monkee in 1968, and with Bowie in 1973–4, during his marriage to Angie. She covered 'The Man Who Sold the World', on which he supplied backing vocals, and the pair recorded several songs together, including the track 'Dodo' – an unreleased duet version of which was recorded during a 1973 John Peel radio session. Destined for but discarded from 'Diamond Dogs', the track was taped for TV during *The 1980 Floor Show* on 18 October 1973. A studio version was recorded the following month. It went unreleased at the time, but appeared on the Rykodisc 1989 retrospective box set *Sound + Vision*.

6 Clem was played by James Corden in the 2008 movie *Telstar: The Joe Meek Story* – an adaptation of the West End play of the same name.

7 French actor and mime artist Marcel Marceau was best known for his creation 'Bip the Clown', and who coined the term 'the art of silence' for the discipline of mime.

8 Mike Smith turned down the Beatles at Decca Studios, 1 January 1962, in favour of Brian Poole & the Tremeloes. His senior colleague, Dick Rowe, who later signed the Rolling Stones, always gets the blame – but Rowe was not present at the audition, and denied the accusation until the day he died.

CHAPTER SEVEN: 1972

1 Natasha Holloway was the author's best friend at Bromley Grammar, and is now a living historian in Wales, demonstrating arts and crafts from the medieval period in Britain.

2 Nicky became artist liaison manager at Polydor: 'a ligger who keeps acts happy. I'd go to Heathrow and get the Osmonds, or look after Slade for the night.' He went on to write and produce hits for Bros ('When Will I Be Famous?'), discovered Ant & Dec and wrote their huge hit 'Let's Get Ready to Rumble', and created *20th Century Boy*, a musical about the life and death of Marc Bolan. It received the 'Best New Musical' award from Broadway World West End, and is slated to open in London's West End.

3 MacCormack was working in ad sales in London when he got the call to go to America. Beginning in 1973, he provided backing vocals and percussion on five albums – *Aladdin Sane, Pin Ups, Diamond Dogs, David Live* and *Station to Station* – and six tours. He became the composer and dancer Warren Peace. With Ava Cherry and Jason Guess, he was an Astronette in *The 1980 Floor Show* TV special, filmed at the Marquee in October 1973, and one of the Diamond Dogs on the 1974 US tour. In 2010, MacCormack published a lavish coffee-table book, *From Station to Station, Travels with Bowie, 1973–1976* (Genesis Publications), to which his old friend David contributed a sardonic foreword.

CHAPTER EIGHT: 1972–1973

1 Mary Hopkin, a contestant on television talent show *Opportunity Knocks*, had been contracted to the Beatles' Apple label. In 1968 she recorded 'Those Were the Days', Gene Raskin's English interpretation of the old Russian love song 'Dorogoi dlinnoyu' ('By the Long Road'), composed during the Stalin era. Produced by Paul McCartney, her rendition went to Number One in the UK and Number 2 on the US Billboard Hot 100 – kept off the top by 'Hey Jude'. She married Visconti in 1971. The couple had two children, musicians Jessica Lee Morgan and Morgan Visconti. Tony later married John Lennon's former 'Lost Weekend' mistress, May Pang, and had two more: Lara and Sebastian Visconti.

2 Suzi Fussey did David's mother Peggy Jones's shampoos-and-sets. It was Angie who hired her to tend her own and David's locks. She became David's personal hairdresser and wardrobe mistress, and later the wife of 'Spider' Mick Ronson.

3 *An American in Paris* was directed by Vincente Minnelli, starring Leslie Caron and Gene Kelly.

4 Linda Lewis was a high-flyer at the time, having scored a hit with 'Rock-a-Doodle-Doo' in 1972, and 'Sideway Shuffle' in 1973. Her cover of 'In His Kiss' ('The Shoop Shoop Song') was to come, in 1975. With a five-octave range comparable to Minnie Riperton's and Mariah Carey's, she worked with many of the greats: Steve Harley and Cockney Rebel, Cat Stevens, Rod Stewart and Rick Wakeman, as well as Bowie.

5 Former Elizabeth Arden cosmetician La Roche also designed the *Aladdin Sane* lightning-bolt make-up, and went on to even greater glory with *The Rocky Horror Show*.

6 'The Hollow Men', T.S. Eliot.

7 *Honky Château* was released May 1972, produced by Gus Dudgeon, who had also produced David's 'Space Oddity'. Dudgeon went on to found, with Elton, the Rocket Record Company. He and his wife Sheila died in a car crash on the M4 in 2002. Elton's 2004 album *Peach Tree Road* was dedicated to their memory.

CHAPTER NINE: 1973–1974

1 'Slaughter on Tenth Avenue' was a ballet choreographed by George Balanchine, to music by Richard Rodgers, which featured in the great 1936 Rodgers & Hart classic Broadway musical *On Your Toes*. In the 1948 film biography of Rodgers & Hart, *Words & Music*, the ballet is danced spellbindingly by Gene Kelly and Vera-Ellen (and is well worth a watch on YouTube). Ronson knew the piece from piano lessons when he was a boy. He took the Rodgers composition to his debut album, and even borrowed the title, changing the word

'Tenth' to figures. Ronson's rendition of the piece is enchanting. He incorporated it in his live performances for the rest
of his life.

2 Marion would continue to be employed by David well into the
late Nineties, resident in Switzerland. She often accompanied
the family on holiday. She received $1 million (£700,000) in
David's will.

3 *Un Chien Andalou* was 1928 silent movie by Luis Buñuel and
Salvador Dalí. The Isolar 1976 show opened with a mash-up of
surreal imagery, including an eyeball being sliced with a razor
blade, taken from this film.

4 A nickname for Amanda Lear, also referred to as 'the Marvel',
after an early Lear jet model.

5 Disco king Giorgio Moroder produced a soundtrack for an
abbreviated version in 1984, featuring Freddie Mercury, Adam
Ant and others.

6 Guy Peellaert had also created the artwork for the Stones' *It's
Only Rock'n'Roll*. For *Diamond Dogs*, he worked from photographs taken by society snapper Terry O'Neill of David and a
live, extremely large Deutsche Dogge (Great Dane). Real
Coney Island fairground freaks inspired the background characters. Photographs of American Josephine Baker, the 'Black
Pearl' star of 1920s Parisian cabaret, who went on to become a
Second World War spy and a civil rights campaigner, receiving
both the French Croix de Guerre and the Légion d'Honneur,
inspired David's pose.

CHAPTER TEN: 1975

1 Dana's recording of David's 'Andy Warhol' was released as a
single. She released two albums for MainMan. Her beauty and
ample charms were exploited by Defries, who promoted her as a
sex symbol. It was something of an injustice: she really can sing.

2 Toni Basil, later of 'Mickey' ('Oh, Mickey, you're so fine . . .')
fame, 1982.

3 Sigma Sound is famous as the crucible of creation of hits by the O'Jays, the Three Degrees, Harold Melvin & the Blue Notes, Lou Rawls.

4 Luther Vandross was an American singer, songwriter and record producer who began his career singing advertising jingles, for products such as Kentucky Fried Chicken, AT&T, GE and Pepsi Cola. 'Discovered' by Bowie, he went on to sing backing vocals for such artists as Diana Ross, Donna Summer, Ben E. King and Barbra Streisand. He became lead vocalist of the group Change, and joined Epic Records as a solo artist, releasing his most famous album, *Never Too Much*, in 1981. He sold 35 million records worldwide, and won eight Grammys, including Best Male R&B Vocal Performance, which he won four times. He suffered from diabetes and hypertension. His career was cut short in 2003 by a serious stroke, which left him in a long coma, and consequently disabled. He died in New Jersey in July 2005, aged 54.

5 *Mardis Gras* at the Prince of Wales Theatre, co-starring Marsha Hunt and Nicky Henson.

6 The title of Graham Greene's anti-colonial novel, published in 1955.

CHAPTER ELEVEN: 1975–1976

1 'I Am . . . I Said', Neil Diamond, 1971.
   Amanda Lear also recorded a song about 'Hollyweird' in 1981: 'Hollywood is Just a Dream When You're Seventeen'. To promote it, Lear was presented as a latter-day Marlene Dietrich. The single was released only in Brazil.

2 *Rosemary's Baby* was a 1968 psycho-horror movie starring Mia Farrow, based on the best-selling 1967 novel by Ira Levin.

3 From 1962 Western classic *The Man Who Shot Liberty Valance*.

4 *Is* there life on Mars? *Stranger in a Strange Land*, the 1961 sci-fi novel by American author Robert A. Heinlein, is the story of a human who comes to earth as a young adult, having been born

on Mars and raised by Martians. 'The most famous Science Fiction novel ever written', its title is a Biblical reference from Exodus 2:22.

5 Ola Hudson designed for John Lennon and Ringo Starr as well as Bowie. She created costumes and looks for David during the Thin White Duke/Station to Station/The Man Who Fell to Earth period. She died of lung cancer in 2009.

6 The Japanese composer's 'Space Theme' was used by the BBC for *The Hitchhiker's Guide to the Galaxy*. In the late Seventies, he formed supergroup Go with Steve Winwood, Al Di Meola, Klause Schulze and Michael Shrieve.

7 According to the Beatles' late producer Sir George Martin, Cherokee was the best recording studio in America. It was said to have 'the vibe': 'an artist-friendly atmosphere that could be felt as soon as one walked through the door'. The first big hit created there was Steely Dan's *Pretzel Logic*, 1974. Frank Sinatra, Barbra Streisand, Diana Ross, Ronnie Wood, Ringo Starr and Bonnie Raitt also recorded there. Michael Jackson recorded *Off the Wall* there, in 1979, one of the biggest-selling albums of all time.

8 I visited 'Point of View' during an assignment to Jamaica for the *Sunday Express*, 1990.

9 Others have suggested that it stood for 'In Search Of Light And Recognition'. It is also an anagram of 'Sailor' . . . which would become David's nickname on BowieNet, his pioneering internet service launched in September 1998. It doubled as an interactive fan club.

10 Egon Schiele was an Austrian figurative painter of the early twentieth century, a protégé of Gustav Klimt, about whom David planned to make a film. It never materialised.

11 Following his own tradition of including a cover version on every album (with the exception of *Pin Ups*, which was all covers), this song was written by Dimitri Tiomkin and Ned Washington for the 1957 film of the same name, starring Anna Magnani. Nina Simone also recorded it. David met her in 1975,

and they are rumoured to have dallied. Other notable covers of the song are by George Michael, Randy Crawford and Barbra Streisand.

12 Oona Chaplin was the daughter of Nobel and Pulitzer Prize-winning playwright Eugene O'Neill. She conducted her affair with David while her husband Charlie Chaplin was still alive. The great comic actor and director died on Christmas Day the following year, aged 88. Oona lasted another fourteen years, succumbing to pancreatic cancer in 1991, aged 66.

CHAPTER TWELVE: 1977–1978

1 Danielle Corminboeuf is the mother of Rick's son Benjamin, born in 1978. When his divorce from Roz became absolute in 1980, Rick married Danielle, but the union lasted less than a year. He subsequently wed glamour model Nina Carter, and fathered Jemma and Oscar. He rediscovered lovechild Amanda, became a grandfather and popular Grumpy Old Man on TV, and is now married to journalist Rachel Kaufman. Musically, he is more in demand than ever. His latest album is *Piano Portraits*.

2 'Wild Eyed Boy From Freecloud' was first recorded in June 1969, released as the B-side of 'Space Oddity', and featured on his second *David Bowie* album – also released as the *Space Oddity* album.

3 It is often written, erroneously, that Brian Eno was the producer on the Berlin albums. While Eno did contribute musically and lyrically, and with his famous Oblique Strategies cards, it was Visconti at the helm.

4 After the Second World War, the north-eastern German city was divided. East Berlin became the capital of East Germany. West Berlin effectively became a West German enclave, surrounded by the Berlin Wall from 1961 until 1989. All around it lay East German territory. After Germany was reunified in 1990, the restored Berlin was once again the capital of United Germany.

5　Coco and Iggy would later move out, into their own separate apartments.

6　The club was named after the seedy cabaret of the same name which features in the 1930 film *Der Blaue Engel*, Germany's first-ever 'talkie', which starred Marlene Dietrich, one of David's idols, in her first speaking and singing role.

7　Journalists don't get to write their own headlines. The piece was published in the next day's *Daily Mail*.

8　*Flesh Color*, or *Couleur Chair* in French, was directed by François Weyergans, an 'immortal' of the French Academy. It co-starred Dennis Hopper, and was presented at the Cannes Film Festival in 1978. It was never released.

9　'Angie' appears on the Stones' 1973 album *Goats Head Soup*.

10　*Life* by Keith Richards, 2010.

11　Dietrich died in May 1992, aged 90.

CHAPTER THIRTEEN: 1979–1980

1　MTV – Music Television – launched in New York in August 1981 with the words 'Ladies and Gentlemen, rock and roll!' voiced over a montage of the Apollo 11 moon landing and the first Space Shuttle launch. The Buggles' 'Video Killed the Radio Star' was the first video shown, followed by Pat Benatar's 'You Better Run'.

2　Chrysalis Records could have been Bowie's label. Chrysalis Music signed his publishing, paying him £5,000 – 'an enormous amount of money at the time for an apparent one-hit wonder,' said Chrysalis co-owner Chris Wright – against future royalties on seventy-five songs he would write over the next five years. Soon after the deal was signed, David's management was taken over by Tony Defries. Chrysalis Records turned him down as an artist on the strength of *Hunky Dory*. Peter Noone's cover of 'Oh! You Pretty Things' set Chrysalis on the path to recouping their investment. The publisher also had rights to the two albums he did for Mercury, *Space Oddity* and *The Man Who Sold the World*, as well as *Hunky Dory, Ziggy Stardust, Aladdin Sane, Diamond Dogs*, and tracks that went to *Young Americans* and *Low*. The deal was renegotiated in 1975, Chrysalis Music holding on to their twenty-five per cent of David's publishing for the full period of copyright – another seventy years after his death.

3 'Mother's Little Helper', Jagger/Richards, 1966.

4 'The End', the Doors, Morrison/Manzarek/Krieger/Densmore, 1967.

5 Darla Jane Gilroy was a student at St Martin's School of Art. A former fashion designer, she is now an academic. Judi Frankland was studying Fashion and Textiles at Ravensbourne College of Art, Bromley (since relocated to the Greenwich Peninsula). As Judith Frankland, she became a designer and nightclub host. Elise was an actress.

6 *The Quatermass Experiment* was a BBC sci-fi serial originally broadcast in 1953, reproduced by Euston Films for Thames TV and aired during October and November 1979, and revived by BBC4 in 2005.

7 Not *John* Merrick: history did the poor man a disservice, not least in getting his birth name wrong. He was probably a victim of neurofibromatosis type 1 and Proteus Syndrome. Merrick eventually escaped terrible abuse and torment to live out his life at the London Hospital, where he was well cared-for. He died there in April 1890, aged 27. As well as this play, written by Bernard Pomerance, Merrick was memorably portrayed by John Hurt in the 1980 film of the same name.

8 At the time of writing, Mark Chapman remains incarcerated at the Wende Correctional Facility, a maximum-security prison in Alden, Erie County, New York. He has been denied nine bids for release.

CHAPTER FOURTEEN: 1981–1984

1 In the Leeward Islands, 300 miles north of the Grenadines – where David would later build his own dream home. Nearly

seventy major rock albums were recorded at AIR Montserrat, by Dire Straits, Police, McCartney, Elton, Duran Duran, Clapton and more. Ninety per cent of the island was devastated, and the studios almost destroyed, by Hurricane Hugo in 1989. They were finished off by a catastrophic volcanic eruption in 1997, and now lie in ruins.

2 Said during a speech to the Berklee College of Music Boston, Massachusetts Class of 1999.

3 *Cat People*, the 1982 film, starring Nastassja Kinski, daughter of Klaus. A new version of the song was included on David's *Let's Dance* album, released 1983, and in 2009 was used by Quentin Tarantino for his film *Inglourious Basterds*.

4 Roger Scott, 23 October 1943–31 October 1989. Many of his vintage recordings have been mounted as a tribute website: http://www.rogerscott.net/

5 The radio network which became America's largest under the stewardship of founder and former chairman, Norman Pattiz.

6 Rodgers co-founded Chic, one of the most influential groups of the disco era, with the late bassist Bernard Edwards. They enjoyed worldwide hits with 'Dance Dance Dance', 'Everybody Dance', 'Le Freak', 'I Want Your Love' and 'Good Times'. In 1985, Edwards formed Power Station, the supergroup that co-starred Robert Palmer, and Andy Taylor and John Taylor of Duran Duran. Bernard's distinctive bass sound was the inspiration for John Deacon's 'Another One Bites the Dust', Queen's best-selling single. In April 1996, Edwards blacked out on stage at the Budokan, Tokyo, and was later found dead in his hotel room. Cause of death was given as pneumonia. He was 43 years old. Rodgers has produced many artists, including Diana Ross, Debbie Harry, Duran Duran, Madonna, Daft Punk, Sam Smith, Lady Gaga and Laura Mvula. In October 2010 he was diagnosed with prostate cancer, but has since received the all-clear.

7 A new recording of 'Modern Love', with Tina Turner, featured

in a 1987 Pepsi commercial. The official video for the original song was filmed by Jim Yukich, using footage from the Serious Moonlight 1983 tour, shot in Philadelphia that July.

8 Tradition holds that a pair of red shoes cause the wearer to dance. Hence, the Hans Christian Andersen fairy story, and the 1948 film *The Red Shoes*. Kate Bush's 1993 album of the same name explored the same theme.

9 The 1953 eight Academy Award-winning film *From Here to Eternity*, based on the famous novel by James Jones, also starred Frank Sinatra and Montgomery Clift. The story is set in Hawaii during the period leading up to the Second World War and the Pearl Harbor attacks. In 2013, lyricist Sir Tim Rice presented a musical theatre version of the same story, scored by Stuart Brayson. It opened in London's West End, closing after six months. The show received its North American premiere in June 2016 as part of the annual Finger Lakes Musical Festival in Auburn, New York.

10 David had spotted New Zealand-born Chinese Geeling Ng waitressing in a café in Australia. She had no acting experience, but had done some modelling. As Geeling Ching, aged 48, she became a contestant on international TV series *Dancing with the Stars* in 2008.

CHAPTER FIFTEEN: 1984–1985

1 Twelve-year-old Mark Feld – Marc Bolan-to-be – carried Cochran's trademark orange Gretsch G6120 guitar to his car in London, on the same tour. Rocker Gene Vincent was seriously injured in the crash. The car in which Cochran died, and his personal effects, were impounded at the local Wiltshire Constabulary station. Cadet David Harman taught himself to play on Cochran's Gretsch. He would make his name as Dave Dee in the band Dave Dee, Dozy, Beaky, Mick and Tich ('Hold Tight!', 'Bend It!', 'The Legend of Xanadu').

2 Padgham is perhaps best known for the Phil Collins single 'In

the Air Tonight', on which he perfected the 'gated reverb' drum sound he'd first experimented with on Peter Gabriel's third solo album in 1980. The three-times Grammy winner has worked with the Bee Gees, Kate Bush, Police, Paul McCartney and many more. He is married to the designer Cath Kidston.

3 Thomas Dolby, new wave/synthpop musician and producer, famous for 'She Blinded Me with Science' (1982) and 'Hyperactive!' (1984), the latter written originally for Michael Jackson. Born with the surname Robertson, he was nicknamed 'Dolby' because of his obsession with keyboards and tapes. Like David, he adopted his stage name to avoid confusion with an existing musician with the same name: David with Davy Jones of the Monkees, and Thomas with singer Tom Robinson.

CHAPTER SIXTEEN: 1986–1987

1 *Blade Runner*, Ridley Scott's 1982 sci-fi picture set in a dystopian Los Angeles, starring Harrison Ford.

2 Australian Janine Allis, the multi-millionaire founder of the Boost Juice smoothie and juice business and a director of Retail Zoo, was a stewardess on David's yacht in her twenties. She sailed around France, Italy, Monaco and the Caribbean, welcoming aboard some of the most recognisable people on earth. 'It taught me that just because you are a famous rock star or incredibly rich does not mean that you are happy, nice or successful,' she wrote on professional networking site LinkedIn in May 2015. 'While working for David Bowie, I was lucky enough to come to understand some of his life journey more. I realised that just because you are famous, doesn't mean you haven't had your financial and emotional challenges, and he had both.'

3 David loved the extensive mythology attached to Deneb, particularly the Chinese love story of Qi Xi in which Deneb makes a magpie bridge across the Milky Way, allowing

star-crossed lovers Niu Lang and Zhi Nü to be reunited one night a year in late summer. Other versions of the tale depict Deneb as the lovers' fairy protectress. Not that we'll know about it, but Deneb will become the Pole star in about AD 9800. Her long-term potential appealed to David, obviously.

4 The biggest blow to Princess Margaret's long-failing health was linked to her beloved Mustique. Having gifted Les Jolies Eaux to her son Viscount Linley to avoid inheritance tax, she was saddened when he decided to sell it and realise the cash. Margaret was mortified to awaken to the sound, one spring morning in 1999, of an estate agent showing social X-ray housewives from Manhattan around her home. In a state of shock, she retired to bed for two days. When she got up to take a bath, still distressed, she accidentally knocked the hot tap. The near-boiling water which gushed from the old plumbing badly scalded her feet. She was flown home to Britain for treatment, but never recovered, continuing to deteriorate both mentally and physically until her death, aged 71, in 2002.

5 William Shakespeare, *Othello, the Moor of Venice*, Act III, Scene IV, Othello to Desdemona.

CHAPTER SEVENTEEN: 1988–1991

1 The Nineties would take Palmer further down the road of alternative music, working with bands such as Pearl Jam and the House of Love – whose band leader and principal writer, Guy Chadwick, is the father of Cydney, the author's daughter Mia's best friend since schooldays. At his own studio in LA, Palmer mixed U2's *All That You Can't Leave Behind* album, and produced, among many others, Ozzy Osbourne's *Down to Earth*. He relocated to Austin, Texas in 2009, where he makes a point of working with local bands.

2 John Pasche famously designed the Rolling Stones' lips-and-tongue logo – perhaps the most recognisable logo in rock history – while he was a post-grad student at the Royal College of Art

in 1970, and sold it to them for a flat fee of £50. He eventually negotiated royalties, which he later sold for a lump sum. In 2008, the V&A purchased his original drawings of the logo for a little over £50,000. He said that he sold the hand-painted work to fund his son's private education. 'Pasche-imodo', as he was affectionately known in the office, also designed for Hendrix, McCartney, the Who, the Stranglers and Bowie.

3 Alan Edwards worked with Bowie for 35 years, and continues to represent his family and the estate.

4 Melissa Hurley would eventually marry American actor Patrick Cassidy, son of actress Shirley Jones and half-brother of Seventies pop idol David Cassidy. They have two sons, Cole and Jack. The family live in Vermont, USA. Patrick is best known for his work in musical theatre, both touring and on Broadway. Melissa has appeared in *Mr & Mrs Smith*, *The Running Man* with Arnold Schwarzenegger, and *Cinderella*.

5 Merthyr Tydfil is also where the Osmonds' family roots lie. The singing group's ancestors left the town in 1868, and settled in Utah, western USA, the seat of the Mormons. The connection is through their late mother Olive. In 2005, production company Yellow Duck made a film with Donny Osmond for BBC Wales, for which they flew him back to Merthyr. Their ancestors were involved in the running of Merthyr steelworks, and their great-great-great-grandfather, Dr John Martin, was chief surgeon there.

6 Until the 1980s, when Margaret Thatcher and Arthur Scargill, leader of the National Union of Mineworkers, battled towards the demise of coal.

7 Ron Howard played Richie Cunningham with the Fonz in long-running TV-series *Happy Days*.

8 Former UK head of Atlantic Records, who later managed Jimmy Page, Robert Plant, Paul Rogers, Foreigner, Motorhead, Yes and others. Carson moved to the US in 1989 to run JVC's Victory Music.

CHAPTER EIGHTEEN: 1992–1993

1 Some of this music would make it onto his next album, *Black Tie White Noise*.

2 A model herself during the Sixties and Seventies, Ms Hardison went on to design swimwear, produce fashion shows, run her own New York model agency, and co-founded, with Iman, the activist group Black Girls' Coalition, to raise public awareness on subjects ranging from homelessness to racism in advertising. She also acted as mother figure to Naomi Campbell, when the teenage model first arrived in New York.

3 Iman would lose her mother just two months after David's death.

4 *The Go-Between*, L.P. Hartley.

5 First referenced by Daniel Defoe in the *Four Years Voyages of Capt. George Roberts* in 1726. Davy Jones also makes an appearance in Tobias Smollett's *The Adventures of Peregrine Pickle* in 1751. He is recorded as a hybrid of biblical Jonah and David Jones, a real pirate who lived on the Indian Ocean in the 1630s. He was also said to have been inspired by Dewi Sant, Saint David of Wales, to whom Welsh sailors prayed, the Jones again from Jonah. Herman Melville, Charles Dickens, R.L. Stevenson, J.M. Barrie and many others wrote about Davy Jones; as did McCartney, in his song 'Morse Moose and the Grey Goose', from the 1978 Wings album *London Town*.

6 In February 2001, 63-year-old Hasselqvist and his son Lukus, 23, were found dead in their apartment in Nassau, Bahamas, after firefighters extinguished a blaze. The celebrated architect had lived and worked on Mustique for many years, designing and building homes for HRH Princess Margaret, Tommy Hilfiger and Mick Jagger, as well as for David.

CHAPTER NINETEEN: 1993–1997

1 Lee Alexander McQueen was a fellow south London boy, from Lewisham. The globally successful designer, whose clients

included rock stars, movie queens and royalty, was only 40 years old when he took his own life on 11 February 2010. After overdosing on a cocktail of drugs at his flat in Mayfair, he sliced his wrists with both a ceremonial dagger and a meat cleaver before hanging himself with his favourite brown belt. His death came nine days after his 75-year-old mother lost her battle with cancer. His ashes were scattered on the Isle of Skye. The following year, the Metropolitan Museum of Art in New York presented a retrospective of his work, entitled 'Savage Beauty'. It was one of the most successful exhibitions in the museum's history. When it travelled to London's V&A in 2015, nearly 500,000 tickets were sold. It proved one of the V&A's most popular shows ever, too.

CHAPTER TWENTY: 1997–2004

1 Eric von Stroheim was an Austrian-American silent movie star, producer and director who played Max von Mayerling in Billy Wilder's 1950 classic *Sunset Boulevard*, opposite Gloria Swanson. The role earned him an Oscar nomination as Best Supporting Actor. A relic of an earlier age and a man of many incarnations, he epitomised the poor European Jewish immigrant who clawed his way to the top. He famously said, 'In Hollywood, you're as good as your last picture.' David owned a copy of a biography of him by Richard Koszarski, *The Man You Loved to Hate: Erich von Stroheim and Hollywood*, which was adapted for the screen in 1979. He died in France in 1957, aged 71.

2 '9/11' was the worst terrorist assault in world history, and the deadliest perpetrated on American soil by foreigners since the Japanese bombed Pearl Harbor, Hawaii on 7 December 1941, leading to America's entry into the Second World War. Weeks after the attack, the death toll was re-estimated at more than 6,000. The remains of only 1,640 had been identified as of 2015.

3 Gerry started as a tape op, and worked with 16-year-old Sinéad O'Connor. He studied classical guitar for five years at Dublin's Municipal College of Music. He performs solo as Spooky Ghost.

4 The popular Looking Glass studios closed their doors for good in 2009, when the lease became prohibitively expensive. Studio manager Christian Rutledge confirmed that its rooms were fully booked when the decision to close was made. 'There's going to be a hole in the New York City musical landscape that I don't think will be filled,' he said. 'We had a big, extended family that rotated around the Looking Glass.'

5 In 1990, Mark Plati worked on the 'Fame 90' remix with hip-hop producer and DJ Arthur Baker. He met David six years later, when he was working on 'Telling Lies', the song for the *Earthling* album which was made available as a single in 1996. More than 300,000 fans downloaded its original internet-only release. Plati has also worked with, among others, Prince, the Cure, Robbie Williams, Fleetwood Mac and Lou Reed.

6 The Living Room was a famous music venue known as 'the incubator of talent', established on Stanton Street, Lower East Side in 1988. It relocated to Ludlow Street in 2003, and to Metropolitan Avenue, Brooklyn in 2015.

CHAPTER TWENTY-ONE: 2005–2014

1 'Do not go gentle into that good night' by poet and author Dylan Thomas (1914–53). The Welshman's best-known piece, it was written in Florence in 1947.

2 Awarded by Her Majesty the Queen to those who have made a distinguished, innovative contribution to any area of British life.

3 'The Love Song of J. Alfred Prufrock', T.S. Eliot.

CHAPTER TWENTY-TWO: 2015–2016

1 Isaiah 32:3

2 The next stop for David Bowie's and Enda Walsh's musical *Lazarus* was London's King's Cross Theatre, October 2016–January 2017.

3 David adored Michelangelo's 'David', perhaps the greatest statue ever created. The breathtakingly lifelike marble master-piece, which can be seen today in the Accademia Gallery in Florence, was sculpted in the early 1500s. The ancient hero David, second King of Israel and Judah and ancestor of Jesus, was a fearless warrior and a prolific musician, poet and composer of many of the Biblical Psalms still sung today.

4 John Bradbury, drummer with ska outfit the Specials, who died on 28 December 2015, aged 62.

Bowie the Minstrel

I suppose for me as an artist, it wasn't always just about expressing my work; I really wanted, more than anything else, to contribute in some way to the culture I was living in.

David Bowie, *GQ*, 2002

Bowie recorded twenty-eight studio albums, twenty-seven of which were officially released, and eleven of which were Number Ones; nine live albums, forty-nine compilation albums, six EPs, a hundred and twenty-one singles and three soundtracks. He also made fourteen video albums and eighty-nine promo videos. There are, of course, innumerable unofficial recordings . . . and, we must hope, a tsunami of unreleased material yet to come.

In January 2017, it was announced that vinyl sales had reached a twenty-five-year high during 2016, with Bowie's final album *Blackstar* being the biggest seller. It sold more than double the number of copies of 2015's top seller, Adele's *25*.

It is estimated that he has sold more than a hundred and forty-five million albums worldwide. His biggest-selling album on original release was *Let's Dance*, which shifted around eight million copies.

He performed around five thousand live concerts across the globe.

His record label is ISO (Columbia Records/Sony/Parlophone/Warner Music/RCA).

SINGLES
Bowie achieved six UK Number One singles:
Space Oddity (1975)

Ashes to Ashes (1980)

Under Pressure (with Queen, 1981)

Let's Dance (1983)

Dancing in the Street (with Mick Jagger, 1985)

"Heroes" (by the X Factor Finalists, 2010)

And twenty-six UK Top Ten singles:
Space Oddity (1969)

Starman (1972)

The Jean Genie (1972)

Drive-In Saturday (1973)

Life on Mars? (1973)

The Laughing Gnome (1973)

Sorrow (1973)

Rebel, Rebel (1974)

Knock on Wood (1974)

Space Oddity (1975)

Golden Years (1975)

Sound and Vision (1977)

Boys Keep Swinging (1979)

Ashes to Ashes (1980)

Fashion (1980)

Under Pressure (with Queen, 1981)

Peace on Earth/Little Drummer Boy (with Bing Crosby, 1982)

Let's Dance (1983)

China Girl (1983)

Modern Love (1983)

Blue Jean (1984)

Dancing in the Street (with Mick Jagger, 1985)

Absolute Beginners (1986)

Jump They Say (1993)

"Heroes" (by the X Factor Finalists, 2010)
Where Are We Now (2013)

But he scored only two US Number One singles:
Fame (1975)
Let's Dance (1983)

STUDIO ALBUMS
David Bowie (1967)
Space Oddity (1969)
The Man Who Sold the World (1970)
Hunky Dory (1971)
The Rise and Fall of Ziggy Stardust and the Spiders from Mars
   (1972)
Aladdin Sane (1973) *Number One*
Pin Ups (1973) *Number One*
Diamond Dogs (1974) *Number One*
Young Americans (1975)
Station to Station (1976)
Low (1977)
"Heroes" (1977)
Lodger (1979)
Scary Monsters (and Super Creeps) (1980) *Number One*
Let's Dance (1983) *Number One*
Tonight (1984) *Number One*
Never Let Me Down (1987)
Tin Machine (1989)
Tin Machine II (1991)
Black Tie White Noise (1993) *Number One*
1. Outside (1995)
Earthling (1997)
'hours . . .' (1999)
Toy (2001) (never released, some tracks absorbed into *Heathen*,
   some leaked onto the internet)

Heathen (2002)
Reality (2003)
The Next Day (2013) *Number One*
Blackstar (2016) *Number One*

The compilation *Changesbowie* (1990) was also a *Number One* in the UK.

Bowie the Bibliophile

What is your idea of perfect happiness?
Reading.

David Bowie to Vanity Fair, 2013

HIS HUNDRED FAVOURITE READS

Interviews with Francis Bacon *David Sylvester*
Billy Liar *Keith Waterhouse*
Room at the Top *John Braine*
On Having No Head *Douglass Harding*
Kafka Was the Rage *Anatole Broyard*
A Clockwork Orange *Anthony Burgess*
City of Night *John Rechy*
The Brief Wondrous Life of Oscar Wao *Junot Diaz*
Madame Bovary *Gustave Flaubert*
Iliad *Homer*
As I Lay Dying *William Faulkner*
Tadanori Yokoo *Tadanori Yokoo*
Berlin Alexanderplatz *Alfred Döblin*
Inside the Whale and Other Essays *George Orwell*
Mr Norris Changes Trains *Christopher Isherwood*
Hall's Dictionary of Subjects and Symbols in Art *James A. Hall*
David Bomberg *Richard Cork*
Blast *Wyndham Lewis*

Passing *Nella Larson*
Beyond the Brillo Box *Arthur C. Danto*
The Origin of Consciousness in the Breakdown of the Bicameral
    Mind *Julian Jaynes*
In Bluebeard's Castle *George Steiner*
Hawksmoor *Peter Ackroyd*
The Divided Self *R.D. Laing*
The Stranger *Albert Camus*
Infants of the Spring *Wallace Thurman*
The Quest for Christa T *Christa Wolf*
The Songlines *Bruce Chatwin*
Nights at the Circus *Angela Carter*
The Master and Margarita *Mikhail Bulgakov*
The Prime of Miss Jean Brodie *Muriel Spark*
Lolita *Vladimir Nabokov*
Herzog *Saul Bellow*
Puckoon *Spike Milligan*
Black Boy *Richard Wright*
The Great Gatsby *F. Scott Fitzgerald*
The Sailor Who Fell from Grace with the Sea *Yukio Mishima*
Darkness at Noon *Arthur Koestler*
The Waste Land *T.S. Eliot*
McTeague *Frank Norris*
Money *Martin Amis*
The Outsider *Colin Wilson*
Strange People *Frank Edwards*
English Journey *J.B. Priestley*
A Confederacy of Dunces *John Kennedy Toole*
The Day of the Locust *Nathanael West*
1984 *George Orwell*
The Life and Times of Little Richard *Charles White*
Awopbopaloobop Alopbamboom: The Golden Age of Rock *Nik
    Cohn*
Mystery Train *Greil Marcus*

Beano (comic, 1950s)

Raw (comic, 1980s)

White Noise *Don DeLillo*

Sweet Soul Music: Rhythm and Blues and the Southern Dream of Freedom *Peter Guralnick*

Silence: Lectures and Writing *John Cage*

Writers at Work: The Paris Review Interviews, edited by *Malcolm Cowley*

The Sound of the City: The Rise of Rock and Roll *Charlie Gillett*

Octobriana and the Russian Underground *Peter Sadecky*

The Street *Ann Petry*

Wonder Boys *Michael Chabon*

Last Exit to Brooklyn *Hubert Selby, Jr.*

A People's History of the United States *Howard Zinn*

The Age of American Unreason *Susan Jacoby*

Metropolitan Life *Fran Lebowitz*

The Coast of Utopia *Tom Stoppard*

The Bridge *Hart Crane*

All the Emperor's Horses *David Kidd*

Fingersmith *Sarah Waters*

Earthly Powers *Anthony Burgess*

The 42nd Parallel *John Dos Passos*

Tales of Beatnik Glory *Ed Saunders*

The Bird Artist *Howard Norman*

Nowhere to Run: The Story of Soul Music *Gerri Hirshey*

Before the Deluge *Otto Friedrich*

Sexual Personae: Art and Decadence from Nefertiti to Emily Dickinson *Camille Paglia*

The American Way of Death *Jessica Mitford*

In Cold Blood *Truman Capote*

Lady Chatterley's Lover *D.H. Lawrence*

Teenage *Jon Savage*

Vile Bodies *Evelyn Waugh*

The Hidden Persuaders *Vance Packard*

The Fire Next Time *James Baldwin*
Viz (comic, early 1980s)
Private Eye (satirical magazine, 1960s–80s)
Selected Poems *Frank O'Hara*
The Trial of Henry Kissinger *Christopher Hitchens*
Flaubert's Parrot *Julian Barnes*
Maldoror (full title Les Chants de Maldoror) *Comte de Lautréamont*
On the Road *Jack Kerouac*
Mr Wilson's Cabinet of Wonders *Lawrence Weschler*
Zanoni *Edward Bulwer-Lytton*
Transcendental Magic, its Doctrine and Ritual *Eliphas Lévi*
The Gnostic Gospels *Elaine Pagels*
The Leopard *Giusseppe Di Lampedusa*
Inferno *Dante Alighieri*
A Grave for a Dolphin *Alberto Denti di Pirajno*
The Insult *Rupert Thomson*
In Between the Sheets *Ian McEwan*
A People's Tragedy *Orlando Figes*
Journey into the Whirlwind *Eugenia Ginzburg*

* It is no longer known where this list was first published.

Bowie the Audiosexual

Herewith, in no particular order, are twenty-five albums that could change your reputation.

David Bowie

The Last Poets The Last Poets
Shipbuilding Robert Wyatt
The Fabulous Little Richard Little Richard
Music for 18 Musicians Steve Reich
The Velvet Underground & Nico The Velvet Underground
Tupelo Blues John Lee Hooker
Blues, Rags and Hollers Koerner, Ray & Glover
The Apollo Theater Presents In Person! The James Brown Show James
    Brown
Forces of Victory Linton Kwesi Johnson
*The Red Flower of Tachai Blossoms Everywhere: Music Played on
    National Instruments* Various Artists
Banana Moon Daevid Allen
Jacques Brel is Alive and Well and Living in Paris Cast Album
The Electrosoniks: Electronic Music Tom Dissevelt
The 5000 Spirits of the Layers of the Onion The Incredible String
    Band
Ten Songs by Tucker Zimmerman Tucker Zimmerman
Four Last Songs (Richard Strauss) Gundula Janowitz

The Ascension Glenn Branca
The Madcap Laughs Syd Barrett
Black Angels George Crumb
Funky Kingston Toots & the Maytals
Delusion of the Fury Harry Partch
Oh Yeah Charles Mingus
Le Sacre du Printemps Igor Stravinsky
The Fugs The Fugs
The Glory (????) of the Human Voice Florence Foster Jenkins

* It is no longer known where this list was first published.

Bowie the Artist & Art Collector

Talking about art is like dancing about architecture.
Art was, seriously, the only thing I'd ever want to own. It can change
the way that I feel in the mornings.

David Bowie confides in the *New York Times*, 1998

Bowie produced more than six thousand works of his own.

His artwork portfolio, his exhibitions and a thumbnail art gallery are featured at www.bowiewonderworld.com/art/art.htm

Self-portraits were a major theme.

His influences included Frank Auerbach, David Bomberg, Francis Bacon and Francis Picabia.

His private art collection included 'a Tintoretto and a small Rubens':

'But the majority of what I have are British twentieth century, and not terribly big names. I've gone for what seemed to be an important or interesting departure at a certain time, or something that typified a certain decade, rather than go for Hockneys or Freuds, or whatever.'

His favourite British artists included Graham Sutherland, William Tillyer, Leon Kosof and Stanley Spencer. He is also said to have owned works by Gavin Turk and Gilbert and George. And his old school friend and lifelong pal, the artist George Underwood, reveals that he sold him a few of his own.

In November 2016, artworks from David's private collection fetched more than £24 million at Sotheby's auction house in London. The highest-selling piece, 'Air Power' by Jean-Michel Basquiat, sold for £7.09 million. All proceeds went to Bowie's estate.

Live Albums & Concerts, Managers, Alter Egos & Groups

LIVE ALBUMS & CONCERTS
David Live (1974)
Stage (1978)
Ziggy Stardust and the Spiders from Mars (1983; filmed 1973)
Serious Moonlight (1984)
Tin Machine Live: Oy Vey, Baby (1992)
Live Santa Monica '72 (2009)
Glass Spider (1988)
VH1 Storytellers (1999)
A Reality Tour (2004)

MANAGERS
Leslie Conn, June 1964
Ralph Horton, (first official manager), 1965
Kenneth Pitt, 25 April 1967–March 1970
Tony Defries, 1970–30 January 1975

From 1975 onwards, Bowie managed himself, with the help of long-serving personal assistant Coco Schwab and a succession of lawyers and business advisors.

ALTER EGOS
Dave Jay
Cloud
Major Tom
Ziggy Stardust
Aladdin Sane
Halloween Jack
The Thin White Duke
John Merrick (Joseph Carey Merrick, the 'Elephant Man')
Tao Jones

GROUPS
The Konrads
The Hooker Brothers (who also appeared as Dave's Reds and
  Blues)
Davie Jones and the King Bees
The Manish Boys
Davie Jones and the Lower Third
David Bowie and the Buzz
The Riot Squad
Turquoise
Feathers
David Bowie and Hutch
David Bowie with backing group Junior's Eyes
The Hype (who also performed as Harry and The Butcher)
The Arnold Corns (the genesis of 'Ziggy')
David Bowie and the Spiders from Mars
Tin Machine
Tao Jones (who performed only two gigs, May and July 1997)

Oddities & Rarities

A SELECTION OF COVERS OF BOWIE'S SONGS

Fame – *Duran Duran*: the 'B' side on the 12-inch version of their second single 'Careless Memories'

Rebel Rebel – *Bay City Rollers*: an album track from *It's A Game* in 1977.

Space Oddity – *Rudy Grant*: a reggae version by Eddy Grant's brother.

Space Oddity and **Life On Mars? – *The King's Singers*:** 'Space Oddity' on their album *Tempus Fugit* and 'Life On Mars?' on their album *Keep On Changing*.

Life on Mars? – *Wall Street Crash*: an unusual version by this harmony group best known for *Royal Variety Show* and *Morecambe & Wise* appearances, released as a single in 1982.

All The Young Dudes – *Travis*: a live version on the 'B' side of their 2001 single 'Side'.

– *The Skids*: a Kid Jensen radio session version on the double pack version of their single 'Working for the Yankee Dollar' in 1979.

– *The Damned*: a bootleg live version during the Eighties.

Fascination – *Fat Larry's Band*: released their version of the *Young Americans* album track as a single in 1976/77.

Golden Years – *Loose Ends*: a single in 1985.

"Heroes" – *Nico*: released as a single in 1983.

– *Billy Preston*: a single in 1991.

Suffragette City – several versions exist, including one by
Frankie Goes to Hollywood, but one of the rarest is a live
version by *Hazel O'Connor* on the 'B' side of the 12-inch
single only of 'Time', released in 1980. The single didn't chart.

ODDITIES

The soundtrack to the film *Just A Gigolo* (released on Jambo
Records) has a track called 'The Revolutionary Song' credited to
The Rebels (though it is obviously Bowie singing). It was written
by Bowie with Jack Fishman.

K-Tel's 1980 *Best of Bowie* album features a rare edit of 'Diamond
Dogs'.

Comparing two copies of *Best of Bowie* – both state that they
were pressed in France, but bear different catalogue numbers. Both
have the same track listing on the record labels, but the labels are of
different colours. Both have the same track listing on the sleeve, but
the second copy's track listing has evidently been 'stuck on' after
the main sleeve was printed. On the second copy, 'Breaking Glass'
on side one is replaced by an uncredited 'Drive-In Saturday', while
'Young Americans' on side two is replaced by 'Breaking Glass' and
an uncredited 'Beauty and the Beast'.

The 'Berlin Trilogy' of albums was released in a stylish French box
set in 1982, under the title *Portrait of a Star*.

Bowie provides a 'Special Vocal Performance' on the 2006 single
'The Cynic' by Danish alternative rock band Kashmir: one of his
rare recordings made during his 'decade off' between 2003's *Reality*
and 2013's *The Next Day* (released on Columbia).

Worth seeking out: *RarestOneBowie* (1995) – a compilation by
MainMan, Bowie's former management company. One of several,
it was released without Bowie's permission, and was later deleted.

RarestOneBowie was the first CD to include a 'hidden' bonus track. Not mentioned anywhere on the CD sleeve or liner notes, the track is 53 seconds of the original 1973 American RCA radio advertisement for the album *Pin Ups* (1973). The ad can be found just before track 1, and accessed by playing track 1 and then using the CD Rewind function to move before track 1 (i.e., rewind to minus 53 seconds).

The Tony Visconti 'Record Producers' CD compiled by Neil Myners with record producer Steve Levine (2007) is the first (and to our knowledge still the only) example of the French language version of "Heroes" – "Heros" – appearing officially on CD.

A 1974 *Record & Popswop Mirror* flexi-disc (LYN 2929) features snippets of eight Bowie recordings: 'Knock on Wood', 'Space Oddity', 'The Man Who Sold the World', 'Life on Mars', 'Starman', 'The Jean Genic', 'Sorrow' and 'Diamond Dogs'.

The *Lodger* album track 'Yassassin' was released as a single in the Netherlands. Its 'B' side, 'Repetition', was the 'B' side of 'D.J.' in the UK. As far as we are aware, 'D.J.' was not released as a single in Netherlands.

'David Bowie Ashes to Ashes (The Continuing Story of Major Tom)' RCA USA only. Vinyl 12-inch 33$^1/_3$ RPM, partially mixed. A DJ promo sampler blending 'Space Oddity' and 'Ashes to Ashes' to give the fictional astronaut's complete story.

Billy Fury recorded a version of Bowie's 'Silly Boy Blue' for Parlophone, released as a single in 1968. It was re-issued on the Billy Fury CD compilation *The Complete Parlophone Singles* in 2010.

There was a Spanish-only 12-inch of his 1977 single 'Beauty and the Beast' (sung in English – but a Spanish release) which runs over five minutes, whereas the original album version is approximately three and a half minutes. It could be found as an import in some UK record stores at the time, though it is more difficult to track down these days. If various uploads to YouTube of an RCA promo bearing the catalogue number PC-1204 is this 1977 release, then the final result is the standard song with repeated sections edited in to increase its length to a duration expected of a 12-inch single.

Peter Noone's cover of Bowie's 'Oh! You Pretty Things' was a hit. Lesser known is the fact that the 'B' side of his follow-up, 'Walnut Whirl', was also a Bowie composition – 'Right On Mother' – which Bowie performed at the Radio Luxembourg studios during the Arnold Corns sessions. (*Lost Beeb Tapes*, the Godfather Records CD, unofficial release, Italy, 2009.)

RARITIES

When the *Black Tie White Noise* album appeared, white-label 12-inch club cuts of the track 'Pallas Athena' were made which are now highly collectable.

The painting created by Belgian artist Guy Peellaert for the 1974 *Diamond Dogs* album depicted a half-man, half-dog creature featuring David's face, and clearly showing the creature's genitals. Few copies with the original cover were released. Those albums are now among the most valuable of all time, into the thousands of pounds per copy. The genitals were airbrushed out for the standard gatefold sleeve. The original artwork and another reject cover showing Bowie in a Cordoban sombrero hat and clinging to a ravenous dog, shot by society photographer Terry O'Neill, appeared in the Rykodisc/EMI re-issues.*

* Guy Peellaert, who worked mainly in Paris, also illustrated the sleeve for the Stones' album *It's Only Rock 'n' Roll*. He designed movie posters for films such as *Taxi Driver, Paris, Texas* and *Short Cuts*. From his painting 'Frank Sinatra: Frankie Goes to Hollywood', the Eighties Liverpool band took their name. Peellaert died of cancer in November 2008, aged 74.

Original copies of 'The Laughing Gnome' are now prized collectibles. In 2011, a Belgian demo pressing from the year of release, 1967, sold for more than £2,300.

In 1980, Bowie released a Japan-only single, an instrumental called 'Crystal Japan', which first appeared in a Japanese TV advert for Crystal Jun Rock sake. The 'B' side was his version of 'Alabama Song'. 'Crystal Japan' has since appeared as a bonus track on CD re-issues, and was also on the 'B' side of UK single 'Up the Hill Backwards'. Decent copies of the original Japanese single currently change hands for around £40.

According to rock memorabilia dealer John Fleming, copies of the 'Space Oddity' single in a mint-condition sleeve are now changing hands for around £6,000.

On 11 January 2016, keyboard maestro Rick Wakeman appeared on Simon Mayo's BBC Radio 2 Drivetime show to perform a musical tribute to Bowie. Rick, a close friend of David's, had played the piano parts on both the 'Life on Mars?' and 'Space Oddity' original singles. The video of this moving performance was viewed on the BBC Radio 2 website more than two million times.

'It was obvious from the listeners' response . . . that they wanted to own a copy of this beautiful piece of music, as well as to make a contribution,' said Mayo.

Rick recorded the tracks for immediate release. All royalties were donated to Macmillan Cancer Support. The tracks can be found on Rick's latest album, *Piano Portraits* (Universal Music Group).

A tape exists of a BBC DJ talking to Rick Wakeman during which they play three songs: 'John I'm Only Dancing', 'Lady Stardust' and 'Star'. They comment on the fact that these are collectors' items and were recorded for the BBC on 21 September 1972. However, the tracks sound exactly like the officially released studio versions, except that 'John I'm Only Dancing' is slightly edited (2´29˝vs. 2´46˝). 'John I'm Only Dancing' and 'Lady Stardust' are found on *Starman In Session* (Silver Rarities SIRA 93); the complete broadcast (including the interview) is available on the *The Rise and Rise of Ziggy Stardust* 4CDR.

Between 1967 and 1972, David recorded twelve sessions or shows for BBC radio, mostly for promotional purposes. When he achieved stardom in 1972, he no longer needed the radio exposure, and did not broadcast further with the BBC until 1991, with Tin Machine. In September 2000, the non-comprehensive double CD *Bowie at the Beeb* was released. For more on the BBC sessions, visit www. illustrated-db-discography.nl/BBC.htm

I am indebted to radio producer and music researcher Neil Myners for his invaluable help with this section. Neil has been writing Ken Bruce's daily pop quiz on BBC Radio 2 since 2003, and is co-author, with Phil 'The Collector' Swern, of the *Popmaster Quiz Books* (Red Planet Publishing Ltd).

Chronology

1912
21 November
Haywood Stenton Jones, David's father, born in Doncaster, south Yorkshire. He will be known as John.

1913
2 October
Mary Margaret Burns, David's mother, born in Folkestone, Kent. She will be known as Peggy.

1932
5 December
Richard Wayne Penniman, 'Little Richard', American musician, singer and songwriter, born in Macon, Georgia, USA. His music will become a major influence on the young David Jones, with hits such as 'Long Tall Sally', 'Rip It Up', 'Lucille', 'Good Golly Miss Molly' and 'Tutti Frutti'.

1935
8 January
Elvis Aaron Presley, 'the King of Rock and Roll', born in Tupelo, Mississippi, USA, twelve years to the day before David. He, too, will become a major influence. David will remark that he first

became aware of the power of music when he watched his cousin dance to 'Hound Dog'. Elvis evolves with the decades – raw young 1950s rocker, schmaltzy 1960s movie star, bloated, jump-suited 1970s live artist – and will inspire aspects of the Ziggy Stardust phenomenon (not least the jump suits).

Presley records with RCA Records, 1956–77. David will record with the same label, 1973–80, overlapping by five years. David's final legitimate manager, Tony Defries, will model himself by the book on Elvis's manager, Colonel Tom Parker.

1937
5 November
David's half-brother Terence Guy Adair Burns born, Pembury Hospital, Tunbridge Wells.

1938
January
David's half-sister Annette born.

1943
29 August
David's half-sister Myra Ann born (she is fostered out, then given up for adoption).

1947
8 January
David Robert Jones born at his parents' home, 40 Stansfield Road, Brixton, London SW9.

5 February
George Underwood born in Bromley, Kent (his Wikipedia birth date is incorrect). He will become David's lifelong best friend from age eight, and will create the album covers for, among others,

Bowie's *Space Oddity, Hunky Dory, The Rise and Fall of Ziggy Stardust and the Spiders from Mars* and *Ziggy Live*; he also illustrates covers for Tyrannosaurus Rex, Marc Bolan and T. Rex, and Mott the Hoople's *All the Young Dudes*. He will achieve notoriety for punching David in the eye.

30 September
Mark Feld, the future Marc Bolan, born in Hackney, London.

1951
12 November
Enrols at Stockwell Infants School, Brixton.

1953
January
Moves with family to 106 Canon Road, Bromley, Kent. Briefly attends a small local private school in Bromley.

5 January
Begins at Raglan Infants School, Bromley.

1954
February
Family relocates to 23 Clarence Road, Bromley.

1955
June
Family moves yet again, to 4 Plaistow Grove, Bromley. David is enrolled at the local Burnt Ash Primary & Junior School.

1955
25 July
Future second wife Iman Mohamed Abdulmajid, daughter of the Ambassador to Saudi Arabia, born in Mogadishu, Somalia.

1958
24 July
David leaves Burnt Ash Juniors.

David and George Underwood perform Lonnie Donegan's 'Gamblin' Man' and 'Puttin' on the Style' at 18th Bromley Cub Scouts' annual summer camp on the Isle of Wight in the English Channel, UK.

8 September
David and George Underwood join Bromley Technical High School, Keston, Kent, where future rocker Peter Frampton's father, Owen, is their art teacher. (The school is known today as Ravens Wood Technical School for Boys.)

1959
Christmas
Aged 12, receives first musical instrument: a Selmer white Bakelite acrylic alto saxophone with gold keys.

1962
At age 15, left eye deteriorates. Pupil becomes permanently dilated.

1963
Popular tea-time ITV show *The Five O'Clock Club* with Muriel Young and Howard Williams (later replaced by Wally Whyton) launches. Musical Director is Alexis Korner. The show presents performances by the likes of Sandie Shaw and Kathy Kirby. Fanny & Johnny Craddock teach the kids how to cook ('And may all your doughnuts turn out like Fanny's'); there are guitar spots by Bert Weedon, and a cool owl and a dog, Ollie Beak and Fred Barker, who are rehoused in 1969 on *Lift Off with Ayshea*. David Jones and Mark Feld (later Bowie and Bolan) become visiting extras.

David and Marc take to meeting for regular coffees at La Gioconda on Denmark Street (London's 'Tin Pan Alley').

1964
5 June
At 17, releases debut single 'Liza Jane' (as Davie Jones and the King Bees, with George Underwood on guitar) on the Vocalition Pop (Decca) label. Despite excellent promo and favourable reviews, it fails to chart.

6 June
Makes TV debut on BBC TV's *Juke Box Jury*. The panel vote 'Liza Jane' a 'miss'. He and George Underwood are introduced back-stage to popular singer Matt Monro.

12 November
Promoting a tongue-in-cheek cause, the Prevention of Cruelty to Long-Haired Men, David is interviewed by presenter Cliff Michelmore on BBC TV's *Tonight* show.

1965
8 January
David's 18th birthday.

5 March
Single 'I Pity the Fool''s B-side 'Take My Tip' by the Manish Boys, on Parlophone, is the first-ever release of a song written by David.

10 April
George Underwood appears on *Thank Your Lucky Stars* (ITV) as Calvin James, miming the track 'Some Things You Never Get Used To'.

15 April
George Underwood as Calvin James debuts 'Some Things You

Never Get Used To'/ 'Remember', produced by Mickie Most, on Columbia. It is the only record he ever releases.

May
David leaves the Manish Boys. The band folds.

20 August
'You've Got a Habit of Leaving' by Davy Jones & the Lower Third, on Parlophone, fails to chart.

16 September
Having tried on a number of stage names for size, and to avoid confusion with stage star Davy Jones, later of the Monkees, David reverts to original Christian name and settles on surname Bowie (after the American knife).

19 November
Debut release by Marc Bolan: 'The Wizard' / 'Beyond the Rising Sun', on Decca.

25 November
Signs to Pye Records label under acclaimed producer/songwriter Tony Hatch.

31 December
David Bowie & the Lower Third perform first gig abroad, at Golf Drouot club, Montmartre, Paris as part of a mixed bill.

1966–9
Records compilation of songs to accompany his 1969 promotional film 'Love You till Tuesday'. Because it was released after he had achieved stardom, and shares some songs with his 1967 LP, it is often mistaken for his debut album. This recording also featured the original 'Space Oddity'.

1966

6 January

Launch party for debut Pye single 'Can't Help Thinking About Me' at Gaiety Bar, Bayswater, is attended by John Lennon's father, Freddie Lennon, who is also signed as an artist to the Pye label.

14 January

Releases 'Can't Help Thinking About Me' (as David Bowie with the Lower Third) on Pye Records. It is the first-ever David Bowie record to be released in the US, and the first time the name 'Bowie' is used in a songwriting credit. Although the single is well received by critics, it fails to chart.

1 April

'Do Anything You Say', by David Bowie backed by The Buzz, released on Pye Records, fails to chart.

August

'I Dig Everything' released. Producer Hatch dumps The Buzz in favour of session musicians, but single is still a commercial failure.

David meets dancer, mime artist and teacher Lindsay Kemp, who trains him to 'express and communicate through his body'.

2 December

'Rubber Band' released, his first single for the Deram label (a subsidiary of Decca). Reflects his obsession with singer/songwriter/actor Anthony Newley (at the time, the husband of Joan Collins). Fails to chart.

1967

14 April

Novelty single 'The Laughing Gnome' released, fails to chart. Re-released in 1973, after David has achieved fame, reaches Number Six on UK chart.

1 June

Releases eponymous debut album on Deram Records – on the same day as the Beatles' *Sgt Pepper's Lonely Hearts Club Band* appears.

11 June

Twenty-year-old David leaves family home, moves in with manager Ken Pitt, at Manchester Street, London W1 for a year.

14 July

Single 'Love You till Tuesday' (second version) released. Widely praised, but fails to chart.

30 September

Saturday, 7 a.m.: the launch of BBC Radio 1.

1968
8 January

David's 21st birthday.

May

John Lennon and Yoko Ono's first joint artwork 'Build Around' exhibited at the Drury Lane Arts Lab. David and landlady/sometime girlfriend Mary Finnigan later visit the Arts Lab, and are inspired.

3 June

Supports Marc Bolan's Tyrannosaurus Rex at Royal Festival Hall show compered by DJ John Peel. Also on the bill are folk rocker Roy Harper and American guitarist/singer Stefan Grossman. Bowie performs 12-minute mime performance, 'Yet-San and the Eagle', to a backing track made with Tony Visconti. Track has a Tibetan sound, made with Moroccan stringed instrument bought on Portobello Road. Marc, 'fiercely competitive', allows Bowie on the bill only on condition that he does not sing.

1969
January/February
Supports Tyrannosaurus Rex on his 'For the Lion and the Unicorn in the Oak Forests of Faun' UK tour, as does sitar player Vytas Serelis.

4 May
With Mary Finnigan, launches Three Tuns Folk Club at the pub of the same name on Beckenham High Street. By the end of the month, it has developed into an Arts Lab, attracting artists from all over London (until 1973).

June–September
Records *David Bowie* album (later versions were called *Space Oddity*) at Trident Studios, Soho, London. Producer is Tony Visconti – but he declines to produce the 'Space Oddity' song (the honour goes to Gus Dudgeon).

5 July
'Space Oddity' receives debut public airing, broadcast to thousands of fans at free Hyde Park concert just before Rolling Stones take to stage.

11 July
'Space Oddity', opening track of his album *David Bowie*, released as a single. BBC will play it during coverage of moon mission and lunar landing. Becomes his first Top Five hit.

16 July
Apollo 11 mission launches.

20 July
US astronauts Commander Neil Armstrong and Lunar Module Pilot Edwin 'Buzz' Aldrin land on moon.

21 July
Neil Armstrong takes first human steps on the moon. Historic moonwalk broadcast live to a worldwide TV audience, who hear Armstrong describe it as 'one small step for (a) man, one giant leap for mankind'. Mission effectively ends Cold War 'Space Race' with Soviet Union.

5 August
David's father Haywood Stenton Jones ('John') dies from pneumonia aged 56.

16 August
Beckenham Free Festival, Croydon Road Recreation Ground, Beckenham, to raise much-needed funds for the Beckenham Arts Lab. Bowie later immortalises the day in his song 'Memory of a Free Festival' (on the album *Space Oddity*).

October
With future wife Angela Barnett, moves into Haddon Hall, Flat 7, 42 Southend Road, Beckenham. Invites Tony Visconti and girlfriend Liz to join them. Living under same roof as David while continuing to produce Marc makes for compromising times.

9 October
Makes debut appearance on *Top of the Pops*, performing 'Space Oddity', wearing silver catsuit borrowed from sometime boyfriend Calvin Lee.

14 November
David Bowie album released.

1970
8 January
On 23rd birthday, David, Visconti, guitarist Tim Renwick and drummer John Cambridge play London's Speakeasy club.

22 February
David and Hype play the Roundhouse, London, dressed in camp pre-glam outfits. According to Visconti, it is the first official night of 'Glam Rock'. Denim-clad Bolan, newly married, attends.

20 March
Marries Cypriot-born American Mary Angela Barnett at Bromley Register Office, Kent.

10 May
Receives Ivor Novello Award for Best Original Song ('Space Oddity').

4 November
Releases third studio album *The Man Who Sold the World* (Mercury Records in the US), and six months later (April 1971) in UK.

Parts company with Tony Visconti for several years. Bolan changes musical direction. Visconti masterminds Bolan's T. Rex hits. 'Ride a White Swan', released 9 October, reaches Number Two on UK chart.

1971
19 February
T. Rex release 'Hot Love'. Soars to Number One, reigns for six weeks. Bolan suddenly in demand.

April
Peter Noone of Herman's Hermits fame releases cover of Bowie's 'Oh! You Pretty Things', produced by Mickie Most, on which David plays piano. On drums is session ace Clem Cattini, who played on Jeff Beck's debut hit 'Hi Ho Silver Lining' in 1967, on more than 40 Number One singles and hundreds of other hits. Noone's solo debut becomes Number 12 hit, making it Bowie's

first success since 'Space Oddity'. Noone enthuses to the press that 'David Bowie is the best songwriter in Britain at this time ... certainly the best since Lennon and McCartney, and you don't hear so much of them nowadays.'

30 May
David's and Angie's son Duncan Zowie Haywood Jones born at Bromley Hospital, Kent, 8lb 8oz.

20–24 June
Glastonbury Festival ('Glastonbury Fayre') held on farm above Glastonbury–Stonehenge ley line. Filmed by future movie director and producer Nicolas Roeg and David Puttnam.

1 August
Signs management contract with Gem.

17 December
Fourth album *Hunky Dory* released on RCA Records, his first for the label which will be his home for next ten years.

1972
22 January
In 'Oh You Pretty Thing', an outrageous interview with Michael Watts in the *Melody Maker* famously declares that he is 'gay, and I always have been' (later insisting it was all a publicity stunt).

29 January
Bowie's UK tour begins. It will evolve, by May, into first Ziggy Stardust and the Spiders from Mars tour.

8 February
Performs with Spiders from Mars on BBC TV's *Old Grey Whistle Test*.

10 February

The date of what has so often been described as the 'first official Ziggy Stardust gig', at the Toby Jug, Tolworth, Surrey, but was in fact just another date on current tour.

11 February

Brother Terry marries Olga, fellow patient in Cane Hill psychiatric hospital, at Croydon Register Office. David is on tour, does not attend. Couple take up residence in a bedsitter off Beckenham High Street, to be close to Terry's mother Peggy, who has relocated there.

Declines an invitation from Freddie Mercury to produce debut Queen album, due to own recording and performing commitments.

6 June

The Rise and Fall of Ziggy Stardust and the Spiders from Mars album released.

17 June

During Oxford Town Hall gig on the Ziggy tour, David's simulated fellatio on Mick Ronson's guitar captured by photographer Mick Rock. Image makes the front cover of *Melody Maker*.

18 June

Dorchester Hotel press conference for US journalists. Future collaborators Lou Reed and Iggy Pop attend.

21 June

Performs 'Starman' on *Lift Off with Ayshea*.

6 July

Performs 'Starman' on *Top of the Pops*.

28 July

'All the Young Dudes', a song written by David for Mott the Hoople and recorded by them, released. Reaches Number Three on UK chart. He performs the song himself during his 1973 tour.

September

Sails on *QE2* to New York with Angie and George and Birgit Underwood, for seventeen-day promotional tour of *Ziggy Stardust* album.

28 September

Ziggy and Spiders perform at Carnegie Hall.

8 November

'Walk on the Wild Side' single by Lou Reed (from his second album *Transformer*) released. David's childhood saxophone tutor Ronnie Ross plays solo baritone sax on the track, produced by Bowie at Trident Studios, Soho, London. David also contributes acoustic guitar, and Mick Ronson is on electric guitar.

1973
25 January

David joins SS *Canberra* in Southampton, to sail to New York, accompanied by school chum Geoff MacCormack in George Underwood's place.

14 February

Collapses from exhaustion after performance at Madison Square Garden, New York.

13 April

Aladdin Sane released, introducing iconic thunderbolt face slash.

5 May

'Camelot' crumbles: the Bowies move out of Haddon Hall.

3 July
Ziggy Stardust tour ends at Hammersmith Odeon, London, with Bowie's shock retirement of Spiders from Mars (182 shows).

12 May
Becomes first rock artist to perform at Earls Court Exhibition Centre.

October
Films *The 1980 Floor Show Midnight Special* for NBC TV in USA co-starring, among others, mysterious mistress Amanda Lear. Show is taped at Marquee Club, Soho, London.

19 October
Covers album *Pin Ups* released, charts on 3 November: the same day as *These Foolish Things,* another covers album, by Bryan Ferry.

1974
24 April
Diamond Dogs released: Bowie's take on Orwellian post-apocalypse, after being refused rights to novel *1984* by George Orwell's widow.

14 June
Diamond Dogs tour begins, Montreal.

2 December
Diamond Dogs tour ends, Atlanta (73 shows).

1975
7 March
Young Americans released. Glam Rock finally buried in favour of a flirtation with Philadelphia Soul. Also kick-starts career of Luther Vandross. Album includes first Number One in US, 'Fame', co-written by John Lennon (also on backing vocals), recorded at

New York's Power Plant. The song is a lament on the nature of celebrity. The famous riff is by guitarist Carlos Alomar.

25 July

Partnership with manager Tony Defries ends.

1976
23 January

Station to Station released: introducing Bowie's 'last great character', the Thin White Duke; recorded after filming Nicolas Roeg's *The Man Who Fell to Earth*, based on 1963 Walter Tevis novel about an alien who lands on Earth seeking a way to convey water back to his parched planet. Not a box office smash, but remains a cult film.

2 February

Isolar 1976 tour begins, Vancouver.

18 May

Isolar 1976 tour ends, Paris (64 shows).

Cocaine-addicted and on the brink of both physical and mental collapse, David escapes from America to Berlin.

1977
8 January

David's 30th birthday.

14 January

Low, first album of his 'Berlin Trilogy', released. Collaborates with Visconti and Brian Eno. The album recorded primarily in France, and mixed in Berlin.

16 August

Elvis Presley dies aged 42 in drug-related circumstances, Memphis, Tennessee.

7 September
Flies to UK from Switzerland to record final episode of Bolan's *Marc* show for Granada TV. Performs ' "Heroes" ', a fortnight ahead of the single's release. Jams with Marc to close the show. Marc falls off the stage. Union restrictions prevent sequence from being re-shot. It is Marc's last-ever TV performance.

11 September
Records 'The Little Drummer Boy/Peace on Earth' with crooner Bing Crosby in London. The partnership is significant: Crosby is the best-selling recording artist of twentieth century, and the world's first multi-media star. Duet is not televised until after Crosby's death, a month later.

16 September
Marc Bolan killed in car crash in Barnes, London, two weeks before his 30th birthday.

20 September
Bowie attends Bolan's funeral at Golders Green crematorium, London, alongside Tony Visconti and Rod Stewart. Bolan's widow June (from whom Marc was almost divorced) leaves funeral with David.

23 September
' "Heroes" ' single released. 'One of the greatest songs of all time' flagged at Number 24 on the UK chart.

14 October
"Heroes" album released – the only album of the 'Berlin Trilogy' to be recorded completely in Berlin. Featuring guitarist Robert Fripp, it inspired John Lennon's *Double Fantasy* in 1980; John would declare that his ambition was 'to do something as good as *"Heroes"* '. Release date coincides with death of Bing Crosby.

1978
29 March
Isolar II – the 1978 world tour begins, San Diego.

5 July
David's step-daughter-to-be Zulekha born, to future wife Iman and her current husband, basketball player Spencer Haywood.

12 December
Isolar II tour ends, Tokyo (77 shows).

1979
18 May
Lodger album, produced in Switzerland and New York, released. Fails to wow critics at the time, later regarded as great underrated album.

Travels to Japan to stay at Togendo, Kyoto, home of American Sinologist (academic specialist in Chinese culture) and teacher of Japanese arts David Kidd (who also died of cancer at the age of 69, in 1996). Taunts Western press with suggestions that he may move to Japan permanently.

1980
8 February
Divorces Angie in Switzerland. Receives custody of their son, then still known as 'Zowie'.

12 September
Scary Monsters (and Super Creeps) album released, his final studio album for RCA. Reaches Number One within a fortnight.

23 September
Triumphs in *The Elephant Man* at Booth Theater, Broadway, NYC

(until 3 January 1981). Records his final album with Tony Visconti for 22 years.

8 December
John Lennon assassinated in New York by Mark Chapman, outside Dakota Building home. Deeply shocked by the loss of his close friend, David retreats to Switzerland.

1981
July
Impromptu jam session with Queen at their Mountain Studios, Montreux, results in collaborative single 'Under Pressure' – mostly recorded in Switzerland, completed in New York.

Begins work on Bertholt Brecht's 1918 play *Baal* for BBC TV, produced by Louis Marks. The play is shot in a week in Acton during August.

September
Returns to Hansa Studio 2 with Visconti. With classical German musicians, records music for *Baal*.

26 October
'Under Pressure' released (EMI-Elektra). Becomes Queen's second UK Number One (after 'Bohemian Rhapsody', 1975), and Bowie's third UK Number One (after 'Space Oddity' and 'Ashes to Ashes').

1982
2 March
Baal broadcast by BBC TV. Accompanying EP is David's last RCA release. Reaches Number 29 on UK album chart.

Begins shooting *The Hunger*, darkly glam bisexual vampire flick co-starring Catherine Deneuve and Susan Sarandon. Based on 1981 novel by Whitley Strieber, directed by Tony Scott. Features

Goth group Bauhaus, and scenes in Heaven gay nightclub, London. Musical Director is Howard Blake, who, with Queen, composed score for *Flash Gordon* (1980) and created music for short animated film of Raymond Briggs's *The Snowman* (1982), featuring classic track 'Walking in the Air'. A departure for him, then.

Purchases Château du Signal, Upper Lausanne, and a flat in the Kincoppal Apartments complex, Elizabeth Bay, Sydney.

July
Attends Montreux Jazz Festival.

Films *Merry Christmas, Mr Lawrence*, directed by Nagisa Oshima, based on factional works of Sir Laurens van der Post, about his spell as Japanese prisoner of war during Second World War. Movie co-stars Tom Conti and Ryuichi Sakamoto, who also wrote score and theme, 'Forbidden Colours', featuring David Sylvian – formerly David Alan Batt from Beckenham. Filming takes place in Raratonga, one of remote Cook Islands in Central-South Pacific, and New Zealand, another 2,000 miles on.

October
Contractual obligation to Tony Defries finally ends.

1983
27 January
Signs new recording deal with EMI America, for 'almost $17 million'.

14 April
Let's Dance, major collaboration with Chic's Nile Rodgers, released. Features Bowie classics 'Let's Dance', 'Modern Love', 'China Girl'.

29 April
The Hunger released, a box office flop, later achieves cult status.

May
Merry Christmas, Mr Lawrence presented at Cannes Film Festival. *The Hunger* is also screened, out of competition.

18 May
Serious Moonlight tour begins, Brussels. It will be his longest, greatest and most successful tour of all.

25 August
Merry Christmas, Mr Lawrence released in UK. David's best-ever effort on screen is yet another box office flop. Has since become a classic. At least Sakamoto wins 1983 BAFTA for Best Film Music.

8 December
Serious Moonlight tour ends, Hong Kong (96 shows).

1984
1 September
Tonight released. Album trashed as 'lazy' features Tina Turner, plus cool cover of Beach Boys' 'God Only Knows'. Stand-out is 'Loving the Alien' (along with 'Suffragette City', this author's favourite), a modest hit, about religious conflict. Also features Top Ten hit 'Blue Jean', for which director Julien Temple creates extended video.

1985
16 January
Half-brother Terry commits suicide. Bowie does not attend funeral.

June
Records for *Absolute Beginners* soundtrack at Abbey Road. Also records, with Jagger, their joint Live Aid contribution, 'Dancing in the Street'. Its video, filmed by David Mallet in London's then-deserted Docklands, will be screened twice on the day at Wembley.

13 July
Performs at Live Aid Global Jukebox, Wembley Stadium.

12 August
'Dancing in the Street' cover by Bowie and Jagger released by EMI. All profits donated to Live Aid charity. Number One for four weeks in UK, Number 7 in US.

1986
7 April
Original motion picture soundtrack of *Absolute Beginners* released, featuring songs by various artists including Bowie, Jerry Dammers, Sade, Style Council, Ray Davies and Smiley Culture, on Virgin Records. The title track is the best thing about the film.

18 April
Release of *Absolute Beginners*, rock musical adaptation of Colin MacInnes's novel, set in post-war, pre-pop London during the 1958 Notting Hill race riots. Directed by Julien Temple, starring Bowie, Patsy Kensit and Sade. Launched to great expectations, is exhaustively covered but, ridiculed by the critics, is a box office flop. Its failure leads to collapse of production company Goldcrest Films, with whom David Puttnam achieved glory, and which had enjoyed hits with Oscar-winners *Chariots of Fire* (1981), *Gandhi* (1982), *Local Hero* (1983), and *The Killing Fields* (1984). Goldcrest has since relaunched.

May
Absolute Beginners screened out of competition at Cannes Film festival.

20 June
Performs 'Dancing in the Street' with Jagger for Prince of Wales's charity The Prince's Trust 10th Anniversary gala, Wembley Arena,

alongside McCartney, Clapton, Phil Collins, Elton John, Tina Turner and more.

27 June
Labyrinth released, produced by George Lucas, directed by Muppets' creator Jim Henson (his last feature before his sudden death in 1990). Screenwriters include Monty Python's Terry Jones. Bowie plays Jareth the Goblin King. Box office flop, but remains cherished.

Buys plot in Campbell Hills on Mustique, West Indies, creates fantasy island hideaway Britannia Bay House.

1987
8 January
David's 40th birthday.

17 March
Fortnight of press and promo appearances for Glass Spider tour in US and Europe.

27 April
Releases *Never Let Me Down* album, recorded at Mountain Studios, Montreux. Critics unmoved.

30 May
Glass Spider tour begins Rotterdam. It is his first tour to visit Italy, Spain, Austria, Wales and Ireland. Becomes romantically involved with one of his young dancers on the tour, Melissa Hurley.

7 June
Returns to Berlin to perform in three-day rock festival at the Berlin Wall.

9 June
Just before Florence show, lighting engineer Michael Clark falls to his death.

10 June
Another crew member falls from set during construction in Milan, but is unhurt.

11 July
In County Meath, Ireland, a fan drowns in the River Boyne while trying to swim to the Slane Castle venue backstage enclosure.

9 October
Alleged assault of 30-year-old Wanda Lee Nichols at Mansion Hotel, Dallas after gig. She accuses David of infecting her with AIDS. He admits to their overnight encounter, denies all other charges. A grand jury declined to indict David on 18 November 1987. Three years later, in February 1990, he was cleared of the rape charges and the case was dismissed, after he was able to prove through blood samples that he did not have AIDS. Attoney Daniel P. Callahan, who represented David, called Nichols's action 'a nuisance suit'.

28 November
Glass Spider tour ends Auckland, NZ (86 shows).

1988
Records with new line-up Tin Machine at Compass Point residential studios, Bahamas. David and Melissa reside at Robert Palmer's beach house.

1989
May
Melissa Hurley's parents announce daughter's engagement to David Bowie. The couple separate soon afterwards.

22 May
Tin Machine album released (EMI): Bowie with guitarist Reeves Gabrels and the Sales brothers.

14 June
Tin Machine club tour begins New York. Band play a dozen gigs in USA, Denmark, Germany, Netherlands, France, finishing in UK. They perform entire *Tin Machine* album, augmented with covers of Bob Dylan and Johnny Kidd & the Pirates songs.

1990
4 March
Sound + Vision Greatest Hits tour begins in Quebec.

2 April
Receives Outstanding Contribution to British Music award at 35th annual Ivor Novello Awards at London's Grosvenor House Hotel.

29 September
Sound + Vision tour ends Buenos Aires (108 shows).

14 October
David and Iman meet on 'blind date' at dinner party hosted by mutual friend, hairdresser Teddy Antolin (who died a month after David, aged 68). They had in fact met before.

29 November
Couple's first public appearance together, at '7th on Sale' AIDS research benefit, 69th Regiment Armory, New York.

1991
2 September
Tin Machine II album released by Victory Music (the cover genitalia airbrushed out).

5 October
It's My Life tour officially begins. 69 dates in 13 countries.

24 November
Queen frontman Freddie Mercury dies of AIDS-related illness.

1992
17 February
It's My Life tour ends Tokyo.

20 April
Performs at Freddie Mercury Tribute Concert, Wembley Stadium.

24 April
Marries Iman Abdulmajid, in Lausanne, Switzerland register office. David is her third husband.

6 June
Formal wedding ceremony held at St James Episcopal Church, Florence, Tuscany, on 20th anniversary of release of *The Rise and Fall of Ziggy Stardust and the Spiders from Mars*. It rains. The couple honeymoon in Bali and in his favourite Japanese city, Kyoto, staying at 300-year-old traditional inn, Tawaraya Ryokan.

1993
5 April
Black Tie White Noise album released on Savage. His first solo album of 1990s. Back together with 'Ziggy' guitarist Mick Ronson, who dies from cancer soon afterwards. Bowie reveals that the album was inspired by his marriage to Iman. Title track triggered by LA riots, which the couple unwittingly flew back into after their civil marriage in April 1992.

30 April
Mick Ronson dies of liver cancer.

June–September
Records *The Buddha of Suburbia* at Mountain Studios, Montreux.

8 November
The Buddha of Suburbia soundtrack album, his first complete soundtrack, released. The four-part BBC2 TV series it partners is adapted from Hanif Kureishi's autobiographical novel about growing up in Bromley during the 1970s. Winner of the Whitbread Award for best first novel.

1994
Iman launches Iman Cosmetics.

April
Hammersmith Odeon Memorial concert for Mick Ronson, in which David declined to perform.

1995
1 April
Launches first, acclaimed, solo art exhibition at Cork Street Gallery, London.

Duncan Jones graduates from the College of Wooster, Ohio, with Bachelor's Degree in Philosophy. David sells Château du Signal, Lausanne. Also sells Britannia Bay House, Mustique, to publishing magnate Felix Dennis for $5 million. Dennis renames property 'Mandalay'.

14 September
Outside tour begins Connecticut.

25 September
1. Outside released on Virgin Records. Concept album based on psychiatric art.

1996
Inducted into Rock and Roll Hall of Fame in NY by David Byrne, accepted on his behalf by Madonna. Other inductees include Jefferson Airplane, Pink Floyd and the Velvet Underground. Marianne Faithfull performs 'Rebel Rebel' in David's honour.

19 February
Outside tour ends Paris (68 shows).

Presented with Outstanding Contribution to British Music BRIT Award by future Prime Minister Tony Blair. Ceremony held at Earls Court Exhibition Centre. Performs 'Hallo Spaceboy', his single from the album *1. Outside*, with Pet Shop Boys. Other live performers include Michael Jackson ('Earth Song'), Simply Red ('Fairground') and Take That ('How Deep Is Your Love').

March
Begins work on *Earthling* album at Mountain Studios, Montreux.

4 June
Outside Summer Festivals tour begins Tokyo.

21 July
Outside Summer Festivals tour ends, Bellinzona, Switzerland (27 shows).

9 August
Basquiat movie released. Based on the life of Postmodernist/neo-expressionist Jean-Michel Basquiat. David plays Andy Warhol. Film also stars Gary Oldman, Christopher Walken and Dennis Hopper. Directed by American painter Julian Schnabel.

19 & 20 October
Performs at Neil Young's annual Bridge School Benefit concert in aid of physically and mentally disabled children, Shoreline Amphitheatre, Mountain View, California. Pared-down set: 'Let's Dance', 'China Girl', 'The Jean Genie', 'Aladdin Sane' and 'The Man Who Sold the World'. Accompanied by bassist Gail Ann Dorsey and guitarist Reeves Gabrels. The percussion is David tapping his foot, with a bottle cap taped to the sole of his shoe. Also on the bill: Pearl Jam, Pete Townshend, Patti Smith, Neil Young, Billy Idol, Bonnie Raitt and Cowboy Junkies.

4 November
'Telling Lies' single released – of which three versions have been made available on his official website, the first downloadable single by a mainstream artist.

1997
8 January
David's 50th birthday. Celebrates with live gig at Madison Square Garden the following night. All proceeds donated to the Save the Children charity.

February
Launches 'Bowie Bonds', an asset-backed security using the current and future revenue from his twenty-five albums recorded pre-1990.

3 February
Electronica-influenced *Earthling*, his 20th studio album. Released on Virgin. Co-produced by Mark Plati. Not a major success.

7 June
Earthling tour begins Lübeck, Germany.

31 August
Diana, Princess of Wales killed in a car crash in Paris, almost a year to the day after her divorce from Prince Charles finalised.

14 October
Releases 'I'm Afraid of Americans' from *Earthling* album, co-written with Brian Eno, originally for *1. Outside*. Also appears in a rough mix on soundtrack of the movie *Showgirls*.

7 November
Earthling tour ends Buenos Aires (83 shows).

1998
January
Launches websites davidbowie.com and bowieart.com

1 September
Launches BowieNet, his own internet service provider. The service wins him a Guinness World Record: as first musician to create an internet service provider. It closes down quietly in 2012.

Begins work on soundtrack for 'Omrikon', a computer game for the company Eidos. Soundtrack develops into full album originally entitled *Dreamer*, which evolved into *'hours ...'*

Invited to contribute a track to the *Rugrats* film, he contacts Tony Visconti to produce his song, 'Safe'. The scene winds up on the cutting-room floor, as does the song, but the collaboration re-establishes the Bowie–Visconti relationship and sets the scene for what will become the definitive work of David's life.

1999
Seventeen albums from Bowie's back catalogue to be released by EMI.

Films lead role in *Exhuming Mr Rice,* a family film about a terminally ill child whose life is saved on a treasure hunt. Retitled *Mr Rice's Secret,* with the tagline 'Only a great man can laugh in the face of death.'

Launch of David Bowie Radio Network on the Rolling Stones Radio website.

16 February
At 19th BRIT Awards staged at London Arena, performs Marc Bolan's '20th Century Boy' with Placebo.

May
Receives honorary doctorate from Berklee College of Music, Boston.

August
Appears at VH1 *Storytellers,* his last performance with guitarist Reeves Gabrels.

Cyber song contest launches as part of promo for forthcoming album, with fans invited to submit four lyric lines for a song. His website reveals the new album cover in stages.

September
Instated as an Officer of the Légion d'Honneur, France's highest award, at the Elysée Palace, Paris.

4 October
'*hours . . .*', final album for Virgin, co-produced by Mark Plati, released as a download, ahead of its physical release: the first ever by a mainstream act.

9 October
Hours tour begins at Wembley Stadium, for NetAid.

7 December

Hours tour ends Copenhagen (8 shows).

In end-of-century media polls, David is voted 'Biggest Star of the 20th Century' and 'Sixth Greatest Star of the Century'.

24 December

Conducts open interview with nearly 20,000 fans online.

2000

13 February

Announcement of Iman's long-awaited pregnancy attracts global news coverage.

16 June

Mini tour begins New York.

22 June

Launch of 'Omikron: The Nomad Soul' (Dreamcast). David makes two cameo appearances, as do selected tracks from his *'hours . . .'* album.

25 June

Appears for only the second time in his career at Glastonbury Festival, before 150,000 fans, the festival's biggest-ever attendance. Performs a 21-song set, opening with 'Wild Is the Wind', closing with 'I'm Afraid of Americans'.

27 June

Mini tour ends at BBC Radio Theatre (4 shows).

15 August

David's and Iman's daughter Alexandria Zahra Jones born at Mount Sinai Hospital, New York City, 7lb 4oz.

22 December
Mr Rice's Secret premieres in New York.

2001
26 February
Performs in Tibet House Benefit at Carnegie Hall with Tony Visconti, their first live performance together since Hype, 1970.

2 April
Announcement made that David's mother Margaret Mary Jones (née Burns, known as 'Peggy') has died in a St Albans, Hertfordshire nursing home, aged 88. David attends her funeral.

11 May
Former lover and costume co-designer Freddie Burretti dies of cancer in Paris.

June
Stays with Visconti at his home in West Nyack, New York State, to begin work on new songs together for what will become the album *Heathen*. Visconti takes David to check out Allaire studios in Catskills. They soon begin recording there.

11 September
Al-Qaeda terrorist attacks on World Trade Center, New York, and Pentagon. A third attack, intended on Washington DC, ends with the hijacked plane crashing in Pennsylvania. 2996 people lose their lives, including the terrorists. David is in the Catskills, Iman and his baby daughter at their apartment in the city. Iman sees the second plane hit the Twin Towers.

20 October
Performs at Concert for New York City Madison Square Garden, organised by McCartney, in honour of lost NYC fire fighters,

policemen and rescue auxiliaries. The show also features the Who, Jagger, Richards, Elton John, Clapton, Bon Jovi, James Taylor, Billy Joel and more. Woody Allen, Martin Scorsese and Spike Lee contribute short films. David opens with Simon & Garfunkel's 'America', followed by a brazen performance of "Heroes". The event is watched on TV by millions around the world.

Leaves Virgin Records, launches own record label ISO. His product will be licensed and distributed by Columbia (owned by Sony).

2002
11 February
Announcement of David's acceptance to act as Artistic Director at London's Meltdown Festival, South Bank.

10 May
Takes part in MTV Rock & Comedy Concert for Robert de Niro's Tribeca Film Festival, at Battery Park City. Performs 'China Girl', 'Slow Burn', 'Afraid', 'Let's Dance', 'I'm Afraid of Americans'. Also sings an excerpt from 'The Wheels on the Bus Go Round and Round' – a favourite of his little daughter's.

6 June
David and Iman celebrate 10th wedding anniversary.

11 June
Heathen album released on Sony. Marks the return of Tony Visconti after 22-year absence. A major success, widely considered his comeback album, reaches Number Five in UK.

Heathen tour begins New York, and is then parked while David honours a prior engagement in London:

14–30 June
David Bowie's Meltdown 2002, with performances by the Waterboys, Coldplay, the Legendary Stardust Cowboy (the original inspiration for Ziggy), Suede, and the London Sinfonietta performing Philip Glass's 'Low' and 'Heroes' symphonies. The final night is 'The New Heathens Night', headlined by Bowie, supported by the Dandy Warhols, with a DJ set by TV presenter Jonathan Ross.

27 June
David's friend John Entwistle, bass player with the Who, dies a rock'n'roll death in Las Vegas.

23 October
Heathen tour ends Boston (36 shows).

2003
January
Begins recording again with Tony Visconti, at Looking Glass studios, on what will become the *Reality* album. Recording completes in May.

28 February
Performs at Tibet House Benefit, Carnegie Hall. Duets with the Kinks' Ray Davies on 'Waterloo Sunset'.

8 September
Performs 'Reality' album live in concert at London's Riverside Studios, Hammersmith, a short walk from the fabled Hammersmith Odeon venue. Show is video-linked to 68 cinemas in 22 countries. Fans' text messages appear on screen during gig. Concludes with Q&A.

16 September
'Reality' album released on his own ISO Records label via Columbia.

David and Iman purchase 64-acre Little Tonshi Mountain, Shokan, Ulster County outside Woodstock, north of New York City, for $1.16m.

7 October
A Reality Tour begins Denmark, his most extensive for half a decade.

12 November
Pulls out of planned Toulouse, France gig with laryngitis. First dates of American run of the tour put back by one week, when David contracts 'flu.

22 and 23 November
Records *A Reality Tour* live album before live studio audience at the Point Depot, Dublin, Ireland.

2004
January
Tour resumes.

6 May
Miami gig cancelled when lighting technician Walter 'Wally Gator' Thomas falls from rig to his death, just before show begins.

18 June
In Oslo, a fan lobs a lollipop at the stage, which lodges in David's eye.

23 June
Abandons show in Prague after just 15 songs, in agony with a suspected trapped nerve in the shoulder.

25 June

Suffers first of a series of heart attacks, backstage during the Hurricane Festival, Scheessel, Germany. Flown by helicopter to AK Altona General Hospital, Othmarschen, Hamburg, where he undergoes emergency angioplasty. Believed to have endured second attack the next day, and at least three more afterwards. Flies home to New York to recover. Remaining 14 dates cancelled.

23 July

Official end of A Reality Tour (113 shows planned). He will never tour again.

2005

8 September

Over a year since his last public appearance, performs for Condé Nast Fashion Rocks extravaganza at Radio City Music Hall, to support survivors of Hurricane Katrina. Suited & booted by young American designer Thom Brown, with a bandaged left hand and a blackened right eye, trousers flapping at half-mast in solidarity with Louisiana flood victims, performs 'Life On Mars?' with Mike Garson on piano. When he returns to the stage, he is in tweed and waistcoat by Agnès B., brings a 12-string and is accompanied by Arcade Fire, with whom he performs his 'Five Years' and their 'Wake Up'. The show heralds New York Fashion Week. He steals it from fellow performers Gwen Stefani, Duran Duran, Alicia Keys, Shakira, Billy Idol, Arcade Fire and others.

15 September

Performs at SummerStage, Central Park, NYC, with Arcade Fire, sporting lilac suit and Panama hat.

2006

29 May

Appears live at Royal Albert Hall, London, in David Gilmour's tribute to Syd Barrett, who will die in July. Joins in on 'Arnold Layne' and 'Comfortably Numb'.

Announces in the press that he has had enough of the music industry, and intends to take a year off.

26 September
Attends opening of Metropolitan Opera's Fall Season with Iman. Anthony Minghella directs Puccini's *Madame Butterfly*. Salman Rushdie, Lou Reed, Meg Ryan, Jude Law, Sean Connery and David's ex Susan Sarandon also attend.

5 October
Announces his participation in *SpongeBob SquarePants*, a favourite of his daughter's.

17 October
The Prestige, sci-fi thriller starring Hugh Jackman, Christian Bale, Michael Caine and Bowie released (10 November in UK).

November
At 3rd annual Black Ball, Hammersmith Ballroom (appropriately), New York, takes part in fundraiser for Keep a Child Alive, supporting families living with HIV. Hosted by Alicia Keys and Iman. Performs 'Wild is the Wind', 'Fantastic Voyage' and 'Changes', the last a duet with Alicia. Accompanied by Mike Garson. He is about to turn 60, and this concert will turn out to be his last ever live performance.

Stars as himself in episode of *Extras*, Ricky Gervais comedy series, aired on BBC and later on HBO in 2007.

2007
8 January
David's 60th birthday.

May
Curates the first High Line ten-day arts & music festival, NYC. A public park created for it from the abandoned 'Els', the elevated train tracks on the city's West Side. Features both superstars and emerging talent, focuses on music, nightlife, visual art, performance and film.

In August 2016, actor and comedian Ricky Gervais revealed that Bowie introducing him on stage at New York's Madison Square Garden in 2007 was in fact the singer's 'last live performance'. During this intro, David sang some of 'Little Fat Man', the spoof song they penned together for Gervais's TV series *Extras*, which echoes Bowie's single 'Little Wonder' (from his 1997 album *Earthling*). *Extras* was also David's last-ever television appearance.

3 June
Honoured at 11th Annual Webby Awards – 'the Oscars of the Internet' – with Lifetime Achievement Award, for 'pushing the boundaries between art and technology'.

August
Former manager Tony Defries announces imminent publication of autobiography *Gods and Gangsters* (which remains unpublished). The project is later dropped when it emerges that he has lost a fortune in a Cayman Islands tax scam, leading to investigation by IRS. Defries was one of the beneficiaries of a fake annuity scheme organised by a Swiss bank and an insurance company. He had bought into the scam, and lost his entire annuity premium of $22 million. Attempting to recoup whatever he could, he then filed a civil complaint in the federal court in Virginia, US. The suit was dismissed for 'lack of jurisdiction'.

2008
David and Iman purchase the Old Rectory, 43 Gilston Road, West Brompton in London's Kensington/Chelsea, SW10, but never live there. The property is sold again in 2011.

2009

Duncan Jones's debut film, the sci-fi picture *Moon*, nominated for seven British Independent Film awards (wins two), two BAFTA 2010 awards, and takes Outstanding Debut by a Director award.

23 January

Attends Sundance Festival, Utah – largest independent film festival in US – to support his son.

April

Attends Tribeca Film Festival New York with Iman, before going to ground for 12 months.

2010

Begins recording, with Tony Visconti, what will turn out to be his first album for ten years, *The Next Day*. They work slowly, over a two-year period, at the Magic Shop studios, SoHo, New York: a 'dark, atmospheric' facility equipped with vintage gear. The studios had previously welcomed Lou Reed and Arcade Fire.

June

Iman wins Council of Fashion Designers' Fashion Icon Award in New York. David attends.

2012

8 January

David's 65th birthday.

27 March

Unveiling of Crown Estate blue plaque at 23 Heddon Street, off London's Regent Street, to commemorate 40th anniversary of *Ziggy Stardust* LP. The location is where the album's front cover photo was shot. Followed by VIP breakfast attended by original Spiders from Mars Trevor Bolder and Woody Woodmansey, Spandau Ballet's Gary Kemp, co-producer of the artwork Terry Pastor, and record producer Ken Scott.

24 April
David and Iman celebrate 20th wedding anniversary.

It is announced that the David Bowie Archive has given unprecedented access to the V&A in London for an exhibition to be curated exclusively by them. Marks the first time that any museum is granted access to extensive and meticulously maintained archive.

6 November
Duncan Jones marries fiancée Rodene Ronquillo.

2013
8 January
Posts video for new single 'Where Are We Now' on his website, with no press announcement, to introduce his first album of new material in a decade. Album is available immediately on iTunes in 119 countries.

8 March
Without fanfare, *The Next Day* album, produced by Tony Visconti, released on ISO Records/Columbia to great critical acclaim. Nominated for 2013 Mercury Prize; Best Rock Album at 2014 Grammy Awards; and for Mastercard British Album of the Year at 2014 BRIT Awards. His first Number One album in UK for 20 years, since 1993's *Black Tie White Noise*.

23 March
'David Bowie Is' touring exhibition opens at V&A, London.

11 August
V&A exhibition concludes, and the show hits the road.

27 October
Lou Reed dies in New York, aged 71.

2014

19 February

Becomes the oldest recipient ever of a BRIT Award, winning Best British Male Artist. It is accepted on his behalf by model Kate Moss. His acceptance speech causes consternation with its references to the imminent referendum on Scottish independence, in which he urges Scotland to 'stay with us'.

3 November

One World Trade Center opens in New York City, on the site of the destroyed World Trade Center.

2015

19 November

'Blackstar' title track from forthcoming final album released as a single.

7 December

Opening night of *Lazarus*, the play, at New York Theater Workshop, Manhattan. His final public appearance before his death.

17 December

'Lazarus' single released as digital download, and is world-premiered on BBC Radio 6 the same day.

2016

8 January

Blackstar, Bowie's final studio album, released on his 69th birthday, on ISO label. Producer Visconti later says it is Bowie's intended swansong, 'a parting gift to his fans just before his death'. Album reaches Number One in many countries. It is his first and only album to make it to Number One on the American Billboard 200 albums chart.

10 January

David dies.

Tributes

What I loved about him towards the end was his incredible privacy during what must have been ten years of incredible bad luck with illnesses, heart attacks, cancer, whatever. He kept it private in an age we're living in with Twitter, when everyone knows everything about everything – he kept it to himself. He made two albums without anybody knowing he was making them. He had treatment for his illnesses without anyone knowing, or anyone saying anything. And that is the mystique of the man. Because we know David Bowie the figure, the singer, the outrageous performer, but actually, we don't know anything about *him*. That's the way it should be in music, and should be in any art form whatsoever.

Sir Elton John

David Bowie was one of the band's earliest supporters and champions. He not only created the world that made it possible for our band to exist, he welcomed us into it with grace and warmth. We will take to the grave the moments we shared – talking, playing music and collaborating – as some of the most profound and memorable moments of our lives.

Arcade Fire

I was listening to his album (*Blackstar*) before he died . . . I thought I must get in touch with him, as I hadn't seen him in a long time. But he died almost immediately after that. I was very upset.
Mick Jagger

A piece of my heart has broken. Not only was David a passionate supporter of my career, but more importantly a very special person in my life. An icon. Irreplaceable, loving friend. I am missing him greatly.
Tina Turner

David wrote some wonderful songs. I was lucky enough to sing one of them – and it changed my life. My heart goes out to his wife, son and daughter. R.I.P., David.
Ian Hunter, Mott the Hoople, to whom David gifted the instant classic 'All the Young Dudes'.

It was the best song I'd ever had the privilege to work on.
Rick Wakeman, discussing 'Life on Mars?'

If 'I Can't Give Everything Away' is the last piece of music we have from Bowie, then it is, in my opinion, the finest goodbye from any artist in my lifetime.
Warren Bennett, musician, composer & arranger

Very sad news to wake up to on this raining morning. David was a great star, and I treasure the moments we had together. His music played a very strong part in British musical history, and I'm proud to think of the huge influence he has had on people all around the world. I send my deepest sympathies to his family, and will always remember the great laughs we had through the years. His star will shine in the sky forever.
Sir Paul McCartney

(After the recording of 'Under Pressure'), the next time we really spent serious time together was at the rehearsals for the Freddie Mercury

Tribute Concert, which Roger (Taylor) and I put together after we lost Freddie. There was one bizarre moment, when I looked around in the rehearsal room and realised that, on some makeshift chairs, in a line waiting for their rehearsal spots, sat Roger Daltrey, Robert Plant, George Michael, and David Bowie. David, as I remember, was very mellow by then, and made a wonderful contribution to the show, including a literally show-stopping moment when he went down on one knee and recited the Lord's Prayer. If you look at our faces on the video for that moment, you can see that it was just as big a surprise to us as it was to the audience! David's duet with Annie Lennox that night is legendary. But pretty much everything David did was legendary.

Never predictable, never classifiable, immensely lateral-thinking and fearless, he stands as one of Britain's greatest musical creators. I'm certainly proud to have worked with him. R.I.P., David.
Dr Brian May

Not everything we worked on together was like *Let's Dance*. David Bowie was always changing, and that's what was interesting about him. He once told me that he felt like he had a responsibility even to himself to change: 'I don't do what people want me to do,' he said. 'I do what I want to do. Not to offend them, but because that's how I hear it.'

He was just incredibly artistic, always inspiring the people around him to do something interesting. His mindset would be: Don't do the logical thing, try the illogical thing and see if that works. And so we would do that. And you know what? Most of the time it worked.
Nile Rodgers, Chic guitarist and producer of Bowie's album *Let's Dance*.

'Great art can show us how we should live. Now it's showing us how we should die. The swansong might just be the greatest achievement.'
Irving Walsh, novelist, screenwriter & playwright

He resurrected me. He was more of a benefactor than a friend in a way most people think of friendship. He went a bit out of his way to bestow some good karma on me . . .

David's friendship was the light of my life. I never met such a brilliant person. He was the best there is.
Iggy Pop

Beyond sad. Difficult to absorb. Deeply moved. He was a sweet, sweet soul. He went out with such a creative bang. Such a privilege to have known and worked with him. Such a remarkable man and artist. I loved him.
Mick Rock, Bowie photographer – 'The Man Who Shot the Seventies' – and video director

He always did what he wanted to do. And he wanted to do it his way, and he wanted to do it the best way. His death was no different from his life – a work of art. He made *Blackstar* for us, his parting gift. I knew for a year that this was the way it would be. I wasn't, however, prepared for it.

He was an extraordinary man, full of love and life. He will always be with us. For now, it is appropriate to cry.
Tony Visconti, record producer

David's death came as a complete surprise, as did nearly everything else about him. I feel a huge gap now. We knew each other for over forty years, in a friendship that was always tinged by echoes of Pete and Dud. Over the last few years – with him living in New York and me in London – our connection was by email. We signed off with invented names: some of his were mr showbiz, milton keynes, rhoda borrocks, and the duke of ear.

About a year ago, we started talking about *Outside* – the last album we worked on together (recorded in Switzerland and New York, released September 1995). We both liked that album a lot, and felt that it had fallen through the cracks. We talked about revisiting it, taking it somewhere new. I was looking forward to that.

I received an email from him seven days ago. It was as funny as always, and as surreal, looping through word games and allusions and all the usual stuff we did. It ended with this sentence: 'Thank you for our good times, Brian. They will never rot.'

And it was signed 'Dawn'.

I realise now he was saying goodbye.

Brian Eno, former Roxy Music star and Bowie collaborator

I'm devastated. David Bowie changed the course of my life forever. I never felt like I fit in, growing up in Michigan. Like an oddball or a freak. I went to see him in concert at Cobo Arena in Detroit. It was the first concert I'd ever been to . . .

I was so inspired by the way he played with gender confusion. Was both masculine and feminine. Funny and serious. Clever and wise. His lyrics were witty, ironic and mysterious . . .

I saw how he created a persona and used different art forms within the arena of rock'n'roll to create entertainment. I find him so inspiring and innovative. Unique and provocative. A real genius . . . Seeing him live set me off on a journey that for me I hope will never end. His photographs are hanging all over my house today. He was so chic and beautiful and elegant. So ahead of his time.

Madonna

I love you, David. You changed my life. I cannot believe it. Thank you for everything.

Boy George

I can't say enough things about David Bowie to show how much I love him. When the *Low* album was out and Iggy Pop was about to tour, David played keyboards in Iggy's band. They asked Blondie to open for them, and, as they say, the rest is history. Without this visionary and his friend Iggy Pop, where would Blondie be

today? . . . There is no doubt in my mind that Bowie played a big part in our future successes. As for now, love you, David Bowie.
Debbie Harry

It feels as if the world has suddenly gone out of joint.
Gary Kemp, Spandau Ballet

I'm deeply saddened by such a sudden shock. David was a true original in everything he did and, along with many others, I'm going to miss him. Another goodbye to another good friend.
Keith Richards

You can't overestimate what an enormous cultural influence he was. (When I was growing up) the music world then was a very masculine world. For David Bowie to come along and to have this expressive theatricality, it was like a beacon of hope and light.
Marc Almond, Soft Cell

No one exists forever, and it seems our elegant gentleman was well aware that his last mortal chapter was about to reach its conclusion. 'Blackstar' was his parting gift. Provocative and nightmarishly 'other-worldly' . . . we are jolted towards the twilight realms of epileptic seizures and voodoo scarecrows. The bejewelled remains of Major Tom lie dormant in a dust-coated space suit . . . It leaves me breathless. You must see it to believe it. He knew. He could see through it all.
Annie Lennox

He was consistent in the quality of what he did. Some things were more commercially successful than others. But you get the overwhelming impression that commercial success wasn't his driving force. Creativity was. Constantly pushing the boundaries, constantly crossing barriers, invisible walls he just seemed to walk through, and move into areas that no one would expect him to.
Midge Ure, Ultravox, Rich Kids, Visage, Slik

He meant so much to me and to so many. He was a one-off, a brilliant outlier, always exploring, challenging and inspiring anyone who wanted to push the boundaries of music, art, fashion and society. There are so few artists who can touch a generation as he did. We will miss him badly. Long live Lazarus.

Peter Gabriel

He came in 1971 with lovely long, flowing hair like a hippy. He was fantastically beautiful, and nobody knew who he was. He played at four in the morning, at sunrise, songs that we'd never heard before, and it was great fun. He's one of the three greatest. There is Frank Sinatra, Elvis Presley and David Bowie.

Michael Eavis, founder, the Glastonbury Festival

I was profoundly sad to hear the news that David had passed away. He's probably the single person that is responsible for me being a musician. Certainly for Duran Duran existing, and probably nearly all our contemporaries of that period. He owned the decade of the 1970s. He was more creative, inventive and innovative than any other musician I could name, so it's an enormous loss. He was fascinating, funny, sharp, eloquent and very caring.

Nick Rhodes, Duran Duran

John and David respected each other. They were well-matched in intellect and talent. As John and I had very few friends, we felt David was as close as family. After John died, David was always there for Sean and me. When Sean was at boarding school in Switzerland, David would pick him up and take him on trips to museums and let Sean hang out at his recording studio in Geneva. For Sean, this is losing another father figure. But we have some sweet memories which will stay with us forever.

Yoko Ono Lennon

If you're ever sad, just remember the world is 4.543 billion years old, and you somehow managed to exist at the same time as David Bowie.
Dean Podestá, aka @jesuisdean, author of a tweet that went viral.

For someone of my age, he provided a lot of the soundtrack of our lives, from the first time I heard 'Space Oddity' to watching our athletes appear in those wonderful Olympics [2012] to the strains of ' "Heroes" ' . . .
So, we mourn the loss of a great talent. We think about his family and friends, who have lost a loved one too early, but I think also we celebrate an immense British talent who has enriched all of our lives.
Rt Hon David Cameron, MP, UK Prime Minister at the time of David's death.

I'm very saddened to hear of his death. I remember sitting and listening to his songs endlessly in the 1970s, particularly, and always really relishing what he was, what he did, the impact he had.
The Most Revd & Rt Hon Justin Welby, Archbishop of Canterbury

The Vatican's chief spokesman on cultural matters, **Cardinal Gianfranco Ravasi,** tweeted the lyrics to 'Space Oddity' on the day of David's death.

I cannot express in words. I am so sad. I'm going to pray something for him. I'll meet him again in the next life.
Tibetan Buddhist Lama Chime Youngdon Rinpoche, who first met David in 1965.

Ashes to ashes, dust to stardust. Your brilliance inspired us all. Goodbye, Starman.
Commander Chris Hadfield, retired Canadian astronaut, who performed 'Space Oddity' from the International Space Station in 2013.

Acknowledgements

I owe a number of David's close friends and associates, and many others within and beyond the music business, for their recollections and revelations both on and off the record. Some of them I cross-examined in the past, for a variety of publications. Most mentioned here were interviewed specifically for this book. A number of them are not quoted directly, but their knowledge and experience informs the text. I am so grateful to them all.

Thank you, Carlos Alomar, Keith Altham, John Altman, Brian Aris, Michael Armstrong, Jonathan Barnbrook, Martin Barden, Brian Bennett, Warren Bennett, Ed Bicknell, Angie Bowie, Dr Noel Brown, Tina Brown, Clem Cattini, Gordon Coombs, Danielz and T. Rextasy, Lisa Davies, Bernard Doherty, Paul Du Noyer, Alan Edwards, Robert Elms, Nick Fitzherbert, Nelson Foo, Karen French, Reeves Gabrels, Mike Garson, Dana Gillespie, Caroline Graham, Nicky Graham, Fergus Greer, Cosmo Hallström, Johnnie Hamp, David Hancock, Bob Harris, Tony Hatch, Andy Hill, Natasha Holloway, Richard Hughes, Julie Ives-Routleff, Allan James, Debbie Jones, Duncan Jones, Julia Jones, Mia Jones, Trevor Jones, the Revd Canon Dr Alison Joyce, Berni Kilmartin, Gerry Leonard, Leo McLoughlin, David Mallet, Brian May, Scott Millaney, Hy Money, Tony Moore, Neil Myners, Simon Napier-Bell, Tessa Niles, Philip Norman, Martyn Palmer, Malcolm Payne, Andy Peebles, Richard Penniman, John Pidgeon, Chris Poole, Tim

Renwick, Sir Tim Rice, Marc Riley, Nile Rodgers, Nicolas Roeg, Philip Sallon, Neil Sexton, David Stark, David Stopps, Phil Swern, Phil Symes, Roger Taylor, Christos Tolera, George Underwood, Tony Visconti, Rick Wakeman, Richard Wallace, Michael Watts, Chris Welch, Stuart White, Caron Willans, Anya Wilson, Olav Wyper and Chris Youle. There are others whom I have thanked privately, because they cannot be identified. They know how much I appreciate their contributions.

Former *Daily Express* showbiz writer Roger Tavener deserves a special mention for having volunteered to accompany me on a Bowie-style rail-sail-rail expedition from London to Rotterdam in May 1987, for the opening of the Glass Spider tour. I was six months pregnant, so I couldn't fly. What an adventure that was.

I am also grateful to Associated Newspapers; BBC News; the British Library; Chartier, Paris; Guardian News and Media; Hansa Tonstudio, Berlin; Johnston Press; Lake Vyrnwy Hotel, Powys; St Brides Spa Hotel, Pembrokeshire; MGMM Productions; Monster! Entertainment; News UK Ltd; the New York Library; *New York Times*; Princess Royal Hospital, Farnborough, Kent; *Rolling Stone*; Trinity Mirror PLC; and Vanity Fair/Condé Nast Publications.

None of it would have been possible without the support and guidance of my publisher, editor and friend Hannah Black. I am indebted to Managing Director Carolyn Mays, Director of Publicity Karen Geary, Assistant Editor Elizabeth Caraffi, Editorial Assistant Ian Wong, Marketing Manager Caitriona Horne, Rights Director Jason Bartholomew, copy editor Barry Johnston, lawyer Kirsty Howarth and everyone else at Hodder & Stoughton who helped. My agent of more than ten years, Ivan Mulcahy, has been a rock. Dan Arthure, 'Dan the Man', has contributed years of good-humoured technical support, and always bales me out at the last minute. Lesley Hodgson has been a relentless and cheerful picture researcher. Jamie Keenan designed this ravishing jacket. Feel free to judge the book by its cover.

Wendy Leigh, who published her own biography of Bowie in 2014, jumped to her death from the balcony of her riverside apartment in Chelsea on 29 May 2016. She was a respected fellow hack and Fleet Street rabble-rouser, in the days when the newspaper industry felt like something akin to the old Wild West. An acclaimed *New York Times* bestselling author of numerous celebrity biographies and racy fiction, she was a beauty, a laugh, and in pain. I wish she'd told us.

Hugh Attwooll and I had many discussions about Bowie and Mott the Hoople after we got to know each other when he and his wife Melissa bought my house in Balham. Turned out we had dozens of people in common. He was also former 'Spider from Mars' Nicky Graham's oldest friend from school. Small world.

Pierre Perrone was a fellow toiler in the vineyard. He was universally loved and is deeply missed.

As is DJ Roger Scott, who meant so much to me, and in whose company I embarked on many a mission. The stand-outs were Montreux for Bowie, Queen and 'Under Pressure', and Birmingham, on the Serious Moonlight tour. It has been my pleasure this year to plunder my archive for his son Jamie Scott, who has created a fantastic website dedicated to Roger's life and work: www.roger-scott.net

Jim Diamond was a one-off. A true lifelong friend. He has left a hole in our hearts that can never be filled.

I first met John Pidgeon at Capital Radio in the early 1980s, where he was producing Roger Scott. He had by then enjoyed a long career as a rock journalist, broadcaster and comedy scriptwriter. He and Roger progressed to the BBC in 1988. After Roger's death in 1989, John launched his own production company, and was made Head of BBC Radio Entertainment in 1999. When I became a member of the biannual Scribblers, Pluckers, Thumpers and Squawkers lunch club for veteran rock stars and hacks some years ago, John was running it. When John fell ill with cancer, Ed Bicknell (who managed Dire Straits for twenty six years) stepped in. John, meanwhile, continued to compile confounding crosswords for the *Daily Telegraph*. He missed a few Scribblers… lunches in a row, but made a triumphant return in June 2016. He died a few weeks later, just as the original hardback version of this book was about to go to press. I'm gutted that he'll never get to read it. He contributed far more than he knew.

Nick Gordon was my Fleet Street mentor; the editor to whom I owe the breaks that gave me a career. He died suddenly in June 2016, at the age of sixty-eight, while on an anniversary walk in Snowdonia in memory of his wife Theresa. He was a fierce deputy editor on the *Daily Mail*, yet uncommonly generous and patient with rookies. When he moved to *YOU* magazine at the *Mail on Sunday*, he took me with him.

Nick first set foot on African soil the day that Neil Armstrong walked on the moon. It was on the Dark Continent that he discovered the culture and environment that would profoundly influence his work for the rest of his life. He campaigned against the tusk traders of Tanzania, and to save the gorillas in Rwanda. He wrote compelling books about his adventures, including *Ivory Knights: Man, Magic & Elephants*, and *Murders in the Mist*, about the killing of American primatologist Dian Fossey.

RIP, Wendy, Hugh, Pierre, Roger, Jim, John and Nick. Save a seat on the bus.

For my mother, Kathleen, and father, Ken; for Sam, Chris, Matthew and Adam; and for Bridie, Henry and Mia. See, Bridie? Sometimes the third-born does come first.

This book is dedicated with fondest love to Nick, Natasha and Hy.

L-AJ, October 2017

Select Bibliography

Ant, Adam, *Stand and Deliver: The Autobiography*, Pan Books, 2006

Balfour, Victoria, *Rock Wives*, Virgin Books, 1986

Cann, Kevin, *Any Day Now: The London Years, 1947–1974*, Adelita, 2010

Currie, David, with Cann, Kevin, *David Bowie: The Starzone Interviews*, Omnibus Press, 1985

Devine, Campbell, *All the Young Dudes. Mott the Hoople and Ian Hunter, The Biography*, Cherry Red Books, 1998

Egan, Sean, (Ed.), *Bowie on Bowie: Interviews & Encounters*, Souvenir Press, 2015

Finnigan, Mary, *Psychedelic Suburbia: David Bowie & the Beckenham Arts Lab*, Jorvik Press, 2016

Gillman, Leni & Peter, *Alias David Bowie*, Hodder & Stoughton, 1986

Goddard, Simon, *Mozipedia: The Encyclopaedia of Morrissey and the Smiths*, Penguin/Random House, 2010

Hadfield, Chris, *An Astronaut's Guide to Life*, Macmillan, 2013

Harris, Bob, *Still Whispering After All These Years*, Michael O'Mara Books, 2015

Harris, Bob, *The Whispering Years*, BBC Worldwide, 2001

Hunt, Marsha, *Real Life*, Chatto & Windus, 1986

Iman, *I Am Iman*, Universe, 2001

Jones, Lesley-Ann, *Freddie Mercury, the Definitive Biography*, Hodder & Stoughton, 2011

Jones, Lesley-Ann, *Ride a White Swan, the Lives & Death of Marc Bolan*, Hodder & Stoughton, 2012

Kent, Nick, *Apathy for the Devil*, Faber & Faber, 2010

Leigh, Wendy, *Bowie: The Biography*, Galley Books, 2014

Lenig, Stuart, *The Twisted Tale of Glam Rock*, Prager, 2010

McLean, Rory, *Berlin: Imagine a City*: Weidenfeld & Nicolson, 2015

Miles, Barry, *David Bowie Black Book*, Omnibus Press, 1980

Morgan-Richards, Lorin, *Welsh in the Old West*, A Raven Above Press, 2015

Morrissey, *Autobiography*, Penguin Classic, 2013

Napier-Bell, Simon, *You Don't Have to Say You Love Me*, New English Library, 1982

Napier-Bell, Simon, *Black Vinyl, White Powder*, Ebury Press, 2002

Napier-Bell, Simon, *Ta-Ra-Ra-Boom-De-Ay*, Unbound, 2014

Niles, Tessa, *Backtrack: The Voice Behind Music's Greatest Stars*, Panoma Press, 2015

Norman, Philip, *Elton*, Hutchinson, 1991

Norman, Philip, *Shout! The True Story of the Beatles*, Hamish Hamilton, 1981

O'Regan, Denis, & Flippo, Chet, *Serious Moonlight: The World Tour*, Doubleday/Dolphin, 1983

Paytress, Mark, *Bolan: The Rise & Fall of a 20th Century Superstar*, Omnibus Press, 2002

Pitt, Kenneth, *The Pitt Report*, Omnibus Press, 1985

Richards, Keith, and Fox, James, *Life: Keith Richards*, Weidenfeld & Nicolson, 2010

Rodgers, Nile, *Le Freak*, Sphere, 2011

Stewart, Rod, *The Autobiography*, Century, 2013

Townshend, Pete, *Who I Am*, HarperCollins, 2012

Trynka, Paul, *Starman*, Sphere, 2010

Various, *David Bowie is Inside*, V&A Publishing, 2013

Visconti, Tony, *Bowie, Bolan & the Brooklyn Boy*, HarperCollins, 2007

Wakeman, Rick, *Grumpy Old Rock Star and Other Wondrous Stories*, Preface, 2008

Weird & Gilly, *Mick Ronson: The Spider with the Platinum Hair*, IMP Publishing, 2003

Welch, Chris, & Napier-Bell, Simon, *Marc Bolan: Born to Boogie*, Plexus Publishing, 2008

White, Charles, *The Quasar of Rock: The Life & Times of Little Richard*, Pan Books, 1985

Wright, Chris, *One Way or Another*, Omnibus Press, 2013

Source Notes

Bowie was loquacious, particularly during the early years: there are hundreds if not thousands of his quotations in the public domain. I have tried to avoid anything too platitudinous. Where the primary source of a quotation is not obvious – many have been recycled so often without credit having been given where it was originally due – I have stated examples here of where else those words can be read.

Also fascinating and informative were the interviews and contributions compiled for the DVD collection *David Bowie In His Own Words:* a collection of excerpts from television interviews with David conducted in several countries, and drawn from his entire career.

An I.V. Production for I.V. Media in 2015.

Statements made by producer David Mallet and broadcaster Robert Elms, used throughout, were aired as part of the globally acclaimed and long-running music television series *Video Killed the Radio Star.* They are reproduced here by kind permission of Scott Millaney, Producer, Owner and Publisher of MGMM Studios Ltd, creators of the sixty-part series, which has been broadcast in some ninety five territories and on several airlines, and which continues to enjoy popularity among audiences of all ages. Scott Millaney owns all rights to all contributors' work within the series. MGMM have produced more than 1,250 music videos, including 'Let's Dance', 'China Girl' and 'Ashes to Ashes' for Bowie, as well as his live concerts and TV productions. Their awards include multiple Grammys, BRITs, MTV and D&AD awards. MGMM's work has been exhibited in museums and galleries around the world.

Page 15:
Marc Riley is widely quoted on the subject of 'Starman' on *Lift-Off with Ayshea*.
 Read more at Michael Harvey's Ziggy Stardust Companion:
 www.5years.com/loa.htm

Page 71:
David talking about Vince Taylor:
 The original source appears to be *Changes: Bowie at 50,* an hour -long interview filmed in January 1997 with the BBC's then direc- tor of programmes Alan Yentob to mark David's 50th birthday.
 David had been interviewed by Yentob before: for 'Cracked Actor', a 53-minute BBC TV Omnibus documentary filmed in 1974 during David's interlude of cocaine addiction, and depicting him as fragile and mentally unstable. Its screen debut took place in the UK on BBC2 on 26 January 1975. This documentary remains unreleased officially, although bootleg copies were made when it was rescreened during the early 1990s, and are widely in circulation.
 These words have been repeated in many newspapers. They can be read on the Ziggy Stardust Companion site:
 www.5years.com/faq.htm and at
 www.thedabbler.co.uk/

Page 80:
David talking about the Velvet Underground and Nico. An inter- view with him conducted by Scott Galupo for the New Yorker magazine in September 2003 can be read here:
 www.bowiewonderworld.com/press/00/030929newyork.htm

Page 84:
Former Bowie manager Kenneth Pitt's book *The Pitt Report* offers fascinating further insight.

Page 87:
Quoted from an interview with Angie Bowie by Los Angeles correspondent Caroline Graham, published in the UK's Mail on Sunday in August 2009.

Page 94:
Angie's words here were widely quoted in the press – in the Sun, the Daily Mail, the Standard and others in the UK – after she sensationally walked out of TV's Celebrity Big Brother house following the death of her former husband.

Page 98:
David's 'Elvis was a major hero of mine' comments, said to have been made in 1996, have been widely quoted, and can be found on the Ziggy Stardust Companion site:
www.5years.com/Triv2.htm
Also at Phil Arnold's www.elvisblog.net and on various other fansites.

Page 100:
David's explanation of the lyrics of 'Life on Mars?' has been repeated extensively. The full quotation can be read here:
www.rollingstone.com/music/lists/david-bowie-30-essential-songs-20160111/life-on-mars-1971-20160111
At:
www.davidbowie.com/news/life-mars-single-42-single-42-today-54566
there is an explanation of how David edited his own comments as to the song's meaning.

Page 103:
Jonathan Barnbrook has been widely quoted on the subject of his design for the album cover of *The Next Day*. See:
www.creativebloq.com

www.musicfeeds.com.au
www.songfacts.com
www.cnn.com
www.ultimateclassicrock.com/
   At:
   http://virusfonts.com/news/2013/01/david-bowie-the-next-day-
   that-album-cover-design/ he elaborates, on his Barnbrook Blog.

On Morrissey's songwriting:
Songs such as 'Certain People I Know', 'Glamorous Glue' and 'I
Know It's Gonna Happen Someday' are widely acknowledged to
have been influenced by T.Rex and David Bowie.
   See Pushing Ahead of the Dame:
   https://bowiesongs.wordpress.com/2012/10/26/i-know-its-
   gonna-happen-someday/
   and https://en.wikipedia.org/wiki/Your_Arsenal
   See also www.soundsjustlike.com/1766/morrissey-sounds-like-
   david-bowie/
   www.uncut.co.uk/features/morrissey-it-sounds-too-much-like-
   waitrose-it-needs-to-be-more-harrods-16913

Page 112:
David's comments about the only pipe he had ever smoked being a
cheap Bewlay are widely quoted. The Mail on Sunday offered a
cover-mount CD compilation in June 2008, and this remark
appears there, under 'The Bewlay Brothers'.
   See also Pushing Ahead of the Dame:
   https://bowiesongs.wordpress.com/2010/04/09/the-bewlay-brothers/

Page 126:
David talking about Ziggy as his Martian messiah; original source
obscure, but can be seen, along with much more on the subject, on
the Ziggy Stardust Companion:
   www.5years.com/quotes.htm

Page 137:

David discussing his Japanese influences; original source unclear, but much more on this subject in Emily Johnson's piece here:

https://www.insidejapantours.com/blog/2016/01/11/kabuki-and-the-art-of-david-bowie/

This blog also features the original page from the 1971 Harpers & Queen magazine which David says inspired his shock-red hairdo.

Page 155:

David's comments were made during *Five Years,* a BBC2 documentary directed by Francis Whately, first screened on 25th May 2013. Featuring personal quotes, interviews, music and previously unseen archive footage. David admits in this film that he came very close to overdosing on several occasions during that period.

Page 156:

Who Can I Be Now? How David spent 1974, Jem Aswad, June 2014:

www.npr.org/secdtions/therecord/2014/06/15/322274193/who-can-i-be-now-how-david-bowie-spent-1974

This also features David's interview on the American *Dick Cavett Show*, November 1974.

See also the deluxe editions of the *Diamond Dogs* and *Young Americans* albums, with liner notes by writer David Buckley.

Page 165:

David talking about extricating himself from the MainMan 'circus':

Much more on this subject on the Ziggy Stardust Companion:

http://www.5years.com/Retire.htm

Page 172/173:

Angie's recollections of David trying to strangle her were told to the press in interviews she gave following her premature departure from television's Big Brother house in January 2016. See here:

The Sun/Sun on Sunday:

https://www.thesun.co.uk/archives/news/213895/angie-bowie-david-held-my-throat-and-began-to-strangle-me-with-his-bare-hands/

International Business Times:

www.ibtimes.co.uk/david-bowies-ex-wife-claims-starman-hit-maker-once-tried-kill-her-1539867

She also discusses the incident in her memoir *Backstage Passes: Life on the Wild Side with David Bowie* by Angela Bowie and Patrick Carr.

Page 174:

Guns N'Roses' Slash revealed his mother's affair with David to Australian radio station Triple M in 2012:

http://www.triplem.com.au/

It has since been blanket-reported across the global press, from the NME and Metro in the UK to www.huffingtonpost.com/ and www.ultimateclassicrock.com/

Page 177:

David explains 'Isolar', as sourced from 'Anoraks Corner':

www.bowiewonderworld.com/trivia.htm

Page 178:

David describing the Thin White Duke as a 'very Aryan, fascist type': widely quoted, as at:

www.independent.co.uk/news/people/remembering-david-bowie-a-journey-through-the-iconic-singers-ever-changing-personas-a6805651.html

http://mashable.com/2016/01/11/david-bowie-character-guide/#Fgz9ROLDaPq5

Page 179:

Angie discussing David's tax affairs in the mid-1970s: as described in her memoir *Backstage Passes: Life on the Wild Side with David Bowie*

More here: www.taxfoundation.org/blog/david-bowie-tax-plan-ning-hero

Page 186:
Tony Visconti discussing David's time in Berlin: quoted from the Uncut Interviews: Tony Visconti on Berlin, the Real 'Uncut' Version. For the full interview, see here:
www.bowiewonderworld.com/features/tvuncut.htm

Page 187:
David talking about Berlin: oft-quoted, for example, here:
www.express.co.uk/entertainment/music/633627/stardust-career-life-David-Bowie

Page 188:
David talking about turning 30: more here:
Bowie Golden Years
http://www.bowiegoldenyears.com/1977.html

Page 191:
David talked about his fear of flying to journalist Lisa Robinson on his arrival in New York. See:
www.davidbowie.com/news/iggy-pop-south-bank-show-special-tonight-25746
Also:
www.bowiegoldenyears.com/1977.html - May entry.

Page 195:
David talking about performing "Heroes" at the Berlin Wall: widely quoted, see Rolling Stone June 2016 for example, here – which includes a clip of the footage from that summer 1987 concert:
www.rollingstone.com/music/videos/flashback-david-bowie-sings-heroes-at-the-berlin-wall-20160609

Page 209:

Christos Tolera, ex-Blitz Kid, singer with Blue Rondo à la Turk, more here:

https://shapersofthe80s.com/2010/05/16/2010-%E2%9E%A4-how-real-did-1980-feel-ex-blitz-kids-give-verdicts-on-tonight%E2%80%99s-play-worried-about-the-boy/

Page 220:

David, Brian May and Roger Taylor have all given a string of conflicting quotes and interviews about the origins of 'Under Pressure', and appear to vary the story each time they are asked . . . probably because it was thirty five years ago, and they can't remember exactly. At times, Bowie's and the Queen members' accounts have contradicted each other. Rock and roll.

Brian spoke at length on the subject in Mojo magazine in October 2008.

David addressed a question about the song from a fan on his own website in 2004, requoted here:

www.alterpolitics.com

More here:

http://www.songfacts.com/detail.php?id=1383

Page 248:

David talking about Mustique: widely quoted in the press; see the author's piece in the Daily Mail, 12 January 2016:

http://www.dailymail.co.uk/news/article-3394969/I-chased-schoolgirl-slept-bed-Mustique.html

Page 268:

David's words here a drawn from a conversation we had in New York, early 1990s. I later recorded the conversation in my notebook, but did not publish an interview at the time.

Page 283:

For the full Daily Telegraph piece about Iman, published in October 1997, see here:

https://exploringdavidbowie.wordpress.com/2013/02/12/iman

In July 2011, the Week published 'The Truth about Iman', drawing on Helena de Bertodano's piece in the London Times:

www.theweek.com/articles/483236/truth-about-iman

'Discovered by photographer Peter Beard in Kenya in 1974, the former supermodel came to the US at the age of 19, where she was introduced to the press as a Somali goatherd . . .'

Page 293:

Morrissey explains at length his decision to quit the European leg of Bowie's Outside tour 1995 in *Mozipedia: The Encyclopaedia of Morrissey and the Smiths* by Simon Goddard, on the book's page 45. He talks about David having put him under a great deal of pressure, which Morrissey found unbearably exhausting. He describes David's behaviour towards him as bizarre, and how he took exception to David's request to sing some Bowie songs in his own set. Morrissey told him that he wasn't prepared to do that. Nor was he inclined to agree to David coming on stage towards the end of his set, meaning that there would be no distinct division between the two artists' shows, and therefore no encore for Morrissey:

'When we played Dublin, I went off and he came on and a lot of the crowd were still calling my name,' Morrissey said. 'He was doing his set and he said, "Don't worry, Morrissey will be back later." But I was 100 miles down the road. I thought it was really showbiz, and really, this is David Showie.'

Page 293/294:

David discusses spirituality and his thoughts about organised religion with writer David Cavanagh, for a piece published in *Q* magazine, February 1997. Read it here:

Changes50Bowie

https://exploringdavidbowie.wordpress.com/2013/02/12/
changes50bowie/

Page 302:
David's interview with Jarvis Cocker was published in the Big
Issue in 1997. It was republished in January 2016, here:
   http://www.bigissue.com/features/interviews/6181/david-bowie-
interview-im-easygoing-about-death-itll-happen-when-it-happens

Page 304:
Richard Wallace's full interview, published in the Daily Mirror,
29th June 2002, can be read here:
   www.bowiewonderworld.com/press/00/0206interview.htm
David discussing the status of the 'native New Yorker': his words
derive from a conversation we had in New York, never previously
published.

Page 307:
David discussing BowieNet: widely quoted, see for example here:
   http://www.independent.co.uk/life-style/gadgets-and-tech/news/
david-bowie-once-set-up-his-own-internet-service-provider-bow-
ienet-a6805481.html
   And here, words from Ron Roy, who co-founded the business
with David:
   http://arstechnica.co.uk/business/2016/01/david-bowies-
isp-as-remembered-by-the-guy-who-helped-create-bowienet/

Page 312:
David discussed Iman's pregnancy and Alexandria's birth in
numerous television interviews all over Europe during the promo
rounds for the Heathen album. The Joneses also gave an exclusive
pictorial and interview to Hello magazine in 2000. Read here:
   http://www.hellomagazine.com/celebrities/2016011429246/
david-bowie-iman-exclusive-interview/

Page 318:

Anthony DeCurtis interviewed David on the subject of spirituality in June 2003 at Looking Glass studios, New York:

http://www.beliefnet.com/entertainment/2005/07/im-not-quite-an-atheist-and-it-worries-me.aspx

Page 321:

David's comments about 'things that they regarded as truths' from 'SOS' by Richard Buskin, October 2003.

David Bowie and Tony Visconti Recording Reality: read here: www.bowiewonderworld.com/press/00/031001sosreality.htm

Page 341:

Director Ivo van Hove has been widely quoted on the subject of David's appearance at the New York premiere of his musical *Lazarus.*

eg, www.mirror.co.uk/3am/celebrity-news/david-bowie-made-emotional-final-7167863

www.dailyrecord.co.uk/news/uk-world-news/terminally-ill-david-bowie-took-7168747#JfrH5dL6YokuiDdY.97

Page 352:

Angie Bowie's words regarding what she would have said to David, had she been able to speak to him one last time, were quoted internationally after his death in January 2016, eg, in British newspapers the Sun and the Daily Mirror:

https://www.thesun.co.uk/archives/news/213895/angie-bowie-david-held-my-throat-and-began-to-strangle-me-with-his-bare-hands/

http://www.mirror.co.uk/3am/celebrity-news/david-bowies-ex-wife-angie-7236015

Picture Acknowledgements

©Bertrand Rindoff Petroff/Getty Images: 23. ©Caron Willans: 39. ©Chalkie Davies/Getty Images: 21. ©Cyrus Andrews/Michael Ochs Archives/Getty Images: 10. ©Dave Hogan/Getty Images: 28. ©David Bebbington: 9. ©Denis O'Regan: 29, 30. ©Dominick Conde: 32. ©Ebet Roberts/Redferns/ Getty Images: 27. ©George Harris / Associated Newspapers/REX/Shutterstock: 11. ©George Underwood: 31, 43. ©Hy Money: 12. ©ITV/REX/Shutterstock: 16, 24. ©Kevin Cummins/Getty Images: 45. ©Lesley-Ann Jones: 1, 3, 4, 5, 6, 8, 13, 15, 34, 35, 36, 37, 38, 40, 41, 42, 47, 48. ©Michael Ochs Archives/Getty Images: 14. ©Mick Rock: 18, 46. ©NBC/ NBCU Photo Bank via Getty Images: 17. ©PA Archive/Press Association Images: 19. ©Pictorial Press Ltd / Alamy Stock Photo: 2. ©Rex/Shutterstock: 7. ©RonGalella/WireImage/getty: 26. ©Steve Schapiro: 22. ©SWNS.com: 20. ©Trinity Mirror / Mirrorpix / Alamy Stock Photo: 25. ©www.brianaris.com: 33.

Index

Do you wish this wasn't the end?

Join us at www.hodder.co.uk, or follow us on
Twitter @hodderbooks to be a part of our community
of people who love the very best in books and reading.

Whether you want to discover r   about a book
or an author, watch trailers and in   s, have the
chance to win early limited edition   browse
our expert readers' selection of th   books,
we think you'll find what you

And if you don't,
that's the place to tell us wh

We love what we do, and we'd love you to be part of it.

www.hodder.co.uk